LISTENING IN

D1612782

LISTENING IN

BROADCASTS, SPEECHES, AND INTERVIEWS BY ELIZABETH BOWEN

EDITED WITH AN INTRODUCTION BY
ALLAN HEPBURN

Edinburgh University Press

Edinburgh University Press Ltd
22 George Square, Edinburgh

www.euppublishing.com

Typeset in 10/12pt Sabon
by Servis Filmsetting Ltd, Stockport, Cheshire and
printed and bound in Great Britain by
CPI Antony Rowe, Chippenham and Eastbourne

A CIP record for this book is available from the British Library

ISBN 978 0 7486 4041 6 (hardback)
ISBN 978 0 7486 4042 3 (paperback)

Contents

CONTENTS

Acknowledgements

While editing *People, Places, Things: Essays by Elizabeth Bowen*, I accumulated more material than I could possibly fit into a single volume. Although my interests lay in Bowen's expertise as an essayist, especially her comments on the craft of fiction and its modern practitioners, I began to notice how much she wrote for radio and how frequently she gave public lectures. Speeches and broadcasts naturally group around the idea of the speaking voice. I owe a great debt of thanks to Jackie Jones at Edinburgh University Press for encouraging me to make these materials available in a discrete volume. James Dale and Máiréad McElligott, also at Edinburgh University Press, offered practical and expert guidance in seeing this book through the press. Donald Glassman kindly located the final version of "The Idea of the Home" in the Barnard College archives when I could provide him with only a hunch and a hope. Louise North at the BBC Written Archives Centre in Reading advised me on archival materials and retrieved a missing detail from microfilm, for which I am very grateful. Phyllis Lassner, steadfast Bowenite, read my translation of "Panorama of the Novel" and pointed out infelicities of style. Claude Deshaies talked over the thornier French passages in that same essay and offered plausible alternatives. Robin Feenstra saved me from errors of judgement in the introduction and editorial notes. Michael Waldron, defying the likelihood of obtaining the documentary "Ireland Today," generously offered his time and resourcefulness.

A Standard Research Grant from the Social Sciences and Humanities Research Council of Canada provided funding for travel and research assistance. Without the support of SSHRC, I could never have completed this book. Initial research for this project was undertaken during a month-long stay at the Harry Ransom Humanities Research Center at the University of Texas at Austin, where I held a Mellon Fellowship in June 2006. A team grant from the Fonds du Québec pour la Recherche en Sciences et Culture for research on "La Poétique du roman" provided further financial support. I have benefited from the assistance of many librarians at McGill University, Firestone Library at Princeton University, the BBC Sound Archives at the British Library, the BBC Written Archives Centre in Reading, the University of Sussex, the Modern Manuscripts collection in the Bodleian at Oxford University, the manuscripts collection at Durham University, and numerous other institutions. During a random database search, Lonnie Weatherby fortuitously located the review of *Things to Come*, which I would never have known about otherwise.

Paula Derdiger, Justin Pfefferle, and Ian Whittington, working as research assistants, read through the manuscript with scrupulous care. Caroline Krzakowski and Shannon Wells-Lassagne shared their insider knowledge about archives. Under the auspices of the Fund for Irish Studies, Paul Muldoon invited me to Princeton University to give a lecture on Bowen's travels in America. Maria DiBattista, who first urged me to read *The House in Paris* and *The Death of the Heart* twenty-five years ago, has kept up an inspiriting conversation about Bowen's fiction ever since. Lastly, I wish to thank the Estate of Elizabeth Bowen, and especially Camilla Hornby at the Curtis Brown Group in London, for permission to publish these broadcasts and speeches.

Introduction

As an essayist and novelist, Elizabeth Bowen wrote for the human voice. A painstaking writer, she was also, by a quirk of fate, a lifelong stammerer. Her voice sounded strange and estranging, even to her own ear. By writing for the radio and by speaking in public, Bowen honed her sense of the acoustic range of the voice in all its accents and intonations. Between 1941 and 1973, she was a regular contributor on the BBC, either reading her own scripts or participating in discussions on a set topic. In the 1940s, she dramatised the life and fiction of three literary figures – Anthony Trollope, Jane Austen, Frances Burney – and tried her hand at writing original plays for radio. Bowen thought enough of her broadcasts to include some of them in the collections of critical prose that she published in her lifetime. The playlet about Anthony Trollope appeared in *Collected Impressions* (1950). Two essayistic pieces, one about Rider Haggard's *She* and another called "Truth and Fiction," were included in *Afterthought* (1962). Many of her radio essays touched on the mechanics of novel-writing or her success as an author, but her range of interests was much broader than that. In the postwar years, she talked on the radio about nostalgia, treachery, the coronation, her favourite book, her next book. Towards the end of her life, she appeared several times as a panellist on "Take It or Leave It," a television game show. In 1961, taking up the challenge of another medium, she wrote a documentary about Ireland for CBS television. Regardless of her stutter, Bowen was a compelling conversationalist and a sought-after public speaker. She lectured throughout Europe and the United States on literary and cultural topics. Her speeches and broadcasts were written, first and foremost, to be heard.

Undoubtedly Bowen had some knowledge of radio technique from her husband, Alan Cameron, who served as Secretary to the Central Council of School Broadcasting at the BBC in London from 1935 to 1945. After his retirement, he advised EMI on educational gramophone records. Bowen confessed that listening to the radio or gramophone relaxed her. The radio was a newfangled technology in the interwar years; the BBC took to the airwaves as a private broadcaster in 1922 and became a public corporation in 1927. Many people in Bowen's milieu wrote for the new medium. Lord David Cecil, Veronica Wedgwood, J. B. Priestley, V. S. Pritchett, Graham Greene, all of whom figured among Bowen's acquaintances, discoursed on various subjects. Priestley's stirring patriotic messages, delivered in a Yorkshire accent, made him a "national sensation" during the Second World War (Briggs, *The BBC* 191). In 1952, Isaiah Berlin, another of Bowen's friends, made an immense impression with six lectures on the Third Programme about thinkers from Helvétius to de Maistre; "hundreds of thousands of people tuned in, mostly from the educated middle classes, to listen to fiendishly difficult hour-long talks, delivered in a clipped, rapid-fire Oxford accent" (Ignatieff 204).

Bowen was not nearly so comfortable in front of the microphone as Priestley or Berlin. Nonetheless, in 1948, Bowen, Greene, and Pritchett jointly broadcast a series of exchanges called *Why Do I Write?* In this three-way conversation about the responsibilities that an author owes society, Pritchett offers modulated opinions in a modulated voice, while Graham Greene blends the gruffness of a gangster with the precision of an Oxford don. Bowen, given far less air time than the two men, claims that writing, for her, is a way to work off "the sense of being solitary and farouche," which every writer feels (*Why* 23). Books attach her to society: "My writing, I am prepared to think, may be a substitute for something I have been born without – a so-called normal relation to society. My books *are* my relation to society" (*Why* 23). The writer might develop an immediate relation with society – or at least a relation unmediated by printed pages – by speaking on the radio.

For Bowen, sound is a form of drama. In her novels and short stories, she attends to dialogue and sudden intrusions of sound as events heightened in magnitude, often devastating in their consequences. The noise of a lorry changing gears on a distant hill or the blare of a gramophone in a seaside house causes fear or dazedness in those who listen. *The Last September* begins with the twang of an iron gate resounding across the hush of an Irish estate. In *The Heat of the Day*, Stella Rodney and Robert Kelway converse in a blacked-out bedroom, their voices held low against the risk of being heard, low enough for Stella to catch the sound of someone in the street shifting his position. In *A World of Love*, Big Ben booms out the hour over the radio: "the first of the whanging blows struck down upon quivering ether, the echo swelling as it uprose" (129). Whanging, quivering, swelling – the sentence registers sound effects within its phonetic construction.

The drama of sound is intrinsic in the human voice and its speech patterns. In fiction, dialogue changes the tempo of narration, heightens feeling, and sharpens the edges between one character and another. Dialogue conveys the ways in which individual characters speak and listen – or fail to. Bowen's characters are often reticent, but they are no less dramatic for keeping their thoughts to themselves. "There is a touch of the sphinx in many human beings," Bowen told her students in a short story class at Vassar College in 1960, "and this 'sphinx' quality is one which – quite often – the [short story] legitimately exploits" (HRC 7.3). She also advised her students that not all fictional dialogue is verbal: "*There is Dialogue* – though it may be unspoken" (HRC 7.3). Whereas dialogue can be muted, Bowen's own virtuosic stories exploit the tonalities in the speaking voice. "Careless Talk" combines social banter and wartime news in a swirl of voices so dense that information pertinent to the Allied cause – evacuees in the country, the Poles and the Free

French in London – mingles with harmless chatter about eggs and good restaurants. No talk can be too careful, especially in the charged atmosphere of war. Around even the most garrulous of characters sneak little ebbs and spates of silence. In *A World of Love*, a couple in an airport lounge, waiting uneasily on the verge of saying goodbye, sit in "twisted silence" (148). In the silences that undergird sound, a great deal happens that is never articulated. In *Eva Trout*, a deaf-mute boy confounds efforts to communicate except through erratic gestures. In the same novel, Eva has very little command of vocabulary and even less of conversation. Mr. Denge's appeals to Eva to make a "Speech!" (267, 268) are, therefore, altogether futile. As in *A World of Love* and *Eva Trout*, Bowen's characters are typically caught between the impulse to speak and the necessity of holding their tongues.

Radio voices have their own agency and identifiable traits: male or female, hoarse or fluty, pedantic or sinister. While preparing an adaptation of *The House in Paris* for broadcast on "Woman's Hour" in fifteen weekly instalments in 1951, H. N. Bentinck at the BBC wrote to Bowen for advice about characters' accents and voices:

> I don't want to go in for a riot of accents for their own sake, but it is always easier for immediate identification of characters on the air for having some easily recognisable characteristic in the way they talk.
>
> Would Leopold have taken on a slight American accent from the Grant Moodys? Does Naomi Fisher speak with a bit of a French accent? Max you describe as having an odd inflection so presumably it is in his inflections that the fact of his not being English is apparent; which is quite sufficient. Madame Fisher also, presumably, has something of a French accent. Should one play her with a rather directly unpleasant implacable sort of voice, or has she rather a devilish charm because of the influence she was able to exert on Max and Leopold [?] Devilish charm may perhaps sound to you rather a dangerous suggestion and I cant [sic] be quite certain what I mean by it until I have heard Patience Collier experimenting; but if I knew what the end result should be like I would know in what direction to conduct experiments. (BBC "Scriptwriter," 1943–62; letter dated 2 November 1951)

Especially in radio drama, characters should have immediately identifiable voices. The voice gives off clues about characters' origins, education, ease or lack of ease with foreign languages, even "devilish charm." In the absence of visual effects, sound intensifies information. Radio objectifies the voice by detaching it from the person who speaks. The radio adds another acoustic dimension to the voice by projecting it through space.

For Bowen, radio induces a sensation of strangeness about the human voice: "Anyone who, having made a recorded broadcast, hears his own voice played back to him for the first time listens to it less with embarrassment than with complete amazement: he hears the voice of a stranger" (*People, Places, Things* 386). Bowen thought a great deal about the strangeness of her voice because of her stammer. She did not just stammer from time to time or trip over awkward consonants; she stammered badly, even painfully. Suddenly beset, she would labour over the initial syllable of "never," uttering a sequence of *crescendo* "n's" before yielding *subito* to a whispered version of the word, like a sigh. Plosives and fricatives were no less treacherous. Her stammer, if one can judge from the few recordings still available, is variable and might happen on almost any word. In the recorded version of "Books that Grow up with One," she attacks the word "Tolstoy," but she sputters on the initial letter: "T-T-T-Tolstoy." Instead of uttering "read," as indicated in the script, she says "re-reads," which might be a stutter or might be an intentional correction.

In any event, Bowen did not always adhere to what was on the typewritten page when she recorded essays for broadcast. "Books that Grow up with One," available at the BBC Sound Archives, indicates the degree to which she improvised on a text by swerving around phrases that presented potential snares for the habitual stammerer. Instead of reading the word "touchstone," for instance, Bowen substitutes "mark." "Memory" becomes "remembrance," and "looking" becomes "glancing." She sometimes rings multiple changes on a single sentence. While recording "Books that Grow up with One," she transformed words and whole phrases. For instance, the typescript offers a sentence with short, erratically punctuated phrases and a comma splice: "At the first meeting our book must engage the erratic curiosity and dream-clouded ignorance of the adolescent, it must give a friendly – not a forbidding – hint of much still uncharted: just because of this it will magnetise, without being wholly understood." The sentence metamorphosed during recording: "At the first encounter of all, our book must engage the erratic curiosity and dream-clouded ignorance of the adolescent, it must give a friendly – rather than a daunting – hint of much still to come: just because of this it will magnetise, without being so far wholly understood." There are at least four substantive changes in words and phrases. Although the alterations are numerous, they do not compromise the syntax, or the gist, of the sentence. To Bowen's ear, some of these verbal changes might have been viewed as improvements. To a listener's ear, some of these changes sound like tactics to avoid troublesome phrases.

Bowen's persistence in speaking in public as a lecturer and over the radio was, given the severity of her stutter, a defiant gesture. She was perfectly aware that her stammer was a liability. Discussing *The Little Girls* with Dorothy Baker in a letter dated 23 December 1963, Bowen acknowledged the particular difficulties she faced in reading on the air:

> The great snag about my reading parts of *The Little Girls* in the "Before Publication" series in the Third Programme would be, that I CAN'T read aloud, because I stammer. Alas. I have done some broadcasting from time to time, and I "speak" when I am in America, but on such occasions I have been "speaking free"; i.e., simply from notes. But something about reading aloud gives me lockjaw (unfortunately) and that would apply particularly, I *know*, to my own work.
>
> If a reader read the extracts and I spoke a short introduction & here & there commentary, I *could* do that. But then, *you* might not think that a good idea? (BBC "Rcont 12," 1963–67)

In the end, Bowen agreed to talk about her novel *and* to read from it. Nevertheless, she recognized the difference between "speaking free" and abiding by the written word as two modes of oral presentation. In certain cases, such as the speech "The Idea of the Home," written for the American Civilization programme at Barnard College, Bowen read aloud from a script. For "The Poetic Element in Fiction," however, she sketched out ideas in the form of notes and let chance play its part when she delivered the speech. In theory at least, "speaking free" made her less likely to stammer, but that did not always prove true in practice.

Bowen's stammer caused headaches for producers and editors.

To reduce or eliminate awkward hesitations, they had to cut tape by tiny fractions. B. C. Horton, a BBC producer, wrote to a colleague on 6 March 1956 about the risks and obstacles involved in hiring Bowen: "Her voice is not ideal but I would suggest that we put her on tape and trim the stammer and, as I said, ask her to arrange the talks so that they could be broken up by readings – or, in the case of dialogue, even by dramatic excerpts" (BBC "Talks," 1941-62). Horton forewarned the woman who was slated to transcribe the three "Truth and Fiction" talks that her task would not be easy: "Elizabeth Bowen, however, is a stammerer – that is why we have never used her on such a big undertaking before we had tape. We believe that she will be able to speak rather more fluently, however, if she is allowed to speak unscripted from notes" (BBC "Talks," 1941-62; memo dated 9 August 1956). When the essays were published in *Afterthought*, Bowen added a headnote to explain that "the talks were recorded as they were spoken; and in that form they are given here. Repetitions, overemphasis, incoherences, etc., must be allowed for" (*Afterthought* 114). The cadence of the spoken voice – the tendency to reiterate and to overstate that can occur in conversation – takes precedence over the accuracy of finely honed prose. The published broadcast is meant to retain some of the spontaneity of its oral delivery.

Because editors cut radio tape to fit specific blocks of time, and because editing out a stammer required painstaking effort, Bowen was not everyone's first choice as a radio guest. Hightoned and affected, her voice lacked common appeal. On tape, her voice has a tendency to dryness, even hoarseness. Her pinched, upper-class accent, with its squashed vowels and tripping consonants, put many listeners off. The Audience Research Department at the BBC conducted a survey of listeners' reactions to "Writing about Rome" in late October 1959. Ninety-two respondents ranked Bowen's talk about Rome very low indeed. It received a score of 50, "well below the average (70) for reported talks on the basic Home Service during the first half of 1959" (BBC "Talks," 1941-62; report dated 29 October 1952). Many respondents disliked the impressionistic, rather than factual, approach to the subject. They called it "highfalutin" and "abstract." Most of all, they thought that Bowen's voice left a great deal to be desired:

Another factor in listeners' disappointment was Miss Bowen's poor broadcasting manner. A small number admired her clear articulation, unhurried delivery, and rich tone of voice, and said she was a delightful broadcaster whose manner was well suited to her material. But half the listeners in the sample considered her only a moderately good speaker while a third classed her as poor. Her main faults, it seems, were a slow, jerky and hesitant delivery and an affected manner. She had a tendency to stutter, which was painful to hear, and her diction was pedantic and over-emphasised, with pinched, distorted vowel sounds. Several said her voice tended to divert their attention from the matter, and a Schoolmaster's wife remarked, "I always feel with this speaker that it would be better to get someone else to read her fine material. Her speech defects make it painful listening – whether they are affectation or affliction." (BBC "Talks," 1941-62; report dated 29 October 1952)

The stammer was an inseparable part of Bowen's persona. In *Pictures and Conversations*, she links her stammer with her father's mental breakdown, which happened when she was six: "I had come out of the tensions and mystery of my father's illness, the apprehensive silences or chaotic shoutings [. . .] with nothing more disastrous than a stammer" (12). Seeking a cure, she saw an Austrian psychoanalyst in 1942. The analyst talked and she listened, with the result that nothing at all changed (Ritchie 142). Despite her stammer, many people described Bowen as a spellbinding talker. Raymond Mortimer told Charles Ritchie, "she has such charm and is so kind and makes most of one's friends seem irremediably vulgar" (Ritchie 130). Molly Keane remembers that Bowen magnetised attention when she entered a room: "Her wit simply flared; she was marvellous. And she made you feel marvellous, she made you feel witty, which was the best way to be" (Foster, *Life with the Lid Off*).

Charisma counters the liability of a stammer. In a BBC memorandum, Jocelyn Ferguson wrote that "Elizabeth Bowen has too bad a stammer to be interviewed; it's sad, but what a blessing for her that she can write" (BBC "Talks," 1963–67; memo dated 6 February 1964). Writing is a way of not stuttering; to write is to achieve fluency, free of the treacheries implicit in the spoken voice. Novels and short stories overcome reticence by revealing what characters think or feel prior to speaking. Bowen's syntax, often torturous and circumlocutious, does not replicate her stammer so much as break free from it. She expresses ideas in complicated clauses that are not necessarily easy to speak aloud, but that are not cumbersome either. John Banville, who describes Bowen's prose as "dense, compacted, full of traps for the unwary, like a spy's debriefing," sees her style as a particular kind of "Hiberno-English," as if English held her Irish tongue hostage (qtd. in Corcoran, "Sunday Feature"). Likewise, writing is a form of escape from a stammer. Whereas a stammer might indicate an interdiction against speaking – what is difficult to say, what cannot be verbalised because of social conventions – written language, no matter how inverted, is always fluent on the page. Reading is another way of not halting and floundering.

Despite her stammer, which was occasionally debilitating and embarrassing for listeners, no matter how sympathetic, she kept appearing on radio. In fact, radio was central to Bowen's self-conception as a wage-earning writer. For a fee, she agreed to participate in all manner of programmes. For a four-minute interview with Bob Waller on 10 February 1964, she received five guineas. In June 1965, her review of Elizabeth Coxhead's *The Daughters of Erin*, which lasted five minutes, earned her a fee of fifteen guineas plus expenses for travel up from Hythe. For a two-and-a-half-minute segment called "Companions of Literature," part of a series called "Today," which went to air on the Home Service in July 1965, she received five guineas. In 1963, she wrote an appreciation of Katherine Mansfield's short stories, which could not have been difficult, given that she had already written an introduction to a selection of Mansfield's stories in 1956. Promoting her own work, she received twenty guineas plus £2.8.0 for introducing and reading an extract from *The Little Girls*. She seldom turned down an offer. When she did, she had legitimate grounds. In 1956, R. E. Keen at the Talks Department of the BBC asked Bowen to participate in a programme about novels that novelists had failed to complete. On 10 April 1956, she wrote to Keen to decline:

I should have liked very much to take part. But the thing is, I do not seem to have any unfinished novel. When I was young, one or two were abandoned after the first few pages, but I cannot now remember anything about them. I suppose the fact that I have written so many short stories, and that my novels have been comparatively few, may account for the fact that I've finished the few I *have* started. (BBC "Talks," 1941-62)

Notwithstanding her status as an author, Bowen could not write and broadcast anything she pleased. She wrote to order on many occasions. William Empson, in charge of broadcasts to China, urged her to submit regular book reviews. On 28 June 1943, Empson wrote,

We would be very pleased if you would do us another 1,000 word book talk for next Monday; we would want it in by Friday afternoon. I am enclosing the recent back numbers to show what has been talked about. We are anxious to have rather more full descriptions of books in these talks now, as the "trends" seem to have been covered, and as the audience won't see the books for some time they can only be interested if the description is detailed. (BBC "Scriptwriter," 1943–62)

Book reviews fulfilled a cultural mission: alerting overseas listeners that British writers continued to publish despite the war. For Bowen, however, reviews were journeyman's labour, done at high speed for a fee.

In an "Autobiographical Note" that she wrote for publicity purposes in 1948 and revised in 1952, Bowen listed her broadcasts and drew attention to the technical demands that radio made on her: "Writing for the air frenzies me: it is such a new and different technique – all the same, its problems are fascinating" (HRC 1.5). She did not easily master its exigencies, such as the judicious use of music and imprinting the identities of characters through speech. In her directions for "The Confidant," she exaggerates the clamour of telephones ringing and doors squeaking, as well as the various timbres of the human voice. In the 1930s and 1940s, when radio plays were in their infancy, manuals flooded the markets with advice to neophyte writers about how to construct dramas solely out of sound. In *How to Write Broadcast Plays*, Val Gielgud, the long-serving Head of Drama at the BBC, advised that "the author must continually bear in mind that he has nothing but his dialogue in which he must not only tell his story clearly and unmistakeably, but also indicate changes of scene, physical traits of his characters, and the essential details of their background" (18). He further remarks that the audience is "a cross-section of society made up of individuals, for the most part by their firesides" (27). Because audiences are accustomed to listening to music, not to plays, Gielgud claims, the playwright for radio should exploit music as a way to focus the ear – within reason, of course. Plots and characters should be clearly delineated and limited in number.

"Dialogue for radio or for the stage," declares Howard Thomas in another advice manual, "is a report of speech as it should be" (69). Thomas counsels the radio writer to vary the tempo and rhythm of sentences and to use sound effects only "if they are essential" (76). Albert Crews, arguing for the clearest possible organisation of a radio talk, states that "the ear has a short memory; while it listens to one point, it is likely to forget the point which it has just heard" (158). The radio appeals only to the ear, but the ear of the audience tunes in and out; at any point in a radio talk or drama, one listener might shut off the radio while another listener tunes in. The radio drama, therefore, has no moment when intensity can flag. The convincingness of a broadcast play depends on its attention to acoustic details: "for radio, the dramatist must study the sound values of a locale" (Crews 284). Seasides do not sound the same as city streets. Erik Barnouw claims that effective radio is built from three elements: speech, music, and sound effects. Although Barnouw acknowledges that speech is the chief among these elements, he adds that "sounds and music are no longer mere accessories or backgrounds in drama, but can occupy the *entire stage*. They become storytelling factors in their own right" (30). Barnouw advocates the careful use of montage, echo chambers, choral speech, and contraptions such as the Sonovox to enhance sound on the air.

While Bowen was writing radio dramas in the 1940s, she was herself listening in. Like other Londoners who lived through the blitz, she was attuned to the changes wrought by radio as a mechanism for disseminating news and culture. In 1969, reviewing Angus Calder's *The People's War*, she singles out the emotive effect of sound on listeners during the war:

> In the main, the voice proved mightier than the pen. Sound made for community of sensation, was emotive (which was required), served

entertainment. Genius came to the surface: ITMA began. Most of all, the microphone built up star personalities. The desideratum was not to *address* the masses but speak as one of them; at that, Mr. Calder suggests, J. B. Priestley was better than Churchill. Press and radio combined in keeping the people's collective image constantly in front of the people's eyes, and did well in doing so. (*Mulberry Tree* 184)

"ITMA," an acronym for *It's That Man Again,* was a BBC radio comedy in which Hitler, "that man again," epitomises the cult of personality. Although theorists deride radio as an instrument of propaganda – Theodor Adorno claims that "totalitarian radio" produces cultural goods that are "transformed into evils" (275) – Bowen understands the democratising function of the medium, especially in time of war. Instead of being an apparatus of state power, the radio unites people and informs them. At the same time, *It's That Man Again,* like other parodies, mocks the abuses of power that the radio, in certain circumstances, engenders. Sound induces a sense of community during the war, and it perpetuates the notion of personal involvement as an obligation of citizenship. As Todd Avery claims, a "moral imperative" (5) motivates public broadcasting.

Transformations in media accelerated in the postwar period, especially at the BBC. The Third Programme, launched in September 1947, cultivated highbrow culture with adaptations of novels, documentaries, learned conversations, and classical music. Via its overseas services, the BBC projected a unified idea of Britishness around the globe. For her part, Bowen thought the Third Programme ripe with potential for raising tone. In her essay on the Third Programme, she writes,

> Language can put out a majesty in its sheer sound, even apart from sense: in poetry and, at its greatest, prose, this becomes apparent. My own feeling is that in listening to spoken (or broadcast) speech, we have listened for sense too much and for sound too little. However, the intelligent listener's wish for *intelligibility* must take first place still – Sartre's *Huis Clos* in English gave him enough to bite on! (102)

Sound can take precedence over speech. By extension, culture, as Bowen understands it, can supersede language. Intelligibility matters, but the listener has to make an effort by listening to *Huis Clos* in French, which puts the onus on intelligent listening rather than intelligibility. Whether the British listener understands French or not, the actors' voices communicate meaning. Neither physical gesture nor *mise-en-scène* assists the radio voice. Endorsing the mission of the Third Programme, which was routinely castigated for being élitist, Bowen wonders whether élitism has limits when it comes to culture and speech: "Stress on style, manner, execution, if necessary virtuosity – can we now, have too much of that? War on the slurred, the sagging, the slovenly – *can* that be carried too far?" ("Third Programme" 76).

By aligning herself with the cultural establishment, specifically the Third Programme, Bowen distanced herself from the young. In her essays and broadcasts, she chastises her juniors for failing in their social obligations. In Bowen's estimation, younger generations in the postwar seldom measure up to their elders. In the radio essay called "On Not Rising to the Occasion," she compares her Edwardian upbringing with the permissive child-rearing techniques that produced, in the 1950s, a crop of spoiled children. In "The Idea of the Home," she criticises American teenagers for their slovenliness. For Bowen, the refusal to grow up – she has *Peter Pan* in mind when she refers to "Never-neverland" in "The Idea of the Home" – has political implications. In "Ireland Today," she spells out the pitfalls of immaturity with the example of the Irish Republic, which remained neutral during the war. In Bowen's view, neutrality "fostered a listless irresponsibility" and thwarted political maturity: "It became first discouraging, later unnecessary, to think. This, at the stage of growth on which Ireland had entered by 1939, was a set-back: it became harder to be adult in Ireland. What was lost, then, still has to be caught up with" (HRC 6.5). Resistance to world politics is like an obstinate clinging to adolescence; it stunts development. It promotes sulkiness as if it were a virtue. Although many of Bowen's stories and novels concern children and adolescence, she held no illusions about youth. In "The Cult of Nostalgia," she is wary of identifying childhood with virtue. While granting that children and adults have different versions of happiness that are not the least bit comparable, she cautions that the "unconscious imperialism of childhood" (225) is really not practicable for grown-ups and should by no means be taken as a model of how to behave. Childhood is no enchanted age, except for those who refuse to grow up.

Bowen worked out her opinions about culture in her speeches, more so even than her broadcasts or essays. When talking to an audience, she was more adventurous in her propositions and formulations. She enjoyed the give-and-take of discussion. On 4 June 1947, she addressed the Oxford University Writers Club, made up of undergraduates. Ludovic Kennedy, secretary for the club, described Bowen's speech in his minutes:

> After a very excellent dinner in Christchurch, S.C.R., the Club moved somewhat unsteadily to the Secretary's Rooms to hear Miss Elizabeth Bowen talk on "The Short Story." Miss Bowen gave a most interesting and scintillating address in the course of which she said that the continental writers (particularly Chekhov & de Maupassant) founded the short story & its development and growth in England were comparatively recent. In conclusion of her address, questions were put by the Club and answered by Miss Bowen: Lord David Cecil proved very active at this juncture, both asking and answering questions himself, though not the same ones. The meeting adjourned at 11.45. (Bodleian Ms. Top. Oxon. d. 1094)

In the 1950s and 1960s, Bowen expanded the ambit of her influence by lecturing in the US. She crisscrossed the continent, with stops in Berkeley, Chicago, Greensboro, Boston, and other cities. By any measure, she set a frantic pace. Between 22 February and 16 March 1954, she travelled to Danville, Chatham, Sweet Briar, and Hollins College in Virginia for speaking engagements. Heading south by bus, she lectured at Durham, Winston-Salem, and Greensboro, then she headed north to Pennsylvania for talks in Meadville and Philadelphia, with detours to Charlotte, North Carolina, and Youngstown, Ohio. In the middle of this tour, she squeezed in a lecture in Washington, DC, on 7 March (HRC 12.5). She gave at least twelve addresses in twenty-two days. It is possible that she hit the road again immediately. She bought a bus ticket on 13 March 1954 for a trip that circled from Norfolk to Charlotte to Atlanta to Jackson, back to Atlanta and on to New York City (HRC 12.5). She may or may not have taken this trip; the bus tickets were never cancelled. She did, however, deliver a lecture in Immaculata, Pennsylvania, on 23 March 1954. In her lectures, Bowen talked on literary subjects: the short story, the poetic element in fiction, character, fictional time. With such a strict schedule, she almost certainly repeated material from one event to the next, with a certain degree of improvisation. In a letter dated 10 April 1952, Bowen recommended that the historian Veronica Wedgwood engage an agent to organise her lecture tours in the US because she could save the trouble of haggling over fees and setting an itinerary. Bowen closed her letter to Wedgwood with some personal tips: "I hope you'll go to Amherst, Mass. (lovely New England place, charming people) also the University of Chicago. I liked the people *there* particularly, & the city itself, though grim, has a fascination of its own" (Bodleian MSS c.6829). Bowen was drawn to university campuses. She spoke at Boston University on 26 May 1953. She spoke at Harvard University on 18 November 1956. At the invitation of Morton Dauwen Zabel, she lectured at the University of Chicago on 1 April 1958 on "The Strength of the Story" (Morton Dauwen Zabel papers; letter dated 3 December 1957). In October 1957, she told Charles Ritchie that she was "a practically full-time female lecturer" (*Love's Civil War* 309). Being a woman who spoke in public rattled her to some degree, or so she claimed. In a letter to Ritchie from London on 23 March 1956, she worried over the trials of after-dinner speaking:

> My date last night was being guest of honour at a large literary dinner called the Society of Bookmen. I was rather scared, as I had to speak for 20 minutes, and I always think after-dinner speeches are so difficult – and particularly inappropriate for women. However I got by all right: one old boy Geoffrey Faber [founder of Faber & Gwyer], who is a Fellow of All Souls so ought to know, said it was the best speech on any literary subject he had ever heard. (*Love's Civil War* 226)

Whether speaking to the Society of Bookmen, Harvard University undergraduates, or the Oxford University Writers Club, Bowen was, more often than not, the only woman in the room. Her speeches and broadcasts demonstrate an acute consciousness of the constraints placed on women in terms of careers and opportunities. Although she disclaims any affinity with feminism in the 1950s and 1960s, such as she understood it, Bowen looked upon women as the equals of men. She liked the clash of opinions in conversation, irrespective of the gender of her interlocutors. She also liked the emotional charge brought about by two people in intimate conversation. Her fiction is unthinkable without intensely realised conversations between two characters: Matchett sitting on the edge of Portia's bed offering starchy advice in *The Death of the Heart*; Louie Lewis accosting Harrison in Regent's Park at the opening of *The Heat of the Day*. Bowen was not unfeeling about women's roles, but she did not champion women just because they were women. Her female characters have many foibles, but so do her male characters. In both men and women, she admires strength of mind, an ingrained sense of social responsibility, and reasonableness connected to feeling. In her broadcasts and speeches, she speaks freely about the changing status of women irrespective of their age. In "Coronation," Bowen considers the expectations placed upon Queen Elizabeth. In her review of *The Daughters of Erin*, she calls upon Irish women to "break through" custom and find fulfilment in art, theatre, or politics. Collectively, these representations of women and comments on women's roles create a wider frame in which to read Bowen's "feminism," loosely construed. Never unsympathetic towards those who suffered, Bowen herself proved exemplary in "breaking through" the conventions that constrained women of her generation. In an important sense, her broadcasts give voice to an ethos of social challenge and change – for women, for the young, and for writers.

Editorial Principles and Selection of Material

To locate Bowen's broadcasts, speeches, and interviews, I used J'nan M. Sellery and William O. Harris's comprehensive *Elizabeth Bowen: A Bibliography*. Sellery and Harris's pioneering work facilitated my research at every step. I have made a few amendments to their bibliography where new information has come to light. For example, instead of using the title "Coronation," as Bowen did for her 1953 broadcast, Sellery and Harris combine the programme title with a descriptive title: "For a Sovereign Lady – Some Thoughts on the Coronation" (283). Bowen clearly preferred "Coronation," so I have adopted that title. Although Sellery and Harris mention that "Ireland Today" was broadcast on CBS television in May and June 1947 (276), I can find no substantiation for this claim.

The materials in this volume have been arranged thematically. Within sections, pieces are arranged chronologically whenever possible. I have grouped essays written for the radio in one section, interviews and conversations in another. Public speeches, mostly but not exclusively given in the US, form a distinct group, as do Bowen's essays about film and radio. As an international celebrity, Bowen repeatedly answered questionnaires for newspapers and magazines; she was mindful of having to promote her books through various media, including the radio spot and the television interview. Her abbreviated answers to questions in "Confessions," "The Cost of Letters," and "Portrait of a Woman Reading" are revealing and teasing in equal measure, and they anticipate the longer answers that she gave to similar questions during radio interviews. While drawing attention to the integral relation of broadcasting to Bowen's career as a novelist and essayist, this collection does not aim to be exhaustive. Instead, it offers a sampling of Bowen's radio broadcasts and public addresses that attest to her diverse interests and social engagement.

Prolific as Bowen was, she inevitably wrote broadcasts and speeches that have disappeared. Many items have been lost because no one saved a typescript or because a tape was not archived. She wrote an essay called "Hythe and Romney Marshes" for the BBC Home Service in 1946; as far as I can discern, no trace of this broadcast, apart from its title, remains. In the same year, she wrote a radio essay about Bloomsbury, which, to the best of my knowledge, does not survive in any version, either typed or taped. Bowen does offer fugitive opinions about Bloomsbury on several occasions. In a 1970 television documentary about Virginia Woolf, "A Night's Darkness, a Day's Sail," Bowen reminisces about the Bloomsbury writer, her senior by seventeen years, dead since 1941. Bowen specifically remembers the breathless way of talking that prevailed in Bloomsbury and Woolf's "hooting" laughter – the vocal expression, Bowen claims, of Woolf's "capacity for joy." Bowen conjures up the past through its sounds. By extension, history is a sequence of acoustic events: a shout in the street, a ringing telephone in an empty house, Virginia Woolf's hooting laughter.

Although such sounds can be recalled in fiction or in memory, they are not, in themselves, lasting. Time and fragility imperil recorded broadcasts. Although the BBC Sound Archives owns a tape of Bowen talking about *The Little Girls*, it is damaged and no longer available for listening, at least not when I visited the archive in June 2009. Although some of Bowen's radio pieces were recorded then shelved, others were explored but never realised. Laurence Gilliam, Director of Features at the BBC, wrote to Bowen on 13 March 1947: "it is the middle of March and we left it that that was the season in which to discuss the Cinque ports idea again. Apart from that I'd like to know if you have any other Feature ideas brewing, how about talking this over at lunch one day soon?" (BBC "Scriptwriter," 1943–62). Bowen answered the next day, agreeing to a lunch date and a chat about the Cinque Ports, but the idea never came to fruition, as far as I know.

While some materials have been lost or never realised, other items have been omitted from this volume. Bowen's book reviews for the radio reflect her engagement with contemporary writing, but cannot be said to figure among her best work. Although I have included two book reviews, I have left out a third review because it is more synoptic than critical. The extraordinary opening to "Book Talk – New and Recent Fiction" justifies its publication. How does the novelist, faced by the magnitude of the war, begin to imagine anything stranger or more comprehensive than history? What does war spare for the imagination? Reviewing books on the radio was a means of extending the parameters of literary culture. At the same time, like her contemporaries E. M. Forster and J. B. Priestley, Bowen dignified the emerging cadre of public intellectuals by the rigour of her literary opinions. Bowen's review of *The Daughters of Erin* rounds out knowledge of her reading in Irish history and culture. The three reviews that she wrote under William Empson's encouragement for broadcast to China seem to have disappeared.

I chose not to include all of Bowen's radio and television interviews in this volume. Her appearances on television quiz shows and "meet the author" publicity spots do not reveal very much about her ideas or methods. In 1948, along with novelist Elizabeth Jenkins and scholar R. W. Chapman, she judged the *Sanditon* competition, for which entrants submitted endings to Jane Austen's unfinished novel. Although the judges' commentary is extant, it is a collaborative, and very brief, document, that bears no trace of Bowen's flair. Although she rose to the demands of being interviewed with grace and perseverance, not every conversation was a success. On 4 May 1955, Walter Allen interviewed her for a programme called "We Write Novels." Other novelists in the series included Joyce Cary, Philip Toynbee, C. P. Snow, L. P. Hartley, and J. B. Priestley. Allen, a literary journalist and critic best known for *The English Novel*, a survey published in 1954, asked Bowen about her Irishness, her sensitivity to place, and her favourite novelists. Allen also asked whether sex – being a woman – played a part in Bowen's writing. She answered in a round-about fashion: "in spite of all the immense changes in the last fifty years, women, I think, tend to lead rather circumscribed lives. You can't generalise but the average woman isn't less free as a rule, either through marriage or children." She concluded her answer with an acknowledgement that writing about places is not a choice, but an imposition on women writers: "I think it needs effort for a woman to shake off her surroundings completely, and possibly part of the effort results in a work of art. You're trying to sever the shackles of your existence." By and large, Allen's questions are unsurprising and, for the most part, badly formulated. The interview is filled with humming and hawing. Almost every one of Allen's comments begins with "Yes, well . . . " Despite his apparent agreement, Allen pays no attention to what Bowen says, which creates disconnectedness in the line of questioning. The transcriber could make neither head nor tail of the interlocutors' syntax; it is a mishmash of run-on sentences and incoherent thinking.

I omitted other interviews as well. On 11 March 1957, Bowen appeared on the popular BBC programme "Desert Island Discs," hosted by Ray Plomley. Whatever her other merits, Bowen was not especially musical. Victoria Glendinning, in fact, calls her "strictly unmusical" (151). She seems to have enjoyed going to the opera from time to time, but she shows no particular musical knowledge or discernment. Her eight choices for desert island music are not adventurous: Paul Robeson singing "St. Louis Blues," "Hallelujah" from *Hit the Deck*, Beethoven's *Moonlight Sonata*, Schubert's *Unfinished Symphony*, Mozart's D-minor Piano Concerto, "Ohne mich" from *Der Rosenkavalier*, the aria "Sheep May Safely Graze" from Bach's cantata *Was mir behagt*, and Jeremiah Clarke's "Trumpet Voluntary." Plomley asked Bowen to name one luxury object, in addition to the eight records, that she would take to her hypothetical desert island. She suggested a kaleidoscope, because it is "perpetually new, perpetually brilliant and can be shaken into a patch of brilliant inexhaustible patterns" ("Desert" 13). She intends to build a hut on her fantasy island and decorate it with mosaics made of shells. "I'd like to civilise the island as fast as I could," she told Plomley (11). Bowen's responses are lighthearted, but not especially revealing. In a similar vein, Robert Waller interviewed Bowen at her home in Hythe about *The Little Girls* in March 1964 for a series called "The World of Books." During the interview, Waller talked a great deal and Bowen spoke briefly about the "magic land" of childhood and the tendency of people in middle age to be "more acquiescent to outside things" ("World" 2, 3). Judging by the transcription of this broadcast, Bowen stuttered violently, causing moments of drastic incomprehension for the transcriber.

Innumerable adaptations of Bowen's short stories and novels – for radio, television, and film – have also not been included in this volume. Her short stories were frequently read on the air without changes. On the other hand, *Friends and Relations*, *The House in Paris*, *The Heat of the Day* and other works required some cuts for the sake of dramatic intensity and length. Although she allowed other writers to adapt her work, Bowen kept a watchful eye on the results. She refused to endorse anything that did not meet her standards. Her novels continue to incite interest from film-makers. Harold Pinter wrote the screenplay for a made-for-television movie version of *The Heat of the Day* (1989), and John Banville adapted *The Last September* (1999) as a feature film.

Broadcasts create a different set of problems for editing than typed or typeset essays. Conversation relies on a different kind of syntax and grammar than written speech does. When transcribers at the BBC typed up interviews, they used their good judgement about punctuation and syntax. Eliminating an "and" and bringing a sentence to a full stop interrupts the conversational habit of linking sentences *ad infinitum* with coordinate conjunctions. In less successful transcriptions, no full stops are used; a bewildering number of independent clauses are pegged together with commas. Some transcribers had difficulty rendering Bowen's speech because of her stammer and accent. She, more than other speakers, caused transcribers to leave ellipses or question marks to indicate points of non-comprehension. In the short interview between Bowen and Waller, the transcriber clearly went over the tape several times, trying to capture Bowen's exact words: "Was not the reality of existence more (unint.) before we fell into this – perhaps one ought not to call it (unint.) ~~wreck~~ but I think it is a ~~wreck~~, it is this world in which we live, in which we analyse ourselves and each other all the time" ("World of Books" 3). The two parenthetical notations, "unintelligible," might be occasions when Bowen stammered or muttered. "Wreck" is crossed out twice, which indicates that the pronunciation was equally incomprehensible. Further guesses about what Bowen actually said have been substituted above the deletions, but the words are too faint to decipher.

The quality of a transcription depends almost entirely on the ability of the transcriber to infer meaning and to apply subtle punctuation that catches tone of voice or inference. Dashes, commas, or parentheses can substitute for each other around a clause to create different degrees of emphasis. The talented transcriber has a supple but precise command of punctuation. Punctuation obscures or clarifies meaning. When broadcasts were edited for publication, fidelity to tone was not at issue. In printed text, punctuation is based on the conventions of written language; grammatical coherence takes precedence over the cadences of speech. Whenever possible, I have used published versions of essays and corrected typescripts as base texts to avoid making false inferences. In general, published texts are more stable than transcriptions. They are not, however, always available. Where multiple versions of an item exist – draft, recording, transcription, publication – I have noted significant variants, but draw the line at listing each and every discrepancy.

Some transcriptions require editorial interventions. In "Conversation on Traitors," the transcriber rendered a comment by Noel Annan with minimal punctuation: "I mean doesn't it make us, for instance, that action of Fuchs' suspicious of people whom we don't really know much about because they've come from a foreign country and settled here." In my understanding of this *viva voce* syntax, the pronoun "it" precedes its referent. Without changing any words, I have re-punctuated the sentence: "I mean doesn't it make us – for instance, that action of Fuchs's – suspicious of people whom we don't really know much about, because they've come from a foreign country and settled here?" The sentence is clearly interrogative, but the transcriber did not put in a question mark. Even inserting a comma before "because" shifts the meaning from not knowing much about people who come from a foreign country to being suspicious of people who come from a foreign country. The comma facilitates sense, although I cannot be certain that such meanings were clear in the mind of the speaker or inferred by the transcriber. In all instances, I have tried to create a clear reading text, not a variorum edition or a strictly faithful duplication of what a typist heard and transcribed in the 1940s or 1950s. The speaking voice, after all, has its inherent ambiguities.

In "Conversation on Traitors" and "Frankly Speaking," someone crossed out long sections of text. These proposed cuts might indicate passages that the producer wanted to omit from the broadcast, or they might be passages that would not be suitable in a published version of the conversation. Without a tape or a published text, I cannot be certain what the deletions signify. In "Frankly Speaking," cuts are so extensive that, were they implemented, little would be left of the original broadcast. These deletions might even be Bowen's. She discloses more in this interview than she usually likes to, and, looking over the transcription, she may have wished to impose a greater degree of discretion on the text.

To create uniformity across this volume, I have adopted British spelling, even when transcribers opt for American spelling. Notes are restricted to significant changes, points of information, and perplexities, rather than a comprehensive accounting of small changes in orthography or punctuation. Where meaning seems self-evident from the context or where general knowledge is assumed, I have not provided annotations. Bowen had a habit of misremembering titles, so I correct such errors as needed. In the four radio dramas, I have tried to impose consistency in presentation, while allowing latitude for differences in each play. Bowen, like most radio dramatists, distinguishes between kinds of sound in her instructions. Directions to actors about how to read the text, which are usually directions about the pitch and quality of the voice, appear in parentheses and italics: "*(eagerly)*," "*(surprised)*," "*(gratefully)*." Directions concerning sounds from other acoustic dimensions are generally placed in parentheses and written in block capitals: "(BALLROOM MUSIC: HUM OF VOICES)" or "(CANNON SHOTS)." These cues are meant for producers rather than actors. They therefore require a different presentation. "The Confidant" is an exception to this general rule; in this play, Bowen used italics for both actors' and producers' cues, which I have preserved.

"Panorama of the Novel" is Bowen's only original publication in French. She wrote the essay in English and Pier Ponti translated it into French. I have, perhaps brashly, translated the text back into English. The original English version is not, as far as I know, extant. In translating, I have tried to capture some of the hesitancies and qualifications in Bowen's style, but grammatical correctness and syntactical cogency take priority over style. I do not aim to invent, or re-invent, Bowen's prose. Should the original English text come to light at some time in the future, I would be very pleased to see it, but I suspect it would bear only a cousinly relation to my translation.

Plays for the Air

The Confidant

Characters:
Hermione Hearthold (the Confidant)
Mr. Antrobus: a Young Man with Love Trouble
Mrs. Billing: a Lady with Husband Trouble
Major James Jeremy: an Old Friend
Mary: Hermione's Maid

The scene is Hermione's small pretty London drawing-room.
Hermione and Mr. Antrobus are seated side by side on the sofa.
They have just finished tea. Near the sofa, a telephone stands on
a glass-topped table.

MR. ANTROBUS: (*his voice fading in, as though he had been
talking for some time*) . . . obvious that you do not feel as I do."
– She came out with this, I may tell you, without warning! Up to
then, the evening seemed to be going well. Naturally, her saying
that threw me right out. Looking back, I see now that I lost my
head. I said . . .

HERMIONE: (*tensely*) – Yes? –

MR. ANTROBUS: I'm trying to remember, word for word, what I did say. You see this was important.

HERMIONE: Don't hurry. – A cigarette?

MR. ANTROBUS: (*absently*) N'thanks. (*Pause*) I've got it now, exactly. What I said to her was –

(*Telephone begins to ring loudly, cutting in upon Mr. Antrobus.*)

HERMIONE: (*apologetic – speaking above ring of telephone*) Oh dear!

MR. ANTROBUS: (*in martyrised tone*) Do you have to answer it?

HERMIONE: But otherwise, wouldn't it go on ringing?

MR. ANTROBUS: Or I could – I could say that you're not here?

HERMIONE: (*still apologetic, but firm*) – The thing is, there's someone it just *might* be – (*Is heard to unhook receiver; bell stops. Over her shoulder, urgently, to Mr. Antrobus*) Now don't forget where we'd got to: it's so important! I particularly want to know what you said to her. (*Into telephone, in neutral voice*) Hullo? . . . (*With feeling*) Oh, hullo – yes, indeed! I've been on tenterhooks. How did it go off – well? . . . No, I'm *not*, as it happens; not just for the moment, no. I'd been hoping you'd ring up earlier . . . You couldn't just tell me in three words? . . . (*Discouraged*) No, I see that would hardly do . . . Perhaps if you rang me later, or I rang you? . . . About seven? . . . Oh dear, will you? Then half-past six, perhaps? –

MR. ANTROBUS: (*cutting in in glum and offended voice*) – I shall have to be off by six, if that's any help.

HERMIONE: (*desperate, over her shoulder to Mr. Antrobus*) Oh, you *mustn't* hurry; there's so much I want to hear! (*Into telephone*) Sorry – I was just saying something to someone else . . . No, I don't think you do: I'll explain later. Six-*fifteen* shall we say, then? . . . I know, I *know*! I can hardly wait to hear how it all went off. Till then, then. (*Click of receiver being replaced. To Mr. Antrobus*) I *am* sorry . . . !

MR. ANTROBUS: (*glumly still*) Not at all. I suppose I *am* taking up an awful lot of your time?

HERMIONE: Of course, of *course* not! I've been so specially keeping today for you. Now, where were we? You promised me you'd remember.

MR. ANTROBUS: Did I?

HERMIONE: You know you did! It was only on *that* condition I took the call. That was someone who – no, it's rather too long a story.[1]

MR. ANTROBUS: (*grimly*) I should imagine so. – Look here, Hermione, this may not be my affair, but don't some of those friends of yours rather prey on you? It may be because I'm reserved myself, but I never can understand that particular type of person who can do nothing but chatter about their own affairs.

HERMIONE: But I think it helps people, don't you, to talk things over?

MR. ANTROBUS: I couldn't say, I'm sure.

HERMIONE: *I* know where we'd got to – you were going to tell me what you said to her when she'd said –

MR. ANTROBUS: Well, exactly what I did say, if you want to know, was. "Look here," I said, "you and I – "

(*Sound of door opening cuts in on Mr. Antrobus' voice. Enter Mrs. Billing.*)

MRS. BILLING: (*in a bedraggled voice*) Oh . . . I suppose I've come in too early?

HERMIONE: (*as though springing up*) Why, Barbara darling, what a lovely surprise! I had no idea you'd be back so soon!

MRS. BILLING: I have had rather a day.

HERMIONE: (*rapidly*) I don't think you know each other? – Mr. Antrobus, Mrs. Billing. (*Mr. Antrobus and Mrs. Billing murmur at one another, without enthusiasm.*)

MR. ANTROBUS: (*dank with resentment*) Well, I must be on the move.

HERMIONE: No, you mustn't! What an idea!

MRS. BILLING: Oh dear, I've been tiresome, coming back here so early. I stupidly thought, Hermione, that I'd find you alone. Don't let me disturb anyone: I'll just slip up to my room.

HERMIONE: (*eagerly*) I really do think, Barbara, that you ought to rest. You're looking sweet, but you look completely all in. – Don't *you* think she looks all in, Andrew? – I'll send you up a tray with some nice hot tea, and then afterwards I'll come up and we'll have a talk.

MRS. BILLING: Well, I should rather like that, if you can spare a moment. (*Significantly*) I've just had *another* letter . . .

HERMIONE: Not *another*? . . . Now, listen, Barbara darling: just go straight on up and take off your shoes and relax. Don't think of another thing.

MR. ANTROBUS: (*to Hermione, with acerbity*) Don't forget, Hermione, you're due to be rung up at six-fifteen.

HERMIONE: (*laughing charmingly*) What a memory! – (*To Mrs. Billing*) Barbara, you're certain you'll be all right? You'll think nice happy thoughts, you promise?

MRS. BILLING: (*tristely*) I'll do my best. (*To Mr. Antrobus, distantly*) Goodbye.

MR. ANTROBUS: Er, goodbye, goodbye.

(*Exit Mrs. Billing: sound of door shutting.*)

MR. ANTROBUS: (*to Hermione*) Didn't realise you had anyone in the house.

HERMIONE: (*sighing*) Poor Barbara. She's in such dreadful trouble. Two days ago, she decided to leave her husband, and she told me she had no place in the world to go. (*Pause*) I did *tell* her you would be coming to tea, and I thought she promised she wouldn't be back till six. But of course, she's strung-up – restless.

MR. ANTROBUS: Keeps popping in and out?

HERMIONE: But if only you knew her story –

MR. ANTROBUS: (*violently*) If a type with a face that length were a wife of mine, she would not get the chance to leave me – I should boot her out of the house.

HERMIONE: (*reproachful*) Oh, Andrew . . . However (*briskly*) let's put the poor dear completely out of our minds. I do want to get back to what we were saying. I mean, I so want to know what you said to her.

MR. ANTROBUS: (*in the tone of one resuming*) Well, I said this to her. I gave her a good straight look and I said, "Now look here, my girl, you and I – "

HERMIONE: (*cutting in*) – Andrew, just one moment: I *must* do something about poor Barbara's tea! Would you be ever so kind and just push that bell?

MR. ANTROBUS: (*frenzied*) What bell?

HERMIONE: (*calmingly*) That bell just right where you are.

(*Brief pause. Then electric bell is heard ringing in distant part of the house.*)

MR. ANTROBUS: (*again resuming, in slightly raised voice*) "You and I," I said, "are going to have this out. – "

HERMIONE: – I wonder if that *was* wise –

MR. ANTROBUS: (*askance*) Why not?

HERMIONE: I mean, wise to have anything out when one's lost one's head?

MR. ANTROBUS: (*indignantly*) Who had lost their head?

HERMIONE: I thought you told me you had, at the beginning?

MR. ANTROBUS: My good woman, the whole point is that I –

(*While he speaks, the door can be heard opening. Maid has entered.*)

MAID: (*cutting in on Mr. Antrobus, though sotto voce*) Madam – ?

HERMIONE: Oh Mary, I want you to take some tea up to Mrs. Billing, up in her room.

MAID: (*respectful but well-informed*) She told me she'd had her tea, madam. I asked when I let her in.

HERMIONE: (*perplexed*) I think she must have forgotten: when I asked her she seemed to like the idea. – Better be on the safe side – she's not very well, you know.

MAID: (*a shade piously*) One can see that, madam.

HERMIONE: (*suddenly, to Mr. Antrobus, alarmed*) Why, what's the matter, Andrew?

MR. ANTROBUS: (*bitterly*) Nothing: what should there be?

HERMIONE: (*hastily*) That will be all, Mary. (*Sound of door shutting, as exit maid.*) Mary's wonderful about people – so sympathetic.

MR. ANTROBUS: (*not without irony*) In fact, *two* wonderful people in one house.

HERMIONE: (*naively, disarming*) You don't mean *I'm* wonderful, do you?

MR. ANTROBUS: Well, you are, er, somewhat amazing, sometimes. I take it this is one of your average afternoons?

HERMIONE: Oh, Andrew, I am so sorry! I do see so horribly well how you must feel. Just when you'd screwed yourself up to the point of telling me things – all this telephoning, then, everyone in and out! I can't help taking an interest in human nature, but –

(Telephone begins ringing again. It is allowed to continue ringing for several seconds, while, presumably, Hermione and Mr. Antrobus confront each other. It ceases ringing abruptly as Mr. Antrobus snatches receiver off.)
MR. ANTROBUS: *(into receiver, furiously)* No, Miss Hearthold is OUT . . . No, I've no idea. *(He replaces receiver with a bang.)*
HERMIONE: *(awed)* Oh, Andrew . . . *(To herself)* Now whoever can *that* have been?
(A click is heard, then an outraged whir from the telephone. Mr. Antrobus has, on second thoughts, again unhooked the receiver, to put it down with a clonk on the glass-topped table.)
MR. ANTROBUS: *(addressing receiver)* And there you can stay, old son. That'll cool you down!
HERMIONE: *(faltering)* Oh but Andrew, *ought* one to leave the receiver off? They say it makes so much trouble for the post office people.
MR. ANTROBUS: Go on, go on, sympathise with the post office! Not that it matters what makes trouble for *me*! – Look, either that thing stays put, or I leave this house.
HERMIONE: Very well, very well, very well.
MR. ANTROBUS: And what did you mean just now by saying I'd lost my head? The whole point is that that's just what I didn't do. I admit I saw pretty red, but I saw clearly. I caught hold of her by the shoulder and pulled her round to face me. –
HERMIONE: *(cutting in)* But look, stop, I'm not quite clear. I thought you told me all this took place in a restaurant. I thought you said you and she were halfway through dinner. You never pulled her about in a *restaurant*, did you, Andrew?
MR. ANTROBUS: I didn't say pulled her about, I said pulled her round. *(Slightly checking himself)* Well, maybe I didn't do that, either – but it's certainly what I'd have done if we'd been alone. As it was, I expect she saw the thought in my mind: she shrank right back and began to –
HERMIONE: *(cutting in, though gently)* I wonder if you *were* right to take such a violent line?
MR. ANTROBUS: But remember what *she'd* just said!
HERMIONE: All the same, Andrew, you can be very frightening.
MR. ANTROBUS: *(deeply gratified)* You think so?

HERMIONE: I expect, you know, she just wanted to talk things out.

MR. ANTROBUS: Then she ought to have had more sense than to start like that. She nearly made me choke over a bit of steak. To say it was obvious I didn't feel as she did! To begin with, I loathe the word "obvious" – it sounds so damn superior.

HERMIONE: (*diffident*) All the same, you don't think that possibly –

(*She has been made to break off by the sound of a bell ringing downstairs in the house.*)

HERMIONE: (*to herself, in quite expressionless voice*) The front door?

MR. ANTROBUS: (*as bell is heard ringing a second time*) All right, come in, come in, never mind about me! (*Rounds on Hermione*) Expecting company, are you?

HERMIONE: (*almost bleating*) I haven't the vaguest idea who this can be – No, truly, Andrew, I'm not expecting anyone. – Oh dear, I meant to tell Mary to say I was not at home . . . However, I expect it's only a parcel.

MR. ANTROBUS: I shouldn't think so. Not at a house like this.

(*Sound, downstairs, of front door being opened, then shut. Voices – a man's and the maid's – below, then ascending stairs.*)

HERMIONE: (*tense but hopeful*) Or it might be Barbara's husband, come round to patch things up. Oh Andrew, that would be perfectly lovely! And in that case we can just send him straight to her room. Then you and I can – (*Door opens*) – What is it, Mary?

(*Mary, presumably holding door open, does not reply. Through open door, James Jeremy's voice can be heard, ascending stair.*)

JAMES JEREMY: (*still off, to maid*) Well, I must say that's funny, Mary. Someone just now on the telephone seemed dead sure she was out. So, all I thought was, I'd come in and wait.

MAID: (*sounding pleased*) Oh no, madam's *in*, sir.

MR. ANTROBUS: (*startled, to Hermione*) What's the matter?

HERMIONE: (*faintly, in changed voice*) Nothing – only, I think it's someone I know.

(*James Jeremy enters.*)

JAMES JEREMY: (*in a voice that can, somehow, be guessed to be not his usual one*) Well, there you are. Here I am.

HERMIONE: (*still in the faint voice*) Jimmy . . .

JAMES JEREMY: I was told you were out.

HERMIONE: I didn't know you were in England . . . That was you just now, then?

JAMES JEREMY: Of course. I was speaking from the box at your street corner. (*His eye lights on telephone with displaced receiver.*) I was lucky, I see, to get through at all. Do you generally keep your receiver on the table?

HERMIONE: N-not always. – Andrew, please put it back.

(*Click of receiver being replaced is heard. James Jeremy now appears, for the first time, to note Mr. Antrobus.*)

JAMES JEREMY: (*his hackles audibly rising*) On second thoughts, I hope I'm not crashing in?

HERMIONE: (*still faintly*) No. – Oh, I don't think you know each other? This is Mr. Antrobus, Major Jeremy . . . Mr. Antrobus had just come to ask my advice.

JAMES JEREMY: (*in the tone of one not seeing*) I see. (*To Mr. Antrobus*) You were so good as to answer me on the line just now?

MR. ANTROBUS: (*in confusion*) It may have been – I –

JAMES JEREMY: Well, just on the chance it was you, I should check on your information another time.

HERMIONE: (*regaining control slightly*) Jimmy, you'll sit down, won't you?

JAMES JEREMY: – Rather depends –

MR. ANTROBUS: (*hastily*) Look, Hermione, I simply must be running away.

HERMIONE: (*vaguely*) Oh dear, must you? Oh dear. (*Rallies*) I am *so* sorry. But you promise to ring me up?

MR. ANTROBUS: (*with a last flash of spirit*) I might, or again I might not.

JAMES JEREMY: As you know, she's not always in.

HERMIONE: (*quavering*) Well, goodbye, Andrew. And, cheer up.

MR. ANTROBUS: Goodbye. (*To James Jeremy*) Goodbye.

JAMES JEREMY: Goodbye.

(*Sound of door opening and shutting marks exit of Mr. Antrobus.*)

HERMIONE: Poor Andrew – you weren't very nice to him.

JAMES JEREMY: That was his look-out, being here. After ten years.

HERMIONE: Ten years?

JAMES JEREMY: You know it is.

HERMIONE: Yes, I know it is. (*Pause: in more steady tone*) Haven't you brought your wife?

JAMES JEREMY: No. She's dead, you know.

HERMIONE: No, I didn't know.

JAMES JEREMY: No, I suppose you didn't. She died abroad, where we lived.

HERMIONE: When?

JAMES JEREMY: Three months ago.

HERMIONE: (*automatically*) Tell me about her.

JAMES JEREMY: Why? I told you about her once.

HERMIONE: You mean, ten years ago?

JAMES JEREMY: You remember?

HERMIONE: (*with a good deal of feeling*) Yes.

JAMES JEREMY: Tell me what you remember.

HERMIONE: (*first with hesitation, then gathering speed*) It was June. I was twenty. You were on leave in England, staying in the next house along the river. I was very happy – except for one thing: it was coming to be near the end of your leave. We had been seeing each other nearly, though not quite every day. The days I didn't see you, I just mooned about. Everyone teased me – I can't tell you what they said.

The last week, you told me you had to go to London for three days. You made me promise that, the evening you came back, I would go out with you on the river. You said to me, to be certain to keep the promise, because you might have something special to say to me.

In those three days while you were away in London, Mary – she was my mother's housemaid then – made me a special new muslin frock. When that evening came, the moon shone, and you came in the punt for me to where I was waiting at the river edge of our lawn. The moon shone all the way down the river, and I waited for what you had got to say –

JAMES JEREMY: – Hermione – !

HERMIONE: No, let me go on. You tied up the punt, and a swan went by. (*Her voice goes dead.*) Then you told me. You told me how you'd been meeting, each time you went to London, a perfectly lovely dark girl, and been falling in love. You told me how it had been, several times, already, on the tip of your tongue to tell me about her, because I was so sympathetic and such a friend. But you'd thought you had better wait till you were quite sure. Tonight, you *could* tell me, because she had just promised to marry you. So I asked again what she was like, and you told me. You said you could go on talking about her all night. I suppose it must have been late when we got in. When you put me back on our lawn, you asked to kiss me – because I understood so wonderfully, you said. Three days after that, you were married in London. I did not have to go, because I had caught a cold.

JAMES JEREMY: On the river?

HERMIONE: (*apologetic*) I get such fearful colds.

JAMES JEREMY: (*fanatically*) I gave you a cold. – It did not take me long to discover I'd been a fool, but for ten years I haven't known that I'd been just that kind of brute. – Yes, as you say, we got married. We sailed next day. There's no "story" – we simply didn't make out. We both saw: we both went on trying. It was very tough on her. I wonder she kept her patience the way she did. On one of the few occasions when she *did* lose her patience, she said: "Must I go on paying for your mistake?" I said, "What mistake?" She said, "Muffing things with that other girl." I said, "What other girl?" She said: "The one on the river."

That sent me off thinking. Since then I've never stopped. The best I could do was, try to be fair to her. I tried hard to hope that you'd never loved me. But of course I always hoped that you did.

So that has been the ten years. She died. I traced your address. Here I am.

HERMIONE: Yes.

JAMES JEREMY: And you?

HERMIONE: Me?

JAMES JEREMY: Yes, that's what I want to hear.

HERMIONE: About me? That's not very interesting. All my friends lead much more interesting lives. You'd be surprised at the things they tell me . . . After you'd gone away, and after my cold got better, I – well, I suppose I thought for a bit. I thought, well, I must *be* something. I remembered you'd kissed me because I was good at listening. Well, at least it's something, I thought, to be good at that. So I sort of took up listening. I got quite interested in it. So many people, you know, have things that they like to say.

JAMES JEREMY: (*grimly*) I'll bet they have.

HERMIONE: (*mildly*) Well, you know, you had yourself.

JAMES JEREMY: Well, what I have to say *now* is about you. (*Door opens: enter Mrs. Billing.*)

MRS. BILLING: (*plaintive as ever*) Hermione? – Oh dear, I am so sorry: I heard the door slam, so I quite took for granted you'd be alone. So I just came down to see when you'd be coming up. I tried and tried to relax, but I haven't succeeded much. And your maid woke me up by bringing a tray of tea.

HERMIONE: (*though with less feeling than usual*) Poor Barbara. (*Automatic*) I don't think you know each other? Major Jeremy, Mrs. Billing.

MRS. BILLING: I'm so sorry I haven't got my shoes on: Hermione advised me to take them off.

HERMIONE: (*to James Jeremy*) Barbara's staying with me.

JAMES JEREMY: Really?

MRS. BILLING: Hermione's been so wonderful. I often ask myself where I should be without her.

JAMES JEREMY: I'm afraid you may have to find out. She's shortly going abroad.

MRS. BILLING: (*wailing*) Hermione darling, what *is* he talking about?

(*She is cut in upon by the telephone, which starts ringing.*)

MRS. BILLING: Oh, for heaven's *sake* – that goes through my head!

(*James Jeremy lifts receiver: telephone stops.*)

MRS. BILLING: Oh, be careful: mind what you say – that might be my husband!

JAMES JEREMY: (*into receiver*) Hullo? . . . Well, she is and she isn't. Who shall I say? . . . Very well, don't, then: it would mean nothing to me. You're not Mrs. Billing's husband? . . . Very well: sorry. (*To Mrs. Billing*) – Not your husband. – (*Into receiver*) What's that? (*Pause of some length*) Right, hold on: I'll tell her. (*To Hermione*) Someone who won't give their name, which they say you'll know, says you specially asked them to ring up at six-fifteen to tell you all about something that's just happened.

HERMIONE: Oh . . . *Is* it six-fifteen?

JAMES JEREMY: So they seem to think.

MRS. BILLING: Indeed it is – I've been lying with my eyes on the clock.

JAMES JEREMY: Then it must be. (*Into receiver*) I gave Miss Hearthold your message, and she asks me to say that she really meant six-fifteen two months hence. She is hoping you will not fail to ring up then. She's afraid this may give you a little extra trouble, as by then she'll be living in South America – also, her name will be Jeremy: please make a note of that. Till then, then: thank you so much, goodbye.

HERMIONE: Jimmy, how *could* you. –

MRS. BILLING: Hermione, honestly, how he *can*! . . . Oh dear, let me go: I want to put on my shoes. I don't feel a bit the same now: this was once such a *restful* house.

JAMES JEREMY: Then don't let us keep you.

(*Sound of his opening door for her.*)

MRS. BILLING: (*exiting wailing*) He's just as bad as my husband. He brings it all back. I should have thought, after all you had heard from me . . . (*Her voice dies away on the stairs.*)

HERMIONE: Oh poor Barbara – Jimmy, I *must* go with her – let go of me – please – oh . . . but darling (*is at this point obstructed, as though by kisses*) . . . But I *ought* to have gone with her . . . Mayn't I?

JAMES JEREMY: You may not: she will have to register somewhere different. This business is wound up. The shop's shut.

New Judgement: Elizabeth Bowen on Jane Austen

NARRATOR: Jane Austen was born at Steventon rectory – twelve miles from Basingstoke, in the pleasant county of Hampshire – on the 16th of December, 1775. The Rectory was set in elm trees – one stormy morning during her girlhood Jane saw two of these trees blown down. Indoors, the rooms were comely, if a little confined. The Steventon neighbourhood, full of small gentle-people, was always lively and often gay. The Rev. Mr. Austen, Jane's father, a happily-married clergyman of good family, saw at Steventon his eight children grow up. Jane herself was to live here till she was twenty-six. She had, apart from her six brothers, one sister – Cassandra –

CASSANDRA: (*In eager affirmation*) – Yes –

NARRATOR: (*Startled*) Miss Cassandra? – I did not know you were here!

CASSANDRA: She would desire me to be present.

NARRATOR: (*A little rattled*) Of course – naturally – I do see – yes. (*Picking up again on more even tone*) Cassandra, her senior by two years. At home, the sisters were much together;

they corresponded copiously when apart. They enjoyed one another's confidence to a rare degree –

CASSANDRA: (*Cutting in*) I had not a thought concealed from her.

NARRATOR: (*After a brief, deferential pause*) Jane, like Cassandra, quitted her parents' home only on visits to relatives or old family friends. She was an affectionate daughter, sister and aunt. When her brothers married, their homes and children provided further extensions of her world. Edward Austen, for instance, with his handsome wife Elizabeth, lived at Godmersham Park, in Kent: it was here that his sisters, Jane and Cassandra, loved above all to stay –

CASSANDRA: (*Eagerly, rapturous*) Ah, Godmersham! – the yellow room, the white room, the little chintz room, the large windows looking out on the park! In the library, Jane was alone in the mornings. She said, "To sit in idleness over a good fire in a well-proportioned room – "

NARRATOR: (*Picking up*) Fanny, the eldest of Edward's eleven children, was to lose her mother when she was seventeen. Mistress of her father's house, distracted with youthful problems, the girl turned instinctively to her younger aunt. Of all the Austen nieces – and they were many – it was apparently Fanny whom Jane loved best. How far did this intimacy create a spell? . . . Though several gentlemen paid addresses to Fanny, we observe that her marriage – to Sir Edward Knatchbull – did not take place till three years after –

FANNY: (*Breaking in, with emotion*) – After –

CASSANDRA: (*Surprised*) – Why – *Fanny*!

FANNY: (*Still with emotion*) After my Aunt Jane died. – "Oh," she said, "oh, Fanny, what a loss it will be when you are married! You are too agreeable in your single state, too agreeable as a Niece. It is very, very gratifying to me to know you so intimately, to have such a thorough picture of your Heart. I shall hate you when your delicious play of mind is all settled down to conjugal and maternal affections . . . Fanny," – she said to me . . .

NARRATOR: The Jane Austen her niece knew was already the authoress of four published novels. *Northanger Abbey*, work of her early girlhood, was with the mature *Persuasion*, published after her death. Interrupted by her illness, the last of her novels, *Sanditon*, was to remain unfinished –

CASSANDRA: – *I* know how it was to end –

NARRATOR: (*Rounding on Cassandra*) Miss Cassandra, we think you know more than *that*! – Those destroyed letters – you know, we hold you accountable! Your sister Jane is known to have written you, day by day, the hopes and the fears involved in her one crucial love-affair. She *did* love, but remained unmarried – that is all we have left. That story – the clue to her life, the key to her art – has been lost to us, through *your* act. You elected to burn those letters. You took too much upon you. Your sister was more than your sister: she belongs to the world.

CASSANDRA: (*Steadily*) She was my sister. Sir, she kept my confidence; I kept hers. A gentlewoman would dread the exposure you seem to desire. My first solicitude was that the secret her heart guarded should not pass, after my death, into vulgar hands. Yes, I burned *those* letters – one packet. The others, Sir, I have left – to you and your world. (*With mounting agitation*) – Fanny – my niece Fanny, *her* dear niece Fanny – *you* will agree that I did right?

FANNY: (*To Narrator*) Sir, you are causing my Aunt Cassandra no small distress. My Aunt Jane, whom you say you honour, would not approve.

CASSANDRA: (*Grateful*) Fanny, she was, I believe, better known to you than to any human being besides myself.

FANNY: Know her? She taught me to know myself. I laid bare to her every shade of my feeling. – "Am I in love *this* time, tell me, *am* I in love?" She always knew – "Fanny," she said . . .

JANE'S VOICE: (*Picking up*) – YOU ARE NOT IN LOVE.

NARRATOR: (*Puzzled*) Miss Cassandra – was that you speaking?

CASSANDRA: No.

JANE'S VOICE: You are not in love, Fanny.

FANNY: (*Rapturously*) Aunt Jane!

JANE'S VOICE: Fanny . . . You are the delight of my life. You are inimitable, irresistible. Such letters as you have lately sent! Such a description of your queer little heart! Such a lovely display – of what imagination does! Fanny, you are the paragon of everything that is silly and sensible, sad and lively, provoking and interesting. – Who can keep pace with the fluctuations of your Fancy, the capriccios of your Taste, the contradictions of your Feelings? –

FANNY: Did I surprise you?

JANE'S VOICE: (*Lovingly*) You are so *odd* . . . (*Pause*) And I? I was languid and dull and very bad company – a minute ago.

CASSANDRA: Bad company – *you*? Jane!

NARRATOR: (*After brief pause, a shade drily*) We share Cassandra's surprise. Jane Austen was known to her family, and has come down to us, as being the soul of *vivacity*. Her youth, that so imperceptibly faded, appears to have lasted a long time. She delighted in dress, dancing, flirtation. (*Pause*) In the gay Hampshire winter when she was twenty-one, the Basingstoke balls and the Steventon neighbourhood were graced by a visiting Irishman, young Mr. Tom Lefroy . . .

JANE'S VOICE: (*Sounding young*) Cassandra . . . We had an exceedingly good ball last night. You scold me so much, I am almost ashamed to tell you how my Irish friend and I behaved. Imagine to yourself everything that is most profligate and shocking in the way of dancing and sitting down together. (*Reflectively*) I *can* expose myself, however, only once more – he leaves the country soon after next Friday. (*Quickly*) On Friday there is the dance at Ashe . . . He is a very gentleman-like, good-looking, pleasant young man, I assure you. But as to our having ever met, except at three balls, I cannot say much – for he is so excessively laughed at about me at Ashe that he is ashamed of coming to Steventon. (*Pause: burst of confidence*) Mr. Lefroy has but one fault – his morning coat is a great deal too light. He is a great admirer of *Tom Jones*, and therefore wears the same coloured clothes, I imagine, as *he* wore when he was wounded. He –

FANNY: (*With laughing severity*) Aunt Jane, I say back to you, YOU ARE NOT IN LOVE.

JANE'S VOICE: O . . .

CASSANDRA: (*Reflectively*) Two days later . . .

JANE'S VOICE: Cassandra, I look forward with great impatience to our party at Ashe tomorrow night, as I rather expect to receive an offer from my friend. (*Quickly*) I shall refuse him of course, unless he promises to give away his white coat! . . . (*Pause*)

FANNY: (*Eager*) Aunt Jane – what happened?

JANE'S VOICE: (*After brief pause, with marked reserve and utter lack of expression*) Mr. Lefroy left our part of the country, after the ball at Ashe. (*Pause: now lightly, reflectively*) I do not want people to be very agreeable, as it saves me the trouble of liking them a great deal.

NARRATOR: Mr. Lefroy was ambitious; he had his career to make. Soon after leaving Hampshire he was called to the Bar: in the end he became Chief Justice of Ireland. To the pleasing young lady who had been his dancing-partner, ambition was – supposedly – quite unknown. *She* merely devoted the year after his departure to (*pause: raised voice*) the writing of *Pride and Prejudice*. Her heroine, Elizabeth Bennet,[1] is her own age – twenty-two. Jane Austen gave her Elizabeth her own brilliant eyes and swift and rallying wit. And – with regard to Wickham – that exceedingly sympathetic young soldier of fortune who appears to be the victim of Mr. Darcy's capricious temper – Elizabeth shows a certain weakness of fancy that could, perhaps, have been Jane Austen's own. Mr. Bingley, tenant of Netherfield, close friend of Mr. Darcy, invites the neighbourhood to a ball. For days the young ladies have been on tiptoe. The officers from the Meryton garrison are known to be coming in full force. There is Elizabeth – with her sisters – arriving: –

(BALLROOM MUSIC: HUM OF VOICES)

NARRATOR: (*As though reading*) – "Till Elizabeth entered the drawing-room at Netherfield and looked in vain for Mr. Wickham among the cluster of red coats there assembled, a doubt of his being present had not occurred to her. She had dressed with more than usual care, and prepared in the highest spirits for the conquest of all that remained unsubdued of his heart . . . The Absolute fact of his absence was pronounced by his friend Mr. Denny, who told them that Wickham had been obliged to go to town on business the day before, and was not returned yet; adding, with a significant smile, 'I do not imagine his business would have called him away just now if he had not wished to avoid a certain gentleman here.'"

(*As though looking up from book*) This is enough for Elizabeth – everything points to the haughty and powerful Darcy's having acted against the defenceless Wickham. Her own dislike of Darcy, formed at their first meeting, seems more than justified. When, without warning, Darcy asks her to dance, she does accept him – but out of sheer surprise.

(MUSIC AGAIN)

NARRATOR: They take their place in the set, and stand for some minutes without speaking, till, suddenly fancying it would be a greater punishment to her partner to oblige him to talk, she makes some slight observation on the dance. He replies, and is again silent.

(MUSIC AGAIN)

NARRATOR: After a pause of some minutes: –

ELIZABETH: (*Jane's voice*) It is *your* turn to say something now, Mr. Darcy. *I* talked about the dance, and *you* ought to make some kind of remark on the size of the room, or the number of couples.

DARCY: (*Smilingly*) Do you talk by rule, then, when you are dancing?

ELIZABETH: Sometimes. One must speak a little, you know. And yet, for the advantage of *some*, conversation ought to be so arranged that they may have the trouble of saying as little as possible.

DARCY: Are you consulting your own feelings, in this case, or do you imagine that you are gratifying mine?

ELIZABETH: (*Archly*) Both – for I have always seen a great similarity in our characters. We are both of an unsocial, taciturn disposition, unwilling to speak unless we expect to say something that will amaze the whole room and be handed down to posterity!

DARCY: (*Indulgent*) This is no very striking resemblance of *your* character, I am sure. How near it may be mine, I cannot pretend to say.

(THE MUSIC LOUDENS AND QUICKENS. DARCY AND ELIZABETH DANCE OUT OF EARSHOT, THEN, DANCING, SLOWLY RETURN. DARCY IS SAYING:)

DARCY: I believe, Miss Bennet, you and your sisters very often walk to Meryton?

ELIZABETH: (*Lightly*) Yes. (*Pointedly*) When you met us there the other day, we had just been forming a new acquaintance.

DARCY: (*Haughtily, well knowing her meaning*) Indeed?

ELIZABETH: (*Firmly*) Yes.

DARCY: (*After marked pause, with marked constraint*) Mr. Wickham is blessed with such happy manners as may ensure his *making* friends. His *retaining* them is less certain.

ELIZABETH: (*With emphasis*) He has been so unlucky, it

seems, as to lose your friendship – in a way that may injure him all his life.

(SOUNDS OF AN INTERRUPTION: DARCY AND ELIZA-BETH HAILED BY ANOTHER COUPLE. CONFUSED QUARTET OF VOICES – IN WHICH DARCY'S REPLIES TO GREETINGS STRIKE AN UNENTHUSIASTIC NOTE – IS BLURRED BY GUST OF MUSIC, SOUNDS OF FEET ON POLISH, RUSTLING SILK . . . AS ALL THIS SUBSIDES THERE IS A MARKED PAUSE.)

DARCY: That interruption has made me forget what we were talking about.

ELIZABETH: (*Very drily*) I do not think we were speaking at all. We have already tried two or three subjects without success, and what we are to talk of next I cannot imagine.

(FAINT MUSIC, HERE)

DARCY: (*Smilingly*) What do you think of books?

ELIZABETH: Books? Oh no. No, I cannot talk of books in a ballroom; my head is always full of something else. (*Pause: suddenly*) I remember hearing you once say, Mr. Darcy, that you hardly ever forgave – that your resentment, once created, was unappeasable. You are very cautious, I suppose, as to its[2] *being* created?

DARCY: (*Firmly*) I am.

ELIZABETH: And never allow yourself to be blinded by prejudice?

DARCY: May I ask to what all these questions tend?

ELIZABETH: Merely to the illustration of *your* character – I am trying to make it out.

DARCY: And what is your success?

ELIZABETH: (*As though shaking her head ruefully*) I do not get on at all.

DARCY: (*Uneasily*) I could wish, Miss Bennet, that you were not to sketch my character at the present moment.

ELIZABETH: But if I do not take your likeness now . . .

(SHE LINGERS ON THE LAST WORD. BEHIND HER, THE DANCE MUSIC FADES UP, THEN QUICKLY OUT.)

NARRATOR: All through Jane Austen's life came that vivid "now." Animatedly moving from scene to scene, in those gay little caps with the bows and feathers, she might have been asked – as Darcy did ask Elizabeth – "The present always occupies you?" How many unconscious people posed for their likenesses to the unconscious, but ruthless, artist in her? Those pretty, fixed, rather frightening dark eyes of hers were to hold, by the end, an entire view of the world – a world that revealed itself in capers cut in a ballroom, the banalities of drawing-room and garden talk. Remember, a ton of feathers weighs as much as a ton of lead. She detected the ruling passion behind the easy remark. In her novels, her polished young men and women confront one another with laughing hostility – one feels, in her little dialogues of flirtation, the rivalry of two vigorous egotisms. Jane Austen's characters show – or, one should say, fail to conceal – the immense intransigence of Elizabethans. If they did not stop at small things, they might accept a safeguard, the restrictions of their polite life. Charlotte Brontë was to give voice, later, to woman's, the sheltered woman's, insatiable rest-lessness. Jane Austen, in her deliberate writing, refused to admit this. Did she perhaps ignore it? Did she ignore the restlessness of her own heart? Her heroines, like herself, seem compliant. And Jane seemed very compliant: she went where she was invited; she threw herself into whatever was going on . . . Here she is, for instance – aged twenty-four, in the May of 1799 – visiting Bath in the company of her brother Edward (who is to drink the waters), his wife Elizabeth and their elder children, among whose number was Fanny. The Austens lodge in Queen's Square . . .

JANE'S VOICE: (*Still very young*) Cassandra? . . . Well, here we are in Bath; we got here about one o'clock, and have been arrived just long enough to go over the house and be very well pleased with the whole of it. It rained almost all the way, and our first view of Bath has been just as gloomy as it was last November twelvemonth . . . (*Murmur-off on to aloof, retrospective plane.*) Last November twelvemonth . . . entering Bath on a wet afternoon and driving through the long course of streets amidst the dash of other carriages, the rumble of carts and drays, the bawling of newsmen, muffin-men and milkmen and the ceaseless clink of pattens, my companions made no complaint. No, these were the noises that belonged to their winter pleasures; all spirits rose under their influence. I did not share these feel-ings; I persisted in a very determined, though silent, disinclina-tion for Bath – caught with the first dim view of the extensive

buildings smoking in rain without any wish of seeing them better
... (*The Voice, having maintained throughout this last passage
its impersonal note, fades out*)

CASSANDRA: (*Almost violently – disturbed*) – Jane – disin-
clination! But you were the soul of cheerfulness!

NARRATOR: Just now – I think – Miss Cassandra, she was
not speaking to *you*.

CASSANDRA: To whom, then? Who else was there? *I* knew
her whole heart!

FANNY: (*Softly*) I wonder – did you?

CASSANDRA: (*Extreme agitation*) Jane, Jane – they are
trying to come between us. Strangers, strangers – who tell me
they are The World. Even Fanny – They pretend you gave me
the lie. Speak to me, speak to them – tell them – (*voice rising*) –
Where *are* you – *Jane*?

JANE'S VOICE: (*By contrast to Cassandra's, sounding
extremely human, youthful, normal, matter-of-fact*) Here I am,
Cassandra – in Bath, still at Bath. (*Calm pause*) I hope it will be a
tolerable afternoon – the pavements are getting very white again.
I am impatient to know the fate of my best gown. We are here
more than three weeks now: it is June. Flowers are very much
worn, and fruit is still more the thing: Elizabeth has a bunch of
strawberries, and I have seen grapes, cherries, plums and apricots
... I spent Friday evening with the Mapletons; we took a charming walk up Beacon Hill. We had a Mr. Gould of our party; he
walked home with me after tea. He is a very young man, just
entered of Oxford, wears spectacles and has heard *Evelina* was
written by Dr. Johnson. (*Pause: different inflection*) Benjamin
Portal is here. How charming that is! – I do not know why, but
the phrase followed so naturally that I could not help putting it
down ... I do not know what is the matter with me today; I am
always wandering off into some explanation or other ... (*With
renewed interest*) We walked to Weston last week, and liked it
very much. Liked *what*? Weston? No, *walking* to Weston ... I
hope you will understand ... (*Voice fades out*)

CASSANDRA / FANNY: (*Simultaneously*) – I –
– Did she –

NARRATOR: (*Commandingly*) – Stop! This may be important! – Miss Cassandra, those letters you say you burned – were
those letters written from Bath, in June?

CASSANDRA: No, sir. (*Impassively*) There were other summers . . .

FANNY: (*Reflectively*) Mr. Lefroy, Mr. Gould with the spectacles, Mr. Benjamin Portal . . . (*Suddenly*) What made her, I wonder – (*breaks off*)

NARRATOR: (*Expectant*) Yes, Miss Fanny?

FANNY: What made her say to me, once, "Your mistake, dear Fanny, has been one that thousands of women fall into. *Poor* Mr. J. P.! He was the *first* young man who attached himself to you – that was the charm, and how powerful it is!"

JANE'S VOICE: (*Picking up from this*) What strange creatures, Fanny, we are! But he would not do for one who has rather more acuteness, Penetration and Taste than *Love* – which is your case.

NARRATOR: *Was* it Fanny's case? Or, in her young niece did Jane Austen see herself in a mirror? She remained unwilling that Fanny should fall in love. Love – how guarded Jane is about the reality, but what play she makes with the illusion, the false dawn! Here, for instance, is one of her heroines, Emma Woodhouse, after handsome Frank Churchill's first visit to Highbury . . . (*as though reading*) "Emma continued to entertain no doubt of her being in love. Her ideas only varied as to how much. At first, she thought it was a good deal; and afterwards, but little. She had great pleasure in hearing Frank Churchill talked of; she was very often thinking of him, and quite impatient for a letter. But, on the other hand, she could not admit herself to be unhappy, nor to be less disposed for enjoyment than usual; and, pleasing as he was, she could still imagine him to have faults. And, farther, though thinking of him so much, fancying interesting dialogues and inventing elegant letters, the conclusion of every imaginary declaration on his side was, that she *refused* him. Everything tender and charming was to mark their parting, but still they were to part . . . It struck her that she could not be very much in love; for a strong attachment certainly must produce more of a struggle than she could foresee in her own feelings."

JANE'S VOICE: (*Now Emma's; picking up*) I do suspect that he is not really necessary to my happiness. So much the better. I am quite enough in love. I should be sorry to be more.

NARRATOR: Emma seems to me the most interesting of the heroines, for with her Jane Austen comes right into the open.

This was the novel of her maturity. We may miss, in it, the bloom and the dancing wit that had been the younger Jane's. But, in the place of this, we have been given, in *Emma*, a superbly adult and classic feeling for comedy. Here are no morning mists of illusion; here are no tender deceptions of evening light. Noon daylight fills the novel all through.

What does Jane Austen show us? A woman in love with power. Young, well-to-do, handsome, spoiled child of a feeble father, Emma Woodhouse dominates Highbury's little society. She has already everything that she wants. Unlike the rest of the heroines, she sees marriage only as an *abrogation* of power. The root of her interest in Frank Churchill is, only, her wish to dominate him . . . Emma meets opposition only from one quarter – that of Mr. Knightly, her neighbour, of Donwell Abbey. Not only is Mr. Knightly her senior by sixteen years but, *his* brother having married *her* sister, she has grown up to regard him as a brother-in-law. Mr. Knightly and Emma meet almost daily, and not infrequently cross swords. For instance, Emma has promoted into her favour a naïve young person of seventeen, Miss Harriet Smith. In the Woodhouses' sunny drawing-room at Hartfield, with its garden outlook and rather too hot fire, Mr. Knightly attempts to charge Emma with having turned the head of her *protégée*.

(FADE UP HASTILY TICKING CLOCK)

MR. KNIGHTLY: I cannot rate Harriet's beauty as you do, but she is a pretty little creature. I am disposed to think well of her disposition. In good hands, she will turn out a valuable woman.

EMMA: (*With irony*) I am glad you think so.

MR. KNIGHTLY: Come – you are anxious for a compliment, so I will tell you that you have improved her. You have cured her of her schoolgirl's giggle.

EMMA: Thank you. *You* do not often overpower me with praise.

MR. KNIGHTLY: You are expecting her again, you say, this morning?

EMMA: (*As though glancing at clock*) Almost every moment.

MR. KNIGHTLY: (*Urbanely*) Something has happened to delay her. (*Thoughtfully*) Visitors, perhaps?

EMMA: (*Impatient*) Highbury gossips – tiresome wretches!

MR. KNIGHTLY: Harriet may not consider everybody tiresome that you would. (*Pause: smilingly*) I must tell you that I have good reason to believe that your little friend will soon hear of something to her advantage.

EMMA: (*Quickly*) Indeed! – how so? Of what sort?

MR. KNIGHTLY: (*Still smilingly*) Of a serious sort.

EMMA: (*Excited*) Very serious! I can think of but one thing. – Who is in love with her? Who makes you their confidant?

MR. KNIGHTLY: Robert Martin, of Abbey Mill Farm, is the man. He is desperately in love, and means to marry her.

EMMA: (*With scornful irony*) He is very obliging. Is he so sure that Harriet means to marry him?

MR. KNIGHTLY: (*Indulgent*) Well, means to make her an offer – will that do? He came to Donwell two evenings ago, on purpose to consult me about it. I was very much pleased with all he said. I praised the fair lady to him and sent him away happy. *Now*, as we may fairly suppose, he will not allow much time to pass before he speaks to the lady. It is not unlikely that he should be at Mrs. Goddard's today.

EMMA: (*With an air of superior information*) Pray, Mr. Knightly, how do you know that Mr. Martin did not speak *yesterday*? – Come, I will tell *you* something. He did speak yesterday – that is, he wrote – and was refused.

MR. KNIGHTLY: (*Thunderstruck*) Then she is a greater simpleton than I ever believed! Refuse him? What is the foolish girl about?

EMMA: (*With spirit*) Oh, to be sure. It is always incomprehensible to a man that a woman should refuse an offer of marriage. A man always imagines a woman to be ready for anybody who asks her!

MR. KNIGHTLY: (*Briskly*) Nonsense! A man does not imagine any such thing. But, Harriet Smith refuse Robert Martin? Madness – I hope you are mistaken.

EMMA: I saw her answer.

MR. KNIGHTLY: You "saw" her answer! – you *wrote* her answer, too. Emma, you persuaded her to refuse him!

EMMA: And if I did? Mr. Martin is a very respectable young man, but I cannot admit him to be Harriet's equal.

MR. KNIGHTLY: Not Harriet's equal? – No indeed, for he is her superior as much in sense as in situation. Emma, your infatuation for that girl blinds you. She is the natural daughter of nobody knows whom. She is only known as a parlour-boarder at a common school – and she desired nothing better, till *you* chose to turn her into a friend!

EMMA: (*Warmly*) Harriet's claims to marry better than this are not so contemptible as you represent them. She is not clever, but she is, in fact, a beautiful girl, with a real, thorough sweetness of temper and manner. I am very much mistaken if your sex would not think such beauty, and such a temper, the highest claims a woman could possess.

MR. KNIGHTLY: (*With extreme irritation*) Upon my word, Emma, to hear you abusing the reason *you* have is almost enough to make me think so, too!

EMMA: To be sure – I know such a girl as Harriet is exactly what every man delights in – what at once pleases his senses and satisfies his judgement. Oh, Harriet may pick and choose!

MR. KNIGHTLY: You have been no friend to Harriet Smith, Emma. I have always thought this a very foolish intimacy; now I perceive it will be an unfortunate one for Harriet. You will puff her up with ideas. Vanity working on a weak head produces every sort of mischief. Men of sense – whatever you may say – do *not* want silly wives.

EMMA: (*Coolly*) We think so very differently on this point, Mr. Knightly, that we shall only be making each other more angry. Robert Martin's appearance is so much against him, and his manner so bad, that if she ever *were* disposed to favour him, she is not now. Now, nothing but a gentleman in education and manners has any chance with Harriet.

MR. KNIGHTLY: (*With vigour*) Nonsense – errant nonsense as ever was talked! (*Pause*) Robert Martin has no great loss – if he can but think so. As you make no secret of your love of match-making, it is fair to suppose you have other projects for Harriet. As a friend I shall hint to you that if Elton is the man, he will not do. He is not at all likely to make an imprudent match.

EMMA: (*Laughingly*) I am very much obliged to you, but I am done with match-making. At present I only want to keep Harriet to myself.

MR. KNIGHTLY: (*Abruptly*) Good morning to you.

NARRATOR: (*Picking up from here, in reading tone*) " – rising and walking off abruptly. He was very much vexed.

Emma remained in a state of vexation, too, but there was more indistinctness in the causes of hers." (*Change of tone*) – In fact, we know that Emma *was* busy match-making for Harriet and Mr. Elton – that rather too pleasant-spoken young clergyman. At most times, she was frank as she was impulsive: only with Mr. Knightly, whose disapproval she dreaded, was she ever at all disingenuous. She only discovers that *she* loves Mr. Knightly when she fancies *he* is in love with Harriet.

"Dear girl, we watch her knot herself up in her own schemes," Jane Austen spoke of Emma, while she was writing the novel, as being a woman no reader would like. I think she released in this novel a frankness she did not elsewhere permit herself with regard to her own nature, her own life. Here, for the first time, we are given a heroine who is aggressive rather than diplomatic. It is at the Box Hill picnic – the scene is a masterpiece – that Emma at last meets her Waterloo. From that social fiasco we see her drive home in tears. She realises that she is likely to forfeit love.

All the other heroines are, in degrees, compliant. Fanny Price, of *Mansfield Park*, and Anne Elliott, of *Persuasion*, are in essentially weak positions. Society, in the form of their families, is always on the point of riding them down. They show courage, but of a despairing kind. To their deference to the superior powers – Sir Thomas Bertram in Fanny's case, Lady Russell in Anne's – they are prepared to sacrifice happiness. It may be noticed that, in all of her novels, Jane Austen appears to be on the side of society. She does not seem to regret her heroines' deference. She believes in great houses, commanding people: she seems to identify those with the moral rule. – Or does she? Great Mansfield Park has to be humbled before little Fanny can live the life of her heart. Only in her last novel, *Persuasion*, does Jane Austen attempt to compute the sacrifice that a woman may have to make to society. In *Persuasion*, we find a poetic austerity; in it the smiling pretences are thrown aside. It is an autumnal novel, summer was over – not only for Anne Elliott, for Jane. Jane Austen was now at the end of her thirties. Ill-health had set in, and was never to go away. Steventon, Bath, Southampton lay behind her, so many pages not to be turned again. With her mother and her sister Cassandra she now lived very quietly at Chawton – another Hampshire village – near to the gates of the great house her brother Edward had inherited. She had time, while she wrote *Persuasion*, to realise how much was gone –

FANNY: (*In protest*) Her youth? She was always the same age.

JANE'S VOICE: (*Sounding tense and tired*) Fanny? – Many thanks for your kind care for my health. I have had a good deal of fever, and indifferent nights, but am better now, and recovering my looks a little – which have been bad enough, black and white. Sickness is a dangerous indulgence at my time of life, Fanny. I must not depend upon being ever very blooming again. (*Voice fades out*)

NARRATOR: Darker than ever, her black eyes looked out of her white face at the black-and-white of her manuscript. She turned to music the different phases of Anne Elliott's loneliness. She –

CASSANDRA: (*Cutting in*) Sir, I must protest – Miss Anne Elliott was *not* my sister! Agree how different their situations were! Miss Elliott's family showed her a shocking hardness. Whereas, in the case of my sister, *we* were always around her – she could be felt to lean on us more and more.

JANE'S VOICE: (*Wearily*) Your Aunt Cass., Fanny, is such an excellent nurse, so assiduous . . . (*Voice fades out*)

NARRATOR: (*As though to himself*) How willingly did she lean?

CASSANDRA: Fame sought her out – for my sister, true to our feeling, had planned to keep secret her authorship. Society courted her, there were demands to meet her. Royalty complimented her. But she turned only to us: she never cared for the world.

JANE'S VOICE: (*Reflectively*) There are no brilliant people nowadays.

NARRATOR: No, in real life – at Steventon, Bath, the London of Sloane Street parties, Southampton, Chawton – Jane met no brilliant people. Yet, in her men and women – no more than little gentry – she has created a race of wits and aristocrats. In her art, all the lights are on . . . In fact, the brilliant world Jane Austen left us was the creation not of her *experience* but of her *desire*.

She could have lived more fully. As to the life she *did* live, her illusions were, I believe, few. Into the novels she wrote with such composure – as another lady might pick up her fancy-work

– her pride, her power of living, her inner fire made their secret escape.

Did she, then, outside the world of her art, permit herself *no* illusions? No, that was not possible – one cannot use up one's whole heart on one's pen. There *was* one real-life illusion, a living illusion – Fanny. Upon Fanny – the niece, the young mistress of Godmersham – Jane Austen projected the role of a heroine. In the person of Fanny, art – for Jane – merged with life. The more Jane wearied and faded, the more she dwelt upon Fanny – warm, living ghost of her own youth, last of her heroines, creature of blood, not ink. (*Change of tone*) Was that not true, Miss Fanny?

FANNY: (*Bewildered*) I do not know what to say . . .

NARRATOR: (*Quickly*) – Leave it at that, then – (*Change of tone*) In the summer of 1817, with Cassandra, Jane Austen left Chawton, in hopes of a cure. For the journey, made in the rain, she was hardly able: one of her brothers rode by the carriage side. Mists of weakness blurred this last departure from home.

JANE'S VOICE: (*Young, dreamingly, as though wandering round in time*) We have lived long enough in this neighbourhood; the Basingstoke balls are certainly on the decline. There is something interesting in the bustle of going away . . . For a time we shall now possess many of the advantages which I have often thought of with Envy . . . (*Voice fades out*)

NARRATOR: Winchester was the destination. There, in the quiet lodgings the devoted Cassandra not quitting her sister's side –

JANE'S VOICE: Languid and solitary –

NARRATOR: – Suffering weakened her –

JANE'S VOICE: – God grant me patience; pray for me, oh, pray for me!

NARRATOR: – She died –

CASSANDRA: (*Catching a breath*) She died. (*Pause*) I lost the better part of myself!

FANNY: That day the letter came from my Aunt Cassandra, I looked in my glass and saw there was no one there.

CASSANDRA: (*On rising note*) She was the sun of my life – the gilder of every pleasure, the soother of every sorrow. I had not a thought concealed from her –

JANE'S VOICE: (*Far away, softly*) To know *you*, Fanny – to have such a thorough picture of your Heart . . . Fanny?

FANNY: (*Wildly*) Where are you, where are you?

NARRATOR: The funeral service was read in the cathedral at Winchester. There were present three of Jane's brothers – Edward, Henry and Frank. Cassandra, being a woman, was left behind.

CASSANDRA: Determined that I would see the last, I stood at the window. I watched the little mournful procession the length of the street, till it turned from my sight and I had lost her forever.

FANNY: Where are you?

CASSANDRA: Oh, hush! Her soul, I presume to hope, reposes in some superior Mansion.

NARRATOR: You are right, Miss Cassandra – a Heaven of brilliant people. Miss Fanny, do not be troubled. She is here. The present always occupied her, to the exclusion of any other scene. The *Now* was always her moment. She is here, where she always dwelt, in the *Now*.

London Revisited: As Seen by Fanny Burney

VOICE: (*which should be impersonal and reflective*) Fanny Burney – later Madame d'Arblay – was fated to live a long time.

King's Lynn was the place of her birth, in 1752, but temperament made her a natural Londoner: she was still a young girl when her family moved to the capital, but from then on she began to realise her destiny. Dr. Burney, that popular, fashionable music master, established himself in St. Martin's Street – running south from the Leicester Square in those days called Leicester Fields – in a house that had been built by Sir Isaac Newton. Now, its parlour hummed with notable people, for Dr. Burney's patrons became his friends. Up top an observatory still remained – and it was to this that Fanny, feeling more than half guilty, stole away from her family in the afternoons, to indulge her passion for writing.[1]

She was small, slight, unobtrusive, short-sighted, discreet to the point of being prim. This was an age of flamboyant beauties, and it was not, I think, until she became famous that anybody thought twice of Fanny's looks. Her short sight was no more than physical: nothing whatever passed little Fanny by. Society, with its foibles, was her target. She became a finished observer while she was still obscure – in fact, an observatory, now that one thinks of it, was the appropriate birthplace for *Evelina* – the story of a Young Lady's Entrance into the World.

Fame came to her early, romance late. She was twenty-six when anonymous *Evelina* broke on a delighted and dazzled London. For some time, only one favourite sister, one brother shared with her the secret of the book's authorship. Dr. Burney, whom his daughter adored, did not in general approve of lady writers: in this he was one with most gentlemen of his time. However, the secret could not be kept forever. Fanny found that she had trembled for nothing, for Dr. Burney, himself not unambitious, looked kindly on his little daughter's success. Fanny became a habituée of the Streatham circle. Mrs. Thrale lost no time in seeking the valuable Fanny out; Doctor Johnson crowned her with friendship as well as praise. *Camilla*, appearing six years after *Evelina*, renewed Fanny's reputation. Not only the blue-stockings fêted Fanny: the unassuming young person was soon present in the most fashionable drawing-rooms of her day.

Queen Charlotte's offer of a place in the Royal Household might seem to be the high point of Fanny's worldly career. Paradoxically, it marked a check in it. As Second Keeper of the Queen's Robes, Fanny led a four years' life of confinement[2] to palace back passages, closets and royal dressing-rooms. George III, his German Queen and their six unmarried daughters espoused – whether at St. James's, Windsor or Kew – an intensive, cut-off domesticity. Moreover, during the time while Fanny held office, the King for the first time became insane. Fanny's health failed, and often her spirits flagged. A German she had little reason to love was her immediate superior, Madame Schwellenberg. She gained, however, as compensation, the affectionate confidence of the Queen, and of the Princesses – those repressed girls.

Fanny so clearly showed the effects of strain that Dr. Burney agreed to her resignation. The Queen, though taken aback, as a parting present made her an allowance of £100 a year. This £100 a year was to be a decisive factor when romance came Fanny's way – as we said, late. The Mickleham neighbourhood, where she stayed with her sister, was enlivened by a group of French *émigrés* – driven from France by the Revolution. Fanny met, loved and was courted by the middle-aged, noble but penniless M. d'Arblay, a general of Lafayette's. Against Dr. Burney's reasoned advice, the marriage – which proved ideally happy – took place, when Fanny was forty-one. Her son was born a year later – to be her only child.

From 1793, the date of the marriage, London saw Fanny, and Fanny saw London, less. The d'Arblays lived in a country cottage; M. d'Arblay gardened and Fanny wrote *Camilla* – she could confess that money was now her aim. In 1802, the brief peace with France gave hopes for M. d'Arblay's career. So the small household moved to France. Here Fanny was caught by the renewed war, but, though an enemy alien, did not fare badly. She was in 1812 permitted to visit England: here she left her son behind with her family, for safe keeping. Napoleon's escape from Elba caused her to fly from Paris; she was in Brussels the day of the battle of Waterloo.

Yes, Fanny's life, her own life, was a string of little events set on a background of large happenings – the Gordon Riots, the War of American Independence, the French Revolution, the Napoleonic War. She was present at the trial of Warren Hastings, she was chased round Kew Gardens by the insane King, she set awed eyes on Napoleon when he was First Consul. She died in 1840, having outlived, but not for a day forgotten, her famous contemporaries, her adored husband and son. Her death, now, seems little more than a fact, for – in her early novels, her unflagging journal, her letters[3] – she has immortalised for us the times she knew, and, by this, becomes immortal herself. Heaven, as found by Fanny, would be a sociable place; both august and kind would be the faces that met her, and eternity would not be too long for talk.

Either chance or genius, during her life on earth, caused Fanny to be where things were happening. She had the knack of slipping from place to place. Her appetite for events was insatiable. It would, I believe, still take her to any lengths . . . (*Voice begins to fade out*) even to (*fades out further*). She was an intrepid traveller . . . (*fades out quite*).

(PAUSE. PHRASES OF FORMAL, EIGHTEENTH-CENTURY MUSIC, SUCH AS WOULD HAVE BEEN

HEARD AT QUEEN CHARLOTTE'S GERMANIC COURT, ALTERNATE WITH THE SOARING SOUNDS OF MUSIC OF A MORE CELESTIAL NATURE. OUT OF THE MUSIC EMERGES A HUM OF TALK – THIS SOUNDING ENERGETIC, PUZZLED, TENSE. THIS GIVES PLACE TO –)

FIRST WOMAN'S VOICE: Your Royal Highness must not be so uneasy –

PRINCESS AUGUSTA: No, I admit no.[4] But I viewed dear Miss Burney's departure with apprehension; I am at pains to account for her long delay. Always so attentive, always so feeling, always so quick to the sound of the Queen's bell. (*Pause – as though turning*) – You said, sir?

EQUERRY'S VOICE: Some final interesting scene, no doubt, detains her – makes her blind to all peril.

MRS. PIOZZI: (*as though bridling*) There can be no interesting *person* – her friends are *here*. (*Sighs quickly*) Estrangements forgotten, rank equalised – Doctor Johnson?

SECOND WOMAN'S VOICE: The Doctor, Madam, is on the look-out. He paces one extreme edge of that cloud. Mr. Burke, at its other extremity, takes upon himself the same solicitous office, but appears to be harassed by his near sight. Sir Joshua Reynolds is adding to his five infant angels the bodies he once thought right to omit, but I can see him halting over his easel, as though overcome by the earthly idea of time. Indeed, Fanny's absence – her visit to the perilous *earth* –

FIRST WOMAN'S VOICE: (*picking up*) – The prime, the principal sufferer, M. d'Arblay, should be taken as our model in fortitude. Affecting a calmness that he cannot feel, the General sustains the duress of Mme. d'Arblay's absence by transplanting the celestial shrubs, exchanging palm for laurel, laurel for palm.

MRS. PIOZZI: – Still limping, I notice, from that injury suffered *near* Waterloo. Not far from the field of battle, he was kicked by a colt.

SECOND WOMAN'S VOICE: (*reprovingly*) Mrs. Piozzi!

MRS. PIOZZI: Oh, all *estrangements* forgotten! Still I cannot forget all Fanny hinted to *me*, when *I* married a foreigner! Thrale to Piozzi. Burney to d'Arblay – well! (*Pause*). The Princess Augusta fears I'm an unregenerate. Indeed, we knew nothing of royal *ton*[5] at Streatham. – Come, Sophy Streatfield, shed two of your pretty tears. Two tears for me, Sophy, and four for Fanny – our Fanny visits the Earth, and is not returned. She is late.

FIRST WOMAN'S VOICE: She is late.

PRINCESS AUGUSTA: Late on a larger Earth than *I* cared to travel.

EQUERRY: (*gloomily*) On worse, Your Royal Highness – an Earth at war.

SECOND WOMAN'S VOICE: (*sighing*) Intrepid Fanny!

MRS. PIOZZI: Obstinate Fanny! – How does her father take it?

EQUERRY: By the General's wish, Dr. Burney has been told nothing. How could we hope to allay his paternal fears? More, he is in a condition to think of nothing, for he has once more lost a page of his – (*breaks off –*)

(A SHOUT IS HEARD IN THE DISTANCE. THE SHOUT IS TAKEN UP BY DIFFERENT VOICES, AS THOUGH FROM CLOUD TO CLOUD. A DEEP HALLOO THAT WOULD BE DR. JOHNSON'S IS, DISTANTLY, AND AMONG OTHERS, HEARD.)

ALL: What's that?

Can it – ?

It must be –

Miss Burney – !

Fanny!

Mme. d'Arblay – !

FANNY!

FANNY: (*Her voice, as she speaks, must louden, as though she were all the time approaching the group. She is very BREATHLESS. –*)

FANNY: (*breathless, unsteady*) Your Royal Highness, my kind friends – you must allow me –

MRS. PIOZZI: Seat yourself; calm yourself! (*To the rest*) Give her air. (*To Fanny*) Miss Burney, your eyes – !

FANNY: (*still confused*) So much *light* here, ma'am – 'tis the sudden light! If you could guess at the dark from which I am lately come – the Stygian black of London . . . (*Collects herself, and goes on in more even tone*) From nightfall the city appeared extinguished and blotted out – not a chink of candlelight, blind streets. Your poor wanderer, all at a loss already, went through an agony of fright. Already, as evening announced itself, I had hesitated in the lee of a building that towered, ladies, to a prodigious height. Surely mankind tempts providence by such an approach in stone to His own sphere! The residences, shops and places of business now overtop the spires . . . but little below the sky mantling with darkness, some illumined windows did for a time appear. Picture my feeling when I beheld these windows, *all* in one fatal moment, quenched – as though by the malign stroke of a wand! What demented new fashion is this, I cried to myself, what diabolic fantasy, what cult of the terrible for its own sake? Shoals of persons, vociferous in their blindness, now pressed past me so close that, forgetting I was intangible, I shrank back against the unfeeling wall.

MRS. PIOZZI: (*with animation*) Madness – not a *light* in London, you say?

FANNY: If I were to tell you *none*, I should not be literal. But, ma'am, those few lights I saw were not only feeble, but, for the greater part, ambulant: they assumed the bobbing movement of walkers or the dashing motion of carriages. It is a fact – the Londoner apes the glow-worm; his beam precedes him, bent stealthily to the pavement before his feet. Others contrive little wicks of tobacco, which they carry burning between their lips. But these, with a great stench, shed but little light. Meanwhile, in the streets, the unnatural surge of the traffic was made more threatening by the onset of night. Only one sight pleased me – or could have pleased me, were it not for my confusion and my fatigue – the streets are now, at their corners, studded with jewels larger than I ever saw in a crown. Ruby, topaz and emerald, propped or suspended by some agency, supersede one another, and, in their blinking, artfully rival the one before. I could see that, at each appearance of emerald, the carriages leaped on, in a greedy rush. Topaz, by shining briefly, appeared to assert a warning; each ruby brought about an affrighted stop.

As for the carriages, – words fail me, my friends, to paint these for you as I had already seen them, by daylight. Horseless, shaftless, they are propelled forward by some infernal interior force. In their fore part the *soi-disant* driver, lolling, no more than languidly thumbs a disc. Their form approximates, I can only tell you, to that of some kind of larva or grub. Their structure slinks on the bloated wheels, and the height of their doors is so insufficient that no lady of fashion could hope to enter without

danger or disarray to her head . . . So much for the private traffic.
As for the *public* – this as tall and bulky as the other is low. I
saw what seemed very *houses* awheel – two-storied, packed
with travellers, garish in colour (and with the windows covered
with gummy stuff). Each bore at the rear an exposed staircase,
on which people, like the angels of Jacob's vision, were without
ceasing in ascent or descent . . . the impetuous tottering of the
vehicle making their peril very extreme. I saw monoliths in
motion, without windows, and vast horseless drays. All these,
in fatuous competition, let out from their vitals such a grinding
and screeching that I was fain to cover my ears. Upon my word,
ladies – the *noise* of London has been as rudely changed as its
plan! I missed the coachmen's shouting, of our time, and the
clatter of hoof and wheel on the cobbles. The streets now are
coated with such a surface that they are sleek as satin and dark
as ink. On this the wheels themselves, the fantastical cushioned
wheels, revolve soundlessly. No, the noise that racked me came
from the traffic's bodies; the monsters are not[6]

A Year I Remember – 1918

NARRATOR: One may live to be a hundred – more than a hundred: it can be done. When I was a child, there were dotted over the country old ladies remembering Waterloo. They dwelled, one was given to understand, upon that memory perpetually, in a mystic hush. The cottage of one such old lady was pointed out to me – Time, to my eye, dimmed the drawn lace curtains; the past, like a ground-mist, lay over the rockery in the front.

"Extraordinary," I thought, "to remember history."

For, *I* was a child before 1914. History, to me, was a book closed – only to be taken out in the schoolroom. The *finale* of violence was, Waterloo.

That interrupted waltz . . .

(FADE IN, WALTZ MUSIC. THEN, BEHIND WALTZ, CANNON SHOTS. WALTZ STOPS SHARPLY. MORE CANNON SHOTS, HEARD, AGAINST SILENCE. CANNON SHOTS STOP. ARE FOLLOWED BY DISTANT BRITISH CHEERING. WALTZ MUSIC PICKS UP WHERE IT BROKE OFF, CONTINUES FOR A BAR OR TWO, FADES OUT.)

NARRATOR: – The interrupted waltz had gone on again. But so had the humdrum days . . . Harmless, humdrum days. (*Pause*) For the Edwardian child, the newspaper was something only for Father: no one else touched it; it had to be clean and crisp. Of course, there was no wireless. Grown-ups were too charming to talk about world events. – No, though: I remember whispers about the San Francisco earthquake. Then, there was to be the loss of the *Titanic* – the iceberg struck the civilised ship. Nature, once having shown her hand, became the villain – thunderstorms were less bearable; once or twice I had nightmares about a tidal wave.

All the same, for a whole afternoon in 1913, I wept, out of temper and boredom. Why? Because nothing *happened*.

Yes, inconceivable as a childhood – *now*.

(*Pause, change of tone*) Interviewed, the old lady in the cottage was disappointing . . .

OLD VOICE: (*fragile and quavering*) Why, yes, I'll tell you, dearie. A rabbit bolted across our garden path. Our dog hot after it. Cruel.

CHILDISH VOICE: (*tense, eager*) But, *that* was Waterloo day? The day the news came?

OLD VOICE: (*vague, indifferent*) So they said.

CHILDISH VOICE: But weren't you very excited? A victory like that! – What else do you remember?

OLD VOICE: (*temporisingly*) Eh now, eh now . . . (*Suddenly agitated*) I tore my little apron. Such a dainty thing – tore it right across.

CHILDISH VOICE: (*slightly desperate*) But don't you remember what they were *saying*? The cheering – wasn't there? Peals of bells? Bonfires? – Weren't you very *happy*?

OLD VOICE: (*slightly outraged at the suggestion*) Eh, why? I was crying over my little apron. "Why, come," Mother said, "we'll soon stitch that up." Still, I broke my heart. That was Waterloo day. Such a dreadful tear – I'll never forget!

YOUNG VOICE: (*on a flat, frustrated note*) Oh . . .

NARRATOR: How baffling, the memory of another person! But, above all, how baffling one's own! Crazy, out of proportion, personal. Storing up nonsense, throwing fact away. If it were not so, the pattern of history would be clearer – but also, perhaps, less coloured?

Now, *why*, for instance, should I remember 1918 so much more forcibly than I remember 1914? True, 1918 is four years nearer to me in time; but so many years are behind me, that ought not to matter. All *reason* argues, that as a child brought up inside the illusion of security, I should have been dinted by the outbreak of war. 1914, that incredible bursting-open of the flood-gates. Noise, danger, fear, hate, horror . . . *Why* were we not – all we people who were alive then – knocked off our balance by 1914? *Was* it, even for children, something of a release? All round us, floating us, was the heroic faith, the trumpet-call . . .

YOUNG MAN'S VOICE:

Now, God be thanked who has matched us with His hour,
And caught our youth, and wakened us from sleeping,
With hand made sure, clear eye, and sharpened power,
To turn, as swimmers into cleanness leaping,
Glad from a world grown old and cold and weary,
Leave the sick hearts that honour could not move,
And half-men, and their dirty songs and dreary,
And all the little emptiness of love!
Oh, we who have known shame, we have found release there . . . [1]

(YOUNG MAN'S VOICE FADES OUT. NOTE OR TWO OF REVEILLE DIES AWAY IN THE DISTANCE.)

NARRATOR: Nothing, ever, to be like that again . . . For us, in 1914, the children at school, war fed a restless wish for the grand. We had found no boots big enough for our growing feet – had not the world grown "old and cold and weary"? This new thing, war, was eased in on us by new treats – Union Jack handkerchiefs; prints of good Albert, King of the Belgians; perpetual whistling of "Tipperary" . . . We grew up inside "the War"; lulled and sheathed by it. Its rules were beautifully simple: we had few problems.

But, behind that wartime peace there grew up, with each year, an imperative. – To live well, because so many were dying that we might live. "Be worthy," they said to us, "of your brothers." How if we fell short?

Every day, the lengthening casualty-lists wrote our debt larger.
(*Break: change of tone*)

I cannot separate the war from my own schooldays. Which would outlast the other? I dreaded leaving school.

(BURST OF ARMISTICE NIGHT 1918 NOISES – ROARING OF CARS, ROARING OF CROWDS. SIMULTANEOUS SINGING OF "TIPPERARY" AND "PACK UP YOUR TROUBLES" AND "THE LONG LONG TRAIL" SUPERIMPOSED ON SINGING OF "OVER THERE." ISOLATED VOICE EXCLAIMING: "TO PEACE – DRINK UP!" ABRUPTLY, FADE ALL THIS OUT. FEW SECONDS OF DEAD SILENCE.)

NARRATOR: Yes, that *was* how it ended, 1918. One forgets that was not how it began. In January, Mr. Lloyd George, Prime Minister, said to *us*, civilians –

SENIOR MALE VOICE: (*cutting in*) *Your* firing line is the works or the offices in which you do your bit; the shop or kitchen in which you spend or save; the bank or the post office in which you buy your War Bonds . . .

NARRATOR: That was *1918* – does it sound familiar? – Then, he was to announce –

SENIOR MALE VOICE: (*cutting in*) It is not our wish to disintegrate Germany or to destroy her great position in the world. The question of her Constitution is a matter for the German people . . .

NARRATOR: Time enough, I thought. One did not think much. In 1918 I was eighteen – had left school, but there was still the war. Being Irish I had returned to Ireland – still, then, included in the United Kingdom (*in parenthesis*) though, 1916 had shown which way the wind blew . . .

Ireland was garrisoned. And, it was full of hospitals. *I* see that 1918 spring full of bright-blue figures of wounded soldiers. In one of those Irish hospitals I worked – a pink, rattled, inexpert V. A. D.[2] This was a special hospital, for men wounded where I had not foreseen – in the mind. Shell-shock cases. Eighty or so of them, up and about all day. Scotsmen, Welshmen, Devon men, Midlanders, North Country men, Cockney Jews – each with some inner queerness a little heightened. Nobody quite mad – nobody, as one came to see, quite curable. A gimcrack house in the country, overlooking a river – that was the place.

Patients slept in huts, under our windows. At nights, the silence used to be broken by the chattering and chattering of a sleeper, or a sudden loud cry. On top of it all, they said that the house was haunted.

All the hospital days, however, went by to music. To music we V. A. D.'s tore about, stacked plates, served dinners, washed up. Whistling, singing, gramophones in the huts . . .

(FADE IN, SUDDENLY, WITH BLARING EFFECT, GRAMOPHONE PLAYING "WE ARE THE ROBBERS OF THE WOODS" [CHU CHIN CHOW, RECORD C. 2562]. ON THIS, GUST OF MEN'S SINGING VOICES PICKING UP A WORD OR TWO OF THE CHORUS. CUT OFF, SUDDEN SILENCE, BOTH SINGING AND RECORDING. UPON SILENCE, FADE IN – FROM ANOTHER DIRECTION AND FURTHER OFF IN THE DISTANCE – ANOTHER GRAMOPHONE, PLAYING "WIDOWS ARE WONDERFUL" [*YES UNCLE*, RECORD C. 852] IN FOREGROUND OF "WIDOWS ARE WONDERFUL," CHINA-CLATTER OF PLATES BEING STACKED. AND A YOUNG GIRL'S WHISTLING, PICKING UP THE TUNE. THE SUBSEQUENT CONVERSATION GOES ON AGAINST A BACKGROUND OF PLATE-CLATTER.)

FIRST YOUNG GIRL'S VOICE: Wonder if they *are* wonderful.

SECOND YOUNG GIRL: Who?

FIRST YOUNG GIRL: Widows.

SECOND YOUNG GIRL: Oh. (*Pause*) Someone said, that's what we are.

FIRST YOUNG GIRL: What, wonderful?

SECOND YOUNG GIRL: No, widows. Without being wives. (*Pause*) There may not be anyone left for us – at this rate.

FIRST YOUNG GIRL: (*with defensive boisterousness*) Oh, shurrup! – And don't have moods before dinner: the troops are hungry. Look at 'em lining up!

SECOND YOUNG GIRL: (*also on the defensive*) *Not* having a mood. Just, thinking.

FIRST YOUNG GIRL: (*briskly*) Comes to the same thing. (*Change of tone*) What's the matter with Sergeant Rose? (*Speaking in the other direction*) Morning, Sergeant! You been seeing the ghost?

SERGEANT ROSE: (*Lowland Scot, in a queer voice*) Hear the guns, Miss?

(SPLIT SECOND OF SILENCE)

FIRST YOUNG GIRL: (*firmly*) No, I don't, you silly – and neither do you. They're in France; we're here.

SERGEANT ROSE: The Germans are through . . .

FIRST YOUNG GIRL: (*placidly*) Get out! – And do *get* out, sergeant, ducky, or there won't be any dinner.

SERGEANT ROSE: There'll never be any dinner. I say, they're through.

FIRST AND SECOND YOUNG GIRLS: (*in unison*) Nonsense!

NARRATOR: But, it was not. It was that month, that 1918 March, that the enemy opened a large-scale major attack along the whole of the British front, in France. The second Somme battle. The news of a British retreat of thirty miles hit the hospital. Here, we were seismographic: nothing was to be kept from the wounded men. What they were not told, they picked up: we saw the battle in their unfocused eyes. Their twitchings got worse; their seizures, one by one, reached a climax.

We could have imagined we heard the guns.

FIRST YOUNG GIRL: (*in startled, bewildered voice*) We can't be *losing* the war . . . ?

SECOND YOUNG GIRL: (*uneasily*) Oh, no. Because, I mean, *no* – how could we?

FIRST YOUNG GIRL: *Somebody's* got to – haven't they?

SECOND YOUNG GIRL: Not *us*. (*Pause*) We're just catching bad morale from these cracky troops. That's all it is. If we were with ordinary people . . .

FIRST YOUNG GIRL: (*tentative*) You think there still *are* ordinary people?

SECOND YOUNG GIRL: Well, you are; I am.

FIRST YOUNG GIRL: *Are* we? – However is one to know . . . ? For instance, I can't imagine myself without a war, – *can* you, honestly? The war's simply come to be part of oneself . . .

SECOND YOUNG GIRL: (*abruptly*) You heard, they're shelling Paris?

FIRST YOUNG GIRL: Mm-mm.

SECOND YOUNG GIRL: And we've *never* been there! You and me – never – have we? (*Passionately*) The capital of the world! My mother's got the most heavenly parasol, *from* Paris

– frills and frills of lace and a rose-pink lining. (*Pause*) You know, I – I could cry, sometimes.

FIRST YOUNG GIRL: You mean, supposing there's nothing left for *us* – no Paris – nothing?

SECOND YOUNG GIRL: (*reluctantly*) Yes, I suppose I do ... (*Abruptly, with revulsion*) No, though, we *are* being awful!

(FADE IN, AT THE END OF HER SENTENCE, SOUND OF HEAVY GUNS IN THE DISTANCE. THIS SOUND IS BACKGROUND TO THE REST OF THE DIALOGUE.)

FIRST YOUNG GIRL: Or, are we just being young? (*Change of tone, briskly*) Better put on the gramophone.

(PLAY, "DO IT FOR ME," FROM *GOING UP* [RECORD C. 861] AT FIRST, SOUND OF GUNS IN DISTANCE IS HEARD BEHIND MUSIC; GRADUALLY GUNS DIE DOWN AND MUSIC LOUDENS. THE YOUNG GIRLS' VOICES PICK UP, FIRST HUM, THEN SING THE REFRAIN. HAVING REACHED LOUD POINT, THIS BREAKS OFF SHARPLY.)

NARRATOR: An overcast spring. The pussy-willows, turned golden, waving in the wind with a lovely indifference, tempting to our hearts. The river under the hospital, swelled by rain, ran fast and darkly. Larks sang; and our patients hated the larks. Everybody was tired; we realised that. At the breaking-point. Even *our* feet ached.

The age for conscription was raised to fifty. Armentières fell. By April 13th, the position of the Allies along the Western Front was "extremely precarious." That, we had to be told. The unbelievable shadow came nearer, nearer.

Field-Marshal Sir Douglas Haig issued an Order of the Day.

SENIOR MALE VOICE WITH AUTHORITY: Three weeks ago today, the enemy began his terrific attacks against us on a fifty-mile front. His objects are, to separate us from the French, to take the Channel Ports, and destroy the British Army.

(PAUSE. FILLED BY SOUND OF A METRONOME TICKING THREE OR FOUR SECONDS AWAY.)

SENIOR MALE VOICE CONTINUES: He has, as yet, made little progress towards his goal. We owe this to the determined fighting and self-sacrifice of our troops. Words fail me to express the admiration I feel for the splendid resistance offered by all ranks of our Army.

(PAUSE. METRONOME AGAIN.)
SENIOR MALE VOICE CONTINUES: Many amongst us now are tired.
(BACKGROUND OF MANY VOICES, MEN'S, WOMEN'S, REITERATING SOFTLY AND FLATLY.)
Many among us now are tired
Many among us now are tired
Many among us now are tired
Many among us now are tired . . .
(THESE VOICES, DISTANT AND OVERLAPPING, SHOULD GIVE THE EFFECT OF A CONTINUOUS SIGN, OR A TIRED WIND HUMMING.)
SENIOR MALE VOICE CONTINUES: (*picking up again slightly more loudly, more firmly*) To those I would say, that victory will belong to the side which holds out the longest. There is no other course open to us but to fight it out. Every position must be held to the last man. With our backs to the wall, and believing in the justice of our cause, each of us must fight on to the end . . .
(PAUSE. METRONOME.)
SENIOR MALE VOICE CONTINUES: The safety of our homes and the freedom of mankind depend alike upon the conduct of each of us at this critical moment.
NARRATOR: The critical moment . . . Daffodils came out; the rough grass round the hospital became white with daisies. This was not a civilian's war. In odd half hours off duty, we girls lay on the grass in a stupor, shading our eyes from the sun. Our feet ached . . . By April 21st, the main tide of the German advance was stemmed . . . But what had we done? (*Pause: faltering*) I cannot remember Zeebrugge.[3]
YOUNG GIRL'S VOICE: (*eagerly cutting in*) Don't you remember? We broke *four* plates! Oh, there was a row . . .
NARRATOR: (*as though straining to be exact*) First American troops arrived on the Western Front.
YOUNG GIRL'S VOICE: (*chanting to "Over There" tune*) The Yanks are coming, the Yanks are coming! (*Young girl fades off into whistling of the tune.*)
NARRATOR: (*impatiently cutting in*) I know – I know – but there must have been more than *that*! (*Sombrely recollecting*) I know the Germans re-opened their attack. By the end of May,

they were forty-five miles from Paris. In June, they crossed the
Marne. The critical moment – how it went on and on . . . [4]
(SOUND OF METRONOME.)
NARRATOR CONTINUES: Then, the tide turned – I
know.[5]
YOUNG GIRL'S VOICE: June, July, August – summer.
Strawberries are coming into the hospital. We are going bicycling
– the country smells of hay. The days are long – long enough for
anything. Bright light in the hospital kitchen when we come
back. Rennie and Rose and Hook are sitting in a row on the
kitchen table; Corporal Deacon's dancing, all by himself.[6]
(SOUND OF "ROSES IN PICARDY" BEING PLAYED ON
A COMB, OR MOUTH-ORGAN.)
RENNIE: (*chanting above accompaniment*) "Nev-er a *rose*
like you." – She's blushing. Who were *you* with last night, miss;
who were you with last night?
HOOK: I'm a married man. That's the beginning and end of
it – married man. I shall go back and rap on the door and say –
"Why, don't you know me?" – I'm not so changed, miss, am I?
I'm not so changed?
RENNIE: How's *she* to know? She's not your old woman.
ROSE: My old woman's not got guns in her head.
RENNIE: Who said she had, then?
ROSE: (*aggressive*) *I've* got guns in my head – what's the good
of that? I've got to go back home, haven't I? I've got to carry
on.
HOOK: (*very gloomily*) Kids too – the little blighters. (*Shrill,
mimicking*) "What did *you* do, Daddy?" – "You think twice,"
I shall tell them, "before *you* pick any more quarrels with the
Kaiser. What did I do? – made the world safe for you." Won't
ever thank me, either – the little blighters. Better go in this river;
that's what I better had. And listen, miss; I'll tell you who else
ought to think twice, miss; *you* ought to think twice, miss –
roaming in the gloaming!
ROSE: (*fatalistic*) All got guns in our heads.
RENNIE: (*bawling*) Forward the guns – hoo-ray! (*Change of
tone: aggressive*) Who said she was roaming in the gloaming?
HOOK: (*still more gloomy*) We won a famous victory.
RENNIE: *Who* won a famous victory?
HOOK AND ROSE TOGETHER: (*sardonic*) British Army.

RENNIE: Show me the famous victory.[7]

Listen to the troops, miss; listen to the troops! Make the most of us, miss; you won't keep us long. Carry me back to dear old Blighty, I *don't* think.[8]

(RENNIE WHISTLES SECOND LINE OF THE TUNE. TUNE TAKEN UP BY COMB, OR MOUTH-ORGAN, CON AMORE. SNATCHES OF WORDS ARE SUNG, ALSO CON AMORE, BUT SATIRICALLY. CORPORAL DEACON, DANCING, SHUFFLES AND HEAVILY STAMPS ACCOMPANIMENT. AT LOUDEST BURST OF SOUND, CUT OFF SUDDENLY.)

NARRATOR: (*by contrast quietly, remotely*) Yes, the tide had turned. With August, everything gathered speed – the Allies recaptured Soissons; the British regained command of the Somme. September, we were back on Passchendaele. October, the French entered St. Quentin, the British, Cambrai. The enemy pulled out of Ostende; we took Lille . . .

But I don't remember; I don't remember. All I remember is the possible Victory coming at us like headlights over dips and hills.[9] To be a young person who didn't know what to make of the world yet, anyhow, under any conditions, was to feel like a rabbit in the middle of the road.

Everybody talked about influenza – "Spanish 'flu." That autumn, it was sweeping the British Isles. Many of us saw the leaves fall, and peace come nearer, through a haze of delirium. Thudding with the sound of our armies moving forward, others in retreat. Meanwhile, the enemy sank the Irish mail boat, the famous *Leinster*[10] – the cleft, the natural tract of danger between the two islands, my own and England, appeared suddenly. That mail boat disaster loomed larger, in Ireland, than all other sinkings – even, the *Lusitania*. We cut the chrysanthemums in our gardens and made them up hurriedly into wreaths and crosses for the very *ordinary* dead people we had known. This idea of war reaching out at random, grabbing civilian victims, never hit me head-on till they sank our *Leinster*. One had felt ashamed, on the whole, of being too safe. Now, that changed: all round us lay the enemy sea.

(REITERATED AND GHOSTLY SOUND OF FOG HORNS. FADE THESE IN TO FIRST AND ASCENDING NOTES OF AIR-RAID SIRENS.)

NARRATOR: In the future, nothing was to surprise us. We of my age grew up with *no* sense of safety. But we tried other things – amazing the experiments we made! –

FIRST YOUNG GIRL: (*eagerly cutting in*) Short hair –

SECOND YOUNG GIRL: (*as eagerly*) – Jazz.

FIRST YOUNG GIRL: Votes –

SECOND YOUNG GIRL: Marvellous modern poetry –

FIRST YOUNG GIRL: Love –

SECOND YOUNG GIRL: Sports cars –

FIRST YOUNG GIRL: Planes –

SECOND YOUNG GIRL: Jobs –

FIRST YOUNG GIRL: Shows –

SECOND YOUNG GIRL: Rows –

FIRST YOUNG GIRL: Romance –

SECOND YOUNG GIRL: Rinks –

FIRST YOUNG GIRL: Art –

SECOND YOUNG GIRL: Frocks –

FIRST YOUNG GIRL: Stars –

SECOND YOUNG GIRL: Dogs –

FIRST YOUNG GIRL: Tunes –

SECOND YOUNG GIRL: Bars –

FIRST YOUNG GIRL: Bands –

SECOND YOUNG GIRL: *Plages* –

FIRST YOUNG GIRL: Proms –

(DURING THE ABOVE, FIRST AND SECOND YOUNG GIRLS SHOULD CUT IN ON ONE ANOTHER FASTER AND FASTER, AND ON A RISING NOTE OF CONVICTION AND EXCITEMENT. FINAL SENTENCE, TO COME, SHOULD BE SPOKEN, IN UNISON, LOUDLY AND DEFINITELY.)

FIRST AND SECOND YOUNG GIRLS' VOICES TOGETHER: Seeing the world – All we mean to say is you're only young once: you've got to have *something*, haven't you! – Got to say something, got to do something, got to *know* something, got to get *somewhere*. So, WE DID!

We did, we did, we did, we did, we did (ad lib).

(BEHIND THE REPEATED, CLAMOUROUS "WE DID'S" CRASH INTO DANCE-BAND VERY LOUDLY AND FAST PLAYING "WIDOWS ARE WONDERFUL" [RECORD C.852] WITH, SIMULTANEOUSLY, HIGH-SPEED CLATTERING

OF A TYPEWRITER. ALSO, SIMULTANEOUSLY, TICK OF
METRONOME. FADE OUT "WE DID" VOICES, DANCE-
BAND AND TYPEWRITER. BUT, KEEP METRONOME
TICKING BY ITSELF FOR 3 OR 4 SECONDS LONGER.)
  VOICES OF THREE HOSPITAL SOLDIERS: (*in the distance,
satirical but encouraging*) Keep it up, miss!
  (DISTANT CLAPPING OF HANDS)
  FIRST YOUNG GIRL: (*suddenly isolated and uncertain*) But
that came after – didn't it?
  SECOND YOUNG GIRL: (*also uncertain*) After?
  NARRATOR: (*tonelessly*) November the 11th.
  SENIOR MALE VOICE: (*speaking evenly, impersonally and
clearly*) Hostilities ceased on all fronts at 11 a.m.
  NARRATOR: Silence . . .
  Where *I* was, it was a silent morning. I was in the top room
of a country house. The sun was dazzling, pale. I stood at a
window, idle, looking down at a stretch of grass just touched
by frost. Two women, my aunts, came walking across the grass
towards the house; I counted the footprints they left behind them
as they came nearer. Then, they stopped, stood still in the sun,
and called up, to all the windows of the house – "Well, the war's
over."
  I was too shy to go downstairs and join them: there was
nothing to say.
  I remained at the window, searching the empty landscape
to see if it looked *different*. I was terrified by the vacuum, the
absolute full-stop, in my thoughts, in my being, in my soul. It
seemed to me, suddenly, that I had grown up without having the
capacity to feel.
  I remembered a poem – but what a strange one . . .
  YOUNG MALE VOICE: (*reciting as it were in the distance,
and remotely*)

  Calm is the morn without a sound,
  Calm as to suit a calmer grief,
  And only through the faded leaf
  The chestnut pattering to the ground.

  Calm and deep peace in this wide air,
  These leaves that redden to the fall;

And in my heart, if calm at all,
If any calm, a calm despair:

Calm on the seas, and silver sleep,
And waves that sway themselves to rest,
And dead calm in that noble breast . . . [11]

(DURING THE LAST LINE, VOICE IS RECEDING, DYING;
SO THAT FINAL WORDS ARE ALMOST INAUDIBLE.)

NARRATOR: It flowed in on me, out of nowhere. I was surprised: thought, but that is wrong, for *today*. "Grief" – why? "Despair?" – I did not know what that meant. What I felt was the sunny empty calm. I felt the absence of all the dead, the young, from this morning I was here to enjoy. It was the end of autumn: no more chestnuts to fall; hardly a shred of leaf left on the trees. Lovely beginning of winter – a day for life. But there were too few of us – where were all the others?

That missing of unknown people – that was grief. I cannot tell you about what I did not see, – the cities' Armistice Day of crowds and flags or Armistice Night of crowds and lights and songs. I finished the day where I had begun it: in the country: the last of the light faded – behind the bare trees. We celebrated – we must have, in that family house – but I cannot remember now. Peace came as such a tremendous shock: it felt like nothing on earth before. It was frightening.

A page had been turned over: here was a great new blank white page waiting to be filled. By whom? By the people of my age. If we made a mess of it – as, indeed, it must seem now that we did – it was not because we did not care enough. We cared too much. In our nervousness we left behind us nothing but nonsense and gaps and blots. To be young *now*, after the Second World War – I am always wondering what that must be like. Perhaps though, there is not so much to learn?

That was my 1918 – made up of large shadows, uncertain visions, and small things. The year I was first grown-up in. A year of history – by now, though, how many more years of history have piled up on it! It is not the year of which I remember most; but it is the one I remember the most deeply. The first, perhaps, of looking life in the eye.

BROADCASTS

Book Talk – New and Recent Fiction

In the last six years, reality – human history – *has* presented a challenge to the imagination. The imaginative writer expects, as a rule, to go one better than life. He has seen it as his business to supply the element of strangeness, of fantasy, lacking in the humdrum daily routine. *While* the humdrum rules, that's all very well. But when – as has happened during the war – daily life itself becomes fantastic and strange, *what* work is left for imagination?

Yes, fiction writers have certainly found themselves in a predicament. But, do you know, I think they have rallied to it extraordinarily well. They have been, perhaps, less inventive; but they have been more critical. They have been less content with simply telling a story – for, *as* a story, history goes one better – and more insistent that the stories they tell should contain some idea that may help to explain life.

Now for the novels actually on my list:

I Will be Good, by Hester Chapman, is, to begin with, a first-rate story. But it is, also, a story built around an idea. It is a romance set in Second Empire France, in the 1860s. The central character, however, is an English lady. But she is more than an English lady; she is a novelist – Blanche Peverence – a Victorian writer of best-sellers. So much for our heroine. The idea? The idea – and to me it's a very intriguing one, is, that if a novelist – a confirmed, professional novelist – ceases, for any reason, actually to write, he or she will make novels out of real life. Instead, that is to say, of controlling the actions and destinies of a set of fictitious men and women, the novelist will begin quite unconsciously to control the actions and destinies of the *living* men and women among whom he finds himself – thereby, forcing *them* to be characters in the novel he cannot help spinning in his own mind. The theory is an alarming one. If it holds water, I'm afraid you may all be giving a wide berth to any novelist you may happen to meet. And, so convincing is *I Will be Good*, that one really feels that the theory does hold water.

Miss Blanche Peverence, because she has sustained a severe shock, lays down her pen and goes to France, to be companion to the young daughter of a millionaire French industrialist. The power of the Victorian novelists was, as you probably know, immense. Following the example of the latest Peverence heroine, an hysterical young English reader had committed suicide. Blanche has been blamed, and whole-heartedly blamed herself: she resolved to lay down forever her dangerous pen. In this mood, she arrives at the fantastic French castle on the Atlantic seaboard. There she is confronted by her half-savage charge, Oriana, by Oriana's hard-boiled father and by Oriana's fiancé, a decadent young nobleman. The young man's father, the Duke, is under the influence of an enchantress who lives in the neighbourhood. In this woman, Blanche meets her enemy, and her only match. One more character – in fact, the hero – a melancholy young Danish officer, Charles Daalgard, is added to the cast of Miss Peverence's non-stop internal novel . . . Need it be said that the respectable Englishwoman's influence on this group of Continental people is disastrous? She not only forms, she over-forms, Oriana's character; she assents to the girl's unpromising marriage, then precipitates her into fatal passion for Captain Daalgard. Left to themselves, these people would have taken their own courses. Woe to them, that they had an authoress in their midst!

As it is, we watch them grow – to a stature they are not capable of maintaining – under the influence of Blanche's suggestive power – through vanity, through simplicity or through self-mistrust they become her prey.[1] "Prey" seems a hard word, for[2] Miss Peverence's own high principles never falter. When her English publisher, Alfred Marchant – who is at the same time her only clear-sighted friend – urges her to return to England and give her victims in France the chance to work out their own fortunes, Blanche, dear Blanche, is genuinely indignant. She replies that she must stick to her duty.

Miss Chapman's fine art as a novelist extracts the last drop of irony from the situation. Yes, *I Will be Good* is absorbing. And in its atmosphere there's something rich and strange. Ornate interiors, of castles and villas, glitter. Voluminous dresses rustle. Sea fogs and orchids, saloons and gardens and wild sea shores, tempestuous love and ruthless intrigue mingle. *I Will be Good*, apart from anything else, is an exquisite period piece. As you read, you breathe the air of the 1860s. None the less, inside their "period" dresses, the men and women here are of all and of any day.[3]

Now for my second novel – *A Fugue in Time* by Rumer Godden. Here we touch something perhaps more than an idea – one might call it a *nerve* of the present day. A house – a London house, a hundred years old, dense and rich inside as a plum cake with the feelings, the hopes and fears of the succession of people who have inhabited it . . . Walls and doors and stairs, windows that have been looked out of, fireplaces round which people gathered, talked, warmed their hands or dreamed in silence, watching the flames . . . "As safe as a house" – one *used* to say! Poor houses, how fragile they have become! Bombs have plucked out the hearts of their mysteries! But do they, perhaps, for this very reason, appeal, today, more strongly to our imaginations?

99 Wiltshire Place, the house in *A Fugue in Time*, is exceptional only in having been lived in by the same family ever since it was built. Young John Dane, prosperous businessman of the 1840s, brought his seventeen-year-old bride, Griselda, here to make their home. Theirs was a ninety-nine year lease; and they had nine children. When *A Fugue in Time* begins, the youngest and last of those nine children, now Sir Rollo Dane, is eighty; the time is the 1940s; the lease is just running out. What had seemed

an eternity is ended. Solitary, the old soldier walks alone, with his memories, through rooms that once teemed and rang with life. The world is at war, the bombers are overhead. Unexpectedly, a young great-niece from America, over here driving with an ambulance unit,[4] comes to join him. *She* is young America to the finger-tips – but none the less, she carries the Dane name. She feels family memories stir within her as, for the first time, she enters the dying house. And she has been christened Grisel, after her great-grandmother.[5]

Miss Rumer Godden gives us a curious, poetic and perhaps rather troubling variation of our old friend, "the family novel." For one thing, as I said, it is the *house* itself that is the central character. For another – she has broken up the ordinary time-sequence. There is no past and present, no "then" and "now." Everything that has ever happened in 99 Wiltshire Place is still happening – and is happening simultaneously. Into one day in this house are packed all the experiences of ninety-nine years. All the way through, we shuttle to and fro in time, and to and fro between character and character – *and*, between the same characters at very different ages. We see old Sir Rollo, for instance, as a baby, as a small boy, as a youth in love, as a disillusioned middle-aged man. We see his mother, Griselda Dane, as a glowing bride, as an anxious mid-Victorian matron, full of buried romantic yearnings. We watch her husband John Dane harden into the Victorian despot-father.[6] We see crowded family breakfast tables; we see the Christmas candles lit each year, by fewer and fewer hands – and by hands that, finally, shake with age . . . [7] Selina, the elder sister. Lark, the lovely foundling. The twins, who died young. Dogs bark, bells ring; the tree, outside the windows, casts the same flickering shadow through the rooms.

All these scenes and people – their births, their loves, their deaths, are, you see, themes in *A Fugue in Time*. This novel aims at – and *I* think achieves – the effect of music. If you want a straight "story," you may find it confusing, or baffling. I found it confusing at the *beginning*, but later on it had a quite powerful effect on me. Miss Rumer Godden shows herself a disciple – though not in the bad sense an imitator – of Virginia Woolf's. She[8] is obviously interested in the technique of writing. If you share this interest, I think *A Fugue in Time* deserves your attention. I do not say that the novel is a complete success, but I do most highly commend it as an experiment.[9]

Obviously, we novelists have got to experiment. New things have happened, whole new ranges of human feeling have been opened up. And for these new things we have got to find new forms. So please, readers, help us by meeting our experiments halfway. Some books may be puzzling because they *are* trying to be too clever by half. But some are puzzling because they are, honestly, trying to say something that has not been said before. And what has not been said before is, sometimes, well worth saying![10]

Again, I do admire the novelist who goes all out and tackles a big subject. So, for my third novel this week, I have chosen *The Horse of the Sun*. The author is L. F. Loveday Prior. Miss Prior has taken for her hero an Indian Prince, and set her scene in the court of a Native State – an imaginary state, of course, as the rules of fiction require; but I feel certain, from the authority with which she writes, that she knows her ground. We begin with the birth of Raemall, the long-awaited heir of the ageing Maharajah of Surthawara, in the grim, fortified castle of his ancestors, above a lake bright with the spring moon. The court astrologers mutter and shake their heads: the Prince has *not* been born under propitious stars! Are their forebodings justified by the Prince's life? Outwardly, fortune smiles on Raemall. He is handsome, beloved, brave; he enjoys fantastic wealth and, inside his own domains, almost absolute power. But, as we watch him, we find him to be his own enemy.

Power . . . power. That, of course, is the trouble. Looking back at the kings through history, we see, don't we, this trouble at work? The kings in the Old Testament – the kings of England, as seen through Shakespeare's clarifying poetic vision. To be royal, to be a ruler, creates, in itself, a predicament – and one that can be intensely dramatic. *The Horse of the Sun* is a dramatic novel. By this, I don't mean that it abounds in "strong scenes." I mean that it takes a magnified, and augustly simplified, view of human behaviour. And, it follows dramatic precedent in balancing the turbulent central figure – in this case, Raemall – by others who are steadier and more sane. One on each side of Prince Raemall – young Maharajah of Surthawara – stand his younger half-brother, Sangram, and Raemall's wife, Tara Devi. Sangram is a thinker: he is patient, speculative and detached. Tara Devi – the wife of Raemall's own choice – for he has refused the traditional unseen child-bride[11] – is not only lovely and loving; she has a sort of intuitive genius. These two, brother and wife, fight on Raemall's behalf against the forces that are ruining him.

And *The Horse of the Sun* has a second claim on your interest which must not be overlooked. Historically, it is important. Raemall, born in 1898, was destined to live through – and, as a Prince, to take part in – what have been for India changing and crucial years. European ideas, with their impact upon the old traditions, add to the conflicts in his character. Miss Prior gives us an unusual angle on Indian affairs. For this reason – apart from its inherent strangeness, drama and beauty, I think the book should be read.

The Next Book

I am always obsessed by the idea of "my next book." I know this to be the case with many writers: is it so with all? The next book seems to promise to be the repository for everything I have not been able to say so far. Or, perhaps, that I have not so far been able to pin down. Books which I have written and published seem to have gone into the blue, like balloons with the cables cut: they have very little further to do with me. All that remains with me of them are the blunders – the ignorance that at the time prevented me gripping my subject as it ought to have been gripped, the imperfect realisation of what I really did mean.

What has been meant, but not yet properly said, still remains to be said. I imagine that if one examined the works of any writer, a carry-over from one book to another would be found. To have finished a book, any book, is a triumph, in one way. But in another way, there is also an element of defeat.

Of course, also, writers are people – and people, unless there is something wrong with them, do not remain static. In the exterior world, something is going on happening the whole time:

consequently, something further is happening to, something is being added to, the person who is a writer the whole time. What is true of any person is doubly true of a person who is also a writer: one simply cannot afford to be either closed or static, to be either is to be dead.

Therefore a double importance, a double hope, must attach itself, for the writer, to his or her next book. The next book is expected to do two things – to make good the deficit left by the books before it, and to embody the further experience which has been added to the writer since the preceding books were written.

In writers of my generation – and, I suppose, of generations younger, down to those who have only just taken up the pen – the recent war and the present state of the world are the experience not to be ignored. It would be impossible for a novelist in these days to write a story purely of private life. At the same time, the novelist's obvious and inevitable domain is the individual. I think that the value of every novelist will be established by the truthfulness by which he or she pictures the impact of the outside world on the individual; and by the honesty with which he or she shows the conflict – as he or she feels it to be – between individual self-absorption and the individual's awareness of the outside world. Myself I would be prepared to stand or fall by this test. But the trouble is, how am I to find a scene, characters or plot which will be the ideal vehicles for my meaning? And by what testing processes am I to arrive at being most certain of what I do mean?

For the ideal layout, and for the ideal expression of what I do mean, and for a clear mind as to what is of the first importance, I am for ever pinning my hopes on "my next book."

Impressions of Czechoslovakia

From my fortnight spent in Czechoslovakia I have brought back clear and lasting impressions. I was there from February 6th to 19th: I spent, first, a week in Prague; then toured through Olomouc, Brno and Bratislava, staying for a short time in each city, then returned to Prague for three days more. Fortunate though I was in seeing so much of the country in so short a time, I wished my visit could have been longer.

I was lecturing, in English, on the novel. I think I have never spoken to audiences whose interest in literature could be felt to be more vital or more sincere. To speak, and to take part in the discussions later was, therefore, for me an inspiring experience. Nor was it only in lecture rooms that Czechoslovakia offered an open-hearted greeting to me as a friend from another land. I was allowed to see vivid examples of social and cultural life. In Prague, Brno and Bratislava I admired the modern housing and the industrial buildings – still greatly in advance of our own. The organisation of public libraries, and their obvious popularity with a great host of readers, particularly impressed me.

A Sunday evening performance, at the Prague opera house, of Smetana's *The Secret*[1] was, for me, unforgettable – I was told, too, the history of the magnificent opera house itself – how, destroyed again and again by fire, it had been, "by the people and for the people," each time indomitably rebuilt. I had been anxious to see Czech films, and I was generously treated in this matter: both educational films – as to which, as I could see at once, Czechoslovakia has pioneered – and the famous puppet films were shown me. As to the last, I spent an enchanted afternoon at a projection of *A Year in Bohemia*.[2] To see the poetry of country life, throughout the seasons, and the traditional dignity of the Bohemian peasant expressed by dolls was extraordinary – *what* great art! I trust that that film, in its entirety, may sooner or later come to us here in England . . . My only regret was that, though I saw some good representative examples of modern Czech painting, time literally did not permit of my visiting any of the picture-galleries.

As a writer, I could but be struck by respect accorded to writers in Czechoslovakia – that they should both play a living part in the life of the community *and* be offered, in "writers' castles," the ideal conditions for creative work seemed to me excellent. Both outside Prague and outside Bratislava I was entertained at the neighbouring "writers' castle" – how I envied the quietness and beauty of the rooms set apart for work, and the surroundings, gardens and woodlands in which one could walk and think. Such retreats, as the pressure of modern city life grows greater, should, ideally, be set up in every country. . . I also was entertained, to my great pleasure, by the Moravian Writers' Association, in Brno. Everywhere I had this same impression – that it was the aim of Czechoslovakian literature to give expression, through art, to the ever-growing national life.

My love of countryside and of landscapes made my motor tour through Bohemia, Moravia and Slovakia a deep pleasure. The great open sweeps of tillage, the mysterious forests, the noble ranges of mountain, the sky-reflecting rivers, the churches perched on hilltops, the villages in the valleys will remain forever photographed in my memory. I remember the large carp ponds, the small ponds in villages with white geese in sunshine and willow trees drooping over them. The prettiness, but at the same time the strength, of the houses along the village streets struck me . . . In Slovakia, it was cheerful to see the vineyards along the sides of the hills – and how excellent was the wine!

Architecturally, what a feast – both in cities and throughout the country! Churches and castles, town squares and streets, monuments and cottages – I could not have enough! My love, particularly, of the Baroque, grew with what I saw: it could never be satiated – but in all its phases the architecture around me seemed to be, though disciplined, full of soul. My eye feasted, not less, on the soft glowing colours of the painted buildings, and the mellowness of the ancient stone ones.

Oh, to have had more time! And there is not enough time, now, to speak of all I saw. First and last, my over-ruling impression was the human one – that I was happy in finding myself among a people who, old in history, were young in energy – full of integrity, courage, strength and promise. I came away with the feeling of having formed a friendship with a great country, and I long to return.

The Mechanics of Writing

Creative writing demands high concentration, and by the end of *my* working day I find that my brain has more or less run out.

On my ideal working day, I have lunch all alone. Talking to any other person does rather somehow break into one's train of thought. Over my sandwich or bread-and-cheese I quite often read a page or two of a thriller, or glance at a newspaper. And before going back again to work, I like taking a turn outdoors.

For the work – the writing – itself, I like an as nearly as possible quiet room. – That holds good, I imagine, with most writers. A big table, not far from a window. Outside the window I prefer to have something not too distracting: a street I find fatal, because I cannot help watching the passers-by. No, I like best to have trees outside the window. As to this, in London I'm fortunate – I live overlooking a park. And in Ireland my old home, where I do much work, is deep in the heart of the country.

A *big* table is so important for me. I'm an untidy person, strewing everything round me. For this reason, it's really ideal for me to have a room specially *for* writing. Because, at the same time, I'm house-proud – I don't like, later on in the evening, to receive friends in a messed-up room. I dust up my table at the end of a day, but prefer to leave my manuscript where it is until next morning.

Yes, I work up to a table, and straight on to a typewriter. I say this because some other authors – specially women – tell me that *they* work curled up in a fireside armchair, jotting down their flow of thoughts into a little pad.[1] – I'm afraid the trouble with me is that I'm so naturally idle that if I were too comfortable I shouldn't get anything done. And it's for that same reason that I keep regular hours. It's been really vital to me both to form a habit of work and to keep up some sort of a continuity. I accept the fact that inspiration varies from day to day – *some* days are exhilarating – the story one's writing fairly flies along – other days are infinitely discouraging: one seems to bog right down. At the best, I write four or five pages (never more, I think): at the worst, I do even less than one. I am most slow when I have to write a description or feel called on to analyse or explain. On the other hand conversation, which I enjoy writing,[2] always goes fairly fast.

The hardest part, I think, about being a writer is that one has got to keep one's own nose to the grindstone. One is one's own master, yes – but that often means being a pretty hard master to oneself! All that, however, is compensated for by the sheer exalting joy of a *good* day's work. In writing a book, one is bringing into existence something which had not been there before: I know of no other sensation to equal *that*!

To grow older is to be conscious of changing values. Some pleasures fade, some questions have no longer the power to hold one's interest. What used to be magic for one no longer works. One finds oneself growing apart from some of one's former friends. With every year, unconsciously, one has been shifting one's camp. One does not know how far one has travelled till some small revelation – some disappointment, possibly – comes as a shock.

For the loyal person, the shock is of self-reproach. "*Am* I, then," he asks himself, "so fickle?" The imaginative person feels, most, a pang of loss, – with which may go, for the moment, fear. "Is some part of me dying?" he asks himself. "Are my sensibilities less keen, my reactions and sympathies less vivid? – Are my interests narrower than they used to be?"

Only reason can answer: thus – We can count our losses more easily than we compute our gains. The intake of knowledge, the growth of powers, the development of the faculty for experience, are – in any life that follows a normal course – inestimable, as the years mount up. Each year adds more. Inevitably, we cannot contain everything; we cannot carry more than a certain load. One must discard to make place for what is new. The discarding is automatic – one need not, really, reproach oneself; one should not be alarmed.

All this holds most true with regard to books. There is, for the reader, a hateful sadness about returning to a former favourite only to find the magic gone. Those pages, now, are nothing but cold print – words, words, words:[1] unevocative! Unevocative, yes, and worse! They are haunted by the ghost of the former joy. Chagrin comes to be followed by an aesthetic distaste. These resounding half-truths, these trumped-up emotions, these two-dimensional persons (if the book be a novel) – how irritating, how embarrassing they are! How could one – oneself, the reader – at any age, have been so far imposed upon, fooled and tricked?

Take it calmly: the fact is, you have outgrown that book. It *was* good, in so far as, once, it seemed good to you. It spoke, once – and who knows what virtue you may not have sifted from it? It revealed, perhaps, something you now accept as a commonplace. For whatever reason, it hit you at the right moment: respect, at least, the power it used to have. What you find wrong in it now is its insufficiency. You expect more.

There are, of course, happier cases – books to which one remains attached because of the powerful element of nostalgia. To such a book one returns, each time, with a feeling of ease and rest; *this* mental landscape remains as dear and fixed as a scene of childhood. And, indeed, as a repository for feeling the book is safer than the physical scene. In real life, the wood may be cut down, the field over-built, the old street corner hideously transformed – but into the book change cannot intrude at all. For me, Mrs. Gaskell's *Cranford*, the juvenile novels of Louisa M. Alcott, and, of all the works of Dickens, most, *David Copperfield*, are of this kind – the books one does not outgrow.

What, then, of the books of which one asks something more: "Grow up with me! Move through the stretch of years that is *my* life, with me, at once abreast and ahead of me!" Of *what* books, what kind of books, does one ask this never in vain?

The specific answer, I think, must in each case be individual. For me, I know, it has been, certain English poets – some

Elizabethan, some nineteenth-century – and a small number of novels. To those let me return. First, I should like to try to establish what I should call the generic qualities of "books that grow up with one."

Let's imagine a book that one reads first (say) at fifteen; again at twenty-two; again at thirty-four; again when one is in one's forties; and again, one hopes, three or four times before one dies. At the first meeting, our book must engage the erratic curiosity and dream-clouded ignorance of the adolescent, it must give a friendly – not a forbidding – hint of much still uncharted: just because of this it will magnetise, without being wholly understood. The young adult of the second reading, and the young-mature adult of the third, will find in the book reflections – yes, and verifications – of his experience. The reader for the fourth time, being into his forties, will find the book raises questions, or contains implications, of which he had not been aware before. His own evaluations will find their touchstone. He will react, perhaps, less to the emotions of the book than to its judgements – or, if you like, philosophy.

And, the readings in the closing decades of life? By this time, the reader's personal memory will present itself to him as a long perspective. He is likely to find himself looking back more often than he finds himself looking forward. His own pace will have slackened. He may hope, at least, to have gained detachment. But, alas, there may also have set in a certain hardening of the mental arteries. His age of intake is over: he has to try – but may fail – not to offer resistance to something new. When he reads, he may tend to return to the loves of youth. And, in the book we imagine, the book read at intervals through his life, he is most likely – *now* – to look for the summing-up.

To endure, then, a book must, like a landscape, have strong features, able to stand out first in the early light, then in the glare of noon, then at last in sunset. That is the first point. Second, it must be able both to anticipate the experience of the young reader and to reflect the experience of the old. Third, the book's truth must be of a hard-wearing quality. Last – and, perhaps, most important – the book must have the power to expand.

The book's expansion keeps pace with the reader's own – or, ideally, should be a little ahead of it. Some new, unforeseen significance should appear with each re-reading. If the book be a novel – and, inevitably, given my own taste, it is novels that I have most in mind – the characters should not only have distinction (in order that we may not tire of their company) but should also have, packed within them, a greater complexity than may, at the first reading, appear.[2] In a sense, a character who is to accompany us through life must[3] be Everyman, containing both good and evil and showing conflict[4] in play. And the same thing – speaking, still, of novels – must hold good of the situations on which the story turns. The great book has depth;[5] it exists layer upon layer, stratum on stratum: we mine down into it deeper each time we read.[6]

One demands, in fact, of a book something more than one expects in the happiest relationship with a human being – universality. In fact, we cannot be commanded by anything that has not something of the poetic attribute.

I have spoken, so far, as though the book came into existence only at times of reading. On the contrary, its existence within us, when it has been even *once* read, is continuous. Absorbed into the consciousness of the reader, the book is at work in him all the time. As, also, the reader's memory is at work on the book.[7] Do you ever find, when you[8] re-read, that you have imagined something not actually to be found on the printed pages?[9] That is an extreme case; but there is no doubt that the action of the reader upon the book is as real as the book's action upon the reader. So that, the book which grows up with you becomes an accretion of yourself. Your comprehension, your vision,[10] have gone to make it.

The books which have grown up with me have not always been, outwardly, searching or grandiose. One, for instance, of them is Jane Austen's *Emma* – comedy of manners,[11] on one of her two inches of ivory. Self-delusion and vanity are the subjects; the scene is small-town; the plot revolves around marriage projects. I have been re-reading *Emma*, on an average, every five years: each time, I am more struck – and struck, perhaps, each time at a different point in the tale – by the sublime evaluation of human motives. I find Shakespearean wisdom in this prose comedy . . . Another novel is French: Flaubert's *Sentimental Education*. The hero, Frederick, is a weakling; tawdry, in general, are the objects of his love. Yet, something educates *me* as I sink myself in this emotional life-story, as I react to the ironical working of time and change. The desire soars clear above the futility . . . A third – so much discussed in the last ten years that by now I have nothing to add to it, is the Russian epic, Tolstoy's *War and Peace*. For me, no higher has fiction ever ascended in its climb for the great panoramic view. The ordeal inherent in being human; the taking-shape of destiny; reconciliation with its great final calm – I find these here.

Yes, there are books which, for me, cannot fail. I come to some new promontory of life and look around me – yes, they are still there; yes, they are still ahead.

The Cult of Nostalgia

Nostalgia: so very much in evidence; such a subject. It has been on the increase;[1] it came to a steady level; I think there is reason to hope it may be on the decline. The hope may sound rather brutal: can we afford in these days, you may ask, to sever any life-line, to break off any continuity? Because of course there could be that aspect to our perpetual dwelling on the past.

The thing is, at the start, to try and see how far this is, or has been, a vogue; or how far it is a real addiction. A very great part of the writing of our own period has served as a carrier – yes, and promoter too – of this nostalgia. Would such writing succeed – which is to say, be acceptable – if there were not a call for it? I suppose, no. One of the dangerous powers of the writer is that he feeds, or plays up to, fantasies he knows to exist. He knows of their existence for the good reason that they are probably active in himself. In contacting the same fantasies in his readers he does something to break down his isolation. If, by so doing, he also may make his living, who is to blame him? But without injustice to him, we should recognize this: that it is easier to recall than to invent, easier to evoke than to create.

It is true, of course, that creation in the literary sense is, must be, to a great extent evocation, the calling up of images, feelings, trains of thought which are recognisable, being common to all men. Accepted human experience is not only the writer-artist's subject; it gives him his terms of reference, and up to a point provides – even dictates – his vocabulary. But am I wrong in saying the inner object of art is not merely to reproduce but to add? Ideally, should not the book, story or poem constitute what has not yet been, what is new? Yet the work of outright imagination sets up, so often, in the first place, some sort of uneasiness or recoil. Why should that be? What is present? It is the unfamiliar, the unforeseen relation between things, the break-through of an unexpected light, the new experience, so far without precedent.

The unfamiliar: really, it may be argued, these days we are having enough of that. Its cold breath meets us at every turn, not only in art, which we may eschew, but in everyday life, which is unavoidable. To live at all, to conduct oneself through a day, week, year, is a matter of shocks, incredulities, then adjustments. If it is true, as one hears, that the British are becoming more tolerant towards art, that may be because there is little to choose between one form of the extraordinary and another: existence is extraordinary, in itself. But at the same time there is in us, I do maintain, a natural strong resistance against all this. Our emotions, even our senses, seek something stable to cling to. How can we not seek, in some form, an abiding city?[2] We continue to cry out for the well known, the comfortable, the dear, for protecting walls round the soul. The resource, we begin to feel, the solution, is to turn back – turn back into the past. The past, now, seems to be the repository of all treasures.

The most concrete, most personal past is childhood. Childhood is a terrain which we all can, or all fancy we can, re-enter, without falsifications, without breaches with honesty. It is a meeting-ground, for have not all childhoods much in common? At a distance, that time of any life seems to have been both simple and dramatic; and also this was a time of fresh, sharp and pure sensation. The favoured scenes of that era – particular street-corners, canal-sides, edges of woods, outlooks from windows, turns of staircases – still hold when one revisits them, if they survive, an emphatic, immortal charm of their own. And, something more, they hold virtue, seem to give out virtue.

Change, in such places, wreaks a personal injury, a tearing out of pages from one's own story: so much so that, knowing how wide and drastic the scope of change is, we may not dare to risk a real-life return, but instead prefer to brood on those scenes in memory – remembrance – which is more insidious, more in-growing, but more safe . . . Just how egotistical, I wonder, are those either actual or imaginary return journeys? Is it one's nascent self, one's in-the-bud identity, that one looks for? Or, better, is one really in search of the thing-in-itself – of that independent clearness with which the flint wall, the flight of uphill steps, the reflected arch of the bridge, used to stand out – stand out not blurred, as yet, by too many associations? We were once – or were, we believe – as children, aware of the delightful and forceful mystery locked up in the existence of outside things. What were they saying, what were they hiding, what were they leading to? What had been or was likely to be, their story? That heaven lying around us in our infancy: was it perhaps in fact, or at least in part, the heaven of impersonal curiosity? If so, it is a heaven we do indeed do well to try and regain. The original magic – perhaps, even, the original truth?

As children, we wanted knowledge. Growing up, we have found ourselves fobbed off with information. We have the answers, but have forgotten the questions which gave them context. It is, probably, that delight of the search, that sense of enigma, that urge towards exploration which a skilful book about childhood does most revive. Or at least, it is by the hope or hint of revival that such a book acts on us most effectively. Yes, but always along with that, though, goes the menace of the sentimental untruth. Then, we may come to believe, the sun always shone. There was happiness.

Nonsense – as we all well know. Frank memory is latent somewhere in all of us: one can check on its records by watching any ordinary child: which is to say, almost any child at all. There were, there are, great stretches of listless boredom. Adventurousness was, and is, intermittent, along with fancy, wonder and curiosity. Anxieties and embarrassments, in a child, may look small to us because its range of existence seems small; but, like our own, they are grimly to scale, therefore, as ours do, loom grimly large. We go on projecting on to the child – on to the state of childhood – what we most yearn for and lack: security. But, in fact, is it too much to say that no child ever has known security? If it had it, it imagined it away: comfortable nurseries were stalked by night fears; grown-ups were incalculable; whole structures of hope could fall at a fatal word. All that is well known; too well known, really – it makes sad repetition. Why, indeed, destroy so much as the last of the fiction of paradise? Or rather, why trample over the ground where once we fancied paradise used to be? Let us leave it that children, as a race, probably are, and probably always have been, more competent at the business of happiness than we are. As humans, they do not do so badly. But neither, for the matter of that, do we.

Our wish for illusion, that is the striking thing. That, and our capacity to be satisfied, however briefly. Whether the world is really less habitable than it used to be is an open question: in the main, we do consider it so – we therefore look for alleviation; and on the whole it is wonderful how we find it. Reading is an aid; and the past, lately, has proved one unfailing source: memoirs, biography, old diaries found in old desks, agreeable works of history, rich historical novels. Everything was, apparently, nicer then: more vivid, less monotonous, more important. The light that never was on land or sea, falls on gardens; the silhouette of the house in trees; the leisurely pair of lovers strolling by the lake; the classic streets of a more orderly London.

Importance – the spot-lighting of the individual figure, the stress on will and choice, the climactic nature of passion – may not that be most of all? It appears – it is made so to appear – that there was a time (fix it when, where you like) when persons were major characters; when a whole world attached to their decisions and actions, to what they thought, felt, achieved, triumphed over, or suffered. What we envy in them also is what attracts us: as we observe, with envy, the unconscious imperialism of childhood. They were themselves, it appears to us: are we? That is, are we ourselves, so fully, to the last risk? No, under present conditions, we fear, not. But might we not have been so, under other conditions? Surely. Those "other conditions," where are they to be found? Our innate perfectionism – for we are all perfectionists – cries out for them. They were to be found, we become convinced, in the Past, rude, unjust, and insanitary though it may have been.

Of course there is always the future, a picture sketched but still to be coloured in. Our moral wills salute the future, subscribe to it and support it; but pleasure is not a matter of moral will; and it is pleasure, or the pursuit of that, which we have at the moment under analysis. And in fact, of course, all pleasure is of the moment: what we desire actually is the "now." During the moment in which we draw the breath, we cast round for what shall pierce us, elate us. The enhanced sensation, the dazzling image, the enjoyable regret, the tear shed looking at a sunset – from our nostalgia we gather an easy harvest. We are masters, however, of the romantic subterfuge. Beware, though, of the subterfuge which outlasts its day. Nostalgia – our nostalgia – is that beginning to decline? Perhaps . . .

Against it, there is the pressing realism of history; the accumulation of evident fact and law. There is the climate of the actual literature of the past, bracing, harsh, shocking, not easy to enter, not always comfortable to breathe. *Tom Jones*: should we have done well in that robust and trenchant world? Compared to the Fielding characters, we are sheltered creatures. We are of a certain intelligence: we dare not not be. We dare not reject the evidence: we must know and judge.[3] Whole reaches of the past were so grim a jungle that it is a miracle anybody survived it; and, at the best, never, we may be certain, did the sky of the day not shed a trying glare. So trying that in each generation there were those who could not – or thought they could not – sustain it. Yes, the nostalgics. We can spot them, perceive them, their heads turned back, all the way down the distances of the road of time. There is something not very exhilarating about their company. They look, somehow, grey, middle-aged, rather mournfully middle-class.

We may, indeed, note today that it is in the younger people that revulsion against nostalgia is most marked. "What is all this?" they intimate. "Nothing, to us. Today is today; it's got to be good enough." Will they stick by that, or will they have to compromise? I hope not. I should like to see a whole generation keep the power of taking its moments "straight" – not half-overcast by fantasy, not thinned-down by yearning. Why, indeed, should not imagination – without which, granted, happiness is impossible – be able to burn up in the air of today? It was out of zest, out of a sometimes blind vitality, out of barbarian energy, that the past was built. There it stands, there it lies, mounting, extending, never complete, in all the nobility of its imperfection. It does not seek to attach us; it does not need us. What of the present, the "now," the moment – so disconcerting, so fleeting, so fascinating in its quivering inability to be pinned down? What has great art done but enclose that eternal "now"?

Coronation

The day rouses an echo: uninterrupted music and beat of feet. From the sky, hundreds of years of light fall on the glitter of *all* the procession. No saying where the occasion begins or ends: it flows like a river come to the surface – a young great day out of an old great past. The answer to expectation is this day.

This island, solitary in the sea, not yet quite alone conserves the idea of Majesty. The idea illumines our human state – so that by crowning we are all crowned: we reflect the act, we enter into the glory. About every destiny, man's or woman's, there is something unique, mysterious – the Queen's, consecrated, is more so. For her, no choice: only one path. Ours, but set apart from us; we salute her.

She goes to the Abbey, comes from the Abbey, through the pressing and burning mist of our sensations, accompanied on her way by[1] a sort of thunder, followed by a long subsidence like a sigh. Where she is not in sight, she is in thought. Something comes in on her from the concentration of the millions of people here but not here in London. The actuality of her movements is being photographed, not only on the consciousness of the bystanders – it is recorded on films as history – and cast from moment to moment, fugitive as real life, on to television screens. Listeners more closely watch with the mind's eye: voice after voice takes up[2] every golden turning flash of her coach-wheels, each inclination of her head. These hours – day here, night elsewhere – focus the world. The size, the intensity, the silence of the global attention can be felt – or, can it? Does the Queen feel it? Is it too vast to feel?

How does it feel, to wake up one morning knowing one is going to be crowned? Because the Queen is young, we imagine for her the sensations inseparable from youth – a sort of eager engagement with what happens, a fervour for experience for its own sake. But here is something outside experience – out of scale with experience as we know it. Because she has an open and natural face, formed for the expression of joys and sorrows which we know about, we comprehend, we share, it must all the more be remembered that, all the same, we, ourselves, cannot go all the way with her. There is a point, today, from which she goes forward: here we stop. Because it seems such a short time since, from the tops of buses, we watched her playing with other children like any other child in a London garden, we feel, today, estrangement – estrangement not from her but from our memories of familiarity. Today? – today she resembles no one.

The stiff, brocaded royal children of history carry, in their portraits, a special look – an expression of being born wary. That look Elizabeth never wore. Neither were we ever excluded; nor are we now.

In view today as clearly as she was in the garden, she passes by us attracting a startled wonder – this apparition of majesty at the height in her – what is it? More than us, she is also more than herself. Gorgeous archaic robes add impersonal beauty – how impersonal is she as to the day? Wonder *at* her gives place to wonder *as* to her . . . Children play kings and queens; children become kings and queens when they act Shakespeare. Afterwards children grow up – but not to this. Does the Queen ask herself, "Can this be true?"

Victorious, happy and glorious . . . Let us recall our victories; let them crown her. The air is haughty with flying flags – and why not? This is a nation great in its endurances. We commemorate the wounds which have been survived, the losses outfaced, the sorrows which ran their course. The Queen's Coronation is taking place in a London of spaces of cleared ruins. The dead who should still be living, the dead of two wars, are among the concourse: the Queen is victorious in their name – she is to reign, also, over a living race of slow but undeterrable rebuilders. This is a day to celebrate, to envisage happiness and lay claim to glory. A summer day.

It *is* true. Happy and glorious, the young Queen moves, also, past the eyes of her generation. She symbolises them – but they do not think of symbols: chiefly, she is a person of their age. This, because it is her era, is *their* era: something new has begun. Naturally, she must smile – do not *they* smile? The young have entered; the young are taking their place – therefore the Coronation procession is not merely splendid, it is triumphal. The Queen's delight in the day, and in being Queen, and in being crowned, is there for all of her age to know – with each look she gathers Elizabethans around her. No mystery separates her and them. They are not shy of her.

The young are natural democrats: their Queen, Elizabeth II, has been educated to share, as far as may be, the ideas of her generation and their time. The possibilities of being a Queen now, and a Queen in her way, seem endless: trumpets may sound and bring down the walls of Jericho. Planets, not merely territories, may be discovered; and, better still, harmony may come to exist between the sexes. The age of science, hitherto unaesthetic, may bring forth subtleties, beauties, pleasures. Something more daring, more interesting than security, as an aim in life, may be first envisaged and then realised. Will Queen Elizabeth launch a space-ship? Will she declare open the Channel Tunnel? What will she see invented – or see abolished? . . . She intends to reign well, and to enjoy reigning.

Reigning should be enjoyable. Woman, on the whole, shows an aptitude for it – there are few who have not desired to try. One cannot, however, reign without dedication – as Elizabeth, child of a King, knows. Coming to the throne so early, so near the beginning of her life, she has far to go – but how rewarding a journey! There attaches to her, from all sides, an extraordinary hope; and she is aware of it – something about her, seriously glowing, shows that she kindles as she responds. Much reaches Royalty that we do not know of – we do not know what reaches them, or how – perpetually progressing between crowds – do they, do the Royal, record vibrations? They are most often amongst us when we, in masses, are at our most extreme: they seldom see us rational. In return, we have the candour and sanity of the Queen's gaze passing over the onlookers. She has been brought up to us; she esteems us. She is romantic.

On Not Rising to the Occasion

Rising to the occasion: I do not remember that it was ever *called* that. No, I am sure it was not. There was no name for what one was asked to do – in a way, this made it all the more ominous. A name, the grown-ups may have thought, would have made too much of it – pandered too much to juvenile self-importance. Children, in my Edwardian childhood, were decidedly played down rather than played up. "Just be natural" – they used to say, before the occasion; "nobody wants you to show off." What a blow to ambition – what a slap in the face! "Be natural"; really, what a demand!

I could scent an occasion coming, a mile away. Everybody was going to be implicated in something tricky. Socially, "they" were about to turn on the heat. It could be some primitive embarrassment was coming a shade nearer the surface than the grown-ups liked. This could have left me cold – *had* they left me out. But no, on what is known as an "Occasion," children are useful. One was to be on tap. One would be on view. One would be required, and tensely watched. One would have to express, to register, something *extra*. Pleasure: "Aunt Emmeline is coming, you know, today: do show her how happy you are to see her." Gratitude, for a present or a party: "And don't just mumble 'Thank you': do smile, too!" Sympathy, with a grief: "Look, here's poor Mrs. X coming down the street: you need not say anything, just let her *see* you're sorry!" Interest, in anything that a senior chose to explain to one, tell one or point out to one. Enthusiasm, for anything one was caused to see – scenery, famous or noble persons, some dreary, intricate curio from the East.

React, child! Demonstrate! That was all they wanted. It was not unreasonable, really – a child like a stuck pig *is* a dreadful sight. I do not want, at all, to give the impression that my childhood was an emotional forcing-house, or, still more, an unduly social one. It was not such a bad preparation for after life. People are always going to expect one to react, in some way: no harm in learning to be quick off the mark. And reactions must be appropriate, not excessive. This cannot be drilled into the young too soon . . . or, can it? The Edwardians considered not. Today, I hear, many differ from them: there are some, aren't there, who go so far as to hold that children should not say "Thank you," unless they do feel a surge of spontaneous gratitude, or "Sorry" – when they tread on anyone's toe – unless they are truly stabbed by remorse. I do not think I can go into the rights and wrongs of it. I imagine there must be in each generation some children uneasily conscious of what is wanted, and uneasily certain they must fall short. They either cannot or will not deliver the goods.

Would this be recalcitrance, or plain nervousness? In me, it was a mixture of both – plus a wary dread of "going too far." If one crossed the very fine line, if one *went* too far, one's behaviour fell into the "showing off" class. To celebrate the arrival of a visitor by whooping, prancing, clashing imaginary cymbals together over one's head was considered hysterical and excessive – I once tried it. And effusiveness, in the matter of gratitude, was, I was to discover, another error. "Thank you, Mrs. Robinson, so very, very much for the absolutely wonderful LOVELY party!" "Well, dear," my hostess would say with a frigid smile, "I'm afraid it was hardly so wonderful as all *that*." And, "Who was that gushing little thing?" I could practically hear her say it, as

I left the room. To this day I remember – and still with blushes, mortification – the awful number of marks that I overshot. After each excess, I had periods of stand-offish caution; I had to resort to the stodgy gruffness of manner allowed, I had seen, to little boys.

I connect so many occasions with stage-fright, paralysing self-consciousness, all but impotence. And, let me be clear, this was far from shyness. I was not a retiring child – I should not at all have liked to be banished from the scene of activity. I had dreams of glory in which I behaved conspicuously well, well to the point of evoking comment. But alas, in real life for a child to behave "well" meant – above all things – never to be conspicuous. An occasion is an orderly grown-up concept, an affair of a thousand-and-one rules. The accustomed actors are old stagers; it is only the child who must walk on without having been rehearsed; though, still, with enough instructions to make it nervous. You see, the poor child is in the picture, but not the centre of it – unless of course, it is at its own birthday party. The child dithers somewhere round the margin.

In my long-ago childhood, it was important what grown-ups thought. They were the censors, the judges. Today, they have less prestige, they have abdicated from power, gone down in status: in some families, they seem like a fallen upper-class. Children, like freedmen going round in gangs, are rather more, today, in each others' power. Well, I say "more," but honestly, looking back, I see that this gang-formation did go on in my childhood also: as an underworld, blinked at by the eye of authority. We children put one another to drastic tests. There was, for one thing, the dire "I dare you . . . " Tree and roof climbing to the extremest heights, blindfold acrobatics on bicycles, one-leg hopping along the tops of walls, balance on parapets over deep railway cuttings – these were the *sine qua non*. I daresay they are today? All the same, physical ordeals were less scorching than non-stop criticism. At day school, we kept a narrow watch on each other – the glances shot from desk to desk in the classroom, and we trailed each other down the streets when we started home. Forever we were keeping each other up to the mark, without committing ourselves by saying what the mark *was*; and this amounted, I see now, to a continuous rising to an occasion which – unlike others – never came to an end.

Friendships, for instance, were exacting: they involved the almost daily exchange of secrets which had to be of a horrific magnitude, and so did plans for Saturday afternoons. This was Folkestone: there was the switchback railway, there was the outdoor roller skating rink, but we looked for something more desperate and more original. Keeping tryst with the dearest friend of the moment, it was fatal not to produce a bright idea. The search – for some reason – always devolved on me. I was forever devising, racking my brains and fancy, tying myself into knots, to think something up. The approach of a Saturday afternoon loomed over me far more darkly than school work.

"Well," the friend would say, "so what *are* we going to do?" A suspicious pause; "Or haven't you thought?"

"Oh yes, I have!"

"I hope it's not something silly."

Thus encouraged, I would unfold my plan. "That does not sound much fun," she would remark. "Still, it's too late to think of anything else, so I s'pose we may as well try. Come on."

An un-thrilling Saturday could cool off a friendship. Folkestone in 1910 was dressy, law-abiding, and well patrolled; the amount of things children could do – bring off without being shouted at – was limited. Bye-laws, prohibiting almost everything, were posted up and down the Leas and along the woodsy paths of the undercliff. Oh, that initiative – why was *I* forced to take it? Yes, it took one's contemporaries, it took other children, to put that particular pressure on one. "You put yourself out too much about your friends!" my mother would declare, as fagged-out, white in the face, I came tottering back to her through the Folkestone dusk. "Why not let them amuse you, for a change, sometimes?" And indeed in my own mind I often wondered.

Would the strain become less as I grew older? No: on the contrary. When I was fourteen, fifteen, the dress-problem raised its ugly head. It was necessary to look nice, as well as be nice. Still more, it was necessary to look "suitable." But, my heavens, suitable to what? For life was to bristle, from now on, with unforeseeable occasions. In advance, these were daydream occasions: I dressed accordingly. In those days, the teenager was unguided. Fashion, now so kind to that age-group, took no account of us. So, trial-and-error it was, for me. Outcome: errors. The rose-pink parasol with which I all but poked out somebody's eye at a cricket match; the picture hat in which I attended a country lunch-party – only to be taken out ratting by my host; the ornamental muslin, with blue bows, in which I turned up at a grown-up beach picnic – *that* I disposed of by slipping off a rock into the sea. The splash was big, though the sea was shallow. The crisis obliterated my frock. Was my accident quite accidental? I cannot answer.

Yes, I think as a child I did better with my back to the wall – in extreme situations, among strangers. Whatever strangers could do to me, they could not bite, and there was the hope I might never meet them again. It was my near ones, my dear ones; the fond, the anxious, the proud-of-me, who set up the inhibition. I could not endure their hopes; I could not bear to fail under loving eyes. I detested causing a disappointment. Perhaps I exaggerated the disappointment? Perhaps I did less badly than I imagined? You see, it mattered too much. I shall never know. For how does one rise – fully, ever – to an occasion?

"What I'd like," I heard myself saying, "would be to write a book about Rome." I had not realised this was so until I said so. It was a sudden answer to a question, one of those "What are you up to?" or "Anything to declare?" questions, which are put to authors sometimes abruptly, and a sudden question does jolt the truth out of one, so I'd expressed a wish, a temerarious, almost aggressive wish, in itself, by the sound of it, almost a boastful one of the kind, which back in childhood, would have brought down on one almost certainly a deflating snub. "You don't want much do you," or "Wait till you're older." I cannot expect now to be much older. Nobody can say wait to me, any longer. What more to wait for?

Off to Rome then. I had been there several times, always, though, for a short time, a few weeks. Now, it was going to be a matter of three months, and, as I looked ahead, I had for the first time the dazzling sensation of having a sum of time to spend. It went, I expect, somewhat to my head, and it embroiled me with a new kind of relationship with Rome – more exciting and more disturbing. How new it made Rome to me, and me in a sense to Rome, I realised when I stepped out of[1] my hotel room into the dazzling sunshine of the winter with, I imagined, plans, ideas, some idea of destination within me, and at once completely lost myself. Why? I should have known the way yet it was now, this morning, as though Rome, during my absence from it, had executed an elaborate dance leaving all the monuments, all the familiar sights, in what to me was a totally new position – and I must explain that I don't mean anything to do with rebuilding, with any clearance, any architectural change. The Rome which was dementing me by having, if I may so express it, swished around, was the Rome which I knew by reason to have existed and been where it was for centuries.

I was adrift on a great, yellow, architectural sea, flapping a map uselessly in my hand, for what use is a map when you do not know even where you are? This, what I call "embroilment" with Rome, this embroilment with my subject, brought about also whole new problems. I had never realised how large Rome was, how chaotic, tumbled about, contradictory and all over the place, and that I think was due to the fact that my memory had simplified the entire place for me into a few delectable scenes, clearly remembered, and, as I thought, joined to one another with no banal intervals in between. But this time, the Rome that I met was standing for nothing of that sort. So I looked at gasworks, wandered through suburbs, eyed ministries, not handsome or beautiful; the great Risorgimento[2] 1871 public buildings; the bald, big boulevards with all the trams. And in the course of these wanderings, I found my way back, or stumbled upon the golden oases I had known, seeing them again with a new eye, and perhaps with more rather than less love.

And was this really a waste? I don't think so. It's breaking up all the self one has brought to Rome, the associations, the sentiments which were beginning perhaps a little to set and settle into tradition.

I took in that everything that is in Rome, is Rome. When we call this capital of the world "eternal," we have in mind, surely, its unceasingness, its going forward, its going on – and going on living is an untidy business. All the kaleidoscopic small things, – and every moment – somebody rising from a table in a café, a child chasing a cat across a courtyard, the petals blowing from a flowery tree onto a statue – every moment one feels and senses its aliveness, adding further to the eternity of Rome.

And so it was that as time went on, Rome's strangeness became in itself familiar – familiar to *me*. I saw with the eye of love. One should never, I think, ask anybody who sees through the eye of love for an accurate categoric description. The eye of love. I have never been indifferent to Rome since first – since that first morning in[3] 1923 – an early, bleak morning in early spring, when seeing everything through a haze of tiredness I stepped out after forty-eight hours' train travel from the great railway station and saw the fountains spraying between the ugly palm trees, and the gardens outside. An immense wave hit me then when I was young. It has gone on playing over me, and I have never recovered from it.

If I had a grand-daughter, she could now be the age I was that morning. She would not be indifferent to Rome, not because she was my grand-daughter, but because she was a human being, and I have yet to find a human being of whatever age, kind or outlook, who succeeded in being indifferent to Rome.

Rome has a very great power to antagonise, assault, oppress, weigh heavy, to get on one's nerves. I know people who immensely dislike the place. Rome does a variety of things to a variety of people. Can one wonder really that this should be so considering the whole thing? What a cauldron of ambitions and passion Rome is! And – for how long on the boil – what a breeding ground and nursery of strong wills and furious opinions, and cold, precise legal thought and hysterical frivolity! All this, mounting up, has made an unmistakable, powerful psychic climate, which one feels all the time in addition to the brilliant and violent physical climate that there is. Everybody one talks to in Rome is feeling strongly on some or another subject. Still more I noticed in my reading how impassioned the writers, any writers on the subject of Rome tend to become, even the mild essayist, who may be liable to a sudden, furious outburst. Augustus Hare, our splendid, English Victorian, uttered from time to time a shriek of wrath and objection.[4] His particular bête noire was Roman trams. William Story's *Roba di Roma* is a lovely nineteenth-century book – he abounds quite unashamedly in violent prejudice.[5] No, the more I read about Rome, the more I[6] realised it was a *danger* subject – one might call it, a mined area – because everything concerned concerned us.[7] Art, human behaviour, religion certainly, and all those tenets and principles and emotions which can amount in some people to a faith approaching religion.

So everything, I realised – everything that I was to say or to write about Rome – was liable to annoy someone, and this could not be helped, probably. I have not at any rate gone out of my way to annoy anybody, but no doubt I shall.

The only Rome I could write about, the Rome I saw and felt, is in one way contemporary and in another it isn't. The today of Rome – while I was there seeking for my book or, perhaps also, waiting to be sought out by my book – was one of streets, squares, charming to dawdle in, restaurants, gardens in which it was delightful to wander, the homes of friends, views from windows or through colonnades, but the thing was too, that the so-called past felt contemporary. The momentousness of so many happenings, many of them centuries back, had not yet worn off the air, characters, events of ancient Rome, and of all the Romes since then, did not feel far away; they did not feel concluded. So much so that often reading some particular page of history, I did so with the same sense of tension and immediacy and excitement, as if I were reading a column in the day's newspaper.

As to history I arrived in Rome very ignorant, and left it only a little less so. At the same time, *less* so, for somehow I got the feel of it. I brought to bear such faculties as I had – imagination, power of reason, interest in cause and effect – on some parts of the past. Which parts? I suppose such parts as chose me, certain characters, also certain regions appealed to me as asking to be looked into. About those I found out as much as I could, which is to say, I found out as much as I could take in. Even if I had known twenty times more, how could I say it? The real boundary is the limits to one's powers of expression, and against those Rome must bring anyone up, head on. I came head on, against the limit of my power of expression.

Yes, though this is a book with which I was not content, yet at the same time it turned out to be the book I am happiest to have written after all. Rome beat me, but what a magnificent subject to be beaten by!

As a country, Ireland is at once old and young. She has a lengthy romantic past, a short modern practical history. Her smallness, her geographic position, outlying Europe on the extreme West, have presented her with peculiar problems, which in her new independence she must meet. The problems are social, cultural and, above all, economic – the Republic of Ireland, though now autonomous, remains linked to the British currency system. The country's principal assets are good agrarian land, faith in herself and a beauty which draws the tourist.

Ireland, as she first meets the tourist's eye, might seem not only pleasing but wholly blessed. Here, there is an illusion of time having stood still; changes work benevolently and gently. The sleepy towns and tracts of unspoiled landscape make the traveller feel he has re-entered the past – there is something nostalgic about the smell of woodsmoke, the rattle of horse-drawn carts, the white-walled farms, the mansions sunk in trees. Here, it seems[1] possible to conduct life on the old pattern: tradition has not been broken, it underlies action, feeling and thought. The mould of existence is narrow, but still strong; the individual feels himself under less pressure. As a compensation – it might seem – for her long past of repression, rigour and deprivation, Ireland has been spared the catastrophes which, within recent decades, have upheaved Europe. Consequently, the country has for the visitor the charm of a sheltered, slow-motion nonchalance – manners are friendly, good humour abounds. To the Britisher, willing to leave behind him strain, regimentation and anxieties, to the American coming from the competitive speed of his own land, Ireland appears an "escape" country.

Everything heightens this illusion. The Atlantic climate, its curdling mists and sweeping rains, confers a brilliant richness of colouring: all tones of green compose the Emerald Isle. To alight from a plane is to feel at once, to arrive by ship up an estuary is to feel more slowly, a differentiation of atmosphere. The air breathed in is soporific; the distances hold other-worldly gleam.[2] Winds, often languid but seldom still, draw a play of light over sheeny foliage, bend the blue smoke from chimneys, carry sea-freshness or pungent smells from bogs. The landscape is at few points not bright with water – hurrying tea-brown streams, mirroring rivers and tidal estuaries, bog pools, farm ponds, blandly romantic lakes. Ridgy mountain ranges, alternately frowning or diaphanous as the light shifts, give out a sense of sleeping Eternity. Ruins – and there are many – by now seem natural to the country, as do rocks, cliffs and quarries: skeleton castles, broken-arched abbeys, mounds where once houses stood are, for the traveller, nothing but picturesque. Nor have these monuments much to say to the modern, utilitarian, growing Ireland – yet, each stands for a scar on history, for a vestige never obliterated. In the climate, as in the temperament of the people, for all the smiles, there is a melancholy, an underlying sombreness.

Contradictions are many, and soon apparent. The Irish face expresses fatalism brightening to animation, eagerness shading into mistrust. Moods change as dramatically as does the light. Expansive, racy, quick, rhetorical talk gives frontage to wary reserve – a reserve actually deeper and more unyielding than that for which the British are famed. The Irishman, outwardly so forthcoming, is in fact not easy to know: his would-be friends, at the start confident, go through phases of discouragement,

disillusionment. Dealing with the Irish, there is more to be overcome than the stranger knows – a race-history of resistance and
insecurity. Not for centuries, it must be recalled, has this country
been in anything but a weak position; not until very lately has
she been quite her own. She has yet, therefore, to learn how to
be herself.

April 1948[3] saw the declaration of the Irish Republic: this,
ending some eight hundred years of conquest, stood for the ultimate severance of the tie with Britain. The declaration savoured
of a symbolic act; for, virtually, Ireland had been autonomous
since the Treaty of 1922, with which went the setting up of
the Free State. But the Irish Free State, given Dominion status,
remained within the British Commonwealth – that the Free
State, as a compromise, might not last was shown by political
restlessness in the country. The movement for unqualified Irish
freedom had behind it an accumulated, ancient, passionate force
– challenging memories of the struggle were not, in the last issue,
to be gainsaid. The 1916 Easter Rising (whose anniversary the
declaration of the Republic commemorated) still lived in the
memories of a generation.[4] There must be no stop on the way to
the final goal.

1916 linked backward on to the former risings, each with its
heroes, each charged with abortive hopes. Executions, reprisals,
repressions were nothing new. Pearse and the others of 1916
joined Wolfe Tone, Edward Fitzgerald and Robert Emmett
upon the national roll of glory. And, alongside secret organisa-
tions[5] had been carried the battle for Home Rule, waged, in
the Westminster parliament, by the Irish leaders – O'Connell,
Butt, Parnell. The constitutional struggle, in its own way heroic,
was too slow for those at home in Ireland. Gladstone's failure,
Asquith's vacillations, John Redmond's heart-breaking defeat[6]
all strengthened the hand of the revolutionary. Talk, parley, had
ended in what? – nothing. There must be action. Action involved
the gun.

For a long time, the shadow of the gunman lay over Ireland.
Fighting against the British garrison troops, brought to a stop
by the Treaty,[7] gave place to the Civil War: dissentients to the
Treaty (Republicans) took up arms against the pro-Treaty Free
State government. Dublin echoed bombardments; the skies
above it, quiet since 1916, were once more crimsoned by fires.

The outlying country suffered no less – there were raids, burnings, sinister midnight movements, accesses[8] of individual violence. Throughout, in the cities and in the country, thousands of Irish people remained passive, tongue-tied, a hypnotised prey to terror. The guerrilla campaigns, whether against the British or in the Civil War, left behind them a backwash of private outrage. There was an era of panic, intimidation – when the men dared speak hardly above a whisper, when few slept quietly in their beds.

To understand Ireland, one must realise how lately she has had to absorb this past. Her roads are dotted with wayside crosses, where ambushed men fell. Memories lie closely under the surface. The last of this, it is true, happened thirty years ago: the generation which has grown up since shows symptomatic revulsion against yesterday. The young would wish to step clear of the tragic story: all the same, the story is in the blood. And, the inflammatory notion will never quite die down while Partition lasts.[9] Partition, the Border agreed by the Treaty-makers, cuts off the six northern, Ulster counties of Ireland from the twenty-six which compose the Irish Republic. Northern Ireland, though having its own parliament, remains by wish and in fact[10] affiliated to Britain. It was the Ulstermen, through their mouthpiece Carson,[11] who at the last successfully blocked up Home Rule. And with Irish fanaticism, Scottish tenacity, Ulster continues to cling to her strange position. Come in to the Irish Republic she will not. If the ruling war-fear were to dissipate, some end to Partition *might* be in sight. But Ulster's usefulness as a base for the Allies during the Second World War reinforces her claim so long as a Third pends. As a whole Ireland forms, willy nilly, a key point on Europe's Atlantic front: the ports, the accommodation for troops withheld by the (then) Irish Free State were provided by Ulster. Alone among the Dominions (of which she was then one) the Irish Free State chose to remain neutral. Her neutrality was, throughout, respected – one has yet to compute at how great a cost.

That neutrality, also, has left its mark. On the positive side, it represented Ireland's first independent decision: at her own risk, the country decided to stand alone. It comprehended readiness for the state of war: the coasts[12] were patrolled, the Free State army stood at alert. A German try at invasion, any British attempt to seize the Southern Irish ports would have been, equally, withstood.[13] With a certain grimness, the Irish faced out their isolation. The isolation, however, was in itself impairing – it made for neutrality's negative, losing side. Travel between Ireland and England was suspended: contacts, communication suffered accordingly. Censorship, of a cautiously nulling kind, inhibited Irish newspapers. Postal censorship (which had to operate at the British as well as the Irish end) clamped down on personal stories of war experience – Dublin, for instance, knew of the London blitz only by bloated, uncertain and ghastly rumour. Gratitude for exemption from the horrors mingled, in certain Irish people, with a sensation of being side-tracked, of being out of step with their generation. The insufficiency of all news produced uneasiness: what might next be brewing? Worst, there was the taboo on judgement – for if one is neutral one must not take sides – fostered a listless irresponsibility.[14] It became first discouraging, later unnecessary, to think. This, at the stage of growth on which Ireland had entered by 1939, was a set-back: it became harder to be adult in Ireland. What was lost, then, still has to be caught up with.

The neutral, cautious years went against the grain, for Ireland traffics very much in opinion. Speech, and speech with a bias, is the nation's delight. Loud, lordly talkers cluster in pubs, congregate in the villages after Mass, mill through horses, pigs or cattle upon a fair day. There is a love of language, an endless enterprise in vocabulary. In no other English-speaking country with so much verve and volume, subtlety or force, Irish-English, as spoken, not only gains charm from the intonation, it has an integral rhythm of its own. Sentence-formations persist in it from the lost Irish; here and there Elizabethan archaisms remain. There is often a vivid, fresh-coined imagery. It is true, the older people speak better than the younger, and the very old people best of all. The present-day young in Ireland are either less fanciful or more taciturn: they are, also, charged with the burden of two languages.

For, that Ireland *should* still be an English-speaking country is a cause of offence. The dying-out – or, say starving-out – of her own language ranks as damage done by her conquered years. It has meant broken cultural continuity, the loss of her ancient Celtic literary wealth. Therefore, the reinstatement of Irish as *the* national language has come, for those who are moulding the new-born country, to be an aim of the first importance – it is viewed as one of the first means of restoring the national identity, of advancing Ireland's self-realisation. The trouble is, Irish cannot merely be fanned back into existence: at the moment, it has to be *imposed*, and, in Ireland, nobody likes compulsion. Compulsory Irish has been, since the Treaty, welded into the State educational system: no school failing to teach it is officially recognized. To qualify for teaching or the Civil Service, or to become the holder of public office, one must have passed a fairly exacting language-test. In the schools, a number of subjects have been taught *in* Irish – an extra tax on teacher and pupils. The child may tend to associate Irish only with the schoolroom. That the country's educational standard is less high than it was prior to 1922 has been asserted in some quarters, denied in others. A further objection is, that the modern Irish language is synthetic, bearing about as much relation to old Irish as modern Greek does to ancient. There has had to be a somewhat grotesque inclusion of adapted twentieth-century words.

Whether the aim is to supplant English, or to make the Irish bilingual (as the Welsh are) does not yet seem clear. What, in fact, are the present aims of Irish education? Are the young to be qualified to maintain their places in a competitive outside world: or, are they formed as the citizens of a future, more intensively Irish Ireland?

Traditionally, many of the Irish have gone abroad to work, and they still do. To the re-builders of the country this is discouraging: there are attempts to halt the outgoing stream. Fewer now (since the quota) go to America, more to Britain. Britain, with her high pay and gigantic need, has for some time been steadily draining off not only the unskilled labour, the boys and girls, but also doctors, engineers, trained nurses, master craftsmen, and others whose skill is wanted at home. The impulse to go is not always mercenary; it may be ambitious – to do well in Ireland is to be reminded that, probably, one could do better elsewhere. The clever, effective or restless person is likely to find his own small island claustrophobic. At the same time, by the simpler country people England is viewed with some dismay – though no longer with animosity. America offered the lure of a fine future; England, in her present vicissitudes, does not. The impression that things are not going well in England is very strong. You make money there, but you may lose your soul. A spectral vision of English cities, irreligious, crime-ridden, immoral, demoralised hangs over anxious parents in homes from which the young[15] are gone. And forebodings gain strength from the attitude of the Catholic Church: the Church does not countenance the outgoings.

This is a Catholic country – having therefore, in aspect, something in common with Italy, France and Spain. A land of chapel and convent bells, of circumspect Mass-going Sunday mornings and dancing evenings, of crucifixes at crossroads, shrines, flower-decked altars in the streets, civic religious processions of a Renaissance glory, young dazzling white muslin processions of first communicants. Catholicism tinges, and in its way enriches, the atmosphere of any Irish society – be it peasant, artisan, farmer, or middle-class. Religion is Ireland's governing social force: nothing can have done more to stabilise Ireland during the uncertain years of her new growth. A country bound to a faith can never wholly fail to be integrated. The Church wields its temporal power wisely. Officially (though, be it said, *officially*) it remained disassociated from the national movement during the phase of violence, blood and struggle. Since then, it has given unstinted countenance to the new regime: in return, most evaluations remain religious – i.e., a man known to be "a bad Catholic" does not get far in public life. And prestige, success in business or the professions rests, more than may be admitted, upon observances.

Catholicism has kept Ireland European: thanks to the Church there has never been, as there might be, a descent to total insularity.[16] Also the Church gives face to the country's innate conservatism – though, in Ireland, "Reds" are hardly there to denounce. It must be recalled that this country has found herself by means of a national, not social, revolution: internal issues of "left" and "right" have not, so far, declared themselves. Strife, any question of a class struggle, formerly centred around land-ownership: this the Land Act of 1923 at least in principal adjusted. By its critics, the Catholic Church in Ireland has been suspected of a reactionary attitude to progress, charged with a tendency to regard improved housing, extended social and health services, and so on, as "materialistic." There seems little concrete evidence that this is so: on the contrary, the Church would appear concerned to keep all aspects of life within its domain. The parish priest and the village schoolmaster maintain a close working alliance; and the Church sponsors – is one to say, restricts? – not only the education but the recreations and pleasures of its children – village carnivals, concerts, matches and dancing are conducted under a watching eye. Catholic concern for family life is well known. At present, the young people are giving trouble; they begin to slip from under control. Till lately, this was a country of cool passions, lasting celibacies, dilatory courtships and late marriages. But sex, in spite of rigorous supervision of reading-matter and films, has lately inconveniently been discovered. Denunciations thunder from the altar.

Ireland's Protestant minority fares well. Numerically, it is said to be on the decline, socially it is stable and compact. Some anxiety as to the fate of Protestants was felt in 1922: the Catholics, then assuming control, had centuries of grievance behind them; they had been victimised by the Penal Laws. Revenges seemed likely enough: in fact, there was equable generosity. The Protestant Church of Ireland, till the British withdrew, had been the official church of the country: disestablishment, halfway through the nineteenth century, did not effectively mitigate its power. All of Ireland's surviving ancient cathedrals were annexed by the British-supported Protestants: not one of them, so far, has been reclaimed. In general, the ugliness of Ireland's ecclesiastical buildings, whether Catholic or Protestant, is to be deplored: the ancient ornate beautiful English village church, with its windows and monuments, is unknown here. Here, a Protestant church is to be distinguished from a Catholic by the fact that its tower or steeple does not carry a cross – a cross is felt to savour of popery. Of the squat grey Protestant churches dotting the countryside, many now are derelict or in ruin – shrinkage of Protestant populations made a re-grouping of their parishes necessary: many worshippers travel distances to their Sunday service.

In fact, the religious irritant, like the class irritant, was removed by British withdrawal – Protestantism had been the religion of the "Ascendancy"; i.e., of the wealthy landlords, kept in place by Britain. Generally, Protestants still are well-to-do – landowning gentry, business or professional people, shopkeepers, farmers (in the cities only are there Protestant poor). Their contribution to the community has been recognized: Protestants, some of whom descend from distinguished Huguenot banking families, enjoy the reputation of being energetic, dependable and honest. In the main, they confine themselves to their own affairs, though some are re-entering public life. Their education receives aid from the State; transport is provided for scattered Protestant children to village schools. Formerly Unionist in their politics, such Protestants as have remained in Ireland give wholehearted support to the new regime. Their number have lately been reinforced by immigrant English – a wealthy new wave of[17] settlers in flight from British postwar taxation. This influx, which began with the 1945 victory of Labour, is known in Ireland as "the retreat from Moscow." "Once," said a Dublin wit on the incoming English, "they conquered us by the sword; now they conquer us by the cheque-book." On the whole, these refugee-settlers have acclimatised themselves – they have repaired mansions and put money into the cultivation of land. Their value to Ireland is not great.

Ireland's sole architectural beauties (apart from surviving cathedrals) are of Ascendancy date. The eighteenth century, carrier of classicism, has left here its august mark. The cities of Dublin and Limerick are Georgian; elegant squares, streets and individual façades of the same epoch beautify dusty, outlying country towns. And, small or large, Georgian country houses are many. This enduring, classic, aristocratic touch is often overlooked by the tourist in search of more haphazard romantic beauties. The visitor may see Ireland as a peasant country with a kindly, somewhat primitive bourgeois overlay: in fact, it is at present a bourgeois country in search of a missing aristocracy. Passion for grandeur dominates many outlooks. The language of grandeur, written in stone and brick, can but affect the mentality. "The fall of the big house" is a popular myth in romantic Irish writing: that it *is*, all the same, a myth should be stressed. Many mansions were burned during the fighting, but those not ruined are now inhabited. Ensconced on their own land, concealed by trees, such homes are mostly out of view of the tourist. They do exist, however: the way of life they preserve is a factor in the complexity of Ireland.

This is a countryman's country. Dublin is not Ireland, in the sense that Paris is not France, and the urbanisation of the provincial cities is only skin-deep. Thousands of Irish go no further than their local country town – and the town, with its low, irregular painted streets is little more than an extended village. The population is not only small but scattered; it sifts away into creeks and pockets, leaving great tracts of emptiness. Ireland breeds lean men, weathered but handsome women, vividly coloured and independent children. The hardiness that goes with the way of life was, till lately, lessened by under-nutrition, and the standard of living is still low. The staple diet – potatoes, bread, black tea, and skimmed milk (the cream goes to the creameries) – may receive, now, more sustaining additions – fatty "green" bacon, a knuckle-end, tinned foods. But agricultural wages, though jacked up, still do not keep pace with the cost of living, said to be generally higher than in Britain. The countryman's sense of hardship is mitigated by physical conservatism: traditionally, he has never expected much – at any rate, he is doing better than his forebears. His isolation has been reduced by the bus services – which, with the trains, form part of the State-owned transport system. He otherwise makes his journeys to Mass, fairs, funeral by bicycle, ass-cart or pony-trap; the farmers are acquiring small Ford cars. Distances, time and weather count for little – respect for occasion, sense of observance, love of festivity or the wish to meet make whole countrysides travel the roads on Sundays or holidays. On summer nights, villages hold their carnivals – fancy-dress processions, decorated hay-wains, swing-boats, flare-lights, gambling wheels. Hurling teams (the game is pronounced "hurley") confront one another on Sunday afternoons. There is coursing, and there are the greyhound-trials. Working days finish in sociability – in the dusk men gather at crossroads or on the bridges; the girls make off in chattering troupes. Cottage doors stand open to calling neighbours.

Irish who move to cities or cross the sea feel the breaking-up of the small, familiar unit – parish or neighbourhood. Until this can be reproduced, in some manner, in the new surroundings there is loneliness, and a threat of disintegration. The race is group-minded, dependent on knowing and being known – hence, in cities, the close-corporation character of the street or tenement. Slow, and not always beneficial, is the adaptation to city life: urbanism is always against the grain. The Dubliner, even the

Cork man, is in physique inferior to his country brothers – looks are less good, morale lower. With this in view, the recent shift of the population from the country into the cities is to be viewed seriously: it is the dangerous side of the de Valera government's pro-industrial policy. Industries, fostered by a protective tariff, are on the increase. Ireland does not bid for an outside market, but the aim is that she should be self-sufficient. Textiles, boots and shoes, glass and china, confectionary, biscuits, cosmetics, tobacco, hardware, paint and wallpaper, and so on, are now being manufactured within her shores. Distilleries and breweries date from further back. British firms have set up and given their names to factories which employ local labour. Ireland has one coal mine, in Co. Kilkenny: coal almost all has to be imported – hence the importance of electrification. The Shannon hydro-electric scheme, masterpiece of German engineering, came into action in 1927; it is soon to be supplemented by another in Co. Dublin – the exploitation of water-power has been one of Ireland's most epoch-making advances: within the next few years it is hoped that districts still without electricity will have been linked with the main grid.

Farming, especially dairy farming, is expected to profit by this aid, though outlying farmers are still shy of it. Agriculturally, Ireland *should* rank with Denmark: she is still, however, held up by divided policy – tillage or grazing? During the late war (known here as "the Emergency"), the spectre of wheat-shortage brought in compulsory tillage: manures were short, and too many crops were taken off the land, which has not quite yet recovered from its impoverishment. Given the good grass, grazing, with the raising of a sufficient crop of roots to feed stock in winter, would appear to be a solution. There is also the matter of feed for pigs and poultry. Sugar-beet (a tricky crop to raise) supplies adequate sugar-factories; and Ireland produces enough wheat to keep her existent flour mills turning – but self-sufficiency as to wheat would, again, shear off land from the dairy-farming. The government cooperative system under which the numerous creameries are run is leaving its mark, on the whole a good one, on Irish small-town and country life. Egg-collection and grading are also organised. The trend to the cities, by draining off country labour, again tends to tip the balance in favour of grazing and dairy-farming: tillage requires more men.

The Dublin Ministry of Agriculture, at this juncture, has in hand what are the country's most vital problems.

Ireland's progressive sacrifice of the picturesque to the utilitarian may be deprecated by the tourist, but is a healthy sign. The reafforestation scheme carries conifer-plantations, like black fur, over former bogs and up the bases of mountains. Land-reclamation schemes are in progress – bogs are being drained, formerly flooding rivers have reinforced banks. In the central rich Bog of Allen, peat-cutting goes on under government aegis – the square black clefts and neat dark stacks may be viewed, from above, on the air-line from Dublin to Shannon. Work on roads extends from the main highways to the coastal and minor cross-country routes: the native or touring motorist, the bus and the sight-seeing char-à-banc thereby profit. The primitive two-roomed "cabin," with its mud walls and thatched top, dear to the artist's eye, has received overdue condemnation from health authorities: working-class Ireland is being rehoused – red-roofed family houses, monotonous in their alikeness but sound in plan, dot the countrysides and, in blocks with gardens, form modern annexes to the older towns. Water-supply – a rural innovation – and drainage follow the new developments. One by one, village schools conform with the approved pattern; the health-clinic and the inspecting medico are no longer strangers. Most important: Ireland is waging war against her deep-rotting enemy, tuberculosis. The endemic habits of over-crowding, hygienic carelessness and fatalism are, however, not easily met. Maternity-centres and child-welfare projects still confront a sort of mystical opposition – who dare touch the sanctity of the home?

Ireland may draw abreast with modernisation; she neither will nor can compete with the modern world. Her traditional assets remain her strong ones – for instance, this is the country of the horse: horse-breeding, horse-coping, fairs, hunting and racing. Horses have an aristocratic timelessness. To fail to attend a horse fair or horse show, to fail to make one of the crowds at races, is to know only half the reality of the country. Sport and gambling are, as you care to see them, either the national passion or the national vice. Dog-racing stadiums spring up almost as fast as cinemas; gambling-wheels whirl at Church-sponsored carnivals; cards flicker, dice rattle deep into nights. Here is a bizarre inverse to the also-prevailing strictness, caution and, in some aspects, Puritanism of life . . . Smoky-toned Irish tweeds, smoky-flavoured Irish whisky, both reaching back in origin, are, again, the most picturesquely popular of her products. As to amenities, there is still a lag: the Irish Tourist Association, bidding for the most promising, possible source of income, has subsidised and attempts to reform hotels, supplies information-brochures and has been forward in pressing for improvement of roads. Chromium, strip-lighting, and plumbing, however, still add little more than a flashy surface to ancient habit. And cooking, when it aims for the higher flights, is not yet to be ranked among Irish gifts. Bacon-and-eggs, mutton chops, boiled potatoes are done sublimely: the sub-Continental cuisine of the more ambitious hotels should be fought shy of. As to food, Ireland is conservative and, beyond that, indifferent. Ireland's tourist hopes have been somewhat dangerously inflated by prevailing currency restrictions: since the war, she has received thousands barred from holidays on the Continent. Her meat and eggs (however rising their cost) continue to lure in the hungry British. *Should* conditions ever return to normal, a considerable and maybe disheartening revaluation of her attractions will be necessary.

The Irish Republic has five principal cities – Dublin, Cork, Limerick, Waterford, and Galway: all are ports. Small picturesque port towns, with vivid if sleepy quaysides, are also niched in the estuaries: these maintain themselves by fishing and minor coastal traffic. Sea-goers breed in such places, and on satellite islands: the British Royal and Merchant Navies receive, annually, Irish recruits. This, with the outgo of workers and influx of tourists, keeps open the relation with Britain. Mutual interdependence is recognized – the exchange basis makes for amicability. Anglophobia, which at the worst of times was more theoretic than personal, has run its course, or died out for lack of fuel. Equally, a sort of political languor has set in – Ireland, now freedom has been achieved, lacks the once inflaming national motive: anticlimax hangs, faintly, over internal politics. Election excitement, whipped up by the press, has not lately been sufficient to feed the polling-booths. The two main parties, Fianna Fáil (Mr. de Valera's) and Fine Gael (in which Mr. Costello succeeded to Mr. Cosgrave's leadership of the once pro-Treaty, 1922 group),[18] have run each other close at recent elections: each, successively, winning by a narrow majority. Proportional representation, whose merits remain under debate, fails to present the countryman with the old, clear alternative – the system is not easy to grasp; at the count, numbers of voting-papers are found spoiled. No apathy, no obscuration of motives have, however, for long displaced Mr. de Valera. His lasting hold on the country is a personal one.

Intellectual, non-rhetorical, and detached, his is not a figure which one would have expected to appeal. Yet Ireland, notably fickle to patriots, has stayed true to him. He has achieved the all-but-impossible task of carrying the past, with its hero-isms, forward into the present, with its prosaic practicalities. Revolutionary memory still invests the figure of this adult statesman – few in Europe have so calmly made the transition from the one to the other. Mathematical professor who took up arms – de Valera was active in 1916, in the subsequent fighting against the British and as Republican leader during the 1922 Civil War – he now brings mathematical philosophy to the art of government. Stubborn and, it has been suggested, authoritarian, he commands respect – Ireland, quickly iconoclastic, has hailed few wholly respected men. There is a touch of the grandee, also perhaps something sacerdotal and medieval, about his tall, thin, Spanish-avised person,[19] on which a raincoat hangs like a robe. This man represents something *to* Ireland, and touches something *in* Ireland, which would at present be irreplaceable. He has dared to ride full-tilt against illusion, illusion on which this country has lived – his "austerity budget" of spring 1952 shook Ireland from her prosperity dream. The expected fall of his government did not follow: in three succeeding by-elections Fianna Fáil not only held but gained seats. From this man, the country takes what she does not like.

Yet ultimately, illusion remains the element. Shift though it may, like light from hill to hill, it is always somewhere – entrancing the visitor, maddening the realist, sweetening and varying life for the simple soul. Ireland has shown, and shows – in her literature, her festivities, her relationships – glints of genius. In whatever country, one must live how one can: it may be seen why Ireland lives as she does.

The Daughters of Erin *by Elizabeth Coxhead*

Elizabeth Coxhead opens *Daughters of Erin* provocatively:

"Ireland," she says, "more than most, is a man's country; and for all the feminine grace of its streets and setting, Dublin is a man's town." . . . Women, she adds, are not welcome in public life – their sphere, still, is taken to be the home: those who wish to strike out into wider fields still find themselves under a certain handicap. This *was* so, certainly, in the life-times of the five Irishwomen who are Miss Coxhead's subjects. Maud Gonne, Constance Markievicz, Sarah Purser and the two actress sisters – Sarah Allgood and Maire O'Neill – all were born in the later decades of the nineteenth century: no one of the five is alive today. Each of them blazed a trail – and the more effectively because the emergence of Woman *was* so unusual. No one of them was, in the doctrinaire sense, a Feminist. Each either crashed the barriers or sailed smilingly over them.

Two were revolutionaries, the three others were artists. In the nature of the art of the three artists, there was more than a streak of the revolutionary; and the two out-and-out revolutionaries had about them more than a touch of the artist. *Is* it in these two roles that women do best? These five, *I* would argue, did what they did not in spite of being women but because of it. Each had an outsize temperament. Each showed an inborn self-confidence, which was justified.

Maud Gonne – English, in fact, by birth – commanded a flaming romantic beauty: she was a born inspirer – not only of Irish revolutionary action against England, but of immortal poetry: Yeats's poems, born of his hopeless passion for her. Handsome Constance Markievicz, formerly Miss Gore-Booth, was a child of the Big House, Ireland's "Ascendancy" class – to her "rebel" drilling, marching and gun-carrying she brought the coolness and toughness of an orthodox long ancestry. Sarah Purser came, too, of Protestant gentry stock: *her* youth was cramped by poverty; she was small, plain, wiry. A fine painter, she was greater still in her faith in art – *she* founded, and maintained, the "Tower of Glass," Ireland's later world-famed stained glass workshop and studio.

The Allgood sisters stepped – with perhaps least effort? – into their natural roles. The then young Abbey Theatre, hub of the Irish Literary Renaissance, had need of actresses. Sarah, with her at once homely and tragic personality, and Maire (O'Neill) with her impish comedy sense, illumined the new naturalistic-poetic drama. Sarah was the original Juno of O'Casey's *Juno and the Paycock*, Maire – earlier – the original Pegeen Mike of Synge's *The Playboy of the Western World*. Both wrote their names, deep, on theatre memory.

Each of these five women had "star quality." No country, and no epoch, could have ignored them. And also intrinsically *Irish* – they all were, though one, Maud Gonne, by choice and devotion only. *As* Irishwomen, they drew on primitive strength – for Ireland *is*, fundamentally, a primitive society; in which there is – I would argue – still[1] more than a trace of the matriarchal. They could cast spells: some through love, some through social genius.[2] Sarah Purser, in her lovely now-vanished house by the canal, was in her later days the greatest, if most alarming, of Dublin's hostesses. And – as a great hostess must be – a creative one: at her *soirées*, everybody who was truly alive in Ireland met.[3]

Maud Gonne and Countess Markievicz were, one gathers,[4]

something of an embarrassment to their more sober-sided, austere, masculine comrades-in-arms. Sarah Purser's admirers spoke of her as "a bit of a terror." The Allgoods' temperaments raged through the Abbey like periodic storms . . . All the more, these five showed what Irishwomen *can* do.

So, take heart, women of Ireland, and break through also! Meanwhile, Elizabeth Coxhead shows us the way . . . This is a fine book, which nobody should miss.

AN ESSAY IN FRENCH

After November 1918, the novelist in England, like the individual, found himself face to face with the great void of peace. The effect, like that of facing a blank page, was intimidating. When war ended, the romantic stimulus that abided throughout the conflict also ended, although it must be said that this stimulus had arisen in great measure as a reaction, even an opposition, to the war. Some intellectuals, few and far between, denounced the war in 1914. Others, more numerous, withdrew from wartime concerns into the austerity of their writing worlds either because they distrusted general feeling or because they wanted to concentrate solely on their work. But among the latter, I think, more than in the case of those writers who had been ready to endorse the war in thought or in deed, a feverish tension obtained. When this feverish tension came suddenly to an end in 1918, it caused something like a halt in sensibility.

Then there was the factor of losses. The heavy tribute exacted by war affected both the heart and the imagination. Just as an entire generation of young women grew up being told that thousands of them could not count on finding a sweetheart or a husband, members of the general public who appreciated art learned that they had to face the exorbitant loss, on the battlefields, of an entire generation of budding artists or artists in their prime. To those who perished, the possibility of expressing themselves had been denied: it was inevitable that a sense of obligation weighed heavily on the artists who survived. They felt responsible not only towards the dead, but also towards the works that those artists had not lived to create. The young people who outlived the war heard the call to art. They strode ahead to fill up the places left empty by the war dead. But they also responded to this call to art with something amounting to fear.

The English novelists of the postwar period can be divided into three groups. First, those whose reputations had been established before the conflict continued to write throughout the years of combat and, when peace came, continued no less impassively to serve their art. This group of writers possessed both the merits and the acquired defences of the "professional." Their technique was assured; they had already been schooled in the rigours of objectivity. They had learned – and, consequently, felt reassured – that nothing in human experience was without precedent. Accustomed as writers to steer clear of every emergency, every sorrow, every loss, they had been able, as individuals, to look at and describe the war from a social perspective: its effects and its dramas, replacing pre-war effects and dramas, became their principal material. Not that they did not feel the impact of the war, but they had already succeeded in not entertaining any feeling that could not be reported. After the war, these writers applied their observation, judgement, and curiosity to newfound peace, as they had done during the war. The 1914 war caused only minor changes to their writing. They were not the least bit disconcerted by the blank page of 1918. These writers included Arnold Bennett, H. G. Wells, and Somerset Maugham.

Slightly apart from this group of writers stands E. M. Forster. Four of his novels, published before the war, were to have a belated effect. I will discuss his works later. However tenuous, his kinship with other pre-war writers should not be rejected as entirely arbitrary.

A second group of novelists began to write and publish during the war. These writers, or at least the most interesting among them, were so fiercely individual that grouping them together is deceiving. Their art was the product of a "climate" of intense isolation. Their bad health, their sex, their opinions made them non-combatants. Among these artists, consciousness of their own existential predicaments eclipsed conscience about the war; paradoxically, however, the war lent poetry to their personal meditations. Such is the case with Virginia Woolf and Dorothy Richardson, whose first published works appeared in 1915. It is also the case with James Joyce, whose *Dubliners* appeared in 1914. D. H. Lawrence published three works prior to the war, but war acted on him as it did with Woolf, Richardson, and Joyce: it accentuated his individualism. All four of these novelists emphasise interior being rather than the exterior forces that motivate feeling and knowledge.

The third group of writers is comprised of those who had not written anything before or during the war. Or if they had begun writing, they had not yet seen their work published. They took up their pens after the war. During the conflict, these young men and women had been adolescents. Their conscience had been troubled, their sensibility, tensile. Instinctively they knew that they would inherit a damaged world. At the same time, their inheritance, whatever its value, had only just been preserved, from minute to minute, by the sacrifices of their older brothers. The position of these young people, some of whom aspired to be combatants, was humiliating. Conscious that they had not suffered much, they remained sceptical of promised utopias, the same utopias in which their patient elders found consolation. Utopia, the young were told, was for them to build: it was the only way that they could work off their debt.

This generation grew up knowing that it had failed. In 1918, they strongly felt that peace was an alarming error. Taken as a whole, women predominated in this generation. Some women attended university during the war. Owing to their sex, they had not been on the battlefields where their contemporaries – brothers and fiancés, the boys with whom they had played when young – had fallen. The men in this group of writers were younger still: when peace came, they were still too young by a year or two for military service. These boys, leaving school around 1918, went to university in the company of demobilised soldiers who had returned to student-life and who, inevitably, seemed superior in manly experience. It was natural that these younger students, resenting comparison with their elders, acted out their resentment, often unconsciously. They drew apart and became aesthetes. In some instances, they became effeminate men.

In their writings, this third group of novelists habitually denigrated masculine values. Ideal art for them meant defensive mockery. The men felt humiliated, the women injured. The women, perhaps haunted by the idea that they would never come fully into their own – the battlefields having claimed so many men – developed a powerful feminism. These women wanted at one and the same time to play the role of men and to show that, to all intents and purposes, men were not indispensable. The war having ended, these women decided that warfare in general was the result of masculine supremacy and the myths that go along with it. To drain masculinity of its power and myths seemed like the appropriate ambition of female novelists. Satire and caricature aimed to demolish the vestiges of masculine authority. No male novelist of any talent took the opposite stance – a defence of masculinity – in the decade that followed.

Aldous Huxley, who had been to Oxford before the war and later worked as a journalist, was the leading light in the postwar generation of male writers. His novels, entirely original, not only reflected, but more, to a certain point, created the spirit of the Twenties. The prevailing attitude in this decade was that postwar life, of still uncertain value, anxiously awaited guidance from art. Fashions – in art, in physical appearance, in love, in decoration, in manners – sprang up with frenetic rapidity. Aldous Huxley, intellectually sophisticated, iconoclastic, romantically anti-romantic in his doctrines, and affected by a hyper-sensitivity due, perhaps, to his defective vision, was the perfect voice for this generation. *Limbo*, a collection of short stories, appeared in 1920. *Chrome Yellow* followed in 1921, *Antic Hay* in 1923, *Those Barren Leaves* in 1925, and *Point Counter Point* in 1928. At the same time, Huxley, as a critic, guided the changing tastes of this generation with his own directives . . . Rose Macaulay, during these years, could be considered the female counterpart to Aldous Huxley. Before the war, she had written several delightful novels. The war, and even more so the ironies of peace that followed, crystallised a new phase in her writing. Unlike her contemporaries', her work was not disfigured by emotional heaviness; her stiff reserve, her laughing disrespect with a touch of spirituality were immediately appealing. She published *Potterism* in 1920, *Dangerous Ages* in 1921, *Told by an Idiot* in 1923, *Crewe Train* in 1926, and *Keeping up Appearances* in 1928.

Katherine Mansfield also figures among distinguished female writers in the first decade after the war. (Her short stories remain beyond the scope of this essay and warrant a separate study.) Other notable women writers included Clemence Dane, who published *Regiment of Women* during the war, followed by *Legend* in 1919 and numerous other novels. Helen Simpson published *Cups, Wands and Swords* in 1928. The repercussions of Margaret Kennedy's *Constant Nymph*, when it appeared in 1924, were not limited to England. May Sinclair and Sheila Kaye-Smith, although they had both written before and during the war, attained the height of their celebrity during the Twenties. As these examples prove, the novel, as was widely recognized, passed into the intellectual orbit of women. *Dusty Answer*, by Rosamond Lehmann, brought an original and truthful note to fiction: youthful and accomplished, this book was the brilliant start to Lehmann's career.

The dominant aesthetic influences continued, however, to come from the second group of writers – the group whose art had witnessed, first and foremost, the effects of isolation from the war. D. H. Lawrence, working relentlessly, became the necessary prophet of the age. People eagerly latched onto his pronouncements. His erotic mysticism quenched the desires of a decade that otherwise derided sex; his idealisation of sexual passion formed a counterpoint to Aldous Huxley's cynicism. *Women in Love* (1920), *Aaron's Rod* (1922), and *The Plumed Serpent* (1926) became touchstones. The attack on *Lady Chatterley's Lover* in 1928 made Lawrence into a martyr: a great part of English fanaticism, stoked higher by Lawrence's non-religious attitude, was directed towards banning his works . . . Virginia Woolf, meanwhile, was perfecting her craft in novel after novel. Her prose, rendered transparent by the concentration of her vision, defined a world in which perceptions replaced plot. External actions were negligible. Woolf's prose was not only the most accomplished of the decade, but also constituted its poetry: few contemporary poets came close to Woolf's intensity or radiance in their respective works. *Jacob's Room* was published in 1922, *Mrs. Dalloway* in 1925, *Orlando* in 1928. *The Waves*, the culmination of her art, opened the way to the 1930s . . . [1] James Joyce, who lived on the Continent during and after the war, published *A Portrait of the Artist as a Young Man* in 1916.[2] *Ulysses*, following a few years later, cultivated the vast domain of individual consciousness. This novel, with its dangers and promises, was snatched from English readers before they could fully explore it. *Ulysses* acquired a fantastic reputation and an equally fantastic hold on the imagination. The cult that sprang up around Joyce, at least for those who could obtain his books, was on a par with the cult that sprang up around Marcel Proust. These two literary giants, one Irish, the other French, exerted immense influence on the evolution of the English novel, an influence that still needs to be examined in detail . . . The novels of Dorothy Richardson, written and published without a break between 1915 and 1931, are the closest English equivalent to Proust's and Joyce's works, and, in their own way, just as remarkable. United under the title *Pilgrimage*, these novels delighted connoisseurs. They have not, however, attained the broader appreciation that they deserve. I do not doubt that they will ultimately receive their just due. In the meantime, no one who studies the English novel seriously can overlook them.

To round out the decade, we should note the belated but enormous regard that E. M. Forster's novels earned. His four pre-war novels, of which *Howards End* (1910)[3] is the most notable, were all out of print in the early Twenties. The originality of these novels had been, perhaps, either too discreet or too profoundly troubling for the era in which they had first appeared. Ten years before such ambitions became prominent in the 1920s, *Howards End* expressed the discord between convention and feeling, the attack on superstition by spiritual means, the desire to synthesise. In 1924, after fourteen years of silence, Forster brought out *A Passage to India*. This book had an immediate success, although its readership was restricted by its controversial subject. Of no less importance, the novels that Forster had previously published were much in demand. Publishing houses filled the need. Forster's rebuttal of D. H. Lawrence's oversimplifications and inevitable absurdities appealed to readers. Without being didactic, Forster expressed, and continues to express, the English desire for civilisation – a desire not always fully formulated or understood, but one that never arises entirely in vain.

Such was the English literary scene until 1930. Among these writers, one finds, more or less, a mixture of masculine wit and rebarbative female passion. Political feeling was absent; religion, outdated. Writers distrusted nationalism and sex. Social classes were not especially under attack. Pacifism was a powerful force. Aestheticism, outwardly frivolous but entirely passionate, held sway; individualism reached an apogee. Cosmopolitanism was of the first importance: the intelligentsia were dazzled by New York, envious of Paris, sentimentally attracted to Weimar Germany. The *beau monde*, in moments of excess, adopted the tone of the intelligentsia and was flattered to find its image in art. Even before the decade ended, brilliant obituaries were being written for the 1920s in the form of novels: *Decline and Fall* and *Vile Bodies* by Evelyn Waugh, as well as *The Memorial* by Christopher Isherwood. Some writers, who have since acquired a larger reputation, belonged to the 1920s because of their age, but they do not share the characteristics of that decade. William Plomer, who lived and worked abroad, is a signal example of an independent-minded writer. Plomer's *Turbott Wolfe* appeared in 1926, *I Speak of Africa* in 1927, and *Paper Houses* in 1929 . . . David Garnett, whose novels, with their fantastic prose resembling Defoe's – *Lady Into Fox* (1923), *A Man in the Zoo* (1928), *No Love* (1929) – found inspiration only within himself. Richard Hughes crowned his original talent with *A High Wind in Jamaica* in 1929.

Between 1930 and 1939, writers reluctantly faced the next war instead of trying to escape the previous one. In the Thirties, no novelist could avoid the influence of propaganda, whether they acknowledged it or not. Younger writers claimed that the novel should serve serious purposes; in particular, they meant that the novel should be wrested from the hands of women. Political, male earnestness took precedence over emotive, female seriousness. The reappearance of virility in novel-writing was, in itself, an excellent influence; virility conferred vigour, and it could have conferred objectivity as well, if the predominant literary style had not been so sombre as to infect subject matter.

Virginia Woolf and E. M. Forster presided over the 1930s as

accomplished craftsmen and as influences, despite the criticism levelled by the younger generation against Woolf's aesthetic detachment and Forster's non-militant irony. There was also a strong reaction against what was judged to be Lawrence's sentimentality. In this regard, Evelyn Waugh and Christopher Isherwood worked to preserve ground already won and to advance even further in the direction of satire. As the Thirties progressed, however, Waugh revealed an increasingly caustic Catholic morality, and Isherwood's political conscience vexed him. Rosamond Lehmann's novels, *A Note in Music* and *Invitation to the Waltz*, being more feminine than feminist, enraptured the reading public. Although Aldous Huxley published the stories *Brief Candles* in 1930 and the novel *Brave New World* in 1932, he produced much more criticism than fiction in the Thirties. Moreover, he displayed signs of withdrawing into mysticism.

Religion was no longer a negligible factor. Two young Catholic writers – neither of whom, interestingly, was born Catholic – stamped the decade: Evelyn Waugh and Graham Greene. Despite their external drama, Greene's mature novels are calls to inaction. The principal characters are, to a certain degree, monstrous; spiritual violence and physical cruelty mark them. The idea of damnation engulfs their being. At the same time, these novels display the technical brilliance of a well-made film. Their high intellectual quality and their spiritual austerity save them from melodrama, a risk that they daringly run. From the beginning of his career, Graham Greene has quickened interest: he established his reputation with *Stamboul Train* in 1932, which was followed by *It's a Battlefield*, *A Gun for Sale*, *Brighton Rock* and *The Power and the Glory* . . . Robert Speaight, first known as an actor, is a third Catholic novelist who has forged a name for himself with a distinguished output.

Since 1930, religious and political sentiments have contributed equally to make the English novel dynamic and to rescue it from the psychological cramp that threatened to overtake it towards the end of the preceding decade. Christopher Isherwood's novels about life in Berlin make insinuations about politics; none the less, their message is loud and clear. Arthur Calder-Marshall's vigorous work – *Pie in the Sky* is a good example – owes a great deal to political pressure. Under the influence of Kafka – who left his imprint on a generation of writers in England – Rex Warner has written poetic allegories that reveal, after their fashion, the same tendency to register the pressure of politics.

Leading up to the Second World War, young middle-class writers with an intellectual bent revolted against their own class, against received ideas, against the attempts made by Public Schools to reinforce tried-and-true notions. Supported by the precepts of psychoanalysis, they dug into the past, especially into bourgeois family life, to uncover the origins of fears and anguish. They denounced the influence of the mother, and with her, women in general. They identified personal injustices, as they saw them, with social ills. Spying the apparition of fascism throughout Europe, they were able to see their nightmares take concrete shape. The arrival of foreign refugees in England, artists and political thinkers, not only worked on these English writers' feeling, but also nourished their art.

Alone among this generation of writers, Catholic novelists did not attach themselves to the left. In the Thirties, the vehemence of poets – Auden, C. Day Lewis, Stephen Spender – made itself strongly felt. In addition to poetry, Auden wrote theatre pieces. Day Lewis and Spender wrote novels. Prose style between 1920 and 1930 had a certain elegance and atmosphere. In the 1930s, prose suddenly became brusque, stripped. Beauty was suspect, or it could only be admitted under the rubric of didactic poetry.

Inevitably, this group of intellectual writers, more and more accusatory and prophetic, attracted no attention from the wider public. Their aesthetic, if aesthetic it was, came across as impure. The obvious absence of creative pleasure impoverished their work – at least for numerous readers. Worried about its own fate and quite tormented by the miseries happening in Europe, the broad English public did not care to be upset any further. During the Spanish Civil War, very few people thanked the poets and their brethren novelists for fanning the flames of partisan feeling, which already burned high in England. Asking for pleasure, entertainment, or, at the very least, an idealisation of a traditional way of life, the English public sought authors who knew how to provide diversion. The novels of Charles Morgan, aesthetically irreproachable but lacking even the remotest seditious idea, were acclaimed. The hermetic beauty of Virginia Woolf's style became even more intensely refined. For less demanding readers, the voluminous novels of Sir Hugh Walpole, who hoped to emulate the achievement of the Victorian novelists, were much appreciated. There was also a great demand for comedies of manners, which the English write so well. Heeding the wise counsel of Jane Austen, several female writers devoted their energies to writing social comedy. The novels of E. M. Delafield deserve particular admiration: they express the social art of Englishwomen at their finest. And, from time to time, come along a few isolated and charming novels, born of what might be called a whim. *National Velvet* by Enid Bagnold provides one example.

"Escapist" novels of all kinds multiplied in the years leading up to the war. They were decried as fast as they accumulated. Among escapist literature, only detective novels incur no blame. For readers they provided universal joy, as they still do, and justly so. The more the novel lost in form and conviction, the more the detective novel gained in dignity. Excellent models came from America and France – Simenon's novels among them – which kept the genre to a high standard. For faultless dexterity, plot, dialogue, the study of local atmosphere, and above all simplified moral values, readers, when they found no satisfaction elsewhere, turned to detective stories. Detective fiction perhaps corresponded to a tormented desire for a solution.[4]

Thus came 1939. The effects of the present war on the English novel surpass the scope of this essay. Personally, I foresee a new energy in the novel; I believe that a new tide of novelists will rise. Nothing could be worse for creative literature than the inchoate fears, the moral self-questioning of the decade prior to the war. Today fears and introspection have given way to the simplicity of great physical challenge. Flaubert predicted a novel of "psychological overflow."[5] In English experience, if not yet in English art, this overflow has begun. At least for the moment, other obligations impose silence on almost every young English novelist. But I should not doubt that present silence will bear fruit in the future; already we are beginning to see fragments, chapters, and sketches of future novels. In these works, we occasionally encounter a new voice, occasionally an old voice that speaks in a new tone. These voices carry.

SPEECHES

Subject and the Time

How do we judge contemporary art? Do we know what we look for? What hope, what particular expectation do we bring to the painting, music, architecture, poetry and prose of our Today? Is our approach open, or is it rigid – that is to say, do we pre-conceive what contemporary art should be, and quarrel with it when it does not conform? If so, we are claiming to comprehend our time – its atmosphere, its forces, its implications – more truly than, and indeed in advance of, our own artists. We shall be adhering to what, though we may not know it, is a conventional set picture – a picture which, by the very fact that it *is* set, becomes false. For Today is fluid; that is its vital quality. A vital reflection of the fluidity, like of water on a Venetian ceiling, cannot but cast itself on to art. To fail to see that is to mistake the very nature of the contemporary.

Our sense of our time *is*, in fact, a sense. As such, it is ever-open, susceptible, and at its least articulate when it is most honest. Today is to be felt rather than known; what we know has already become yesterday. Our existence, at its most nearly pure, is a thing of sensations and apprehensions. Yet the wish to know, to define, the need for order, the desire for meaning cannot be denied: these are instinct in our human state. The brain strains after evaluations. So, we enter the danger-area of the concept – the acceptable theory, the plausible explanation, the ingenious idea. It is to our fixed wish, to our wish to envisage "life" that we sacrifice what is most true and meaning in the momentary spontaneities of existence. And the result of the sacrifice is estrangement; we cannot but wonder, from time to time, how it is that we seem to be cut off from some great part of our power to be. Somehow, somewhere we have lost freshness; a sort of eager immediacy is gone from our reactions, from our response. Today, the sensation of living *now*, eludes us, or only is to be felt as a balked experience or an obscure trouble. Realisation of it, in the acute sense, fails – yet, it was realisation we thought we sought. To regain realisation, we need expression. It is in hope of that that we turn to art – yet it is a fact that the very hope may be refractory and confused. For, what we seek for, in many cases, is affirmation of what we believe we know. We expect restatement, made with sublime authority. But art is not restatement; each work of art is a statement made for the first time.

The art of the past eases us by a sort of sublimated familiarity. We have inherited it; it has indeed become a best and noble component of our experience. Anything disconcerting, anything harsh in the impact it may have made on *its* contemporaries had died away; there has come about, within the years, an evaporation of inconvenience, though not of meaning. Such art – although it perpetuates a moment which was for it *the* moment – we call "timeless." It has extracted, it has distilled, it proceeds to simplify and idealise, then return to us, what we most wish from the sensation of living – a living inspired by strength and faith. We salute the "timeless" because it seems to exclude our own nagging modern disorder – our frustrated, our haunted, taunted uneasiness with regard to what is our own time. But, for that very reason, the art of the past has a lacking element – an element only to be supplied, at whatever cost in harshness or inconvenience, by art which *is* contemporary with us.

Today, having never happened before, cannot be contained in what is already said; it exceeds the vocabulary of yesterday. The artist's language, whether of colour, sound, shape or words, continuously requires an addition – such addition as in the course of art has constantly gone on being made, but which is only sharply apparent when made in our time. In so far as Today is without precedent, it has always demanded to be expressed in a manner, through a medium or by a means for which no aesthetic precedent can be found. And yet, there has seldom not been a protest, a mistrust of what seemed convulsive about change, reckless about extensions and innovations, drastic about abandonments. That these are not made for their own sakes, that they are necessary – necessary, that is, if there is to continue to be expression – has never yet been accepted easily. That is a commonplace. The traditional opposition to what is not traditional need not concern us – what is interesting is that it should, still, come from those (or, more fairly, from some of those) who believe they want contemporary art. No, it is not possible to make a statement of the new in the old terms. The statement, if statement there is to be, must be allowed to come at its own expression – if there be not that, there can be no other. Contemporary art is not merely a statement not made *till* now; it is in essence a statement *of* now.

One aim of art, I take it, is at once to concentrate and to deepen our sense of the "now." The artist is there to reclaim for us our original freshness of apprehension, that direct and eager susceptibility which, by the habit of long denying it, we had all but forgone. He puts us through the ordeal of pure beholding; he is demanding of us the pure response. We are more than claimed or confronted, we are involved – involved in the unexpected surge of our own awareness, an awareness we did not know we had. How has this happened? Some sort of disconnection, either within ourselves or between ourselves and the outer world has, at least temporarily, been healed. Some sort of haunting suspicion of unreality – either that we are not real ourselves, or, that if we are real ourselves, nothing else is – has been laid low. We need no longer feel the estrangement of sense from senses.

The reconciliation of the individual with his world can, it may be argued, be brought about by the action on him of *any* great work of art, out of any epoch. What peculiar value is there in the contemporary – often more cryptic or more abrupt, less pleasing, more troublesome to receive? . . . Contemporary art, we may dare to say – or, better, art through being contemporary – accomplishes what is still more difficult, still more valuable: therein its value lies. Contemporary art – not perhaps at once but by the continuous effect of its absorption – reconciles the individual with his time. And it is that, in *our* time, which is the crux. Of the Todays which went to compose the past, each one must in its turn have been at once pervasive and evasive, intractable, mysterious and disturbing. Few can have been less friendly, less directly attractive to heart or senses, indeed more nearly inimical than our own Today. It is a time of scientific threats, sense-deadening scientific concessions, loud null words, unruly demoralising passions. It is a time hard to inhabit because it is hard to love; yet we must inhabit it. It is a time difficult to know because of its mechanical uniformity; yet it *is* our time, in which we as humans live – we are dwarfed, we are shorn of humanity if we fail to know it. In spite of all, it offers its own kinds of fulfilments and errant joys; even at its most withheld, abstract and calculated it throws off a perhaps not quite accidental beauty. In spite of all, it has not quite ceased to make, as the simpler times did, antique claims on our honour, courage and duty.

Our hope of anything from our time must depend on our perception of what it is. Our hope of fruition in our Today must be bound up in our willing awareness of it. We cannot live in anything but fear if we live negatively, which is to live blindly. Art does not merely offer to lend us vision; it calls on us to freshen and use our own. The artist who is our contemporary shares Today with us; with him, let us perceive what there is to see. Let our apprehensions tell us, as his tell him, that in spite of all, this is still a time of experiences, not all sad, and of mysteries, not all hostile ones.

At no time can man have been more aware of time – of his own time, its climate, character and potential meaning. Our art plays intensely, endlessly on our time-consciousness. To an extent, our time is our art's subject. In so far as – in the novel, in the non-abstract picture – there must also be an ostensible, concrete subject, that is so chosen, and so placed, as best either to illustrate time's action, to reflect time's colour, to register time's pulse. And yet how few, for the painting, the lyric or the narrative, are subjects, and how few subjects are not still traditional. Apples on the plate, the shadow on the ground, the house at the street-corner, the sensations of infancy, the triumphs or deviations of the affair of love. If our day, in its insistence on realisation, seems to insist that *it* dictate art's subjects – still, how narrow the choice is!

At work in this area of small choice, we sheathe the subject inside the statement. The fruit with its interlocking curves, the anonymous figure in the doorway, the street-scene, the pattern of actions, the light on landscape or the lovers' embrace become charged with more than their own significance. There is a possibility of the symbol in every object. Language, made concrete by imagery, evokes something further than its immediate meaning; style gains a second voice from its overtones. There is an effort so to impart proportion as to indicate values; and the discovered speakingness of relationships is more felt – indeed, the deciding of the relation between thing and thing, between act and act, is in itself a great part of our artists' expression. The angle of vision may, by its choice, be no less eloquent. All this serves the creative purpose.

The novel, which is my province, nominally stands at the edge of art. Yet it too feels the tie between time and subject. The actual telling of the story is conditioned by what the story is *about*; and the novel, however prosaic and factual it may appear – indeed, should appear – now has almost always an inner content, an internal theme which is, in effect, poetic. The novelist is faced by a double task: he must, like his fellow-artists, attempt to break through again, or break back again, into pure sense; he must recall freshness to apprehension; but he must not risk or forfeit intelligibility. From him, the statement is expected to be direct; the implications of it – though it is for these he cares – may to the reader remain secondary. The novelist's reaction to his time, and judgement of it, are bound to be manifest in his work: he commits himself, all along the line, if not by words at least by clear implication – and he may antagonise, more closely than other artists, when he least intends to. His proceedings must, in the main, be perfectly overt. He cannot but seem to embark on argument, to imply attitude. Yet he is reinforced by more inspiring contact with other arts than may have been possible till now: painting, music, architecture aid him to extend the bounds of his medium – or, better, cause him to feel it need not be bounded. He feels a fusion between all manners of saying; he is aware of his own part in the convergence, from every aesthetic quarter, upon truth. Thus, the contemporary novel, apparently informal, is stayed upon an inner regard for form; it is visual, and in feeling musical; and in sense and intention it is at heart poetic.

Today is the present climax of time – the extreme, so far, to which experience can go. Today is the outcome of the enormous past: when we feel this, no moment seems disconnected, no single sensation seems accidental. How can we consider Today unmeaning when we look back at all that went to formulate it, and us? In the main, we are surrounded by what is constant – what is new, what is singular, what is without precedent in our contemporary consciousness. The genius of every preceding age came from fresh beholding – a beholding in the unique light of the age itself. In that sense, we have a genius of our own. We need not seek subject; subject is found by Time.

The Poetic Element in Fiction

I speak this evening in a series given to poetry. I speak as a writer of stories – as a person confronted at once by the limitations and the possibilities of narrative prose. In its infancy, the sheer, actual story was, surely, immersed in one kind of poetry, the primitive poetry of people. It was simple, and tended to be heroic. It was not so much invented as expressive, in itself a natural coming-to-life of man's awareness of his existence, and of its consequences – emotions and actions. When the novel came, the story began to diverge from poetry, lose height, and become entangled with minutiae. The novel compelled the story to take to itself a whole new function – that of explanation, and then analysis – it became, if not anti-poetic, unpoetic. It took on the character of a document.[1] Factitious elements had to be introduced. Losing the spontaneous veracity of its childhood, the story began to struggle to be grown-up – reflective, ethical, and, lest it be not credited, circumstantial. We must not decry the novel – but since its day we have been less often given a "pure" story. The novel gives one the sense of a story *used*.

The novel came into being some two hundred years ago, in the Age of Reason.[2] It concerned itself with, and reflected, modern society – as it then was, and to a degree is still. It dealt with the growing complexities of consciousness. Immediately (and rightly) sought for its entertainment-value, the novel could also demand praise as an[3] aid to man's understanding of fellow-man. It stood for psychological exploration; it examined motives and kept a watch on the passions – showing them, in the main, to be anti-social. Out for justice, though seldom revolutionary in trend, the novel was a liberalising influence – through causing the reader to feel, it induced him to think. It was not, however, expression in the old, pure sense – it was invention. It was the result of a process.[4] If the intuitive-imaginative stream ran, in the novel, comparatively low, this was atoned for, for its delighted readers, by something else it had which *was* semi-miraculous. The original novelists of the eighteenth and nineteenth centuries could reproduce life, and, somewhere in the course of this reproduction, suggest criticism.

The novel seemed bound to be circumstantial. It relied, for its effect, on the building up of a picture absolutely convincing[5] of the practical considerations which Piast[6] was rounding. It dealt with rank and income; it dealt with social ambition; it dealt with all the minor but powerful influences, the practical considerations which run counter to, or well up in man, the current of the more majestic and simple apparitions. In fact, the ideal of the century which gave the novel birth, the ideal of the Age of Reason, of both bloodless and violent revolution, the ideal which Henry Fielding expressed in a speech in *Tom Jones*, was the ideal of the rational passion. It was felt possible to line man up, to make him accord to the scientific, to the informed, to the considered due of life. Romantic in its expression, the novel was surely classical fundamentally in its intention, in its first wish. And it was inevitable that in taking to itself so many, as one might say, stage effects, in imitating life so closely, in cataloguing the minutiae of existence, in conjuring up for the reader all the circumstances of domestic or social life which surrounded the characters, the novel should place itself at the very remote distance, from the standpoint of poetry; it was inevitable that the story, as encased in the novel, should be summed up contemptuously, distinguished by the poet Shelley from poetry, as a combination of facts, a combination of facts set arbitrarily in the frame of a chosen time, artificially placed in their time and liable to dissolve and to lose virtue and reality when the time of the chosen story had gone by.

It was not with this narrow view of the novel, of the story in the novel, that the greatest of its practitioners embarked. And it was, in fact, ironical, that exactly when it was found that the novel could be technically perfected, could be brought out of its original, somewhat incoherent, somewhat lavishly documented state, into the disciplined form of a work of art; it was when this discovery had been made, that the artists who applied themselves to the story, in the form of the novel, began to rebel, began to wish to escape from the almost irritating possibilities of neat, technical perfection, the potential possibility of a wholly rational and order due of man.[7]

Flaubert was a very great instance of this. We know the agonies of the process by which he applied himself to the novel, to the first realistic novel that he wrote – *Madame Bovary*[8] – and how, at the end of the day, in which he had squeezed from his brain, from his judgement, from the finest of his faculties, the most precise, and the best word, how at the end of that day, he wrote to a friend, speaking with a certain excitement and a certain desire, of what he described as "the psychological overflow" which he saw ahead. He predicted – he would be the last to say that he prophesied – what has, in fact, come about since his time, what was to begin to signalise itself in the work of the Russian novelists. Even in Flaubert's lifetime, this psychological overflow, this sense on the part of man and on the part of the artists that there are irrational and unregimentable elements in mankind and humanity which no hard set form of the classical, of the disciplined story can hope to contain.

The novel had begun in the English language. The contagion of the idea of the novel was to spread through Europe. And it was by the French, by Balzac, with his almost Elizabethan parade of the major passions in his work, and by Stendhal, with his preoccupation, his pride and ambition, by Flaubert himself, and considerably by the more ungirt and fluid gigantic novelists of[9] nineteenth-century Russia. It was by these people that the mould of the novel, having been formed originally with such intention, began to be cracked. The disciplined form of the novel, the rational language, the circumstantiality and the detail, and the social landscape, and the intelligent analysis of persons, was not enough.

In England this was realised, even when the most[10] apparently dominating and genial of the Victorian novelists held their form. Something happened when Emily Brontë seized and broke the apparent form, the apparent story of an isolated family in a house on a bare midland and surged through across the frontiers into poetry, with *Wuthering Heights*. It was the scene, again, in England, when Thomas Hardy affronted the public of his day with those awkward and formidable and primitive masterpieces – masterpieces in which the person of the region, the peasant, the schoolmaster, the simple and local man, showed himself capable of strange and cosmic and dramatic behaviour. The scene in *Jude the Obscure* when the sick man who watches the perfection of the sunset in his bedroom glass, when the woman broods over the fire on the horizon of the heat,[11] and when Tess of the D'Urbervilles, after the innocent murder which she has committed, falls asleep on midsummer night, on the Stonehenge[12] sacrificial stone.

Yes, it had come to be recognized in England, as elsewhere, by the end of the nineteenth century, that the rational and circumstantial telling of the story by the deliberately prosaic means of the novel, was not enough. Fiction must breathe in a more deep air, and fiction, if it was to survive, if it was to see the nineteenth century out into the formidable and uncharted future of the twentieth century, must recognize the poetic necessity. This came with Henry James, with his extraordinary production of the overtone of prose. His confluence of unstated things arising from his stated remark, from those very intellectual complications which he passed in the middle and late periods,[13] came this desertion of the plain, straight, comprehensible fact, and this transition into a sort of no-man's land, which had ceased to be clear prose and was not yet explicit poetry.

This was to progress, as you know, with Proust, with his tapestry of this sensation, with his cult of the impression for its own sake; with his extraordinary evolution from the fact of the remembrance, the identifying of the memory with the art; the passage from the minute and life-like social documentation into this – a pioneer of unreasonable sensibilities, it was so powerful. It was to move forward, also, with James Joyce.

It was, I suggest, with the appearance – for one can only call it the "appearance" – of the short story, so much a product of our own century, that fiction was able to shed, to discard, a great deal of the dragging hiddenness which it had had to carry. Whether the short story was a conscious abandonment of some of the positions held by the novel, of some of the virtues or the destination claimed by the novel, it is impossible to say. The short story is so much part of the art of our time, it partakes so much of the nature of our time, that it is hard to account for its presence among us, for its prominence in art, and for its future in art, except by saying that our generation, in its desire for the story in general,[14] required from the short story something in which the novel had failed; or else, that our generation required the short story to advance to a point to which the novel could not. The short story had the advantage, and one may say again, the virtue, of being non-explanatory. It is not the business of the writer of the short story to place, to analyse, or, in fact, to impart information, and the creative writer who has, for years before he approached the simplicity of the short story, become increasingly restless at this, as it were, information desk of the novel, has turned with very great happiness and very great sense, not only of relief, but of reality, to the shortened story.

The story does return, the short story, to, in a way, that early primitive state. It is not concerned with the detail, with the social circumstance, or with the minutiae, unless, of course, it may happen to hinge, as certain excellent and realistic and photographic stories do, on a practical circumstance of everyday life. It must be realistic. There is something poor and thin and invalid about the short story which neglects place, which neglects time, which does not take as the base of its imaginative flight, some actual and practical circumstance. But the circumstance of the story is very quickly established, and the matter or the substance of the story is preeminently imaginative. It is expressioned,[15] it is an imaginative act, and an imaginative conception of action. The mechanisation, which the novel must have, the bridge passages, as we have come to call them, which are, I believe, even trying to the poet himself, as a means to link between illuminations – the bridge passage is mercifully eliminated from the short story, with its presentation of sensation at the moment, in the scene for its own sake. That is not to suggest that the writing of the short story is in any sense easier, is in any sense an abandonment of the discipline which is inherent in the writing of any prose which is to have fibre or truth at all. In fact, the story, because of its real perks to poetry, because of its stress on language, is a very much greater imaginative test, is a very much higher trial of the fibre of the artist behind it, than the novel, with its smoother surface, its more easy equilibrium. I do consider the story to be a searching and a very trying test. It would be too much to say that the short story has usurped altogether the prominent place, the leading artistic position for the prose story in our time. It would be an untrue assertion in the practical sense and it would give a very poor and unsatisfactory account of what is actually being done in fiction now. It would be accurate to say that the simplifications of the story and the concerns of the story have very much influence on the novelist who now writes, and that, partly, perhaps, because of the extraneous elements of social change, of the breaking up of the established scene, of this forward movement through scientific change, through the various frustrations and arbitrary events of the century.

The novelist can no longer rely on the full picture, the crowded canvas and the circumstantial account. It would have to be a reduction of the novel in any case, and it does appear that the novel is learning its simplification and its concentration on the imaginative side to a certain extent from the short story, to a very great extent, I think also, from the cinema. The great flux of information, of pleasing pictorialness, the manipulation of history and of small, personal dramas, in order to provide what will be an entertainment, what may be a kind of alleviation, what may be, as we wearingly say, an escape, but which has no really alive contribution to make to man's knowledge of himself or to his awareness in art.

There seems to be now no halfway in the writing of the novel or the story between the flood of documentary writing and the internal story imaginatively told, simplified and taking to itself this new language for its expression. And this new language is bound in inference, if not in outward style, to be poetic. It is really to be desired, in these days, that we should be able to pin down whatever is unique in our age and unique in ourselves. It is very much to be desired that we should separate the experience of the man, of you, or of me, from this great generalised flow of conventional experience which we are told we have. We are constantly under the influence of this hypnosis which comes from the press, from some part of the radio, from this mass opinion, which tells us that we are this or we are that, which suggests to us that we proceed like a shoal of fish or crowd of sheep.

We could be very easily numbed and very easily made anonymous, unaware of ourselves, by this heavy looming up of invention, of buildings, of process of speed, of similarity, of mass production. It is an accumulation from which the ordinary, the old-fashioned novelist, with his love of the outwardly individual peculiar, may well stand back in despair and awe. We can no longer manufacture for ourselves the exterior, romantic story. The pretty scene and the romantic circumstances of life are to be found in creases of the countryside, in outlying tracts. But they are no longer the scene of the ordinary action, the ordinary emotion, and the ordinary thought. We are being deprived, in most of the world, and as a generation of what was outwardly attractive to the fancy, and delightful to the sentiments, and riveting to the eye. We remain, like personable, like passionate actors, on a scene from which the,[16] or stage, from which the ordinary charming scenery has been removed and the surroundings are abstract – for the background is abstract, and casts very formidable shadows. We cannot really rely, for our interest in life, our magnetism to life, or our absorption in life, on any exterior, charming circumstance. That is true about it in the main, true of the big cities, and true of most of the people who have been wronged by their energies and their powers into the narrow forward movement of distance. Still we have in the outlying parts and the smaller of the countries this freeness, this naturalness, this outward inspiration from which Thomas Hardy wrote, from which the romantic poets wrote. But, for most of us, on the main stage of life, there is not anything but dependence on what I should call the internal scenery, the sensation, the imaginative thought, and the continuous emotion which is great enough by what is happening day after day. Out of that, how is there to be made a story? Is the storyteller to withdraw altogether and finally from the scene? Is it to be allowed that the only spokesman for our time, the only remaining voice for our time, and a voice which may not always be easily heard, should be the voice of the poet, and of the lyrical and self-contemplative poet, at that? I don't think that that is an end, is a future which we can altogether concede. I should be unlikely, of course, to concede it, because it would mean I should withdraw from the scene myself. At the same time, I don't think it is only egotism, only the wish for accomplishment which keeps the teller of the story still active, still convinced that life contains this material and that he has in the building of the story, in the relating of the story, some part to play. There must be the outward action, however placed and however staged. There must be the conflict between consciousness of the one and of the other person. There must be the movement and the impact of the passion upon the passion, the project on the project. We cannot really accept, even in our most introverted individualism, the idea of a one-man world, of the solitary consciousness reflecting everything else. And that really, that fact that it concerns itself with two people, with three, with an unnumbered cast of persons, placed in a pattern relating to one another and acting upon one another, does constitute the hold and the future promise of the story, whether it be in the novel, the novel of sensation, whether it be in the novel of allegory, the Kafka novel, or whether it be in the short story with its simplified invisible view, the fact of reaction and opposition,[17] the consequence of one person upon another and one action as following another, will always be desired and will always be needed to be made plain.

How, however, is this to be done? How is language, which in the course of two hundred years of inventive storytelling, to be restored to the immediacy and aliveness which will return, if that may be, the action and the story of now to its place in primitive experience? For that we are still capable of the primitive experience I cannot for a moment really doubt. Here it is, that we who tell the story, find ourselves surging up against, fighting against the apparent restrictions of prose language. We have been aware of them, we have been trying to break through them, and I think, that just as happens on the line of a rather indeterminate battle in a campaign, the break-through has been made by writer after writer. It was clearly made by James Joyce. It was clearly made, of course, by Gertrude Stein. It was made by them with a certain sacrifice of intelligibility. It was made by Proust and by Henry James, but without the sacrifice of intelligibility, but merely at the cost of a demand for more intuition and more understanding in the reader. This frontier line between prose with its precision, and poetry with its infusion of what cannot be precise – that frontier line, as I feel it, as a number of us feel it, unsure and tremulous, is certainly beginning to yield or beginning to fade. I dare not speak for the poets or from the poet's point of view, but it would appear to me that the poet, on his side, is borrowing more and more for his imagery, for his language, even for his subject, on the domain of fact, that he is drawing his images from what used to be considered not assimilable by poetry, that he turns his back on no technicality, no prosaic or everyday scene, and that poetry is reinforcing itself from what was once considered to be, in so far as it was the material of anything, the rather gritty material of prose. If that is so, the debt would be an equal one, because we certainly, who attempt now in these days to crystallise the story, to find our internal stronghold for the story, and yet to keep the drama, the shape, the primitive action of the story clear. We are making our demands on the imagery of the poetic language, we are trying to fuse our words, not only in their meanings, but as Shelley said, they could be fused also in their sounds. We aim, perhaps, for the concatenation, for the overtone, for what is apparently inharmonious. We take words with our roughness, for their unacceptability just as much for their smoothness or their grace. Our idea of style, when we write or we tell a story, is not purely suppleness and surface for its[18] own sake. It is something of a muscularity and a strength, but it is also a style which should be capable of being luminous and transparent. Poetry has a transparency of glass; prose, according to its value, can have anything up from the heavy, unresounding opaqueness of earthenware. But, if we are to continue to tell stories, and I do believe that it will always be required that the story should be told, we must be able to use the narrative language at white heat, and if in our experimentation we bungle or fail, if our language offends and seems incomprehensible, the allowance for the attempt, the hope of capturing, not for ourselves but for art and comprehension, a new position, a new forward post for the story must be allowed for. As storytellers we seek and we must have the poetic element now. We need to be subject to that force, that poetry, of which Shelley says, "It compels us to feel what we perceive and to imagine that which we know."

The Idea of the Home

By "the idea of the home" I mean, a partly conscious, partly unconscious image of what is to be desired – an image always a little modified by existing circumstance. For it is not in human nature to desire – or to desire, at least, for long – what cannot possibly be achieved. "Home" connotes to people an institution which has a practical-economic base, but which tapers up towards a moral ideal: there is involved, when one speaks of "home," at least some notion of the ethics and the aesthetics of living. The habitat, whether large or small, is the container of the essential elements of life; what goes on within four walls has a continuous and creative effect, whether good or bad, on the individual inner being. Here it is that we allow ourselves to be sheathed in the mystery of sleep; here we wake to that slightly changed world which is another day. Here proceeds the routine to which we nail our sense of reality – the very monotony, the certainty that certain hours will bring with them familiar happenings and acts, keeps the anxious, nervous infant in us secure. The dependence on home is one of the few dependences which are not weakening: on the contrary, this is an origin of strength. We not only require, we are as humans completed, by what the home gives us – location. Identity would be nothing without its frame.

The home implies the family unit. Where there is not actual blood relationship, roommates or housemates begin in their adjustments to one another, their accumulating habit of life together, to approximate to the family pattern. Psychologically, there must be an accommodation, a compromise, between what dwellers under the same roof *have* in common, and what they have *not* in common, with one another. The home, most intensive community, must – like the larger, looser social communities – allow play for the pull, the occasional lack of harmony, between the individual and the group. Harmony, whatever may be the dissidences from it, is the integrating force – instinct, therefore, urges us to preserve it, at whatever cost, on whatever plane, in whatever manner, under whatever guise. Different sexes, different generations, different temperaments have to accept the modifications created by the nearness of one another, the operation of diversified factors within the same space. What must be achieved is, living together – inherent in the plan of the home is, at least some notion of how this may be done; and, ideally, of how this may be done best.

In the main, the plan is inherited. There is the great base of racial experience, upon which is superimposed the successive experiments made by civilisations. The primitive cannot be lost sight of – home is the scene of birth, marriage, death. Nor, though the existence of human beings often can and always should be idealised, can it ever be rationalised completely. Ultimately, the strength of the home tradition lies in its realism: we absorb, we are sustained by, we take for granted the knowledge that human beings *have* found it possible to live, and have continued to do so under conditions in some sense equivalent to our own. In spite of blind pressures, in spite of disintegrating forces, something has not only held firm but gone on. And, better still, not only have the primal, harsh and insistent needs been satisfied; there has been an expansion into desire – i.e., an envisagement of what it is not necessary to have but would be good to have. Realisation, however partial, of such desires has left its imprint: we inherit concepts of form, style, grace, manners, decoration, and social usage. Tradition, with regard to the home, provides us not only with a directive but an incentive. At the same time, it would appear now that tradition, if it be too strong, may prove in some way adverse to modern life – by being too hypnotising or too binding, by being reactionary or inelastic, by failing to allow for or take account of the altering nature of our universe, by riding too hard against the new psychology, or by acting dangerously as a stimulant to needs we desire to cease to have, since they are needs we can no longer satisfy.

How far is this so?

The question arises in all countries, all continents, with regard to the way of living and, most concretely, with regard to the home – as mould of the way of living. A sort of crux has been reached. It is not so much that we contemplate any thought-out domestic revolution, or would commit ourselves, at a given point, to anything drastic, radical in the way of change. More, we feel it necessary to take stock, to make some analysis, to attempt to be clear both as to what *is* happening, and what *should* be. It is not so much a matter of whether we should or should not promote change; more, we must take an objective attitude towards it. We must keep in mind, however, that change, though lately speeded up, is *not* the especial attribute of our century: on the contrary, change has ever been at work.[1]

America, for those of us who see her from the outside, stands for dynamism. For the Old World, as you no doubt know, there is a touch of the fabulous about your country – we conceive of her in terms of size and speed. At the outset, it is the dissimilarity – or, I should say, the reputed dissimilarity – of the American scene to ours which is arresting. The magazine, the cinema, and a certain amount of American "export" fiction are – or too easily tend to be – our mentors. We of the Old World tend, I think, to be too much at the mercy of our own fixed ideas on the subject of you: it is easier for us to aliment these than to break them down – actually, admirable, sometimes first-rate information, documentation as to the realities of your country *is* to be had, but we either do not know how to come at it, or are slow to. Nothing does, nothing can take the place of an actual visit to this country – a visit which, if circumstances allow, should be prolonged and, best of all, repeated from time to time. For, by the fact of coming here, one embarks upon an almost entire re-education. One discovers, at least, the immensity of what still is waiting to be discovered – and here, in this country, I should like to say, the atmosphere of discovery is infectious. For here, at once, one is among people immersed in the discovery of themselves – questing, testing, comparing, querying, analysing, looking back, looking forward. This growth of American self-consciousness is a no less important, no less decisive thing for the world than the growth of America in organic strength. It is an affair of civilisation.

We other people who want to know you are aided and met by your self-discovery – though it can but be that we lag some way behind. It can but be that, because we are not American, we remain outside the main body of your experience. All that we have to offer, against this, are our observations, impressions, and deductions; many of which might strike you as incorrect, irrelevant, or absurdly naïve. You must, however, accept them for what they may be worth. They are to us of a certain value from the fact of our having arrived at them, and in good faith. And the possibility that, from the outside, at a tangent, and out of our very freshness to your scene we may have hit on some aspect of truth, may make them of a certain value to you. If we utter truisms, we must be forgiven.

To me, America's newness is on the surface: beneath that I feel the submerged action of her past. Elsewhere, the past has force because of its length; here it has force because of its nearness and its intensity. I would suggest that civilisation here was, in the first place, a matter of reproduction – the reproduction of an image brought in with them by the original settlers from the Old World. The instinct was to imitate in a new land the way of life from which settlers had come – though that way of life was to be conducted in better circumstances, with promise of freedom and of expansion. It also was, at the start, to be modified by primitive roughnesses, difficulties, endurances, risks, and dangers. The immediate necessities – a degree of security, food, shelter, warmth, protection – had to be found first: in the first homes, the expression of the idea of living, though the idea *was* present, was rudimentary. Protection and warmth had to predominate over any notions of ease and space; for the family, survival must be established before there could be any question of an expressive pattern. The early houses, massive in their smallness, contracted into themselves by the need for strength, seem, with their over-hanging second stories, to be darkened by a resolute frown. Yet they contained, already, the classic idea – inside them were not only tables and chairs but books and thoughts; a comely English was being spoken, and still more an order of being was being worked out, inside these defending walls. Physically, the original American civilisation was primitive; ideologically, not – it had the authority of centuries of civilisation behind it. The lamp which had been carried so far and with such care was with still greater care kept burning. Each home, integrated by resolution, was a world in embryo, each family a potential tribe.

One might, I suppose, call that first phase one of establish-ment: it was functional. Once there *had* been establishment, there could be expression. Settlements became villages, villages towns, towns cities; homesteads could sun themselves in fear-less isolation upon hillsides or by the curves of rivers. Now could, and did, enter the social idea – and with that the home came to be seen as not merely a unit but a manifestation, not merely an entity but a face. The idea of the desirable could be entertained: it was still a sedate desire, tempered by classicism, expressing itself in columned porches, in symmetrical whiteness, fluted doorways, amply windowed rooms, shining hardwood floors. Here, both in the architectural and the moral sense, was order; something propitious but at the same time disciplined and austere. The marvel, to the European eye, of these eighteenth-century and early nineteenth-century American homes, is their equitability: they give the impression of being for *all* people – the small have the dignity of the large, the large have the simplicity of the small. Also, facing each other across wide streets, each itself a pattern, each contributing to the organic pattern of the village or town, they seem to have struck the ideal halfway between the sense of identity on the one hand, the sense of community on the other. For a space, it would seem, for a century and a little more, home life – in the Eastern, settled, already maturing parts of America – expressed what it desired to express. It was also modelled, perhaps, on the original vision of the forefathers: was there not a touch of "the promised land"? – an existence free from oppression, but still strongly held within moral bounds; an existence purified (as compared to that in the Old World) by its very simplification.

Expression, then, in this second phase was arrived at. The formula for the home, and for the domesticated society which surrounded it, may well have seemed to be a sufficient formula for life. For the family, did not the Biblical injunction still hold good: "Honour thy father and thy mother, that thy days may be long in the land"? The adult, having within his own day achieved so much, had unshaken faith in the value of his experience; it would have occurred to almost no one that authority did not increase with age. Life was still ambitious enough to be rewarding; that is, to keep alive the sense of reward – there was something ethical, meritorious about the having of what one had, for it was deserved. Above all, those American homes of the middle period, of what I have called the "expressive" phase, must have embodied, for those within them, the consciousness of America as *America*. The imported home-idea was giving place to the spontaneous[2] flowering of the native one; not because there had been a break but because there was being an evolution. Reproduction, having played its initial part, was at an end: furniture was shaping the native wood into its own styles (expressive now, not derivative); homecrafts brought their own colours to decoration – something the more vigorous, the more inspirational for being naïve. The emergence of a tradition was to be felt. Life had a positive, unique, pungent, and urgent quality, which, as it were, forged a mould for itself. I think of this epoch as culminating about halfway through the nineteenth century.

There had not been, so far, *more* than could be expressed.

Or, at least, so it now seems.

One can see how, for America, the home came to be invested with ideality. One hears it said, "The Englishman's home is his castle." The American does not think in terms of castles, which he may well associate with the feudal evil from which America broke away: instead, he conceives of the home as the seat of virtue, the symbol of independence, the source of strength. Also, perhaps, as an assertion of fearlessness – since the stockades came down there have been no fences: this in particular strikes the British eye, accustomed to the high fences and thick hedges inside which the equivalent British home maintains an almost impassioned seclusion. The Currier & Ives[3] domestic print – product, already, of a nostalgia – seems to aim to capture a stalwart lyricism: already, however, a sentimental etiolation has set in; one seems to be viewing a lost Paradise. Since Currier & Ives, the idealisation has taken different forms; but it goes on, becoming more rather than less intensified, keyed to an ever higher pitch. *Does* the idealisation, now such a force, tend to diverge too widely from reality?[4]

The idea, at its best, was prolonged by the practical repetition of the simple, stalwart pattern as the pioneers moved West, into tracts, again, of infinite possibility. The phases of establishment, then expression, were to recur in zone after zone across the continent: the pioneers, like the original settlers, also carried with them and were to give body to an idea of life; but by now the idea was American – the recollected civilisation[5] was that of the East. Had the entire development of America been simultaneous, her ideological-moral youth might have lasted less long: as it was, youth seemed to be given a well-nigh endless term by the continuous feeling of expansion: the East, already far from Paradise, already in the modern grip of complexity, could be still braced, still inspired, still stimulated by the physical enterprise of her children, however far away. And at the same time, in from across the ocean came pouring the immigrants to the Land of Promise: each arrival constituted an act of faith, a faith which renewed, confirmed, swelled America's own. The continuous absorption of races, the continuous processing of these into a type not yet ready to be defined produced, I suppose, a state, a pressure of consciousness which was at once enigmatic and overcharged. Ideas were to be adhered to for their very simplicity – a simplicity which in itself, it seemed, vouched for them, constituted their worth. What was simple could not but be salutary. One retained therefore, perhaps for just too long, the unicellular, self-regarding concept of the American home.

Should one say[6] that America has been slow in facing the multicellular concept of society? And, along with this, the outgoing relationships of the home – centre now, as it is, of a stretching nexus of aims and interests, pulls and responsibilities? One may put three questions: –

How far has the change in living conditions shifted the balances of home life?

What, and how important, a contribution should the home be able to make to the world as it is today?

How far should the home resist, and how far admit, exterior influences, pressures, theories, and trends?

Life flows into the cities: the norm is urban, or suburban. Mechanisation has altered the face of the countryside: the villages and rural areas are populated mainly by ageing people, with a few young folk waiting to take wing. Former groups, family or neighbourly, are now broken up by the immense distribution over the continent: the great majority of the population no longer live where they were born. In the new environment – or, it may be, the succession of new environments – there are social regroupings, a formation of new ties, but always against a background of the feeling that such ties are likely to be impermanent: one no longer expects to strike deep roots. External continuity is broken; any internal feeling of continuity must therefore be more difficult to achieve. Most environments lack associations – there has not been time, and there is unlikely to *be* time, for those to form – therefore emotional attachment to scenes, things, places becomes rarer, which may set up one sort of emotional inanition: it is *not* natural to feel neutrally towards one's environment. "Home" is no longer to be identified with a fixed set of physical surroundings. House-moves, changes from apartment to apartment, from suburb to suburb or from city to city (sometimes with thousands of miles between) no longer cause, as once they did, acknowledged emotional-psychological upheavals – either this is a sign of atrophy, or the American race is really becoming nomad. The installation of the family in the new place is, practically, so much less troublesome than it once was as to appear, these days, almost automatic; and, the new surroundings are likely to be, in effect and layout, almost confoundingly similar to the old: there is a perpetual substitution of the not-quite-the-same for the quite-the-same. In fact, nothing in the home remains continuous but the *idea*, on which too great stress may therefore come to be laid. The idea may either harden into a fixation or degenerate into a fantasy, which as such offers itself to exploitation.

Such a fluidity, such an unfixity as to surroundings may affect the relations between persons – husbands and wives, children and parents. Perpetual readjustments, however facile, habitual, automatic these may appear, can but impinge upon fundamentals.[7] Very much fewer children now see their parents as monoliths in an unchanging landscape – landscape, that is, either social or geographical; and in big cities the social landscape, which is to say the *felt* community,[8] may barely exist at all. The child sees the parent, for better or worse, as an *individual*, and as that only: the institutional aspect of parenthood, which was localised, which to an extent derived from the parent's place in a tribal pattern or scheme, is gone. Adult prestige is less, and the adolescent if not the child is quick to feel this. Also, the greater speed, ease and mechanical smoothness with which the home is run, the short-circuiting of what were once patient and skilful processes, tend to demolish the mystery, one might say mystique, which before now used to surround home-making – there is little the adult does that the child cannot do, or could not do if it wished. Domestically there is, or ought to be, more leisure; but in turn leisure creates its problems: there may ensue a vacuum, or a neurotic expectation of some happiness which, unspecified, is impossible to attain. The adult – in view, it may be, of the adolescent – is himself, or herself, in an adolescent state through loss of the sense of adult function or restricted outlet for the adult capacity.

However well planned, the contemporary house or apartment is small; the house may have a yard or surrounding space; in the case of the apartment there is no outlet. The effects of constriction and contiguity demand to be overcome; but how? The impact of people, of two or it may be three generations, on one another may come to be deadened, dangerously, by indifference; or, unless it can somehow be humanised, harmonised, may wreak havoc. Conflicts become more difficult to evade, tensions more difficult to ignore; lost control sets up endless reverberations. Above all, growth for the child and the adolescent requires living-space. Can psychological living-space be achieved when physical living-space is restricted?[9]

The balances, the stresses of home life *have*, inevitably, been shifted by modern living conditions – shifted, but not necessarily fatally displaced. The essential is, to recognize what is happening. A new equilibrium must be sought for.

What of the home's contribution to the America, to the world of today? How creative can be the existence of the family unit within four walls; how far can that existence generate strength? In so much as asking this, we may seem to query the accepted moral-ideal status of the home. Popular fiction, propaganda, advertisement all promote[10] the idea that the home is good – blameless no less than it is idyllic. An immense, bright-coloured, smiling fantasy of sheer satisfactoriness is built up as we turn the pages of magazines: this fantasy not only sells itself but sells goods. Comfort, "graciousness,"[11] prettiness, hygiene are to be had, and are had, not only by the masses but in the mass; and the effect, one is given to understand, of what is agreeable is ethical. Here is depicted a Never-neverland;[12] all the more alluring because it *is*, one can see perfectly well, attainable – more and more closely does actuality, in the matter of furnishings[13] and habit, approximate to those images on the glossy pages. What, then, is sinister and disquieting? Is there not a suggestion that the home is simply a consolidation of the ego? – a gratifying, warranted insulation of the self and dear ones (who are attributes of the self) from the world's complexity? In the pictures, smiling mated adults entertain friends who are their almost exact replicas; over the romping children hangs no threat of any greater or more testing maturity. This hermetic picture-home, is it self-sufficient? Not quite, for it requires not only to be admired but to be rated: it rates high for its success in the competition. Insulated, competitive, it stands – good in the sense of being not evil, but good for what?

The Never-neverland excludes psychological oddity, deviation, passion, intellectual or social adventure. Attempts to conform with the Never-neverland distort or break marriages and wreck temperaments: here one can be lulled by radio, hypnotised by television, but one cannot think, feel, act or, indeed, *be*. Happily, I believe in a generation, whether a minority or otherwise, to whom the Never-neverland is not to be sold.[14]

There are in existence persons who not only resist but persons who mock at it, deride it, challenge it, and see through it – the recalcitrants, the high-spirited non-conformers,[15] or the sheer unpretending possessors of commonsense. These, who also have homes, face inherent problems – how at once to conserve and maintain the essential privacy, and keep participations alive; how to share;[16] how to be independent without dissidence; how to abide by individual standards without making those manifest too aggressively.[17] The home offers itself as a merger for variants, a meeting-place for strangers due to become friends, as a "free zone" for talk, as a friendly guardian for what may be nascent originality.[18] In aliveness, awareness and, once again, expressiveness, unlost domestic genius may find outlet. Not merely what goes on *in* the home, but what proceeds *out* of it is important.[19]

To this links the third question: How far should the home resist, and how far admit, exterior influences, pressures, theories, and trends? To an extent, we have the answer above – what else does "aliveness" mean, or "awareness"? One might infer that there should be *no* exclusion – yet, it is not so simple as all that. A degree – I say, a degree only – of conservatism is so inseparable from the home concept that it cannot be altogether wrong: there is, also, the instinct to keep watch – that is, on behalf of the young and children. To conceal, deny or mitigate any truth is, clearly, to be unjust to the growing mind: on the other hand, one must recognize that a statement is not necessarily valid, or a theory necessarily of worth, simply because it happens to be contemporary. As for influences, their temporary strength and pervasiveness are not the measure either of their importance or of what is likely to be their long-term effect. The ideal is, to discriminate, not arbitrate; in order not to be arbitrary, one must encourage people to discriminate for themselves. At any age, one is entitled to experimentation, to trial-and-error, to growing pains; and of these the young are entitled to full measure. Should one, however, discountenance what does seem trash? Should one exclude what could be subversive?

The adult abdication, the unselfconfident shrinking from authority, may go so far in the matter of non-exclusion as to promote chaos: as to right and wrong, as to truth and falseness, *someone* has got to dare to say they know. We are less likely to err in the reverse direction, that of the Latin countries, where windows are metaphorically and actually shuttered and parental or adult authority is absolute. The one infection strenuously to be combatted is fear; the one attribute to be denied to any subject is fearfulness – and this, probably, holds as good in dealings with other adults, in so far as they are affectable, as it does in dealings with the young or children. Given that, the more the home takes count of the world, the stronger and more firmly established the home is; and, above all, the more innocent it is in the fearless[20] sense. Discussion, and discussion not in an atmosphere of prejudice, in the long run is the solvent of almost anything – the difficulty as to that is, hurry, pressure of business, sheer lack of time.

The idea of the home seems, at this stage, to be in a consciously tentative relationship to reality – if, that is, we may apply the term "reality" to America's mid-twentieth-century living conditions.[21] The idea, now, seems to alternate, or to fork – on the one hand, there is aspiration to an ideal future; on the other, nostalgia for an idealised past. I gather, from friends with whom I talk, that a sort of dissatisfaction, one might say a sort of anxiety, as to the *character* of existence does prevail; but also, that the dissatisfaction and anxiety are in themselves healthily symptomatic: they imply refusal of what might be a purely material[22] solution. Domestically, America's needs would appear in the main to be satisfied, her desires not – those desires being the more disturbing because they are not yet quite formulated to suit the day. With increased convenience – the cities' vertical and compressed plan, the suburbs' horizontal, interconnected one – has come a threat of stultification, due to overall similarity, mechanical repetition, and monotony. How is a clean-edged sense of identity to be preserved, and not only preserved but developed further? How is that reflective repose which the self needs – if it is to *be* a "self," as apart from a mere "ego" – to be obtained, maintained, in view of the rush, pressure, friction, and strain of outside life? The home should be asked to provide the answer.

The idea of home – that is, the desideratum – now seems also connected with an idea of tempo: inside the four walls there should be *enough time*, temporal if not physical space. Inside the four walls, there should be abatement of the psychological tyranny of the clock. There should be enough time for relationships to develop fruitfully, for impressions and memories to be digested, for feelings and thoughts to connect themselves into a meaning pattern. Modern consciousness, constantly overcharged, requires a resting-place, an unloading-place – that, should not home provide?

America is in the throes of an education: education heightens every demand the individual makes upon his surroundings. But contemporary American surroundings, because of their now mass-produced uniformity, in some cases almost their anonymity, tend these days to give out less rather than more: one kind of expressive period has come to an end. A new kind of expressiveness – concrete in architecture, furniture and regional planning based on a social idea, unconcrete in modes and rhythms of living – is being sought: but first, what there actually *is* to express must be known, felt, and in the main agreed upon; and as to that there are divergences. The divergences only do not cause more conflict because, it would appear, in America groups of all kinds, in particular age-groups, are apart from each other in interest and in activity: absence of conflict is obtained at the price of absence of contact. Schools, colleges, clubs, recreation-centres, the profession or business, at present drain off interest, energy, personality from the home: like seeks like, and seeks it outside the domestic four walls – the young go one way, men another, women another. Yet the ideal society is the composite; the integration of differing kinds in harmony. The home should, as a unit, represent mixed society.

The wish to integrate – or, rather, re-integrate – seems to be once more present in the idea of home. The coming-together of different generations and unalike characters should be pleasurable and voluntary, not merely enforced by lack of room-space. A richer blend, a greater cross-fertilisation of ideas and personalities in the home would in its effects, extending outward, produce a richer, more various, interesting and therefore satisfying general society: there would be more *to* people. In fact, the civilised individual is the one who is at once developed and disciplined by interplay with what is not himself and perhaps unlike himself: as to this, the home could again be, as it once was, the social nursery. America's fast-growing sense of responsibility demands adultness, knowledge of direction, and that perceiving awareness which makes for civilisation, for each person – and the person is the product, conscious or not, of what goes on inside the four walls. This may not need to be stated; it is now recognized. The idea *of* the home – for some time hazy, sentiment-fed, fantasy-threatened, and, it may be, even anachronistic – gives place, in America as I see it, to a constructive if not yet clearly blue-printed idea *for* the home.

I. You will forgive – I hope? – my speaking of language this morning –
  from my own angle
  that of the writer

II. I should not presume to do this if I did not feel –
  not only that language concerns us all – but that its
  (1) problems
  (2) its pleasures,[1]
  (3) our vital awareness of its past
  (4) and, our sense of responsibility for its future
are the same, whether we write or teach

III. *Perhaps there never has been a time when the state of language was not giving cause for concern*
  Flux, change, in anything both so alive *and*
    so life-reflecting as language *can*
  surely, never *not* have[2] been

at work?
Everything that we recognize as history
must have left its mark on language
	violating fixed ideas on the subject,
	making further exactions and new demands

IV. *True, till lately language was defended by the idea of Polite Usage*
	It was a matter of *Manners*
	There was an *élite*, which talked or endeavoured to talk as it knew it should
	Outside lay the Masses, who talked as they best might.

V. *Now, the barriers – to an extent artificial barriers – are down*
	Language is for all
	It may be regarded as more *imperilled*
	But also – by having become *democratised* –
	it *could* develop a great width and depth and a new force.

VI. *Let us now – in our own day – consider Language*
	in terms of
	its possible loss, its possible gain
	Loss: – ?
	The going of words into disuse
	The collapse – or at,[3] increasing erosion *of style* – spoken and written style

VII. *Loss of words – the terrifying shrinkage of vocabulary*
	This – I suppose – comes from a blend of *hurry* and lazy-mindedness?
	Lack of *precise* thought
	Or, *mistrust of precision* (as likely to seem "affected," pompous or priggish)
	Preferred are "sort of" or "you know – you know what I mean."
	Some nouns, verbs, adjectives disappear because they stand for things that no longer exist
	This is inevitable

VIII.[4] *Collapse of Style*
  (1) Failure of sentences to *direct themselves*
  (2) Failure in *emphasis*
  (3) Failure in power to give *proportion*

IX. *Gain*
As against those losses, what are – or can be – the Gains?
  (1) *Entrance into language of New and expressive words*
      (a) *Slang*
      (b) coming from *technical vocabulary*
      (c) from *dialect*
One must distinguish between the *slovenly, general-purpose* new word
  and, the word supplying a felt want

X. *Necessity to Hear Language*
I am talking to people – you – who know more about this than
I do myself
  (a) Reading aloud
  (b) Broadcasts and Records
  (c) Conversation
I am convinced that there *is*, in people, *a fundamental desire to
  be articulate*
and that *inarticulateness* is the cause of *damage and pain*
I also think it is wonderful how articulate people CAN be
There is something sad in the expression "a dead language"
Is there fear that our language will be become[5] "Dead"?
I *think* not.[6]

The Fear of Pleasure

Do I exaggerate if I say that there is something challenging – not to say truculent – about the title chosen for my talk? Pleasure ranks, surely, amongst the highest of human goods; it is in essence honourable; it stands for the full expansion of man *as* man – for the due play and the proper fulfilling of faculties. Perception plays a great part in it. In the rare consciousness of living the perfect moment, there occurs a widening sense of illumination, even of nobility. Indeed in all true pleasure there is an element of the sublime – in the pleasures of art and intellect, of travel, of friendship, love and home life, of duty and accomplishment. Is there not even a sort of pleasure, far from perverse, in our ability to confront and surmount pain, to bite upon and then rally from failure?

Pleasure in any of the forms I have already mentioned is not only ideally human, it is in itself humanising. So much so, indeed, that to cease to envisage pleasure, or to desire it, must involve a distortion of outlook, a misdirection, even a dereliction of our inherent power to live well.

Can it then be true that there has crept in a mistrust of pleasure, a mistrust amounting to fear? If so, surely there are questions to be asked. How prevalent is this fear? What may be its causes and what forms does it take? How does it make itself evident and what are, and may be, its consequences? I fear that, in our day, the strongest evidence of the fear of pleasure resides in the degradation of the very notions of it. The desperate value of time, the demand for a plan of life, the need to conserve energy all tend to militate against pleasure. There is a tendency on the part of strenuous, thinking, ambitious or idealistic persons to outlaw it, to suspect it, to write it off. All the more so because of the two incontrovertible facts that pleasure is non-rational and non-utilitarian. It is, we may feel, irrelevant to the sterner issues: it is as distracting as were the golden apples![1]

It is difficult not to be aware of this hardening of attitude – of a certain impatience with the apparently senseless pleasures of other people; of a revolt against fruitless and mechanised amusement, against idle gratification, time consumed to no purpose, energies blunted and individualities lost; of distaste for the vague, stupid beam on the face of the trooping crowds. Nothing is more isolating than the contemplation of pleasure one is not tempted to share, nothing more bewildering, more disheartening.

All this is, in fact, a reaction to the situation in which a great part of the present-day fields of pleasure has been commercialised. The innocent, fluid desire is exploited, the faculty for play, corrupted. The pleasure-seeker has fallen into wrong hands and in reply there has come to be a touch of bewildered defiance in his attitude. He is on the run from a repressiveness, from a rigidity, which he suspects to be operating *somewhere* – a "schoolmaster" attitude to life. "What is the harm," he asks, "in a bit of fun?" What, indeed?

What is harmful, what is deplorable, is that the idea of harm should be entertained at all! The connection of harm with pleasure makes it harmful, or at least makes it barren, stupefying, an expense of spirit,[2] a dead loss. It brings it into opposition with our fundamental certainty that pleasure should be a gain.

On whatever plane we approach it, pleasure should and, indeed, must raise questions of selectivity – the satisfaction of the *real desire* as opposed to submission to the *received idea*. But this exercise of choice, this power to make distinctions – what a degree of maturity they require! Can it be, perhaps, that we suspect pleasure because the capacity for it, as an active personal thing, seems to mature so slowly, because human wishes and fantasies lag (it seems) so far behind the human intelligence? There is a naïveté, an inconsequence, a touch perhaps of the barbarous in the human make-up which – for any of us who attempt to think of human nature constructively – is confounding. One does not know its limits: it inspires dread.

One cannot, I believe, be either effective or honest with oneself or in one's dealing with people without recognizing these elements – the persistence inside the apparent adult of the unrewarding recalcitrance of the child. We have continually to ask ourselves, "Is there nothing of that in me?" And how many of us, I wonder, can be quite certain of the answer!

Were we certain, our uneasiness with regard to pleasure might be less troubling. For it is pleasure, we suspect, which removes the controls; which offers this poltergeist element endless and dangerous play; which issues in extravagances that represent an undertow away from civilisation. We suspect on our own behalf and on behalf of others what may be enjoyed too much.

Yet if I am right in my estimate of the life-fulfilling quality of true pleasure, we have to reckon with the unsatisfied capacity for it. The question we have to answer is nothing less than whether people can and should be taught to live. And in the present crisis in human development there can be nothing except an affirmative answer. The assertion of pleasure as a positive good is part of the response to the threat of atrophy of the rational faculties. It is part of your task to recognize, to instate, to educate the faculty for pleasure. You have to coordinate – or rather to open and point the way to coordination of faculties – so that in the growing human being – and what *living* being is not a growing being? – nothing may be left adverse or astray. What is needful for this, in what measure imagination must supplement intellect, only you through experience can assess.

Who, in our time, dare aspire to be quite fearless? But we may diagnose fears and by so doing may at least conquer some of them – and we should do well to conquer the fear of pleasure.

A Novelist and His Characters

The novelist and his characters . . . This relationship is one of the mysteries which surround authorship: it could be the greatest, I think sometimes. And is so not only for the reader but – is this recognized? – for the writer himself. An enigma, to which he does not feel qualified to supply the key. He finds himself under pressure from endless questioners: he is unable to answer them – or, unwilling? At the root, there is something primitive and ambiguous. One might say, he has an instinctive guardianship of his own secret: at the same time, is *he* so sure what that secret is?

Where do fictional characters come from? How are they made? – or, *are* they "made" (that is, deliberately constructed)? If not made, are they found? Where are they found from: recollection, individual memory, chance encounters? Are they drawings from life? If not, then – what? They were invented, were they? "Invented," purely?

All the author can tell you is one thing: there is no formula.

And, the question of origin is unsettled.

I am taking it that all fictional characters are fictitious. This may sound a sweeping statement: it could be challenged. What I mean is, they are in essence fictitious. If they were not fictitious in origin, they become so by entering the extraordinary element of the novel. They acquire fictitiousness. They take on a size, a significance, a disturbingness lacking in people in outside life. Or, lacking in the generality of people in outside life. That must, I think, be so: for, when one encounters an exceptional person who *has* those attributes, does one not find oneself saying (or at least, thinking) "He – or she – is like somebody in a story"? . . . Undeniably, actual men and women have served to spark into existence some of the striking members of the fictional tribe. Or have – is it better to say? – inspired them. That they did do. But that was the most they did. Once within the book, a great trans-mutation took place. A sea change. One knows, for instance, that the characters of such giants as Proust and Tolstoy are traceable back to members of their families, to friends or lovers, to neighbours, acquaintances, to luminaries of some particular social world. One *knows* this – as a matter of information: one has been told so. But does one *feel* it? No. At least, not where I am concerned. These inhabitants of the pages of Proust and Tolstoy have about them the authority, the singularity, and the wonder of having been *created*.[1] Re-created was what they, in fact, were.

Above a certain level of imaginative performance, the char-acter who has had origin in "real life" – that is, in the author's human experience – is indistinguishable from the (nominally) invented one. He or she is neither more convincing nor less so. If anything, there is a tendency to be less convincing: why, I wonder?

And what, now, about that other great race of characters: those who take form (apparently) out of the blue? Those known, I mean to say, as "invented."

To begin with, "invented" is the wrong word. A word of convenience, which easily comes to hand but is injurious and misleading. It suggests *conscious* contrivance, and ingenuity. Invention is something that goes on at the top of the brain. In its own way, a fascinating pursuit – I can think of few of us who have not tried our hand at it, particularly in childhood. But far distant from the creative process as understood in the art – *and* the life of fiction. One cannot "invent" a man or woman as one might a new kind of mouse trap, or whatever. What would result from trying to? A clockwork figure, mechanised, empty of breath. A creature without impulses, made to order. Predictable, as might be a wound-up robot. Altogether sterile and unconvincing . . . An instinctive novelist does not "invent" his characters; no, not even the most minor of them: he not only knows that he should not, he knows that he cannot – he does not try to. Celebration is useless, in this instance. The character either *is* there, beside him, within him, or it is not. No amount of thinking, the hardest thinking, will ever bring the creature into existence. A character can be summoned, but not by thought.

Summoned . . . "invoked" might be better? But that suggests a genie out of a bottle, or a ghost raised by some expert in the occult. I don't mean that, or anything of that sort. I think of a character as being called into being by the desire of the author that he (or she) should exist.

Called into being from where? "Out of the blue . . ." But what is the blue? *I* see it as anything but an azure transparency; rather, as a profound, rather dark mist. A mist in which forgotten experience mingles with forgotten and reabsorbed dreams, a mist of hitherto dormant imagination. Out of this the character, at the beginning shadowy, takes form – like a ship coming forward out of a fog at sea. Continuing to come forward, nearer the author, it takes on an almost overpowering distinctness. Its identity becomes as strong as his own. And not only this, but he *knows* this creature – for whose origin he cannot account.

So – having swept away the word "invented," I should like to substitute "perceived." Meaning, that the character begins to come into existence at the moment when it is first *perceived* by the author. As he contemplates it, it grows, it intensifies. Physically, it materialises. Both in its inner being and in outward form it takes on for him an urgent, pressing reality. A reality which (it is to be hoped) he will convey to, make felt by, others: his readers.

In saying that a character cannot be *thought* into being, I do not mean that, once *in* being, it should not be thought *about*. Very much the contrary. The element of reflection is a vital one – vital, and therefore essential. The novelist – surely? – is constantly thinking about his characters, observing them, analysing them (though he need not necessarily re-analyse them for the benefit of the reader!). He evaluates them, to an extent he judges them; he sees them first in one, then in another light. He explores them, to find out how they would react to this, that or the other circumstance – and still more (for this is very important) how they would be most likely to react to each other. He takes note of the inconsistencies, the variability, without which they would not be valid as human beings . . . This reflection upon his characters by the author, though in part intuitional, emotional, demands also the best of his intellect and the whole of his judgement . . . In reading a novel *we* are most aware, probably, of the degree of "lift," illumination, and force given it by imagination. It is indeed a work of imagination – but not that only. Behind it there had to be a controlling mind. The size of the vision gives a novel its scale. But is great vision possible without true judgement?

How far are a novelist's characters really *his*? Myself, I find something distasteful in the proprietary, possessive attitude. Moreover, I do not think it to be an attitude of which any proper novelist is guilty; it is, rather, wished on to him by his readers – who would, themselves, consider it eminently natural, rightful and fitting. Paternalism, and so forth. I am one author, and I think one of many, with whom this is anything but the attitude. The characters with whom I have to contend are stormy inhabitants of my being: they are not *mine*. If anything, I am at risk of becoming theirs, for they take over my faculties for their purposes. I think that for many novelists – I am one – there is something demonic about characters. One's attitude to them, when one is feeling low, is subservient – at any rate, fatalistic. One chronicles them and, with them, their inherent destinies.

Do characters, then, run riot? No, they do not.

There is the plot: that is, the author's intention. And inside that plot (or, situation) and in it only can the characters operate. And, that they may operate the better, the novelist subjects them to an inhuman pressure – keeping them at the alert, and extracting the utmost from them, forcing them along. He exposes them, night and day, to a relentless daylight in which nothing is hid. No human being, other than a fiend, would treat with his fellow humans, in daily life, in so ruthless, uncompromising a manner.

So – the pressure is mutual: fifty-fifty?

One last point. The idea that a novelist's characters *are* "his," and constitute an ever-increasing family, may derive from this – that the characters of even the most excellent, the most fertile, the least repetitive novelist do come to show, onward from book to book, a certain alikeness (almost, a family resemblance) to one another . . . This comes, I would suggest, from the fact that it is by his way of regarding character, characters, that a novelist, inevitably, characterises himself. Also, that his notion of character, characters, may be dominated by some underlying myth – having its source, probably, in childhood. The myth may lead to a re-embodiment of obsessive figures. Vary as his cast does and his plot must, from novel to novel, that myth is a constant – submerge itself deeper and deeper though it may. Hardy, Dickens, Lawrence, the Brontë sisters, to an extent Flaubert, were, surely, myth-dominated novelists? . . . The ideally non-dominated novelist was, I would say, Jane Austen.

The answer to my first question stays in the air: how *are* fictional characters brought about, made effective, given such phenomenal power to affect – to affect us no less than they do each other? What does go on; what is the interlock between characters and their (in name) creators? There *is* – who dares to deny? – the creative process. And this, though it is not magic, cannot be wholly divested of its mystery. May I leave with you my idea? – you may find your own – that the creative activity exercised by the novelist with regard to those characters is a triple one. That is, it has three stages. First, perception of the character *as* a character – whether the origin be conscious memory or the depths of an anonymous mist. Next, reflection: the realising and thoughtful gaze under which the character develops. Third, presentation: the showing of the character in action, throughout the story, as he or she is, within and without – at the full.

What an undertaking! – Forgive us our shortcomings.

FILM AND RADIO

Things to Come

Mr. Wells's *Things to Come* is, above all, spectacular. But it is unlike the run of "spectacle" films, such as Cecil B. de Mille's, with their teeming casts and ultra-gorgeous settings, that excite the eye and stun the imagination and culminate in some monster cataclysm. The technique of *Things to Come* is controlled and quiet, the cast, all things considered, unexpectedly small; the actors being used with such intelligence that not a figure appears without effect. Though the horrors of war, most notably an air raid on an Everytown that is the London of today, appear in the film early, *Things to Come* is memorable not for its use of horror, its power to wring the nerves, but for its command of two important elements: size and rhythm. Detail is used also, with feeling and precision, but dramatic use of detail is not an innovation; it is for its power to present *size* emotionally, to make one feel either an object or an event to be unprecedented, extraordinary, that this film seems to me chiefly remarkable. Except in one or two of the major Russian films (e.g. the shot in *The Fall of St. Petersburg* of the equestrian statue rearing over two peasants' tiny figures) I have never seen sheer enormousness photographed before. Our feeling for size is odd; it is childish and non-rational; one beholds very large objects with feelings of dread and pleasure. Given even the most expert photography, the dimensions of the screen make the representation of size difficult. The Eiffel Tower photographs like a toy. On the screen, the best models, the most (in their first conception) impressive sets too often appear tame, or suggest trickery. Machines and buildings seldom command the screen, dwarf the actor or make us feel their majesty: here they do.

Mr. Wells is a romanticist with a vital attitude towards science. He is an artist with a profound mistrust of art. He is a humanitarian and a moralist first of all: his conception of *Things to Come* lacks both the sternness and the frivolity of an artist's. If the film has a "message," it shows that passion wrecks us, that it is fatal to rate too high a person or an illusion. It is as novelist that his touch here seems to me least happy. He oscillates between the heroic and the domestic. The close-ups of personal drama are not telling; the Cabals and the Passworthys gain little by having been particularised. The women could have stayed cyphers; he chose to make them bores. The dialogue beside the impressive action sounds trivial and once or twice grotesque. Colloquially didactic, almost all sentimental, much of the talk is cackle and I wish he had cut it. His imagination, which is gigantic, works visually: all the drama is here implicit in the actors' movements, and in the situations Mr. Wells creates. There should be less talk – more of Mr. Bliss's magnificent music, with its doomful pulse like distant savage drumming, more sirens, chimes, deadly drone of planes, ruined silences of the old world, humming dynamos of the new. Rhetoric, with a loud-speaker-like, impersonal quality, has, it is true, its place here, and there are some fine passages. But in the best sequences sounds and images fuse, heightening the rhythm.

Some of the shots are beautiful; significant in the high poetic sense. The film might well be seen for these alone; they woo the imagination instead of bludgeoning it. The door of the festive house thrown open on Christmas evening, above it, the anxious searchlights crossing in the sky – the shadow of deadly planes falling on sunny white cliffs – the child running along the cheerful grassy skyline to the crashed plane exuding fatal gas – the savage Boss holding court among cracking pillars and gaping domes, the mutilated architecture of an extinct world – the march of the New Men, black steely figures, up the grass-grown streets of ruined Everytown – the shots of machinery –

The opening passages of the film are realistic (and, consequently, unnerving); the middle is picaresque, with rescues and counterplots. The end seemed pure fantasy; its intention was (at least by me) forgotten in an amused delight of the eye. As the story marches on into the future, ever further from a present that we know as reality, it becomes more abstract. The material, at its outset, is the familiar; at its close, the unknown: then images have to be at once amazing and possible. In making sets for the future Mr. Vincent Korda had so much scope that he might well have lost his head. He seems to me to have kept it admirably. Size – as I said before – and a kind of inexorability make the *mise-en-scène* of 2036 impressive. The dresses were less good – the padded togas for men, the women's cellophane haloes – and came dangerously near the sentimental and tawdry. The most future-like element in the 2036 sequences was the sound: a sort of sea-shell humming inside the galleried, shadowless white town. But unhappily there was again a good deal of talk. The people of 2036 seem at once smug and null.

Mr. Wells being a moralist, it is futile to quarrel with him on account of aesthetic flaws. If this film fully came off it might knock one flat; it does not fully come off because of a constant conflict between moral and poetic intention. It tries to be too comprehensive; its aims are confused. Mr. Alexander Korda has worked magnificently, but he, too, was perplexed, or allowed himself to be sidetracked. All the same, *Things to Come* is a film that grows in the memory. It should be seen for its rolling boldness, the excellence of its lighting, its naïveté, its drama and the unforgettable beauty of some of the shots.

Why I Go to the Cinema

I go to the cinema for any number of different reasons – these I ought to sort out and range in order of their importance. At random, here are a few of them: I go to be distracted (or "taken out of myself"); I go when I don't want to think; I go when I do want to think and need stimulus; I go to see pretty people; I go when I want to see life ginned up, charged with unlikely energy; I go to laugh; I go to be harrowed; I go when a day has been such a mess of detail that I am glad to see even the most arbitrary, the most preposterous, pattern emerge; I go because I like bright light, abrupt shadow, speed; I go to see America, France, Russia; I go because I like wisecracks and slick behaviour; I go because the screen is an oblong opening into the world of fantasy for me; I go because I like story, with its suspense; I go because I like sitting in a packed crowd in the dark, among hundreds riveted on the same thing; I go to have my most general feelings played on.

These reasons, put down roughly, seem to fall under five headings: wish to escape, lassitude, sense of lack in my nature or my surroundings, loneliness (however passing) and natural frivolity. As a writer, I am probably subject during working hours to a slightly unnatural imaginative strain, which leaves me flat and depleted by the end of a day. But though the strain may be a little special in nature, I do not take it to be in any way greater than the strain, the sense of depletion, suffered by other people in most departments of life now. When I take a day off and become a person of leisure, I embark on a quite new method of exhausting myself; I amuse myself through a day, but how arduous that is: by the end of the day I am generally down on the transaction – unless I have been in the country.

I take it that for the professional leisured person things, in the long run, work out the same way. Writers, and other inventive workers, are wrong, I think, in claiming a special privilege, or in representing themselves as unfairly taxed by life: what is taken out of them in some ways is saved them in others; they work, for the most part, in solitude; they are not worn by friction with other people (unless they choose to seek this in their spare time); they have not to keep coming to terms with other people in order to get what they have to do done. They escape monotony; they are sustained in working by a kind of excitement; they are shut off from a good many demands. Their work *is* exhausting, and by human standards unnatural, but it cannot be more exhausting than routine work in office, shop or factory, teaching, running a family, hanging on to existence if one is in the submerged class, or amusing oneself. I make this point in order to be quite clear that my reasons for cinema-going are not unique or special: they would not be worth discussing if they were.

I am not at all certain, either, that the practice of one art gives one a point of vantage in discussing another. Where the cinema is concerned, I am a fan, not a critic. I have been asked to write on "Why I Go to the Cinema" because I do write, and should therefore do so with ease; I have not been asked to write, and am not writing, *as* a writer. It is not as a writer that I go to the cinema; like everyone else, I slough off my preoccupations there. The film I go to see is the product of a kind of art, just as a bottle of wine is the product of a kind of art. I judge the film as I judge the bottle of wine, in its relation to myself, by what it does to me. I sum up the pleasure it gives. This pleasure is, to an extent, an affair of my own palate, or temperament, but all palates and temperaments have something in common; hence general "taste," an accepted, objective standard in judgement of films or wine. Films, like wines, are differently good in their different classes; some of us prefer to seek one kind, some another, but always there is the same end – absolute pleasure – in view.

Cinemas draw all sorts. In factory towns they are packed with factory workers, in university cities with dons, at the seaside with trippers (who take on a strong though temporary character), in the West End with more or less moneyed people with time to kill, in country towns and villages with small tradespeople and with workers scrubbed and hard from the fields. Taste, with these different audiences, differs widely, but the degree of pleasure sought is the same. A film either hits or misses. So affectable are we that to sit through a film that is not pleasing the house, however much it may happen to please one personally, causes restless discomfort that detracts from one's pleasure. (Avoid, for instance, seeing the Marx Brothers in Cork city.) This works both ways: the success of a film with its house communicates a tingling physical pleasure – joining and heightening one's private exhilaration – a pleasure only the most weathered misanthrope could withstand – and your misanthrope is rarely a cinema-goer. There is no mistaking that tension all round in the dark, that almost agonised tension of a pleased house – the electric hush, the rapt immobility. The triumphantly funny film, hitting its mark, makes even laughter break off again and again, and the truly tragic suspends the snuffle.

The happily constituted cinema-goer learns to see and savour a positive merit in films that may do nothing to him personally, films whose subjects, stars or settings may to him, even, be antipathetic. To reject as any kind of experience a film that is acting powerfully on people round seems to me to argue poverty in the nature. What falls short as aesthetic experience may do as human experience: the film rings no bell in oneself, but one hears a bell ring elsewhere. This has a sort of value, like being in company with a very popular person one does not oneself dislike but who does not attract one. Popularity ought to confer a sort of hallmark, not have to be taken up as a challenge. I speak of the happily constituted cinema-goer – I mean, perhaps, the happily constituted, and therefore very rare, person. The generality of us, who hate jokes we cannot see and mysteries we are out of, may still hope to become sophisticates in at least this one pleasure by bringing with us, when we go to a cinema, something more active, more resourceful than tolerance. This is worthwhile: it doubles our chance of that fun for which we paid at the box-office. To my mind, any truly popular film is worth seeing – granted one happens to have the time and money to spare. I say, *truly* popular film, the film that after release has triumphantly stayed the course; not the *should-be* popular film, the film stuck with big names or inflated beforehand by misleading publicity. If nothing else, the popular film I don't like adds to my knowledge of what I don't like and don't want. One's own apathies are complex and interesting.

Films have – it is a truism of the trade – a predetermined destination. Every film made makes a bid for the favour of certain localities whose taste has been gauged in advance, correctly or not. Local appeal, at its strongest, is strongly delimited. If one is to go to a film for its popularity-interest, one should go to it in its own country – its areas may be social, not geographic, though largely they *are* geographic, for climate and occupation do condition an audience. For instance, my great respect for Miss Gracie Fields[1] does not alter the fact that I would not willingly see, for its own sake, at my nearest London cinema, a film in which she appeared. But I should feel I had missed something if I missed seeing a Gracie Fields film in the Gracie Fields country. There she operates in full force, and I cannot fail to react – to the audience, if not to her. I see a great girl in play. The comedian's hold on his or her own public is hard to analyse: in some cases (such as Miss Fields') it has a strong moral element. Or it may have a healthily anti-moral element. The determining factor must, I think, be social: hard-living people like to have someone to admire; they like what is like themselves. The sophisticated are attracted, titillated, by what is foreign, outrageous, by what they may half deplore.

But it would be misleading, as well as precious, to overstress this rest-of-the-audience factor in my reaction to films. I do really only like what *I* like, I go to please myself, and when I sit opposite a film the audience is *me*. My faculties are riveted, my pleasure can only be a little damped down or my disappointment added to by the people cheek by jowl with me in the dark. I expect a good deal, when I go to the cinema: my expectations absorb me from the moment I enter. I am giving myself a treat – or being given a treat. I have little spare time or money, the cinema is my anodyne, not my subject, and my objective interest in its emotional mechanics is not really very great. Nine times out of ten, it is alert, exacting expectations of pleasure that carry me to the cinema. The tenth time I may go from abstract curiosity, or at random – as when I have hours to pass in a strange town where it is raining or there are no buildings to see. This tenth time I will discount; it is seldom serious – though it does sometimes turn out to have started up a new fancy, or left a residue of interest behind.

I expect, then, to enjoy myself. This end I do all I can to further by taking as good a seat as my purse, that day, will allow – a seat giving room for my knees, in which I need not tip my head back or keep craning my neck round, and from which I have an undistorted view of the screen. (In the up-to-date cinema this last, of course, is all right in all seats.) Cramp or any other physical irritation militates quite unfairly against the best film: if a film is worth seeing at all they seem to me worth avoiding. Sometimes I can't avoid them: if a film is booming I'm lucky to get in at all, and have to sit where I can. But there is a good deal in waiting till the first rush is over, then seeing the film in comfort: a film, I try to remind myself, doesn't lose quality in the course of its run, and the urge to see it at once may be sheer vulgar topicality. Anyhow, I seek comfort – and how important smoking is. I start slightly against the best film in a foreign cinema where I am unable to smoke. Very great films (generally Russian) and moments in any good film do suspend my desire to smoke: this is the supreme test.

I have – like, I suppose every other cinema-goer – a physical affection for certain cinemas. In London the Empire is my favourite; when I settle down in there I feel I am back in the old home, and am predisposed to happiness. May it never come down. I suppose I could rationalise my feeling for the Empire by saying I like Metro-Goldwyn-Mayer films – but though I have enjoyed these all over Europe, the last drop of pleasure is added by being at the Empire. However, one must take films not only as but where one finds them. In the provinces, I have often had to desert my favourite cinema in order to see a promising film elsewhere: this gave the evening, though the film might prove excellent, an undertone of nostalgia: "I wish this were at the Such-and-such." The sentiment was absurd, and is only mentioned because I think it is general. Pleasure is at its best when it has in it some familiar element. And the pleasure-seeker has a difficult temperament; he is often as captious as a spoilt beauty, as whimsical as a child, and given to fretting against conditions not in his power to change. This may be because, in most cases, he goes to his pleasure tired. He does not know what he wants, but he knows when he does not get it. It is for him – myself – that the cinema caters; and how much the cinema has to overcome!

I hope never to go to the cinema in an entirely unpropitious mood. If I do, and am not amused, that is my fault, also my loss. As a rule, I go empty but hopeful, like someone bringing a mug to a tap that may not turn on. The approach tunes me up for pleasure. The enchantment that hung over those pre-war façades of childhood – gorgeously white stucco façades, with caryatids and garlands – has not dissolved, though the façades have been changed. How they used to beam down the street. Now concrete succeeds stucco and chromium gilt; foyers once crimson and richly stuffy are air-conditioned and dove-grey. But, like a chocolate-box lid, the entrance is still voluptuously promising: sensation of some sort seems to be guaranteed. How happily I tread the pneumatic carpet, traverse anterooms with their exciting muted vibration, and walk down the spotlit aisle with its eager tilt to the screen. I climb over those knees to the sticky velvet seat, and fumble my cigarettes out – as I used not to do.

I am not only home again, but am, if my choice is lucky, in ideal society. I am one of the millions who follow Names from cinema to cinema. The star system may be all wrong – it has implications I hardly know of in the titanic world of Hollywood, also it is, clearly, a hold-up to proper art – but I cannot help break it down. I go to see So-and-so. I cannot fitly quarrel with this magnification of personalities, while I find I can do with almost unlimited doses of anybody exciting, anybody with beauty (in my terms), verve, wit, style, *toupet*[2] and, of course, glamour. What do I mean by glamour? A sort of sensuous gloss: I know it to be synthetic, but it affects me strongly. It is a trick knowingly practised on my most fuzzy desires; it steals a march on me on my silliest side. But all the same, in being subject to glamour I experience a sort of elevation. It brings, if not into life at least parallel to it, a sort of fairy-tale element. It is a sort of trumpet call, mobilising the sleepy fancy. If a film is to get across, glamour somewhere, in some form – moral, if you like, for it can be moral – cannot be done without. The Russians break with the bourgeois-romantic conception of personality; they have scrapped sex-appeal as an annexe of singularising, anti-social love. But they still treat with glamour; they have transferred it to mass movement, to a heroicised pro-human emotion. I seek it, in any form.

To get back to my star: I enjoy, sitting opposite him or her, the delights of intimacy without the onus, high points of possession without the strain. This could be called inoperative love. Relationships in real life are made arduous by their reciprocities; one can too seldom simply sit back. The necessity to please, to shine, to make the most of the moment, overshadows too many meetings. And apart from this – how seldom in real life (or so-called real life) does acquaintanceship, much less intimacy, with dazzling, exceptional beings come one's way. How very gladly, therefore, do I fill the gaps in my circle of ideal society with these black-and-white personalities, to whom absence of colour has added all the subtleties of tone. Directly I take my place I am on terms with these Olympians; I am close to them with nothing at all at stake. Rapture lets me suppose that for me alone they display the range of their temperaments, their hesitations, their serious depths. I find them not only dazzling but sympathetic. They live for my eye. Yes, and I not only perceive them but *am* them; their hopes and fears are my own; their triumphs exalt me. I am proud for them and in them. Not only do I enjoy them; I enjoy in them a vicarious life.

Nevertheless, I like my stars well supported. If a single other character in the film beside them be unconvincing or tin-shape, the important illusion weakens; something begins to break down. I like to see my star played up to and played around by a cast that is living, differentiated and definite. The film must have background, depth, its own kind of validity. Hollywood, lately, has met this demand: small parts are being better and better played. Casts are smallish, characters clear-cut, action articulated.[3] (Look at *It Happened One Night*, *She Married Her Boss*, *My Man Godfrey*.) There is family-feeling inside a good film – so that the world it creates is valid, water-tight, *probable*.

What a gulf yawns between improbability – which is desolating – and fantasy – which is dream-probability, likeliness on an august, mad plane. Comedy films show this fantasy element more strongly than tragedies, which attempt to approach life and fail too often through weakness and misrepresentation: comedies are thus, as a rule, better. A really good comic (a Laurel and Hardy, for instance) is never simply improbable: it suspends judgement on the workaday plane. Comedy-drama needs some verisimilitude.

When I say verisimilitude, I do not mean that I want the film to be exactly *like* life: I should seldom go to the cinema if it were. The effective film (other, of course, than the film that is purely documentary) must have at least a touch of the preposterous. But its distance from life, or from probability, should stay the same throughout: it must keep inside its pitch. The film that keeps in its pitch makes, and imposes, a temporary reality of its own.

Any cinema-goer, however anxious for peace and for his own pleasure, may detect in a film a *gaffe* that he cannot pass. I quarrel most, naturally, with misrepresentations of anything that I happen to know about. For instance, I have, being Irish, seen few films about Ireland, or set in Ireland, that did not insult and bore me. (*The Informer*[4] was one remarkable exception.) But I could sit through a (no doubt) equally misrepresenting film about Scotland, which I do not know, without turning a hair. I know only a very small part of America – and that superficially – so that American films can take almost any licence with me. In fact, years of cinema-going probably did condition my first view of America: I felt as though I were stepping into the screen. Dreamlike familiarity in the streets and landscapes not only endeared the country but verified the cinema. But I cannot know how greatly Hollywood's representations, however idyllic, of New England small towns may offend New Englanders, or how cardboardy, to the Southerner, may seem the screen face of the Old Colonial Home. I cannot challenge falseness in setting, detail or manners past the point where my experience stops. As a woman, I am annoyed by improbability in clothes: English films offend rather badly in this way. Dressy at all costs, the English heroines hike, run down spies or reclaim lovers from storm-girt islands in their Kensington High Street Sunday bests. An equal unlikeliness blights the English film interior: I revolt from

ancestral homes that are always Gothic, from Louis Seize bed-
rooms in poverty-stricken manors, from back-street dwellings
furnished by Mr. Drage. The frumpy and unsatirical flatness of
the average English stage-set is almost always transferred by the
English film to the screen. The French make *genre* films in which
every vase, tassel and door-handle thickens the atmosphere,
makes for verisimilitude and adds more to the story: why cannot
we do the same?

Why are there so few English *genre* films? All over this
country, indoors and out, a photographable drama of national
temperament is going on, and every object has character. By-
passes, trees on skylines, small country town streets with big
buses pushing along them, village Sundays, gasometers showing
behind seaside towns, half-built new estates, Midland canals, the
lounges of private hotels, stucco houses with verandas, rectory
tea-tables, the suburban shopping rush, garden fêtes and the
abstract perspectives of flyblown, semi-submerged London are
all waiting the camera and are very dramatic. English interiors
are highly characterised; English social routine is romantically
diverse. As it is, the same few shots – which might, from their
symbolic conventionality, have been made to be exported to
Hollywood – drearily re-appear, to give English films their local-
ity: Westminster Bridge, crazy gables stuck with oak beams,
corners of (apparently) Oxford colleges masquerading as Great
Homes, clotted orchards (that might be faked with a few rolls
of crêpe paper), the spire of always the same church, and those
desolating, unconvincing, always-the-same rooms. There are
exceptions to this – Anthony Asquith shows feeling for landscape, and Hitchcock gets humour into interiors – but not
nearly enough exceptions. Generally speaking, English films lack
humour in the perceptive, sympathetic and wide sense. They lack
sensibility; they do not know how to use objects. Are we blind
to our country? Too many English films are, humanly speaking,
dead. Character in them is tin-shape and two-dimensional. The
whole effect is laborious, genteel, un-adult and fussy. Comedies,
technically "clean," are unbearably vulgar; there is no fun, only
knockabout and facetiousness. It is true that we are beginners,
that we have admittedly much to learn, still, in the way of technique. But we fail in more than technique; we fail, flatly and
fatally, in conception.

At present it appears, discouragingly enough, that to make outstanding films one must either be sophisticated, like some Americans; disabused and witty, like the French; vividly neurotic, like the Germans; or noble, like the Russians. One must know how to use convention, and when to break with it. One must either, like the Russians, take the heroic view, or else be iconoclastic, racy, though still know what to honour. One must have an eye for what is essential, telling, in action, scene or face. One must know how to hitch one's particular invention on to the general dream. Human fantasies are general; the film, to live, must discover, feed and command these.

I am discussing, throughout, the "story" (or "entertainment") film. That is the film I go to see; I go to the cinema for amusement only; my feeling for it may be exceptionally frivolous. I more than admire, I am often absorbed by, good "interest," or documentary films that may occur in a programme, but, as these are not the films I seek, I do not feel that I am qualified to discuss them. I go for what is untrue, to be excited by what is fantastic, to see what has never happened happen. I go for the fairy story. I state – I do not see why this should rank as a confession – that I would rather see a film in which a (probably doped) lion brings a tense plot to a close by eating a millionaire than the most excellent film about lions in their wild state, roving about and not furthering any plot. If I am to see a documentary film, I prefer what I can only describe with Lower-form vagueness as "films about foreign countries" – preferably, European countries. I like to get some idea how foreigners spend their day – and the incidental beauty of "interest" films is often very great, their rhythm admirable. But I have very little curiosity, and an inordinate wish to be entertained. If many more cinema-goers were as lazy-minded and fantasy-loving as I am what a pity it would be – but I take it that I am in a minority. I hope that the cinema may develop along all lines, while still giving me many more of the films I like – grown-up comedies, taut thrillers, finished period pieces and dashing Westerns. I want no more American tragedies, Russian comedies or crepitating Teutonic analysis. I should like still more dramatic use of landscape and architecture. I like almost any French film – perhaps I have been lucky. I have rather dreaded beforehand, as one dreads drastic experience, any Russian film I have seen; have later wished, while it lasted, to protract every moment, and finally found it, when it was over, more powerful than a memory – besides everything else, there had been so much more fun than one foresaw.

I am shy of the serious aspect of my subject, and don't want to finish on an unnaturally high note. It is, of course, clear to me that a film, like any other attempt on art, or work of art – all being tentative – can have in it germs of perfection. Its pretension to an aesthetic need be no less serious than that of a poem, picture or piece of music. Its medium, which is unique to it, is important: fluid pattern, variation of light, speed. In time, the cinema has come last of all the arts; its appeal to the racial child in us is so immediate that it should have come first. Pictures came first in time, and bore a great weight of meaning: "the pictures" date right back in their command of emotion: they are inherently primitive. A film can put the experience of a race or a person on an almost dreadfully simplified epic plane.

We have promise of great art here, but so far few great artists. Films have not caught up with the possibilities of the cinema: we are lucky when we get films that keep these in sight. Mechanics, the immense technical knowledge needed, have kept the art, as an art, unnaturally esoteric; its technical progress (more and more discoveries: sound, now colour) moves counter to its spiritual progress. An issue keeps on being obscured, a problem added to. Yet we have here, almost within our grasp, a means to the most direct communication possible between man and man. What might be a giant instrument is still a giant toy.

How much I like films I like – but I could like my films better. I like being distracted, flattered, tickled, even rather upset – but I should not mind something more; I should like something serious. I should like to be changed by more films, as art can change one: I should like something to happen when I go to the cinema.

Third Programme

It is news for Britain that culture should make news. As a start, of course, we are shy of the word; and perhaps we always shall be; and perhaps rightly. Rather than "culture," then, let me say "art." The metamorphosis of wartime with regard to music, literature and drama has been commented on; but comment must still be delicate and go slowly.

George Barnes is the Third Programme's Head; Etienne Amyot is in charge of planning; Leslie Stokes in charge of presentation and publicity. Close teamwork was essential from the beginning. Because the Programme is not merely a loose, hopeful assemblage of good ideas; it is a concept, a whole, and must have its own kind of unity. It must combine range with consistency, progressive elasticity with character. To talk with George Barnes is to realise how definitely the Third Programme is a unity for him. Not, be it said, something set, closed, static; on the contrary, something receptive, open and on the move. He aspires not merely to see it stay the course; he envisages, constantly, its development. He is aware twice over of the vitality of relationship – that of the part (or individual broadcast) to the whole, and that of the programme as a whole to its public.

Its public – the idea of "specialness" in the exclusive sense is, George Barnes made me feel, to be combated. Be clear: the aim is not to discriminate between people (thereby grading listeners, invidiously, into classes) but to make people discriminate for themselves. Creativeness, the creative use of radio, is the function and *raison d'être* of the Third Programme. But this implies interaction – how can it not? To an extent, the programme is to create the listener: not less, the listener is to create the programme – by his response, mobility, curiosity, sensitiveness and willingness in approach to the not yet known. Third Programme is out to take long chances and risk wide shots: anybody in sympathy with that is the potential Third Programme listener. It is up to the planners and artists to see that perspectives keep opening up. Here is a chance to answer the "But-why-can-we-never-have . . . ?" school.

One idea, or ideal, is dominant: performance – not merely the *what* of the broadcasting but the *how*. It was high time that, in Britain, we had again what Third Programme is not ashamed to stand for: a demand for the best. War and the slow recovery have been in all fields threatening us with a loss of standard: isolation, restrictions, substitutes and make-do's bred a resignation, or thankfulness for anything in any form, which could affect art badly if we were not pulled clear. Aesthetically our senses need resharpening: the Third Programme's perfectionism (as some see it) may be hard to take, may be antagonising, but it is bracing. Stress on style, manner, execution, if necessary virtuosity – can we, now, have too much of that? War on the slurred, the sagging, the slovenly – *can* that be carried too far? In music, demonstrably not. So far, Third Programme towers on its musical side – the policy of extending knowledge and taste, of inviting and inducing discrimination, has been declared and stuck to: it may be felt at work.

Third Programme will soon have completed its first six months: already there is, to note, one novel exciting trend – a Europeanism of outlook. This shows in the fair – though still, necessarily, cautious – proportion of contemporary foreign work; drama, music, poetry, philosophic discussion. War having set up a time-lag in our artistic contacts – yes, and our intellectual contacts too

– we have an immense amount to catch up with. We need exactly the stimulus outside thought can supply. Continental artists come to Third Programme studios – and, as soon as it becomes technically possible, performances from theatres and opera houses of the Continent will be to be heard. As fast as Europe is opened up, Third Programme hopes to extend its range. Hopes, also, to be reciprocal – to give back: at present it cannot be heard across the Channel.

In these directions it will be necessary, of course, to go gently – and persuasively gentle is still the pace. George Barnes has high hopes of building up a British public for foreign language listening: why not, for instance, one act of Barrault's (Paris) *Hamlet*, in Barrault's French, followed by the same act as played here by, say, Gielgud? The interest of comparing the two techniques, the two different applications of emotion pressure, would – even for those who may not understand French – be endless. Language can put out a majesty in its sheer sound, even apart from sense: in poetry and, at its greatest, prose, this becomes apparent. My own feeling is that in listening to spoken (or broadcast) speech, we have listened for sense too much and for sound too little. However, the intelligent listener's wish for *intelligibility* must take first place still – Sartre's *Huis Clos* in English gave him enough to bite on!

In the matter of drama, Third Programme is always casting around. The high merits of a play *as* a play still may not make it suitable as an air form. The air-performed drama should have this aspiration: not only not to lose but to *gain* from the invisibility of the actors. This rules out any play that relies, for instance, on purely visual effect – the significant tableau, pose or grouping.

Obviously, poetic drama must score, from the fact of its pace, movement and colour being in the words and the delivery of the words. The dramatic formality of the classics has made these ideal – the *Agamemnon* of Aeschylus and the *Hippolytus* of Euripides have not only been superb experiences for the listener, they have taught lessons. Lessons, because it becomes clearer and clearer that we need drama writing, on a high plane, specially *for* the air: in response, our contemporary dramatist-poets, excited by the possibilities of the new form, are coming across. Patric Dickinson's *The Wall of Troy*, Laurie Lee's *The Voyage of Magellan*, Louis MacNeice's *The Careerist*, Henry Reed's adaptation of *Moby Dick* have been high-watermarks: they have put broadcasting right in the forefront with a new kind of contemporary theatre.

In fact, to have missed the above, and other Third Programme features, is to be nowhere. Let's face it, there *is* a considerable influence in fashion, and Third Programme looks like making listening to radio the fashion, instead of a mere domestic resort.

With regard to this, one must note a highly intelligent, and often emphasised, factor in the Third Programme policy: that of "repeats." Any important item goes back again on the air, a number of times: if you missed it one evening, you can hear it the next. (None the less, "planned listening" does remain an imperative: the broadcast date of the item you want to hear should be ringed round, in your engagement book, just as much as the dinner or lunch engagement.) "Repeats" have worked splendidly all along the line – they give more base and point to radio criticism (which used to be totally retrospective) and they are encouraging to the creative writer, who used to regret the hour-short life of the piece into which he had put so much.

To attract in writers – hitherto recalcitrant or suspicious – and to kindle them with the idea of new possibilities, has been the aim of George Barnes and his inspiring team: they are more and more succeeding.

Rightly or wrongly – I think in the main wrongly – writers have feared constraint from the BBC. Highbrows have shied away from the ordeal of a vast, mixed, popular, unseen audience, to whom repugnant concession in matters of style, approach or ego would have, apparently, to be made. This inhibition had to be broken down.

Third Programme issues a sort of psychological invitation (or is it challenge?) which is exciting – "Go on: be yourself!" A warming blend of freedom and intimacy. Up to now, one would *not* have called the British a race of natural broadcasters – a stilted or patronising caginess tends to rule; spontaneity is lacking. The literary artist, in particular – addict of small circles and private life – tends to mutton-freeze in front of the microphone, as in front of the camera. Now, perhaps, Third Programme's ice-breaking technique may have vital results?

Yes, Third Programme is now well away on its course. Like a not yet expert cyclist, it has wobbled and described a few wild loops; but it is headed the way it means to go. As listeners, how are we coming along? At present for five rather than six hours every evening, Third Programme is on the air. Radios are still in short supply: if there *is* more than one in this winter's average home, there is usually only one room heated in which to listen, which comes to the same thing.

Conflicts of "family listening" have to resolve themselves. The two other programmes, "Home" and "Light," both show a rise in quality and attractive power – Third Programme has *not*, as some people feared, stolen thunder or skimmed the cream from the other two: on the contrary, it seems to have given stimulus, so that "Home" and "Light," on their merits, are bidding more and more worthily for attention. So, in the family, the would-be Third Programme listener must (which will do him no harm) manœuvre for listening time. The solitary, with his radio to himself, or the dweller among congenials, naturally scores.

Again, it must be taken into account that the hours Third Programme is on the air *are* those of the brainworker's recreation – to engage him, broadcasting must compete with books, periodicals, movies, party-going, conversation and the pursuit of love. Quite a challenge . . . Third Programme, however, as has been set down, does *not* desire hypnotised non-stop listening. It plans to be planned for – and to reward the planning. Socially it is beginning to be a factor, by crystallising, defining around itself a classless new class – the perceptive seeker of pleasure.

I offer my impression of what Third Programme is, aims at and stands for. As to what it *ought* to be, aim at, stand for, controversy, of course, does not cease to rage.

Radio critics, as to this issue, have taken the field with zest. At present, battle is joined between W. E. Williams, of the *Observer*, and Edward Sackville-West, *New Statesman*. Williams accuses Third Programme of narrow aestheticism: it caters exclusively, he says, for that out-of-date exquisite, "the man of sensibility." Does, he asks, Third Programme truly claim to be adult? – then, not perhaps all but considerable programme space should go to economics, social science, science, world affairs, political free debate. In brief, W. E. Williams wants Third Programme to be more adult-educational, less aesthetic; more, as *he* sees things, contemporary. (He also thinks the tone too intense; *would* like a few experiments in the funny . . .)

Edward Sackville-West, for his part, supports Third Programme's present policy and would like more of it: he looks on aesthetic radio, the creative broadcast, as keeping a torch alight: Third Programme is giving something that nothing else can; something essential to the survival, and to the growth as certainly, of the inner man. Sackville-West cannot see why Third Programme need, or should, act as substitute for journalism, the lecture platform or the debating club. This critic finds Third Programme, as now shaping, the most important civilising influence of our day. He comes out strong for performance, as against information – in this programme he says, "broadcasting aspires to the condition of opera."

Lawrence of Arabia

It was in Seville last January that I first encountered the men who were making and acting in the film *Lawrence of Arabia*. They were a company as bleached and bony as Desert Rats,[1] and as knit-together – veterans by that time of a campaign which, in toughening bodies and spirits, had bred a confederacy quite like no other. They had come together through a dread desert summer, against the advice of all the experts, where the heat mounted to 125 degrees. They had been known in Jordan where the first part of the picture was made as "Lean's Mobile Maniacs." Now, they were back amid amenities long foregone. Orange tree planted squares, streets lively yet leisured, friendly hotels, baths, bars, restaurants, luxury shops give Seville all civilisation's gloss – and glamour.

The story of Lawrence is a story of desert wastes, but it is also a tale of three cities: Cairo, Jerusalem and Damascus. That same Jordanian desert, which forty years before had seen the exploits of Lawrence and his Arabs, served in the film for the desert sequences. The city episodes presented a problem. Since

Lawrence's day, these three Arab centres had been so transformed that the 1916–18 settings no longer existed in them. In Seville the director, David Lean, found his substitute. Today, in architecture and atmosphere, old Spain is more Moorish than the modern Middle East. Seville still has sunken courtyards, drowsy fountains, mysterious archways and twisted, cryptic streets. And to the palm-plumed skylines, Lean and Sam Spiegel, the producer, added minarets and Mohammedan-looking domes.

A small, self-aware city in which an important picture is being made grows, psychically, larger by one dimension. A sort of hallucination was in the air, thrillingly – Lawrence of Arabia pervaded Seville. Bizarre, beautiful, ancient monuments – already dating back through how many centuries, the scenes of how many momentous doings – now were stage turning points in the Lawrence drama. Casa de Pilatos (which has its still more ancient original in Jerusalem) and the Alcazar, eleventh-century Arabic fortress, were God's gift to Lean and his cameramen for the shooting of several confrontations between Lawrence and General Allenby. One night, the Alcazar's water gardens mirrored crimson skies: "Damascus" was burning. And here in Seville streets was re-enacted the other city's liberation.

Hallucination headquarters were, however, at the edge of the city, and it was there that I met Peter O'Toole, the film's Lawrence. O'Toole, a twenty-nine-year-old star of the Royal Theatre, Stratford-on-Avon, is taller than T. E. Lawrence was, and, though a little more than a year older than Lawrence was when the adventure opened, is younger looking. He is blessed (though also possibly burdened in this context) with effulgent good looks. Against those, presumably, he had to play – for the reason that Lawrence's physical personality, though not bad, counted for little. That spare, smallish, energy-taut form was dominated, surely, by its intensity. With it went long head, bone-carven features and jutting brows which encaved the commanding eyes. As a type, he was cerebral. His "youthful look" sometimes referred to seems to have been a matter of ruffled hair, whippet-like quickness, non-weighty build and, in general, mannerism. Flowing Arab getup conferred a majesty unknown to his figure in other guise – it brought out a latent majesty. Fascination he did exert, glamour surely not.[2]

O'Toole's own inadvertent glamour had to be sternly played

down. O'Toole, brachycephalic, has a wide face compared to Lawrence's – but it is an actor's face, so much in itself a theatre that, when emptied for a moment, it appears unlike itself. Something about this actor at once dispels any doubt that he can play Lawrence – and not only play him, be him. He checked out Lawrence, he told me, when shooting stopped for a day, and returned to reminding himself that he was himself. He was scarred by one Lawrence habit, that of extinguishing matches by pressing the flame to death between thumb and finger. The O'Toole thumb and finger, by then, were thickly calloused, but it still hurt. He had not yet, he said, learned the Lawrence "trick" of not minding pain.

My Seville visit, by chance, coincided with the shooting of the Town Hall scenes and gave me a chance to see O'Toole at his peak. In the Robert Bolt script, Damascus has been but yesterday freed from the Turks by the Arabs. The Town Hall – the Casino of the Teatro Lope de Vega – is packed with a delirious mob electric with pent-up forces – clash on clash could break out, chaos could follow. From a dais, the triumvirate responsible for the Arab victory (Lawrence, Auda Ibu Tayi, Ali Ibn El Kharish) dominate those below them. Lesser Arab chieftains, arms ready at hand, are seated around a horseshoe table. White-robed and white with tension, Lawrence sits at the centre; on his right, the great overweening arrogant old Auda (Anthony Quinn); on his left, the fiery, proud young Ali (Omar Sharif), his nerves a hair trigger. Enmity has long smouldered between these two. Should it break out now – what? Victory thrown away, Lawrence, impaled on a crisis, glares at everyone and at no one, beating a pistol on the table, crying aloud: "We are Arabs." The Robert Bolt script reads excitingly. The dialogue is hard-hitting and economic: terse in the British sequences, more oblique in the Arab ones. Not a "big speech" throughout. Now one sees in action all the virtue of the script's restraint, a restraint that serves to build up an effect of contained force dangerously often nearing explosion point.

The actors break. Out in the winter sun on the garden terraces Bedouin-garbed extras chain-smoke or snooze in cocoons of drapery. Of the close on 2,000 Spaniards hired for the crowd scenes, the largest recruitment came from Spanish gypsies, faces narrow with melancholy. From Jordan, Lean and Spiegel brought three somewhat jaded camels. Outside the Casino, the camels, always in profile, sneer at spectators plastered, entranced, against the gates. The gates are set in fences bushy with jasmine – beyond them a new-type boulevard stretches into the distance: all is pale-bright. What and where is reality? Out here, or in there?

In the Casino again, under the gaudy glaze dome, passion-pressure mounts – will the dome blow up? Cameras sweep, dip, over the hot-lit multitude intermittently hotly roaring – heaving there on the floor or wedged in balconies in Moorish arches upborne by Ionic columns. Gilt-and-bright-green, the Casino's interior glitters, groans in the throes of chimeric agony. Again, again, the pistol thumps on the table. Everybody is sweating – in the desert, even, can they have sweated more?

Lawrence of Arabia will be great cinema or it will be nothing. I cannot foresee that it will be nothing. A Shakespeare subject, handled in a screen-Shakespeare manner. Words at the minimum, silences are soliloquies. Visual is the poetry: torrential action acts like torrents of language.

Lean says, "Every motion picture has a point at which an audience feels it can relax and light a cigarette. I should like to present *Lawrence of Arabia* in such a way that no audience will ever be able to get a cigarette lit."

He means for almost four hours. Shall *I* be able to get a cigarette lit? If I get a cigarette lit, I shall be surprised.

APPRECIATIONS

Downe House Scrap-Book 1907–1957

I was at Downe from September 1914 to the end of the summer term 1917. This was "the old Downe House" – final home of Charles Darwin, at the edge of Downe village, near Orpington, Kent. In another sense, it was the *new* Downe House: the school had been in existence for not more than seven years. There were still girls there who had been there "at the beginning," or from at any rate near it. I remember this interest attached to Augusta Burn, who was in the Sixth Form when I arrived, and to my own contemporary Mary Winkworth – who must, if this *was* true about her, at the start have been one of the very little ones.

To me, as a new girl, the school did not feel new – looking back I suppose that it hardly could have. Even so, I can see it had taken only a short time for Downe to acquire identity and meaning. I found it hard to believe that generations had not been there before me: everybody seemed very sure of themselves – and for some reason, to the comer-in from outside, this was not alarming but reassuring. One was plunged straight, deep, into the middle of *something*. The absorption with which everybody lived – and, with that, the curious, quick, characteristic, psychological pace – made one unselfconscious; or, at any rate, as nearly so as it is possible to be in one's teens. The only nightmare at that transitional age is a shifting universe: Downe seemed a deep-set stable one. I remember feeling up against several things, but it pleased me that there things *were*, for me to be up against. Even resistance helped me to get my bearings.

Architectural growth marked the growth of the school in more concrete ways. Almost every term, certainly every year, there was further building activity on the part of Miss Nickel – concrete-floored, metal-roofed annexes, from whose wood-lined walls winter heating drew out a smell of creosote, swastika-ed farther and farther out into the garden. The gaunt passage in which we hung up our purple overcoats and seemed to be for ever changing our shoes, the high pea-green Gymnasium with the stage at the end, the washroom and the three or four music-rooms already existed when I arrived; the Chapel came into being during my second year – an austere achievement in naked concrete. In a way, I was sorry to have this supersede the original "Chapel," a white-washed ex-bedroom up on the top floor. For everything slightly irregular, improvised, amateurish about the original Downe was dear to me. I suppose I had from the beginning a sort of dread of anything which could feel like "an institution" – therefore I feel it a tribute to Miss Nickel to say that her outbuildings had a Kafka-like oddness. Their acoustics, their perspectives, their ventilation were peculiar to themselves. Not less, there was something in an elegant way ramshackle about the main Downe House – one of those vaguely Regency country houses with amorphous, large-windowed, Victorian extra rooms, which suit the vague, airy, flowing landscape of Kent.

I understand that one reason why the move from the "old" Downe to the present Downe was made was that, apart from increasing numbers, we girls were beginning to wear out the fabric of the house. (I suppose that the British Association have made it good again.)[1] There cannot, I suppose, even when I left, have been many more than seventy of us, but even so, at release-points during the day and evening, our cattle-like gatherings and stampedings were sufficient to make the structure rock. "Need you *rush*?" Miss Willis constantly used to say, looking at us with a distaste which concealed affection.

Miss Willis's attitude, throughout, was far less "Don't" than "Need you?" There was always something speculative, detached, about her criticisms, which was probably why they took such deep effect with us. In fact, they were not so much criticisms as invitations – to be taken up or not, as we thought well – to criticise ourselves, plus suggestions (only just not tentative) as to what lines to take if we chose to do so. I recall no feeling that she was "managing" us. And this power to indicate, to set going, was, I suppose, some part of that other side of her genius – that of the teacher. Her feeling against direct "instruction" must have influenced her choice of the teaching staff – in the former family sitting-rooms which were Downe classrooms, I remember having no *facts* drilled into my brain – which did not mean we were not expected to know them. "Bitha,"[2] exclaimed Miss Morgan-Brown, swooping on me in the course of a lesson, "you are not listening." "I'm sorry, Miss Morgan-Brown," I said, "but I'm still thinking about what you said last." "Well," said Miss Morgan-Brown, "you must think later."

Miss Heather was so great a mathematician as never to humiliate the stupid – that is, the stupid as to her subject. Respecting any desire to understand, she allowed for inhibitions which worked against it. She honoured the mind, of whatever kind it might be. Science lessons with her, in the tiny laboratory which had been the final domain of Darwin, were memorable. I imagine that in these days, those afternoon sessions would be called "elementary physics." I at least learned how not to blow myself up with a retort – but chiefly the lessons gave occasion for philosophic dialogues with Miss Heather. The Laboratory, with its burners, was also used for the mystic cooking lessons of Miss Nickel – nothing since has ever tasted so good as those beefsteak-and-kidney puddings, infiltrated (under her instruction) by many cloves. Originating – we gathered – in central Europe, Miss Nickel taught us that suet *can* be flavourous. Her brown, belted, monk-like robe (one could not say overall) strongly exhaled a smell of machine-oil. Spying through the windows of the small engine room, on the way to the orchard, one saw, often, Miss Nickel obsessed by her central task.

How taxing it must have been to keep a school "running," in any or all senses, during the First World War, we did not compute. I cannot imagine the Downe House of my day without "the war" – Miss Willis's address to us, my first evening, was based on the outbreak, and the thing still was a year short of its conclusive agonies when I left. My generation, accordingly, grew up with a horror of being *bouches inutiles*.[3] I can't claim, however, that the war was borne in upon us the whole time – I don't think Miss Willis intended it should be so. She was in favour of our thinking of everything as transient, including and particularly our schooldays. She reminded us, we would not be at school for ever. This may be why Downe (as far as I know) has not turned out that saddest of English products, "the perpetual schoolgirl."

The greatest crime, as I remember Downe, was silliness. Or it was at least the crime of which one was most aware, as being the most dreary, the most mortifying. Some of us tried to get the silliness out of our systems by travestying it – mock cults, mock crazes, cultivated inanities of speech. The bad thing was to be "affected" without knowing it – that was, without deliberately affecting to *be* affected. In the main, the view we took of ourselves was drastic. I fancy this did no harm. And we were eased, the school being in the country, by all round us the beautiful superabundant sillinesses of Nature. Lovingly do I remember the cuckoos, too near, too many, too non-stop, making themselves cheap, flumping and battering on the tin roof of Miss Nickel's ultimate masterpiece, the Chalet. Summer at Downe was full of the smells of hay; clumps of azaleas smouldered on the enormous lawn. In the Cudham valley, there were reputed to be nightingales.

I have written about Downe House before, for a Graham Greene collection entitled *The Old School*. My piece was reprinted elsewhere, as "The Mulberry Tree." I do not want to repeat myself, so I omit from here what I there said. Actually, there is still so much to say that I could go on for many, many pages before repetition, really, became a danger.

Alfred Knopf

Writers are difficult to know; it is to be doubted whether they entirely know themselves – that is, as writers. The deepness of their involvement with their work often creates a block when they try to speak of it; thus, to the average person who seeks him out the writer may seem recalcitrant or secretive. Aware of this psychological impediment, and regretting it (for by it he is the loser, also), the writer is grateful to anyone who can break it down for him – but how few can! Failing that, he knows himself doomed to disappoint, or, at the best, to be treated as a gifted alien. When I was young, I found it alarming to meet a writer; I now realise that it is alarming for a writer to be met. He may learn to adopt a manner, as time goes on, but behind that manner lingers a shy monster.

How immensely indebted, therefore, is the writer to that rare person who *has* a capacity for knowing him – which is to say, to an extent taking him for granted. Such a capacity is to be recognized from the first instant. That it establishes friendship goes without saying; it makes also for an increasing confidence, steadiness, naturalness and calm. The shyness evaporates; then, there is no more monster. Any human being requires such reassurance; it is simply that the requirements of the writer, in this regard, are less often because less easily met: memorable it is for him when they are! His internal life, with its exhausting endeavours and often obsessive preoccupations, from now on has no longer to be explained; it is perceived, and, still better, it is respected. While being accorded its true mystery, it is at the same time set free from its false ones. Realism, turned upon what a writer is, what a writer does, by an imperturbable yet understanding outside observer does more than anything else to build up morale, a morale apt to fluctuate or be shaky. To how great a degree a creative person needs himself (or herself) to be created, and how great a part in the creation of a creative person is played by the investment of faith in him, or her, few know. Alfred Knopf does, or should. Somewhere in his relationship with his authors must lie the reason – and this *is* the reason, surely? – for the relationship's being what it is.

Knopf authors must be something of a family, or a race, in the sense of having a fundamental in common, what we have in common being the more marked by our otherwise great divergence in age, nationality, habitat, origin and outlook. Some of us bear the stamp of a conscious and positive Europeanism, others of us range up and down two Americas. Some of us may have met; many others, because of our wide dispersal, have not, and probably never will. Irrespective of meeting or not meeting, we know each other, we scattered kinsmen. Some of us are dead; in spite of which I think the important thing is that no Knopf author is not a living author – for this reason: no one of us has been allowed to suffer the one and only death that an artist does dread, the death of his work. To fade away out of the knowledge of living man into that remoteness which is the verge of oblivion, till one is a name, then less than a name, only, could be a bitter fate. This has not been the fate of any author of any stature or any virtue with whose destiny the house of Knopf has charged itself. An artist's lifework could not have better guardians. There is no morgue, in this business, for any reputation to be consigned to, however respectfully. On the contrary, names continue to blazon forth not less freshly on fresh and arresting book jackets because those names are also graven on tombs. It is the book itself (one is reminded) rather than the man or woman who was the instrument of its writing, which is creative – affecting and giving extra energy to and extending the vision of the world in which and about which it was written. To such creativeness, time need set no bounds – only, the books must be *there*, they must be in print, they must be to be had. Alfred Knopf sees to it that this is so. A great publisher has a dual responsibility, as he is aware: he has in his hands not only the destiny of the writer, dead or living, but also the destiny of the reader. Looking down the Knopf list of re-publications, I see that no reader is likely to go without any experience which is his heritage, as a child of this century, and his due.

Also, as men and women my fellow Knopf authors remain living, close up and vivid in the conversation of Alfred, their friend and mine, with his photographic memory, eye for character, relish for what is speaking in an environment, uncannily retentive ear for what makes good talk. Also there is his camera, with its gift of immortalising moments. Thanks to him, neither distance nor death cancels out these people, with whom I claim a bond. I am in their company when I am in his.

I became a Knopf author in the 1930s, the first of my novels to carry the Borzoi imprint being *To the North* (1933).[1] It was not long after that that I first met Alfred, on one of his visits to London. He had asked me to lunch with him at the Savoy; we were to look out for each other in one of those large foyers (or salons, or lounges) overlooking the Thames. The month was November, the day was bright; through the windows facing me as I walked in streamed dazzling, river-diluted light, which, catching me straight in the eyes, blinded me – I could not only not see Alfred, I could see no one. Wraiths moved or stood in the haze of their cigarette smoke – and *which* of these (now that I came to think of it) might be Alfred? Extraordinary though it may now sound, I had in no way envisaged him in advance. I had never, knowingly, seen a picture of him – I can only think that photographs of the great were not so freely in circulation in those days as they now are. Though I already knew Blanche[2] well, it had not occurred to me to ask her what her husband looked like – indeed, who would? What possessed me, to come to this meeting, so momentous for me, without briefing myself? I can only say, that was how it was.

Circling the room, I succeeded in getting my back to the windows, put on my spectacles (I am near-sighted) and again looked round, more worried if less blinded. There seemed to be several women in their thirties (my then age), any one of whom might well have been I. It struck me that Alfred might be in the same quandary as myself: possibly he might have become bored by the puzzle and gone home?[3] Or, had something gone wrong, had he not come? He could not possibly be anyone I had looked at so far.

Then, my eye lit on a tie, some distance away. The sun glinted on it. The tie was not so much magenta as the dark-bright purple-crimson of a petunia, and it was worn with a shirt of a light green, just too blue to be almond, just not blue enough to be verdigris. Tie and shirt were at some height from the ground; their wearer stood leaning in a doorway or archway, a vantage-point some way away from the throng. He looked almost sleepy. With an onlooker's great calmness, one might say indolence, he was considering everybody, including me.

"I wondered how we should find each other," I said, as we shook hands.

"Why?" asked Alfred, with what I now know to be his usual equanimity. This was my first intimation that he does not waste his mind over petty problems, and is surprised that anyone else should.

We went in to lunch.

On the whole, surprise was on my side, that Savoy morning – the opening of a procession of surprises which have in themselves been an education during the thirty years (by now) of my association and friendship with Alfred Knopf. As I said at the beginning of this piece, a writer recognizes, instantly and instinctively, anybody who is going to be able to be straightforward with him or her, and thereby break down the internal solitude: therefore, even before we sat down to table, that glad recognition had taken place. But there still was a vast adjustment ahead of me, to be made. I think, my still-youthful ideas of people had, up to that morning, been hard-and-fast. I had been unused to thinking of an outstandingly intellectual person in terms of colour: those I had known, so far, resided rather in the fastnesses of the brain, "seeing" mathematically or philosophically. A subject, to them, was a proposition set out in black-and-white. Up to now, accordingly, it had been artists rather than thinkers who shared my awareness of and my joy in that whole extra dimension given to existence by the senses. Here, however, seated with me at a table, was a being no less cerebral and able for having expanded also into a world of colour and light, a world fully musical (in the sense that all art, it is said, aspires to the condition of music), visual and tactile, a universe of texture and shape, landscape and climate, gardens and trees and animals; and a being also for whom humanity of all kinds, of all avocations, in all places, was a likeable and unwearying panorama.

Then, and since, I had also to learn from Alfred not only how many subtleties but how many austerities go to make up what we all seek after: excellence – whether in the quality of a performance, the taste of a fine wine or a faultless dish, in a degree of wit or degree of learning, in perfected companionship, or in an act of integrity on the part of a person. And as a writer I was to learn something further. I had yet to realise what a book can become.

A book when it leaves the writer and goes to the publisher is only about to begin[4] its effective life. Away goes the manuscript, by the hand of the carrier or through the mail: left behind, the writer finds himself in the throes of a strange mixed sense of triumph (at having concluded something) and bereavement – it is over; *his* part has been played. He has now to wait; and as the waiting-time ends he feels a stir of renewed excitement. Though I have been writing since 1920, the sheer prospect of anything of mine "going into print" continues to awe me. Each time, it is at once incredible and exalting to have what one's outlandish manuscript has become, an actual *book*, placed between one's hands. When the book is not only a book but a Knopf book,[5] the effect of what I should call the benign shock is doubled, and more.

A book's potentialities for beauty as a thing-in-itself, as a concrete object, could have seemed to come to an end with the antique world *cognoscenti*, patrons and leisured craftsmen, mellowed leathers and jewel illuminations and gilded tooling. But that there in fact was no end, nothing more than a pause in the aesthetics of book production, the house of Knopf shows. Part of the splendour of a Knopf book is that it does not revive or cling to an old tradition, it founds a new one. *This* is a beauty which is contemporary, at work through contrast, pure and clarified colour, angle, surface. A book of this kind is not only to be devoured by the eyes but handled: it is a pleasure to the fingertips. It gains weight from the fine solidity of the paper, yet lightness from the set-out of the distinctive type on each spacious page . . . I love words, and for years have done my best to honour them as they should be honoured; I pursue meaning, and have done all that I can to make meaning clear. Words have their due of honour, meaning becomes enhanced, when the eye lights and rests on a Knopf paragraph . . . Thus to send forth a book, thus to give it life, seems to me the final manifestation on Alfred Knopf's part of faith in the writer, that steadying faith. This is affection, speaking in terms of art. This is friendship, indeed.

Blanche Knopf

You ask about Blanche. Yes, about somebody who for the world is a vivid image there always is, I expect, something more to know. A diversity of people's diverse impressions go to the making of the image, and hearsay and legend also enter in. It is known that Blanche Knopf, wife and partner of Alfred, is remarkable, and that her role is unique. It is known – though I sometimes wonder how fully? – what a part she has played, and plays, in the Borzoi story, and how the great house of Knopf, this year celebrating its fiftieth birthday, was from the start the product of a duality. To know more, it is necessary to know her.

My friend Blanche is famous. Fame means that practically everybody you meet has already heard of you. A stranger may be a stranger to you, but you are already other than that to him. Wherever you arrive, wherever you go, there will be an atmosphere of keyed up expectation and preconceived ideas, whether right or wrong. Could this be oppressive and claustrophobic? Whether or not Blanche finds it so (I have never asked her), it has made no mark on her, has left her neither jaded nor automatic – a fresh encounter for her *is* a fresh encounter; her reactions are quick, her curiosity as to the newcomer unabated. She's a rapid summer-up, never a damning one; I find her more charitable than I am. Does she ever wish she could go about incognito? That would mean, to break completely out of her orbit, and there's little time for that. Yet, there are situations when one can be incognito by chance – say, on a journey. How would it be to be somebody setting eyes on Blanche Knopf, and later maybe falling into talk with her, without having a notion who she was? Another passenger, seated across the aisle of a plane on one of those intercontinental air journeys, looking sideways across at her, then looking again?

It would be clear, from the first glance, that she was Someone – that she cannot escape. She gives off this aura of being Someone unconsciously, I would say inadvertently. What would hold the eye would be her look of unusual physical distinction, of clear-cutness, and with that an equivalent of stature – a stature irrespective of size, and in its effect on one made more startling by the fact that she's far from tall and so slight she could almost blow through a keyhole. There is no other word for this look but aristocratic. At the same time, what would be unmistakable *as* elegance (even to the most naïve, unaccustomed eye) would be the elegance, what is worn but still more the manner of wearing it, the supple suit and angular jewellery. Also the looker across the aisle would note the slow, intent turn of the hatless head, with its shaped hair – either abstractedly towards him or away off into the bright monotony of the sky. He would note the attitude, with its quiescent vitality, and the gestures, which are more an extension of movement than means of emphasis. A Someone. And whither bound (that is, beyond the destination airport) and for what purpose?

So much of the artist is in Blanche that in some of her aspects, in some moods, one might take her to be wholly temperamental and dreamy – and possibly in the passivity of an air journey she might seem so. She is not, we know; but neither is she nor would she desire to be a cerebral being wholly. Her forceful will is reined in; her impatiences are sheathed, though they can break out. Her wondering neighbour on the plane could not be blind to her air of ability, though he might take it chiefly to be a tactile one, her way of taking a cigarette from the packet, and so on. She would continue to puzzle him by her mastery – though, of what? – without masterfulness. His overall impression would be fragility: he would decide that she needed and deserved to be taken care of; and she does. It would stun him to learn that she is a publisher. He had understood all publishers to be men.

It is being a woman that makes Blanche Knopf the publisher that she is. Saying that, I mean more than that she complements her husband and fellow-publisher, Alfred: of course she does, and that is very important. But also, by what might seem the contradictions within her nature, she complements herself. Her strength, though exercised with a coolness which could be called masculine, is feminine in its fibre, nerve and tenacity. Her understanding is feminine in its character, intuitive flashes followed by slow reflection. I have known her to act or decide like lightning, but when Mrs. Knopf says, "Do you know, I have been thinking . . ." she *has* been thinking. In speech Mrs. Knopf is unwomanish in that she knows nothing of wiles or guiles; she is downright, direct, can be blunt, indeed disconcerting. That dispassionate side of her keeps in balance the other, its opposite – her temperament, vibrant, susceptible to harmony and beauty, mortally accessible to feeling. Idle or aimless – *could* she have been either? Let us for an instant suppose that possible – here could have been a destructive woman. As it is, she has constructed, and a great part of her construction is that she has inspired.

I should think it a poor tribute to say, "She has a mind like a man's." She has not: had she, what an anomaly! Better say, an unfettered, relentlessly honest, vigorous mind. Yet this is accompanied in her by subtleties and unexpectednesses, an uncanny perceptiveness, and (as friends know) genius touches of sympathy. She invites confidence and, having gained it, honours it: she is a great ally. This may be one of the secrets of her memorable relationships with people, of whom many are writers.

Under her touch, the publisher-author relationship blossoms out. Blanche Knopf respects the executant in the writer, and deals well with it, but is it the artist in the writer that she loves.[1] She divines that X quality which is more than talent, strikes sparks from it, nurses the sparks she strikes. Her long journeys are not geographic only; they carry her into little-known hinterlands of the creative imagination. She and Alfred together, as youthful exploring publishers, showed an effrontery in their early lists; and they have maintained a far-ranging boldness. Blanche, American-born but of a family Viennese in origin, has a complex birthright: with this goes a perception of Europeanism, what it has suffered, how it is growing, what trends it is taking, and what it means, that many a Europe-bound European is denied.

There is no so happy a pride as pride in a friend. I think with awe of Blanche's achievement: so should the world. But I think also of what perhaps fewer people see, not only what she has done but what she is. I am one to whom she is dear as a personality. To talk about her (perhaps for that very reason) has not been easy, but you asked me to – and with it has gone a certain pleasure: that of at least for myself evoking the warmth she kindles, the aliveness she generates, the grace she has. She is a subject for a book, not these few pages. What one could say is endless. This must be all.

QUESTIONS

Confessions

What has been your greatest personal deficiency in life?
Laziness – what they at school called "slackness." Result: sins of omission.

What century or period is your spiritual home, and why?
Late seventeenth century in England – provided one had been "fortunately" born. Should have enjoyed small country house life of that period, with what one takes to have been its mixture of tranquillity, formality, style, grace, and intelligence.

On what occasion have you been most frightened in your life?
By a V1. Or when I thought a plane I was in was crashing. Also went through awful phases of sweating-fear of the dark in my childhood, when I had been reading ghost stories.

What was the most momentous interview of your life?
With my first publisher, Frank Sidgwick, when I was twenty-three. I had gone to see him in response to a letter saying he was interested in my book of short stories and would like to discuss them. During the conversation the idea that the book really *was* going to be published dawned on me.

231

Where and when did you have the most memorable holiday of your life?

The first time I went abroad – as a child, in the summer of 1913. Night and day in Brussels; night in Cologne; journey along the Rhine by river steamer; rest of the time in Switzerland – Wengen in the Bernese Oberland. Nothing particularly exciting happened: it was the sheer new sensation of "abroad-ness" which was exciting. A temperamental traveller's first taste, as it were, of blood.

Where and when did you have the most memorable meal of your life?

My first grown-up dinner party, at which I met an Archbishop.

Have you any pet reforms?

Income Tax. Under three headings – (a) adjustments for authors, (b) husbands' and wives' incomes to be taxable separately, (c) greater distinction to be made between earned and unearned incomes.

Are you urban or rural by temperament, and what is your conception of the ideal house or flat?

Rural. House in the country; enough but not too much garden. Friends within reach but not on one's doorstep. House should be, ideally, eighteenth-century: not too large. Countryside should be as quiet and remote as possible; and should have kept as far as possible its indigenous people and traditional way of life. Travel to or from the outside world should be not too difficult or expensive. Self-sufficiency, but not isolation, seems to me to be the ideal. It is probably well to have lived in a big city for some years at one or another time in one's life.

Are you a host or a guest?

Hard to say: I enjoy being either. Perhaps, on the whole, host.

To what do you attribute your success?

Power to concentrate when I *am* working. Good temper; in the main, goodwill towards other people. Power to throw things off.

What lessons has life taught you?

To allow other people to go their own ways. To discard extraneous wishes and concentrate on what I really do desire. To cut my losses.

Is there any other profession you might have been good at?

I should like to have been an architect. Or (if I had been a man) a barrister.

The Cost of Letters

Q. How much do you think a writer needs to live on?

A. I should say that, as in the case of any other kind of person, this depends on his liabilities and his temperament. In my own case, I should like to have £3,500 a year net.

Q. Do you think a serious writer can earn this sum by his writing, and if so, how?

A. I should say that, with *all* past books in print and steady production still going on, a writer, if his or her name is still of value, should be able to command two-thirds of the sum I have named by the time he or she is sixty or sixty-five.

Q. If not, what do you think is the most suitable second occupation for him?

A. I should say in a man's case a suitable second occupation would be either medicine, architecture or law. Very few women would have time to carry on two professions simultaneously as their personal life and domestic responsibilities take up a good deal of time in themselves.

Q. Do you think literature suffers from the diversion of a writer's energy into other employments or is enriched by it?

A. I should think that a writer's writing would be improved by any activity that brought him into company other than that of his fellow writers. Literary sequestration, which seems to be increasing, is most unfortunate. On the other hand, the diversion of energy is a danger. If a writer is doing two things at the same time he is likely to have more to write *about*, but runs the risk of writing with less high concentration and singleness of mind.

Q. Do you think the State or any other institution should do more for writers?

A. I find this difficult to answer, as I am not clear how much the State does already. Writers who have worked hard and shown distinction (in any field, or of any kind) should certainly be entitled to some help, or even a degree of support, in the case of illness or old age. And, equally, some sense of responsibility should be felt by the public towards the dependants (young children, etc.) of such writers. As far as I know, an extension of the Literary Fund, and possibly a contribution to this from the State, should meet the purpose.

Q. Are you satisfied with your own solution of the problem and have you any specific advice to give to young people who wish to earn their living by writing?

A. I doubt if one ever does arrive at a specific solution of the problem – it is a matter of getting along from year to year. My advice to young people who wish to earn their living by writing would be to go at it slowly, with infinite trouble, not burn any boats in the way of other support behind them, and not either expect or play for quick returns.

Portrait of a Woman Reading

You are Anglo-Irish?

Yes, the original Bowen who came to Ireland was a Welsh squire who fell out with the king's party and came over as a Cromwellian general. My mother's people came over in Elizabethan times, but we have a little pure Irish blood on her side. We lived in Cork and were completely Irish really. We couldn't afford to go to England and didn't know what we would do if we had gone over. The Anglo-Irish that I knew were not at all bad. They weren't the cavorting kind who kept popping over to London.

Where did you go to school?

I would have started school in Ireland, but when I was six or seven, my father had a breakdown and it was decided my mother should take me to England to school. I would have gone to school in England in any case when I was thirteen or fourteen. People thought that would give you a larger view of the world and would prevent you from having a brogue. In 1914, when I was fourteen, I went to school at Downe House in Kent, where Charles Darwin had lived.

What was the effect of the First World War on you and your friends?

It affected our point of view enormously. You had the feeling that everyone you knew was being killed. All the brothers of the girls. An awful toll of death, death, death going on all the time. When the wind was blowing in our direction, we could literally hear the guns firing from France. The war made us feel that all this death should not be for nothing. Not so much that we were determined to change the world. But it gave you the feeling that whatever you did, you should do it jolly well.

What kind of books were you reading in your younger years?

All the girls' books I remember were American. Louisa May Alcott and Susan Coolidge's *What Katy Did*. I read a lot of what were technically boys' books. Henty's wonderful stories about India. H. Rider Haggard. And the Baroness Orczy's *The Scarlet Pimpernel*. You know, that created a Scarlet Pimpernel complex. People are still running into countries to get people out. It was exquisite. It made me hate the French Revolution and made me a tory for life.

What did you read during your teenage years?

We read Arnold Bennett, though he was considered rather risqué. H. G. Wells was too. I remember lying on my front on the school lawn one sunny Sunday afternoon reading one of Wells's lesser known books called *Marriage*. One of the school mistresses passed by and said, "I'm sure that is of no particular interest to you at the moment." But she didn't take it away. And we read P. G. Wodehouse. He was clean. Later in my life, my husband and I had the good fortune to live next door to Wells on Regent's Park. He was a heavenly man. Oddly enough, Henry James died during the time I was in school, in 1916, but I never heard of him until 1920.

What do you think of James?

I think his stories are wonderful. If I had known him, though, I would have sent him a blue pencil. Oh, those endless scenes in drawing-rooms of sympathetic young ladies listening to neurotic young men. But his style is powerful. I would never read him while I'm writing. He's infectious, like a rash.

What were you and your friends reading during the Twenties?

The world we grew up in, the war, made for a complete break

with the pre-war people. I suppose we were angry. I get so bored with this business of "angry young men" that was all the rage fifteen or twenty years ago. All young people get angry. We all do our own things and start our own tradition.

But during the Twenties we were reading a lot of French authors in French: Malraux, Proust and a man who's now in eclipse, Paul Morand. We were reading translations of Chekhov and Turgenev. The Americans, led by Hemingway, had a terrific impact on my generation. The only English writers I can recall who had any influence were the Bloomsbury people, Virginia Woolf, Lytton Strachey, E. M. Forster. We admired Joyce like anything. He was a bible. People used to make journeys over to Paris to buy *Ulysses* and we would wrap it in our undergarments to get it past customs. *Dubliners* is the best book of stories ever written. We were reading D. H. Lawrence, too, but we used to make a lot of jokes about him. Do you know who had no, absolutely no influence? Freud. No one cared at all about the fact that we all wanted to sleep with our fathers. Nothing could shock us. We were all worn down by the war.

Who were you reading during the Thirties?

We kept on reading Lawrence. And Faulkner. We kept following Hemingway. Aldous Huxley – I read everything he wrote during the Twenties and Thirties. And we followed the people who emerged under his influence, like Isherwood.

Do you read while you are writing?

While I'm writing, I can hardly read at all. I can do a bit of poetry or a mystery, but if I get a minute, I'm more likely to go downstairs and watch a game on television. I found Wimbledon fascinating this year. I watch cricket, too, but there is a terrible foreshortening of the pitch on the telly, though you do get a good idea of a batsman's form.

If I'm having a holiday, I will read more. I read the novels of my friends, or some recommendation I've picked up from a review or a friend. I have a passion for Dickens and for memoirs of the era of thirty or forty years ago – the Strachey epoch. I love Jane Austen, a book you can move straight into the middle of. I like the California school of mystery – Dashiel Hammett, Raymond Chandler, Ross Macdonald.

Who were your favourite novelists?

I like the sure-fire people. Anthony Powell, Iris Murdoch,

Muriel Spark, Graham Greene. Any new book by Greene excites me. It's awfully hard to take the novel as a classroom subject. I'm completely ignorant of "trends" in the novel. I only know trends in myself.

My next book is going to be what Mr. Malraux rather portentously calls an anti-autobiography, so I have been reading Anglo-Irishmen. Richard Brinsley Sheridan's plays are marvellous. I don't turn tables or anything, but I'd like to get in touch with Sheridan. He had such a weird, outside view of the English.

Do you keep up with contemporary writing in England?

Very erratically. But since I finished my latest novel *Eva Trout*, I've had a chance to catch up. I've read Edna O'Brien. There's a fine Irish girl for you. She writes beautifully. I think she's obsessed, but she writes beautifully.

And I've been reading Margaret Drabble. Such an unpromising name – it kept me off her for years. She's of the generation after Muriel Spark. I think I've read all her books, except the last one. She's a gay, lively young woman, middle class from the Midlands. Took a first at Oxford and married somebody she went to university with. There's always that theme in her books – young marriage. She writes in the first person and it's difficult to know how far she is taking an ironical view or how far she is embroiled with the main character. She is a combination of a writer who could serialise in the women's magazines and a very intellectual writer.

What else have you been reading lately?

I've read Henri Troyat's new three-volume novel about an upper-bourgeois French family. He's the man who wrote that marvellous book on Tolstoy. His novel is the best book on the generation gap. There's a Phèdre situation, with a young, handsome stepmother seducing a boy of twenty. Then the boy, Jean-Marc, becomes the tutor of a rich, sheltered eighteen-year-old and they have a very close relationship, but not homosexual. When Jean-Marc is going to get married, the younger boy kills them both in a car crash, saying "I love you, I can't let this happen." All of this is taking place in this ultra-respectable – couldn't be more respectable if they were Irish – family. The book hasn't been translated yet, but I'm afraid that in cold English, it will antagonise the WASPs. Frightfully hard to translate the colloquial way the French talk. I'm afraid it will end up full of phrases like "my dear old chap."

Any other recent reading?

During the summer I read George Kennan's *Memoirs* and a book on Washington by Stewart Alsop. I've been trying to get hold of Robert Conquest's *The Great Terror*, but haven't been able to.

Do you keep up with contemporary Irish writing?

I read all the new Irish novels. They're all about tormented lads or decaying old families. I wish Ireland had a more solid bourgeois kind of literature.

Aidan O'Higgins' *Langrishe Go Down* is a brilliant novel. Brian Moore is wonderful. He's from Northern Ireland and I think the writers in the North might be a bit superior at the moment. Seán O'Faoláin is a fine writer. I think some of his stories are, after Joyce, the best around. At his best, he beats Chekhov twenty times over.

You know, Ireland is frightfully dull. Unless people get drunk or go to the races, they don't inspire literature. One gets the idea that all Irishmen have the same character, like the Chinese. All those inscrutable, endless farmhouses. Unless you beat up some personal fantasy – a feud or something – it's hard to get subject matter. One's better off doing what Sheridan does or what I try to do – swoop down on the English.

Interviews and Conversations

The Living Image – 1

Sykes-Davies: I think we've a more difficult job than you had, Pritchett, when you talked about painting.

Pritchett: Eh! Do you, why?

Sykes-Davies: You touched on it yourself when you pointed out that non-artistic considerations are bound to play a bigger part in reading books. You talked about the novelist's "stock-in-trade of men and women, character and situation." I suppose you meant that books and life are very much tangled up together. If that's true, it's going to be very much more difficult for us to show the difference between life and art in books. And by the way, Pritchett, what about words? How do they compare with shapes and colours as a medium for art?

Pritchett: Well, words are the signs of things spoken, just as a picture is the sign of things seen. I don't think a writer really needs necessarily to see things intensely.

Bowen: Yes, it matters much less what he sees with his eyes than what he discovers with his imagination.

Pritchett: Yes, it doesn't matter if he hardly sees at all – if he's frightfully unobservant. But as Sykes-Davies said, since words are his medium, his hearing should be acute. If it comes to that, we really learn more, I think, about human beings by listening to them than by seeing them.

Bowen: But to the average person words have an immediate connection with the purely superficial part of their mind, much more than shapes or colours have.

Beales: Yes, people talk so much and mean so little. We do, in fact, learn to speak before we learn to observe. I mean, we learn to speak before we learn to think about the things we see.

Bowen: That may be partly why people do use words so superficially. I think that in conversation with a person you get about one sentence in twenty-five which is infused by some spontaneous thing in the mind of the speaker. The remaining twenty-four sentences are just routine symbols of communication.

Sykes-Davies: Certainly, and that's one of the very worst ways in which books are so closely tangled with life. Words are used for so many purely routine purposes, and they get debased and blunted.

Beales: Eh! Do you mean that they lack precision? I know as a teacher I have to compel people to use words to convey exact meanings, to describe definite facts. When as a historian I talk about the "Constitution" or "the State" or "Capitalism," or whatever it may be, the words have fixed associations, and that's why I use them.

Pritchett: Yes, but that's a special case altogether. You don't use those words for private purposes, and you learn them much later, you know, than the nice words like "glamorous" and "adventure." Eh! No, I don't think that it's a matter of how precise or exact the words are. It's a matter of the use they're put to. Or rather, the kind of use. Because there's a sort of unuseful or practically useless language, the whole train of images with words to fix them which run through your head in daydreams and fantasies – like those of Leopold Bloom, you will remember, in James Joyce's *Ulysses*. It's an unuseful process – done for one's own pleasure, I suppose.

Beales: All right, but it seems to me that in this process even the ordinary man tends to be a bit of an artist.

Pritchett: Oh! I grant that, though at a low level. For instance, I know a very commonplace man who used to go to the Lord

Mayor's banquets as a sort of servant there, and he was absolutely captivated by the Toast Master's cries – you know – "My Lord Mayor, My Lords, Ladies and Gentlemen, pray silence," and that sort of thing. Well, once or twice when I've been with him, walking in the country, just for the pleasure of the rhetoric of it, I suppose, he's suddenly spoken one of these toasts out loud. Well now, he's obviously been seeing himself either as the Lord Mayor or the Toast Master, or someone very grand. Well, in a way, he's writing a novel, he's using words to create, to see himself in an imaginary situation – something totally unlike real life. Is that the sort of thing you meant, Miss Bowen, when you say that some sentences are infused by some spontaneous thing in the mind of the speaker?

Bowen: Absolutely. Your friend was doing something creative with words, although they were somebody else's. He took somebody else's words, but he related them to a feeling and a fantasy of his own – they became something spontaneous in the mind of the speaker.

Sykes-Davies: Then what about slang and swear-words, and the sort of language people use when they are trying to describe the way they feel?

Pritchett: Yes, certainly they are creative – even expressions like "browned off" and the "loony bin," I suppose, are creative in a way.

Beales: I like expressions like that – the American language is full of things of that sort – it's got a lot of the Elizabethan quality – it's vital and graphic. And you know the Air Force is creating a new language which is intensely rigid.

Sykes-Davies: What we are all really saying, I think, is that words can be made to play as well as work. When we use them ordinarily, it's for some more or less practical purpose like "please pass the pepper." Very occasionally, we do make them play tricks – we amuse ourselves with them. And that's the sort of way the artist uses them. As a matter of fact, a lot of the conversations you hear in the street (you must have noticed it) consist in reporting other conversations: "I said to him," "he said to me," and so on. It's obviously a very fundamental thing for people to live over again in words something that they've lived through in fact. In a way, they're transforming work into play. And, of course, when you play, you can create a world according to your own rules. In all those reported conversations you have a chance of improving on what you really said.

Bowen: It's a form of egotism too, because in the reported conversation you always make yourself dominate the situation, if you notice, even if what you really said was quite ordinary and what the other person said was fantastic. You can arrange the whole way of telling it just as you like. But may I go back to something I said before? About those conversations. Even in conversation, it's only very occasionally that you do hear something really creative. I'm not sure, in fact, that one in every twenty-five sentences isn't on the generous side. Words may be very much mixed up with life, but that doesn't mean that the sort of art you find in books is very much mixed up with life too. They're very different things. You realise that when you look at the dialogue in a novel. It isn't just the ordinary conversation of people written down. If it were, anyone who had a good memory or who knew shorthand could write novels. As a matter of fact, good dialogue is very non-realistic, and it's very difficult to write because you are trying to get the unconscious emotional content of your character into the words, and the whole structure of your book depends for that moment on what he says.

Beales: Yes, the trouble is, though, that whatever purpose the author may have in mind, the words he uses are going to have private associations in the mind of his readers.

Sykes-Davies: Oh yes, Beales, so they may, unless the writer's somehow managed to disinfect his words, to objectify the language he's using. I think one of the reasons, you know, why you yourself find a sort of Elizabethan quality in the American language is that the words aren't in daily, dreary use by you yourself. There are lots of ways in which an author can disinfect or objectify the words – your historical words again, Beales. They're carefully tied up to one particular meaning. Or sometimes a writer has such a sharp and intense meaning to convey that he manages, as it were, to wrench the words into it, in the face of their ordinary everyday use.

Beales: Yes, a writer can appropriate a whole language to his style. You know, like Doughty in *Arabia Deserta*.[1]

Sykes-Davies: Yes, yes, and you often hear people say, don't you, "Oh! if only I could write, what a book I could make of it!" as if being able to write were quite a small matter, a sort of little knack they didn't happen to have. The trouble is that familiarity with words breeds contempt. People don't realise how tricky they are, and what a huge gap there is between the ordinary language of life and the language of art. I think it's very probably the same with characters, you know. In ordinary life, you've got to sum up the characters of the people you meet for purely practical purposes. You want to know if you can safely swindle them or fall in love with them or spend time with them without being bored. It's very easy to carry that habit over into the novel. I think it must be one of the biggest obstacles novelists have got to overcome, you know, because readers will seize on just a character or two, and concentrate everything on them so that they miss the rest of the book. There are thousands of people, you know, Pritchett, who've never read a word of Shakespeare who think they've a perfectly good idea about Hamlet's character. It's the same with Dickens. They don't even think of a whole book, they think of someone like Mr. Micawber.

Beales: Yes! Yes! And if they do that they're certainly getting the book quite wrong. Micawber wasn't meant to be just a character study – he was meant to teach the great Victorian virtue of thrift. The chief point in a novel isn't any single character, it's the whole set of circumstances which go to make up the people and the situation.

Bowen: Yes! Yes! I think you only use people and their emotions and their make up to express or give point to an idea; probably an emotional idea, rather than a logical thought. Sometimes it's purely an image that happens to have become extremely important to you. Somebody was asking me yesterday what I consider to be my best novel and I talked of one called *The House in Paris*, and I said that the original idea was simply two children isolated in the house. Now that isn't an intellectual idea at all. Perhaps an emotional idea. But it seems to me better to call it an image – existing just for its own sake, though it includes certain things – the children, they're helpless, they're outside their own control, and so on.

Sykes-Davies: And the characters of the children, they've nothing to do with it?

Bowen: No, the characters of the children were only made to give more force to the idea.

Sykes-Davies: Well, if you say that, Miss Bowen, then it's no use our trying to keep up a hard-and-fast distinction between prose or novels, on the one hand, and poetry on the other hand, is it? Because what you've just said is a perfectly good description of the sort of image, or emotional idea which makes poetry. You know Milton's line, "In vain the Tyrian maids their wounded Thammuz mourn."[2] That's the sort of emotional idea on which your kind of novel might very well be built. And, of course, the characters of the Tyrian maids don't matter in the least, or of Thammuz, whoever he might be.

Beales: And what on earth is a "poetic idea" if it's going to be common to the novel?

Sykes-Davies: Oh! I don't think it's anything much to do either with the novel, or verse, or anything of that kind. It's a concentrated kind of play, something without any practical purpose that happens to get hold of you completely. You don't know why, and you don't have to ask why.

Bowen: And when you do want to express it, your difficulty is then to narrow your audience down so that they can only do one thing – in fact, only see the idea from your point of view. Vernon Lee, in her book *The Use of Words*,[3] says that every adjective applied to a noun narrows down the significance of the noun to one exact thing – for instance, the sea, the grey sea, the grey uneasy sea. You have to "precise" – is there such a word?

Sykes-Davies: Oh! Yes.

Bowen: Well you have to "precise" the general idea of sea, and create a direction, as it were, in which your reader has to go with you. And if a reader picks out a single character, and falls in love with her, for example, he's probably not going in my direction at all. Don't you think that's right, Mr. Pritchett?

Pritchett: As far as the characters are concerned, yes, I certainly do. If I write a story I think of it as, well, all sorts of things. It may have behind it a simple moral idea, like, let's say, "good people aren't as good as they look," or "goodness isn't as good as it looks," or "badness isn't as bad as it looks." And, of course, I have to use people to illustrate the idea. I don't think I'd write a story and put people in it without any sort of explanation – I think I'm really writing little parables, or allegories or poems or interpretations in which people are necessary, but they aren't the main thing.

Beales: Well, you may agree with Miss Bowen, Pritchett, about the comparative unimportance of characters, but you seem to me to have a rather different conception of this central idea round which the whole book turns. She calls it a poetic image, but you talk of a moral idea, don't you?

Pritchett: Well, moral-social-symbolic – they're all mixed up together. I suppose Zola's *Germinal* is a book based on moral ideas. I don't know whether its moral or social ideas are good ones, but they certainly enabled Zola to look at a coalmine, which was his subject, in a totally new way. I don't think his moral idea was a very simple one. He's read a great deal of scientific literature – Darwin, and things like that – and he's applied Darwinism rather than any political notion to the struggle of life. He sees his men, like seed, planted into the earth and toiling there, and then blossoming forth out of the pit. It's all rather confused, and there are probably a few poetic notions mixed up with all the political, social, and scientific ones. But the point is, all together, they make a sort of white heat which gives the book its driving force. In a rough way, I'd call it a moral idea, and it fuses all the other elements of the book together like a furnace so that they come out quite different in the end from the sheer raw materials of a coalmining life. And that's, incidentally, what I don't find in modern novels about coalmines although they're written, very often, by people who have actually lived and worked as miners which, of course, Zola never did.

Beales: What bothers me is that you are bound to get a confusion between things which are accidental, historical if you like, and things which are really creative. As far as *Germinal* is concerned, I'd just as soon read the 1848 report on coalmines in England. Mr. Micawber, too, and Victorian thrift. It was no doubt a very good and necessary thing at the time, but who bothers about it now? You, Pritchett, and Miss Bowen, you move on from there. You are dealing with a new set of moral ideas, or poetic images, and quite rightly. But in another hundred years, people will have moved on again, and then where will you be? [Laughter]

Sykes-Davies: Oh! No! No! Beales, I don't think we ought to ask them that. I see what you mean all right, but I don't think it works out quite in that way. Books have been written round all sorts of moral ideas, feelings, even just manners, ways of behaviour. And, of course, all those things change. But what matters is that the writer should have a terrific feeling of the importance and urgency of what he's doing. That remains long after his particular notion has faded away. For example now, the moral idea in Defoe's *Moll Flanders* is altogether too naïve and simple for us. At the time, no doubt, Defoe felt it was of supreme importance – and rightly, because a new set of morals and manners had to be worked out just then.

Pritchett: Are you suggesting that *Moll Flanders* is good because of Defoe's moral interests?

Sykes-Davies: Oh! No! Pritchett, on the contrary I think that he was merely "cashing in" for his own creative purposes on a habit which people happen to have, you know – reading pamphlets and tracts. I didn't mean that the moral was the main thing at all. I meant that the feeling of importance is what really matters, that makes books last long after their particular historical problems have disappeared, you know. I think that this sense of urgency and importance is really the white heat in your notion of a furnace, Pritchett, which I absolutely agree with. And I don't see that it matters at all to what sort of thing the feeling is attached. And, of course, by the way, the man who thinks that he could write a wonderful book if only he had the knack of stringing words together is completely without this feeling. He wouldn't be held back by such a trifling thing. And without this feeling he's miles away from being an artist, even in embryo.

Bowen: Yes, and without that white-hot feeling of importance he couldn't even learn to write well, he couldn't even put his words together in the sort of way a good novel needs. I'm not thinking of a "good style" in the schoolmaster's sense at all – no split infinitives and prepositions at the end of the sentence, sentences of varying length, and that kind of thing. You can see that very clearly in writers like D. H. Lawrence, whose actual style I should say is awful, but the ideas have such force and luminousness that they come through it and fling themselves at your mind. Hardy too – I should call his style sometimes in the main creaking or pedantic, but there are moments when I feel that I am being dive-bombed because of the sheer power behind his words.

Sykes-Davies: Yes! And there's Poe's nasty rhetorical journalese too, you know, like local papers, as far as the style goes, but the images – the poetic ones (of course, not moral) come breaking right through the style. Poe reminds me of another point too. I suppose he's not an absolutely first-rate novelist, but he does manage to give an impression of terrific intensity, and he happens to do it without dragging in love very much. It seems to me rather striking, because the situations in most novels certainly deal with love affairs. And most people have love affairs in actual life. I think it's another of the ways in which books do get tangled up with life.

Bowen: Then it's another way in which they've got to be disentangled. Poe is interesting as an example, because among other things he invented the detective story, and I must say I do think the growth of the detective story habit is a very good sign. You go back to sheer excitement, there's no false illusion and muddle with your own life and feelings. The detective story writer isn't trying to trick you into any false emotional participation in the characters or scenes of his story.

Pritchett: Oh! Of course, I agree that love isn't the main thing in good novels, although it certainly is in most bad novels. But even in the good ones love can be quite useful because reading about it puts people into a creative state of mind. I think they often come, in fact, nearer to a creative use of words, for example, in love affairs.

Beales: You mean, Pritchett, that love interest is just another of the writer's tools, like words and characters. But it isn't the central idea at all, the white heat in your furnace.

Sykes-Davies: Yes, well, look here Beales, you and I have a good deal to do with young people. Wouldn't you agree on the whole that until a young person has been thoroughly in love once and equally thoroughly out, it's not much use our expecting them to think of anything else?

Beales: Oh! Surely, that's universal experience, and that's why as a mere editor I have been trying to screw up standards all the time. To get people to understand the novelist – I mean the artist – the good novelist, we've got to feed them more and more with non-fiction. It's no good if they just go on reading about the sort of love affairs they'd like to have, or imagine they'd like to have. I think we can build up a public for the good novel by education in science or politics or history or what-not.

Sykes-Davies: Oh! Yes! I'm sure you're right there, Beales. Somehow or other, people have got to be jerked forward, made to move on from a youthful interest in idyllic love affairs. After all, you know, they never get any further by having a series of imaginary love affairs all very much alike anyhow. I'm afraid the trouble with love is that its problems are simple, and considered just as "simple" they're very boring. The bad novel merely passes the time, and then leaves you just where you were, facing just the same simple boring problems. Before very long you've got to read another – that's probably why there have to be so many bad novels. It seems to me, Beales, you know, that this business of making people move forward, what you and I mean by education – that's the novelist's main problem too. Of course, they don't educate people in the same way to think about your constitution or state or capitalism. They're concerned with making people more skilful in feeling or in living, and their job is at least as difficult as ours, because art isn't the same thing as life.

Beales: No, indeed! Do you remember Henry James's horror of being too much entangled in the facts of real life when he was developing a plot, the germ of which, of course, he'd taken from actual life or fact?

Sykes-Davies: Quite! Quite! What people do in a novel certainly mustn't be confused with what they do in life. Any more than "thinking," what you and I hope we mean by "thinking," Beales, is the same sort of thing that usually goes on in people's heads!

Bowen: And I suppose your difficulty is that people won't see the difference?

Sykes-Davies: Yes, that's the trouble with us.

Bowen: I am sure it's the novelist's trouble too – they won't see the difference – I mean the difference between life and art, between their way, which is perfectly good, of using words and people and ideas, and the novelist's way. They try to keep art down at the level of life, so of course they miss real art altogether, and I shouldn't think they gain much in life either.

Beales: No! No! I shouldn't think so.

Sykes-Davies: But now, let's see if we can agree on anything. As far as I remember, first of all, we talked about the words the novelist uses, and I thought we all pretty well agreed that until people grasp the idea that they're going to use words in quite a new way, or read words in quite a new way, they haven't the faintest hope of reading, much less of writing any novels.

Beales: Well, I still believe that if people are to understand what the novelist is talking about there will have to be something common to the novelist and to the reader, and that the novelist's aim should be to find universal expressions. But still, you're so far right, Davies, that unless the writer "disinfects" or, so to speak, objectifies the language he uses he can't hope to cut his readers loose from their own associations and get them to recognize the universal principles or truths, or whatever it is he's after in his novel.

Sykes-Davies: No, I'm glad you agree there, Beales. Right! Well, now, then after the words we got on to the characters, and there it's the same difficulty. People have got their ordinary day-to-day practical interest in sizing up the people they meet, but that isn't what the novelist wants characters for at all. He has them, but they're not in the middle of his picture. They're just things he uses, and at the same time they're a sort of concession to his readers.

Bowen: I think he creates a character for an almost mathematical reason because that's going to operate his plot. In order to establish contact, in order to make this creature live and do the work he wants it to do he – in the imagination of the reader, that is to say – he gives it certain characteristics, and he gives it emotional appeal.[4]

Sykes-Davies: Yes! Yes! I think that's completely right. And then we were talking about this business of love and the fact that so many novels are love-novels. I thought we all pretty well agreed on that too, but this is a sort of accident – it's a useful accident to the novelist because he likes to catch his reader in a particular mood and the introduction of a love motif rather helps him there. But again, the words, characters, love, situations, style, all the rest of it, all those things are just the instruments with which the novelist has to work. He takes them over from ordinary life, and they're in very poor shape, very often, when he does take them over. They've got to go through a pretty long process before they become precision tools.

Pritchett: And when he's got his precision tools, what does he do with them?

Sykes-Davies: Well, just what you do with tools in general, Pritchett, I think – that is, you make something which is quite different from the tools themselves of course, and has nothing much to do with them. You know when you're making some-thing in a factory after all, you remove the tool marks rather carefully before you let the thing go out. What the novelist is really doing is adding something new to the world, something that wasn't there before. He is just making something, quite simply. I know some people like to call this art – creating a work of art – and of course if they like that I don't mind much. Personally, though, I've got the feeling that the shortcomings of art in the last fifty years or so have given the word a rather bad odour, and I'd rather not use it myself. I'd just rather say quite simply that the writer makes something new in the universe. Now words are obviously tools; characters and situations partly tools, partly raw materials, but the main thing is the total result at the end of it all is something quite different both from the tools and the raw material. The words happen to be spoken in daily life and the situations may be pretty much like things that actually happen. But the contents of the novel mustn't be mistaken for the contents of daily life, and certainly mustn't be judged by their closeness to daily life.

Beales: Exactly! Well, might one even hope to get from the novel a clearer idea of life than one could get from living it?

Sykes-Davies: No! I don't like your word "clear," Beales, because it suggests something simple.

Beales: Well, all right, would "simplified" do for us? One can get from the novel what one can get from any universal – namely, an essential view, in this case of life, the result of detachment and looking at the thing from a distance and in perspective.

Pritchett: Well let's define the novel then, as life after the acci-dental has been removed.

Sykes-Davies: Yes! Yes! Or a concentrated comment on life, so concentrated that, in fact, it's become something quite new.

Beales: I feel I'm at a disadvantage in talking with you three about books. I'm not a literary person. The rest of you are that, if you don't mind my saying so.

Sykes-Davies: Well, I don't mind being called literary. But I'm sure Miss Bowen and Pritchett have come across that particular opening gambit before. I certainly have; so we're all on our guard and you can go on. But I do hope you'll try to be modest about not being a literary person, Beales.

Beales: Oh, I wasn't going to boast about it. I was only going to say that you literary people have always puzzled me a good deal with all your talk about the novelist's idea, the force behind his book and all that sort of thing. You talk as if he writes books simply because this idea or this force makes him do it. No, I can't help thinking – and I'm sure it's the ordinary man's point of view – that you write in order to be read. In fact, I might go further – you write so that you can make some money.

Voices Together: Oh no, no sir . . .

Sykes-Davies: Now look what you've gone and done, Beales.

That's very painful. While Miss Bowen and Pritchett get themselves fully mobilised, I'd like to deal with your simplest point – the one about money. I don't think this gets us any further in understanding why and how books get written, because you see it isn't only writers who have to make money: that's just the common lot of suffering mortals. I think it's particularly unjust to accuse writers of wanting to make money, because nowadays no one's supposed to act from that particular base motive, you know. Businessmen, stockbrokers, company promoters, bankers – surely you don't believe that they're just out for money? – not since Carlyle called them all "Captains of Industry." They're public servants, surely. They're working just to keep things going, not to make money. No, no, Beales, as far as the money goes, everyone's in the same boat. The point is why does a man choose one way of making money rather than another? Why does he become a pawn-broker rather than a bishop, or a tinker rather than a tailor? Now I say because he has certain abilities and qualities which fit him for one job rather than the other. And I think it's just the same with the writer. He has certain qualities which enable him to write. It may happen, of course, that he gets money this way, but that's not essential to the business of being a writer. What matters is that the writer should have these qualities: should be a particular sort of person. Now that's what the rest of us are talking about.

Beales: All right, you mustn't mind me being sceptical about it. I still think you're rather flying in the face of facts. Take Shakespeare: you surely agree that he was a good writer. In fact he is, but he made quite a lot of money out of it: enough to retire in ease at Stratford as he grew old.

Sykes-Davies: Oh yes, true enough that he was a great writer and that he made money. But that isn't the same thing as to say that he wrote in order to make money. I read somewhere in an introduction to Shakespeare a sentence which has stuck in my mind. I suppose I find it rather funny. It went something after this kind, you know: "It's unlikely that Shakespeare, with that massive commonsense which characterises his plays, was unaware of the pecuniary advantages of being a genius." [Laughter] I think, you know, that puts the horse in the proper place, Beales – not where you put it. Being a genius – a particular sort of person – comes first, and making money follows if you're lucky.

Bowen: I certainly agree with that. And you can say it in another way, too. Even a genius has sometimes tried to write things he really doesn't want, to make money or to please somebody, and he generally writes things below his usual level. Didn't Queen Elizabeth ask Shakespeare to write another Falstaff play – one all about Falstaff – because she'd enjoyed him in the Henry IV plays? As a result, *The Merry Wives of Windsor* isn't up to the other two at all.

Pritchett: There's a rather similar sort of thing about Tennyson, you know, in his poem about "The Charge of the Light Brigade." Apparently there was a heavy brigade, too, and it did very well in the battle, and they felt very sore at being missed out; so according to the story, they went along to Tennyson and asked him to write another poem, this time on "The Charge of the Heavy Brigade." Well, he did his duty, but the result only shows that even a good writer can't always write to order.

Sykes-Davies: Yes, it's a nice example, Pritchett. I remember the poem. It is rather heavy. But I hope Beales will remember "The Charge of the Heavy Brigade" if he's ever tempted again to think that people write books simply to make money.

Beales: All right, all right. We'll leave the money out of it. But you still haven't said anything about my other point, you know, that a writer intends to be read, that he writes books so that people can read them.

Bowen: Well, I think it's an over-simplification to say simply that you write to be read. I do agree, though, that the reader – the possible reader – comes into the process of writing somewhere, probably in a different way with different writers. With some, the reader is rather in the foreground, and they write really carefully so as to get a definite response; but others have the possible reader lurking much more dimly in the background, and so their approach is much less definite. I should say that you really write to invite an approach from your reader like feeding a wild animal – you put down your saucer of milk and you keep hoping it will drink some.

Pritchett: Yes, I think it's rather like that. A few years ago, I remember, a man wrote to various writers and asked if we'd mind – I was one of those he wrote to – he asked us if we'd mind his reading a chapter or two from our books in Hyde Park. Well, I was a bit puzzled about it, and before I replied I asked a friend of mine if he knew exactly what happened in Hyde Park when he did it. But my friend told me that the man was perfectly serious and sincere. He stands up on a chair, he said, or bench in the park and then he opens your book and he says: "Here's an extremely good writer and I'll now read you something from him." Well, apparently at first he read to the open air; then about five people came up, and the next Sunday he had about fifty. Then he told them if you come along the next Sunday you'll hear some more and then there were about two hundred. Well now when I heard about this, I realised that this man was, in a way, myself. I never ask anyone to read my stories. I don't really particularly want them to be read. What really goes on in my mind as I write is that I'm reading out loud to people. I don't want to be read: I want to write *at* people. My role in the business isn't passive at all; it's active. I hope I've made it clear to you – this difference between writing for the public and *at* a public.

Beales: Oh, I suppose you have, Pritchett, and I've no doubt it's true enough as far as you and Miss Bowen are concerned, and true enough of a good many other people as well, but I still think that the impulse to write is an impulse also to write something that people will read, and though I don't insist upon the purely commercial aspect after being trodden under foot by your Heavy Brigade, I still think that no writer would be sorry to write a best-seller.

Sykes-Davies: No, no, of course not, Beales. Even writers aren't complete fools, but I still think you get things the wrong way round. I mean you should say that no writer would be sorry to find that he had written a best-seller. I don't think that a writer can actually set out to write a best-seller, at any rate with any reasonable hope of success, because as far as best-sellers are concerned, the public taste is extraordinarily capricious, and I've certainly never been able to make out why from the hundred or so novels a year more or less of the same kind and about the same level of merit, one or two are picked as best-sellers. Can you make that out, Miss Bowen?

Bowen: No, I'm not sure that I can. I'm pretty sure it has nothing much to do with reviews. Good reviews don't necessarily make a book sell. Really I think there's something pathological about the best-seller. The book happens to be based on some craving or daydream and it happens to chime in with a similar mood or ways of feeling among the public. I've always wanted to try an analysis of this sort of thing. I should call it "The Pathology of the Best-Seller."

Beales: Well, it's all very mysterious. I don't know if you really mean to, but you seem to be a bit hard on the best-seller. Some of them, of course, are worthless, and they succeed, as you say, because of some freak taste and they're soon forgotten. But there are others with real merits of their own. Take a delicate and skilful thing, for example, like *The Bridge of San Luis Rey*. Or take that more recent one *Gone with the Wind*, which was in many ways a good book. It certainly had a solid and well worked-out historical background. There again, it's quite possible for a book to become a best-seller because it's based on some contemporary question. Dickens and his debtors' prison scenes, for example. I don't mean that the book's a great one because of its use of these temporary interests. If it's great at all, it's great because it has a universal appeal quite apart from the immediate one. The temporary questions may carry it into the best-selling class – I almost want to say "through no fault of its own," because I can't help feeling that you literary people look down on the best-seller as a matter of principle.

Sykes-Davies: Oh now, not as a matter of principle, only as a matter of fact. I certainly wouldn't despise a book simply because it sold well. As a matter of fact I don't think much of most of the best-sellers I've read – I mean the real "book of the year" sort of best-sellers. But I agree with Miss Bowen that there's a pathological element in most of them. They're based on psychological ramps or the sort of journalistic interests that you have in mind, Beales. But, on the other hand, a lot of books which I admire a good deal have sold very well without being in the top best-selling class. Several novels by Hemingway, for example, and Steinbeck's *Grapes of Wrath*. And look here, Beales, anyhow, I'm not going to be put down by being called a literary person. Even if I am one, I've got a right to my own opinion. There's a tendency, you know, to think that only the man-in-the-street has got a right to have opinions about anything. Now I've nothing against the man-in-the-street at all, but if you won't allow me to be one myself and make me into a literary person, I don't see at least why I shouldn't have equality with the man-in-the-street.

Beales: Oh, I don't mind you having opinions.

Sykes-Davies: Well, if you don't mind that's very nice of you, Beales. I'm only saying, you see, that among all the books I've read I've picked out some that I think are really good. I couldn't help doing that, and then – well, it's not exactly a question of setting standards that can be defined. I think it's a simpler matter than that. Once having had the experience of the very best kind of book, my approach to any other book isn't quite the same. Some sort of comparison is quite inevitable. I suppose in a way I have my own standards, though I should certainly hate to have to define them exactly.

Bowen: Yes, the books that you do go on reading, the books that you really admire, have some quality that's definite enough, but it's awfully hard to describe. A friend of mine uses the word "mad." She recommends a book by saying, "You must read it; it's really a great mad book." It's a quality extremely rare in English writing, I think.

Beales: Now what about Thackeray?

Bowen: Well, I think his books are bad examples of insufficient madness.

Sykes-Davies: Yes, I agree, Miss Bowen, they're not mad, they're just rum. [Laughter] *Henry Esmond*, you know, in a quiet sort of way, is an awfully rum book.

Beales: Well, I don't quite see that, you know. Why is it so rum?

Sykes-Davies: It's rum, Beales, because the hero gets married off to his mother-in-law. [Laughter] I mean, the mother of the woman you expected him to marry right until the last chapter.

Beales: Yes, well, I suppose that is pretty queer, but do you mean with all this talk about madness that there's something to the old saying about genius and madness?

Sykes-Davies: No, no. After all, that isn't quite what Miss Bowen's friend says. I rather like the way she puts it. She doesn't talk of a mad writer, she talks of a mad book, though, of course, she doesn't mean "insane," "lunatic," I take it.

Bowen: No, no. She just means it gives a powerful distortion of life, a distortion that isn't essentially untruthful at all but super-truthful. It puts things before us so intensely and powerfully that it gives one a shock – the sort of distortion you get from seeing things in a very strong light. And I do agree too, about the book being mad, not the writer. Generally speaking, people attach too much importance to the writer himself. They give him too big a place in the production of the book. A great book, I think, is produced by a whole concatenation of circumstances. Some emotional experience is ready to explode socially – I mean in society – and when it goes off the good artist just happens to be there, but he doesn't provide the main part of the explosive at all.

Sykes-Davies: Yes, well, most of the good writers who've succeeded in saying anything intelligible about the way they've worked have made roughly the same point, that the really good writer is a man who has a special ability for keeping his own personality out of the way, so that he can act as an agent, as it were, for much bigger forces than those which can live inside any one human skin. Keats certainly thought and said that, and the Brontës, whom you just mentioned, Miss Bowen.[1] I suppose, by the way, that we literary people would all agree without any hesitation that *Wuthering Heights* is one of the greatest novels –

Bowen: I certainly would.

Sykes-Davies: Well, in her preface to *Wuthering Heights*, you know, Charlotte Brontë makes this point very well, and she talks about the nominal artist – the person who happens to write the book. She says that the nominal artist's share in the business is to work passively under "dictates," she calls them, from outside, that can't be controlled or questioned.

Bowen: Yes, I remember, and that's where she says that very striking thing, isn't it, about the writer who possesses the creative gift owning something of which he isn't always the master.

Pritchett: Oh, I very much agree with this. I think the writer, really, is almost an accidental figure. A good book is produced by something beyond yourself. I don't know exactly what it is, but I suppose it's probably society, as Miss Bowen says, the life around you, or some special part of it, and the writer is just a person through whom society can talk to itself, as it were – but of course in an unusually clear and forceful way.

Beales: You don't know exactly what it is, Pritchett, and I'm not quite sure that I've got you quite. Why not give me an example?

Pritchett: Well, I think I can do that. Now there's a story that's always interested me, James Joyce's *The Dead*. It's very well known and people usually plump for the last paragraph;

it certainly is beautiful – the snow's coming down outside, a woman's thinking about someone who's dead. Well now, I've always though how platitudinous this last bit is compared with the earlier part of the story. The whole story, you will remember, is nothing more than a description of a Christmas party, or a New Year party, with the sort of absurd and awkward things that happen at them. It's not the ordinary conventional picture of a party, however, that might have been written by almost anyone – the conventional party handed down in literature from Dickens' Pickwick Christmas and all that. It's an astonishingly new, fresh picture of a party in 1911, and no other time, among a section of people in Dublin, and no other place. There's a really profound understanding of those particular people at that particular time. It's very much as if that section of society had – how shall I put it – suddenly been able to write itself down and Joyce happened to be able to act as its secretary, though, of course, an extraordinarily intelligent and imaginative secretary – there's no question that it's a mere shorthand report, of course.

Beales: Well, it's an interesting example, and I suppose even I can more or less get at what you mean by it. But if you're right it seems to me to lead into a difficulty. Your good book, you say, is a case of a set of people writing themselves down. But, as usual, I think of the reader. I want to ask him this. Why is it possible for a reader who doesn't belong to that section of Dublin society, or to that time, to admire and enjoy the story? Even yourself, Pritchett, you say you like it: but you're not a Dubliner; you were only a boy when the story was written. You see what I'm driving at. I don't think that books are read simply because they have this rather temporary quality. The fact is that they often continue to be read because they have in them something, well, perennial, permanent, universal. People still go on reading Dickens long after we've got rid of debtors' prisons.

Pritchett: Oh, I agree about that, and I make the same sort of distinction between those parts of a book which have a merely temporary interest and those which have their roots much deeper in human life. Take Dostoevsky, for example. You've a whole lot of more or less journalistic notions running through the books, all about the union of the German and Russian souls, in *The Possessed*, and the redemption of the world this union will bring about, a sort of crude race theory, which looks very strange in the light of present-day events; but it doesn't matter because underneath these there's a real motive power, a real force. And I'm quite willing to put up with the journalism for the sake of the real power behind the novel.

Beales: Maybe so, but I think that the majority of readers work it the other way about; they put up with your real power for the sake of the journalism. And after all, what's wrong about journalism anyhow?

Sykes-Davies: Well, there's nothing wrong with journalism, Beales. We're not using it as a term of reproach, but on the other hand I think it's rather important. I think it's one of the reasons why we enjoy the books of our own day in a special sort of way with a kind of vividness, a tang, that you never really get from reading the classics. After all, with a book written in our own time we have the same sort of ideas and feelings, even the same sort of journalistic interests. It's a piece of our own society, almost of ourselves, writing itself down. Now with the older books we're bound to miss something, if it's only the flavour of the journalism. Of course, we can try to piece together again the original background, but at best it's only a kind of Hollywood set, it's really a fake. That's one of the reasons why I think a writer's best critics are always his contemporaries.

Beales: Good heavens alive, do you mean to say that we're the best people to tell if the books being written today will last or not? I shouldn't have thought there was very much truth in that, you know.

Sykes-Davies: Oh, no, I don't think that at all, Beales, but nor do I think that the business of criticism is to put books in order of merit and say whether they'll last and all that sort of thing. It's like a habit someone once told me that women have, of arranging their friends in order, "my greatest friend," "my second greatest friend," and so on. [Laughter] I think it's a silly thing to do, either with your friends or with your books. I don't see the need for it. Your friends and your books all contribute to your life in different ways and they have different qualities, and I'm for leaving things like that. I don't think, you see, that criticism's really concerned with ranking. I think it should just describe books, help the reader to see their real merits; for example by describing the way the books have arisen out of particular social circumstances. I thought that Pritchett's comments on Joyce's story were a good piece of criticism – what I mean by criticism – and I think that comments of that sort are generally best made by a man's own contemporary.

Bowen: Yes, I think that this contemporary element is very important. But I also think it's important that the other more permanent things should be there as well. With the best-seller it's rather like pretty annual, you've got a nice show of flowers and leaves, but when they wither there's nothing left at all. The other sort of book is more like a tree. It's quite true that while the leaves are out it looks especially attractive, but even when they're gone there's a trunk, a solid shape left.

Sykes-Davies: Yes, I entirely agree, Miss Bowen. I didn't mean to say that the contemporary element's the only one, you know. There is, of course, the solid element as well in any good book. By the way, I think your illustration does enable me to say roughly what I mean by "standards" – why we literary people make this distinction between the best-seller and the good book. It isn't that we want to put an end to the best-seller – we couldn't even if we wanted to. It's simply that we don't want people to miss the good things because they pay too much attention to the leaves, as it were. If they're only used to looking at showy annuals, then they look at the leaves only, and they'll miss the rest. You see what I mean, Beales? We don't want to take away your best-seller from your man-in-the-street – we want him to have something in addition to what he's already got. I hope you don't mind that.

Beales: Oh no, no, why? That sounds to me quite a respectable occupation. But how do you actually apply it in practice? Let's take a modern novelist. Take E. M. Forster. I should have said that his books *A Passage to India* and *Howards End* were among the most revealing works of contemporary fiction. What have you literary people to say about that?

Bowen: Well, they've both got a certain amount of what could be called "preaching" in them, and sermons tends to date rather quickly, however good they are. *Howards End*, too, I think, was written in 1912 and its heroine is rather a feminist, which you'll agree might seem absurd now. Even people I should expect to take an interest in feminism have told me that they do find it rather out of date. But there are other tremendous things in the book as well. There are some young men – one particularly who went for long walks. I think people who read it now don't mind the sermon. They read it and enjoy it from a poetic point of view.

Pritchett: Yes, but I think *A Passage to India* is a bit different because the sermon still has a good deal of force. The problem it deals with hasn't actually been solved. But still one can see it may be solved before very long and then it'll begin to date like the feminism in *Howards End*. But I should say that people will still read that book in a hundred years' time because of the lasting things in it. They'll probably dislike the sermon part of it, but they'll enjoy it – the account of how the people felt, and thought, and behaved, even although they may think their problems rather silly and unnecessary.

Beales: Well, you may be right, and luckily for you it's a prophecy and we shan't live long enough to see whether you're right or not.

Sykes-Davies: No, I don't think it's such a rash prophecy either, Beales, because this distinction we've been making between the temporary and the permanent elements may be useful but it mustn't be pushed too far. The fact is, surely, the more fundamental characteristics of human beings change very slowly, though the actual outward forms of behaviour change quite quickly. As long as a book reflects the life of its time profoundly and not just superficially – as long as it gets down somewhere to really important things – its chances of lasting are very good.

Beales: So you do think some of our present novelists will last?

Sykes-Davies: I do indeed. I shouldn't like to say which ones, but the chances of some of them are exceptionally good, because if you look back over the history of literature it's very striking that the great things have all been written in certain well-defined periods – in fifth-century Athens, for example, Elizabethan England, Russia towards the end of the last century. And it looks to me as if these outstanding literary periods tend to coincide with the main historical turning points of civilisation. Of course I know you'll tell me, Beales, that history and change go on all the time: but every now and then there's a real crisis when the old ways of living have to give place to new ones. Now it's at these "turns of the tide," as it were, that people become specially aware of themselves; they begin to question their old habits and assumptions. They see themselves from a fresh point of view. They're more keenly interested in writing themselves down, to use Pritchett's very good expression, and it's easier for the writer to do his job well too because, of course, he's in with the rest of them. His habits of prejudice are breaking up, so that he can write down the life of the time more directly and profoundly. He has a better chance of getting down through the layers of temporary things to something permanent.

Beales: And so I take it that we're living in a critical period of history?

Sykes-Davies: I think there's no doubt about that. And some very good books are bound to come out of it. Why, Beales, I think today it's almost possible for a best-seller to be what even we literary people call a good book, and for that matter I don't see why a good book shouldn't be a best-seller too. I hope that'll satisfy you, Beales.

Beales: Yes.

How I Write: A Discussion with Glyn Jones

Jones: I think that the reading public, Miss Bowen, when they hear your name think of you as a novelist.

Bowen: Yes, I think they do. What I don't think is actually often realised is that I am deeply interested in the writing of short stories – I began with short stories – and but for the challenge, from all sides, to try a novel, I might never have had so many sleepless nights. "Sleepless nights" is perhaps an exaggeration. What I mean is that a novel involves continuous strain over a long time, whereas a short story rises to a sort of poetic peak; it almost completes itself and so satisfies me.

Jones: How do you get a long novel – like *The Heat of the Day* – down on paper?[1]

Bowen: I work straight onto a typewriter. My typing's slow and bad. About thought speed. I like to see a sentence or paragraph; also I like the impersonality of typescript.

Jones: And how long do you actually take to write a novel?

Bowen: The writing of a novel takes me about two years. I've generally been brooding over the *idea* for a length of time

– unspecifiable – before I start . . . A short story takes from two to four weeks! I hate being hurried over one.

Jones: Do you keep office hours?

Bowen: Yes, and as rigidly as possible. With me, the state of mind necessary for writing has to be induced; and I induce it by an association with particular hours. Half-past nine to one; two to five – ideally! I know this is shorter than an office day; but it does stand for all-out concentration.

Jones: Tell me, Miss Bowen, do you find it easier to write at one particular time of the day? And do you enjoy the act of writing?

Bowen: I dislike – and suspect – working late at night: I only do that under high pressure. A sort of feverish facility sets in, but the super-tax on energy isn't worth it. Not only do I feel like death next day, but next day, from the point of view of working, goes more or less to loss. I enjoy writing novels and stories – though there are days of impotence and nightmare. Criticism I find an undue strain, which I resent – I feel I am doing what's *not* my business; and fundamentally I doubt my right to pronounce judgement.

Jones: What usually starts you off writing a short story, say, is it a situation, a bunch of characters, the desire to convey a mood you've experienced, or what?

Bowen: With me, a short story starts from an impression – most often a house, stretch of road, scene of some kind, poignant reaction to some hour of a day or time of year. Yes, I suppose the beginning of a short story, for me, is some unexplainable connection between a mood and a scene. The characters in the story come last with me: they are brought into being in order to be "carriers," or expressers, of the mood. Fundamentally, I doubt whether I have any great interest in character. Which is one reason why I prefer the short story to the novel. In the short story characters can be shadowy and impressionistic.

Jones: Can you think of your characters and your scenes as you walk about the streets, for instance, or play a game of cards?

Bowen: I must sit down to my task before I *begin* to write. Once a story or novel is on its way, it so much commands me that it returns to me at all times. So much so that it can be agony for me to be out of reach of my manuscript; I find myself wanting to dash back to make some alteration or note some new idea. I find walking, driving myself in a car alone around lonely roads, or a train journey ideal for continuous reflection on the story I'm working at.

Jones: What about these images and apt phrases which you use in your work? Do these derive from the inspiration of the actual writing or are they the fruit of previous observation and experience?

Bowen: No, I don't keep notebooks, if that's what you mean. Occasionally a flash of a phrase or an image comes to me when I'm away from writing; but generally these arise from intense concentration while I'm at work. As Flaubert pointed out,[2] the contemplation of the writer and the contemplation of the mystic are not unlike. Both may precipitate a sort of flash.

Jones: How many drafts of a novel (or of a short story) do you normally do?

Bowen: I make from three to five drafts of a short story – apart from particular passages which I may re-cast from six to ten times. In work on a novel, I re-cast individual chapters, as I go along – the number of times varies according to the chapter's difficulty (for me). When I've come to the end of the novel, I revise it from beginning to end. Unforeseen alterations suggest themselves when one is able to see the novel as a *whole*.

Jones: Could I ask you something about the way you revise? What exactly is your method of revision? Could you say *why* you alter during revision? I mean, what makes you take out one word and substitute another? How do you *know* that the substituted word or phrase is superior? Are you a writer who cuts down? Or one who adds on?

Bowen: Changes I make, in revision, are for the sake of clearness. I hate opaque, thick passages in prose. I revise best when I have not seen the story or chapter for some time. It's extraordinary, then, how clarifications jump to the eye. People who don't know about writing imagine that one revises for the sake of adding a final gloss. I revise like one prunes – snipping away dead wood. It's ironical how a paragraph, sometimes a whole passage, to which one has given days of work, which one may have re-written a dozen times, becomes dead wood ultimately. What I mean by "dead wood" is anything too cerebral, too confused – anything which fails to convey sensation. I make particular war on analysis. My first drafts are always over-analytical.

My ideal is, to replace analysis by a pure image – as in poetry. I tend, in revising, to reduce rather than add. Just occasionally, things work the other way. What had been a rather "dead" sentence or statement suddenly flowers out, on re-reading – showing a potentiality to expand into something further. In that case, let it expand. Result, I break open a paragraph in the middle, to insert a new one. As a rule, these late-comer paragraphs *do* add some vital sense to the book or story. Now I come to think of it, my entire process of writing *is* revision. I rough out a few pages, contemplate those, work on them. Then again, rough out a few more.

Jones: How different is one of your novels in its final appearance from your first conception of it?

Bowen: My novels almost always "break shape" as they go along. By now, I take this as inevitable. Either a character exerts more pull, generates more force, than I had expected: or, an unforeseen emotion sets up, displacing the structure of my original thought. On the whole, this is to the good. I should detest shapelessness; but I feel a respect for a novel which insists on re-casting its own shape.

Jones: And is your writing a closed activity? I mean, Budgen says that Joyce was continually adding to *Ulysses* words and ideas that were arising out of his life in Zürich although what he was writing about had taken place of course many years before.

Bowen: No, my writing is not a closed activity. Any book or story I have on hand is affected by what is going on around me at the time of writing. At the same time, it magnetises much that is going on around me into itself. Life round me, while a book or story is on hand, assumes a new, queer proportion. Slight incidents, scenes, or phrases overheard in talk, suddenly dart forward at me, significant, because in some way they *apply* to my theme.

Jones: Do you plan out a novel before you begin to write? In any detail, I mean? Or are you content with a general idea which can be worked out more fully as you go along?

Bowen: No, I don't plan out a novel ahead. Partly because, as I've said, it almost always insists on breaking out of *my* preconceived shape into its own. I try to keep myself focussed on the central idea – the idea which has been the germ of the book – then, while working, I cast about me, from chapter to chapter, to see how the idea can best work itself out. The middle parts of my novels unfold by stages. I know the beginning, the end: that's about all.

Jones: Have you got any special stimulus to help you on when you are writing? Something like Schiller's rotten apples or who-was-it's best wig? Or something of that sort?

Bowen: While I write I chain-smoke. Occasionally I get up and walk about the room, and, if I can, put a record or two on the gramophone. The wireless is useless,[3] as there's almost always something I don't want to hear. I like to work on pink paper. When I get thirsty – from either smoke or exhaustion, I drink lime juice. If I had the sense to drink tea out of a glass, like the Russians, I'd probably drink more tea; but having a cup-and-saucer on my writing-table irritates me . . . I roll up my sleeves when I work, however cold the day, because I like the feeling of bare forearms.

Jones: And how conscious of an audience are you when you are writing? What effect does this have on your writing or on your revising?

Bowen: While I write I'm reader-conscious – which I suppose is the same as being audience-conscious. I don't quite know who my reader is: simply "X," I suppose. "X" is several degrees more critically intelligent than myself, and a quick jiber at anything likely to stand out as "a fine phrase." "X's" power of sensuous reaction is about the same as mine – which I consider average . . . With each revision, I try to approximate more to "X," less to myself.

Jones: What exactly is your attitude to your audience? I mean, what do you wish to *do* to them? Do you wish to make them experience certain emotions when they read your work? Or do you wish them to behave in a certain way as a result of reading you? Or is your aim to present them with an aesthetic pattern satisfying to yourself and so perhaps to them?

Bowen: I differentiate "my readers," to whom the book or story will ultimately go, from the "X" watchfully present at my writing-table. What do I want to do to my readers? Convey to them an idea, an image or a sensation – I suppose, really, all three simultaneously – to which they shall react with my own intensity. I want them, as they read, to experience a series of reactions, of which the effect shall be cumulative. I desire, in fact, that when my reader has finished the book or story, all the reactions experienced in its course shall run together within him, to form *something*. I want my book to crystallise, in and for the reader. Failure to have crystallised means aesthetic failure.

Jones: What would you say was the most powerful element in you as a writer? Is it your sense of character or your sense of language? Is it your sense of pattern or design?

Bowen: I would say that the most powerful elements in me as a writer are my sense of atmosphere and my sense of language. The latter, however, is too often faulty. Proust says, all writing is translation: there are times when I fail to translate clearly.[4] At their best, my short stories seem to me good in shape: I am less happy as to the shapes of my novels. The most "shapely" novel I have written is *The House in Paris* . . . I should never take my stand on treatment of character.

Jones: I wonder if you've ever had this sort of experience? You work hard at a section of a book, you feel really inspired when you pen it, you believe you've got the best in you into it. And yet critics and your friends ignore it and praise something that you threw off rather thoughtlessly. Could you give any explanation of this?

Bowen: Yes: I have often killed myself forging out passages which escaped the notice of ninety-nine readers out of a hundred. The last thing a writer seems able to impart is his own interior sense of what is significant. The reader most dear, and most rare, to me is he or she who, instead of merely praising the book, *perceives* it. What I might cold-bloodedly call my "descriptive pieces" (e.g., the opening passage of *The Death of the Heart*, or the 1940-London pages in *The Heat of the Day*) seldom are overshot by anybody who cares for my work at all. As against that, for instance, a good deal of the middle (seaside) section of *The Death of the Heart* has seldom been commented on except as rattling comedy. Passages in this section are as near to tragedy (apart from pathos) as I have ever come. I can only think, that the sheathing of tragedy in comedy must be baffling to English people. The Irish are better at it; so are the Russians.

Jones: Would you regard your own particular upbringing and education as favourable to you as a writer?

Bowen: I think my being a hybrid – Anglo-Irish – has had a certain effect on my writing – whether good or bad I can never say. I am perpetually having to re-adjust myself. I gain by a sort of quickness as to impressions; I lose by never having had continuous absorption in any one region . . . Teaching of literature at my school was good! It made me style-conscious. I never went to college: I semi-consciously tried to repair that by extensive reading between the ages of eighteen and twenty-five.

Jones: You are a very experienced writer by now, Miss Bowen. Would you say that you find your aims, your methods, your style, changing much as you go on writing?

Bowen: Yes: after thirty years of writing I still find myself, as a writer, in a fluid state. I'm glad of that: I should hate to "set." It would be terrible to fix oneself to a formula – actually, I've never been tempted to do that, as I've never found any formula likely to attach me. Each novel or story I write seems to ask something new of me: each time, I seem to have to start from scratch. Writing becomes more rather than less difficult as I go on – at the moment, there doesn't seem to be any fear of my acquiring "facility"! Indeed, there have been moments when I've felt I could do with some of that. I find myself with my head in my hands, groaning, "*Why* should it still be so difficult?" The truth is, I suppose, that any magnetic subject carries with it its own unique problems. For that very reason it *is* magnetic. There's no such thing for a writer – unless he or she be utterly cynical and commercial – as the old bag of tricks.

A Conversation between Elizabeth Bowen
and Jocelyn Brooke

Brooke: Well, it's always struck me that there are two kinds of novelist. The kind who's primarily interested in character and plot, and the kind whose interest lies chiefly in a sense of place or in what's commonly called atmosphere. Novels of this kind seem to me to spring from a vision of a landscape with figures, rather than from a direct interest in the figures themselves. Now I'd say that your novels, Elizabeth, are very much of this second kind. I tend to remember scene and atmosphere, landscape or the interiors of houses, especially interiors in your case, in any novel of yours, much better than the characters themselves. Would you agree about this?

Bowen: Yes, yes I think you're right. Several of my novels and a very great number of my short stories have come from a sort of a vision of a place. Some sort of a vision of a place, not perhaps an upsetting, but all the same an insistent and a compelling one, a vision that seemed to draw one into itself. The [. . .]¹ of the story is to me a very great part of it. The characters take shape later and far more slowly. For quite a long time they are, as you say, not more than figures in a landscape. I daresay I think of characters last and not first. Of course, that may sound a rather damning admission for a novelist, I don't know if you think so. I mean to say I suppose it's generally taken that a novel arises out of interest in human character. I suppose I feel more, I feel the dramatic possibilities of character. A novel can't be static. It can't be purely contemplative. It must have movement, action, combustion of some sort. In fact, it must have what one conveniently calls plot, and to make plot therefore one must have characters. However, I believe I've said that already, haven't I, when I wrote the "Notes on Writing a Novel."[2]

Brooke: Yes, I was reading those notes again just the other day. To tell you the truth I was really quite alarmed. It seemed to me so astonishing that anybody could be so conscious of the process of writing as you seem to be. Of course, there's always Flaubert and Henry James for that matter, but I can never quite believe that anyone can be quite so aloof and detached from the writing process. Would you say you were really as highly conscious as the "Notes on Writing a Novel" seem to imply?

Bowen: Oh no. No, no, far from it. That is to say naturally far from it. The notes, I suppose, were an attempt to externalise or to pin down, or to bring up on to the plane of consciousness what is, in the main, an unconscious process. In the actual process of writing the most the brain can do, I find, is to hold its own against the imagination. The brain, perhaps, translates, but like any other translator it's the servant of the original in making the best of the matter, although it cannot perhaps entirely comprehend or handle. At any rate the brain tries for precision, so I say. But don't you agree that any theory of writing must be more or less retrospective? I have noticed, as you say, that other writers have had the wish to stand back from what they do, to externalise. There are two examples, as you say, Flaubert and surely, quite outstandingly, Proust.

Brooke: I'm glad you mentioned Proust because he was rather running through my mind. One can see his attempt to externalise or justify, if you like, the process in his, the last volume of his novel, *Le Temps retrouvé*. Incidentally, I must say I'm rather relieved that you aren't quite so conscious of[3] what you're doing. But as far as Proust is concerned I've always felt that, as you say, his apology, his justification for his whole book is a purely secondary affair. I mean I don't for a moment believe, as one might infer from *Le Temps retrouvé*, that he had this sudden vision of a complete work. You know when he was at that party given by the Princesse de Guermantes[4] at the end of the book. I'm quite certain in my own mind that *À la recherche du temps perdu* really sprang from his immense nostalgia for his childhood. And particularly the places he knew in his childhood: Combrey and Balbec. It wasn't any Bergsonian theory about time or anything like that that made him write. I should think, I'd rather say it was the madeleine dipped in tea, and all the other sudden illuminations of the past throughout the book. I suppose, by the way, James Joyce would have called these epiphanies?

Bowen: Yes, probably. You now, Jocelyn, you, are you a conscious or an unconscious writer?

Brooke: Oh, unconscious. One hundred per cent. I forget who said it, but do you remember that remark somebody made: "How can I tell what I think till I see what I write." That seems to me absolutely true for me. I find the writing process easy once I've begun. Things I want to write that is. Things I feel I've got to[5] write write themselves almost, like under a trance, but any purely conscious writing I find painfully difficult. Writing a review for instance, or even an ordinary business letter. But don't you think any writer of the kind we're discussing, any serious imaginative writer, that is to say, writes largely in this way, unconsciously?

Bowen: Oh yes, yes. And another thing apart from its unconsciousness, I should say that the state or the continuity out of which and in which one writes are so very interior as to be insulated to a great degree from much of the rest of one's ordinary life as a human being. Indeed, so much so that any imaginative writing seems to me only quite indirectly, if in fact at all, the product of the time in which the writer actually lives. The writer, surely, creates a time of his own, all with its own morality, its own values, its own perspectives. I don't even call that a privilege: it's a prerogative. It gives the man's or the woman's work that unique stamp without which it can't be said to be creative. That's not to say that as a human being the writer is unconscious of the crises and the extremities of the world he shares with other human beings, or that he should be absolved, again as a human being, from confronting problems or bearing burdens.

What I do mean is that in so far as the outside world, that is the world of his immediate day, does pass through him, through the writer into his art, he's probably most honest when he writes in symbols.

Brooke: Yes, I quite agree there.

Bowen: And feeling that, feeling as I do, I'm always rather nonplussed by these questions and discussions as to this predicament of the writer in our day. Concretely, practically, economically, of course, they can look enormous, but in the purely writing sense, the creative sense, I should seriously doubt whether the predicament's greater now than it ever has been. You don't even think there's possibly a danger that we may use the badness of our time as an alibi.

Brooke: As an excuse, yes. I was thinking something of the kind.

Bowen: I'm glad because I thought you might think I was going rather far. About this predicament, this special contemporary predicament, I would like to know is it real to you? Or rather, of course, every writer has his or her unique internal predicament. You have yours; I have mine. What I want to know is do you connect your own internal predicament with the external state of the world?

Brooke: It's a very difficult question. On the whole I think I'd say no. Surely the writer was always in a predicament: the original writer anyway, which is the kind we're talking about. I think the writer was always a kind of outlaw and still is, and I don't think I'm very much in favour of making things easier for him. I don't think I believe in state patronage and all that business. It might be a good thing for some writers, but in general I don't think so. But you once said, Elizabeth, I remember, that writers form a kind of perpetual resistance movement. I quite agree that they ought to anyway. But in actual fact I think the writer's position today is even easier in some ways than it's been in the past. I think it's easier on the whole for a young writer to get published. That may be a good thing or a bad thing. Of course, we know there are special difficulties at the moment. Shortage of paper and people reading less, perhaps. And there's the competition of the cinema and the radio and television. But the fact remains that people still want to write. Goodness knows why they should. Certainly not to make money because if you want to do that you'll make a lot more in almost any other profession, I should think. I'm sometimes inclined to agree with the psychoanalysts who say of all writing, of all art for that matter, there's a kind of neurotic over-compensation for some sort of insufficiency. In fact, it looks as if we're coming back to the old, old question: why one writes at all. Why does one write, do you think?

Bowen: Why does a beaver build a dam? There's no option, it's a predisposition, I think.

Brooke: Yes, yes, I agree with you. You could call it instinct, though a biologist wouldn't. That reminds me, I was thinking when we were talking about writing consciously or unconsciously that some of your novels seem to me to be written much more easily than others. One I'm thinking of in particular is one called *Friends and Relations*. I don't know whether you agree with me about that.

Bowen: *Friends and Relations*. Yes, it's funny your saying that. I suppose that is a book of mine which most nearly wrote itself. I say, of course, "most nearly." Is writing [. . .] not extremely difficult.[6] Oh, but in some ways that novel was more exterior to me than any other I've ever written before or since, and that did make for a sort of psychological ease. On the whole I looked on the story rather than felt it. But then again, one can't have it both ways. Frankly, I've got less feeling for *Friends and Relations* than I have for any other of my books. I quite enjoy a book when I re-read it and in a way I could be impressed by it. In so far as I have any abstract conception of what a novel should be *Friends and Relations* seems to conform to that. Perhaps it reminds me slightly of the Edwardian new novels I used to read when I was a child.

Brooke: Yes, that's very interesting. I felt very much the same about that. Which of your novels, Elizabeth, have you most personal feeling for?

Bowen: Feeling, you mean almost tenderness?

Brooke: Yes, yes.

Bowen: Oh, *The Last September*.

Brooke: Yes, well that happens to be my favourite novel of yours. Well, I think that brings us back to what we were saying about novels which spring largely from a sense of place. *The Last September* always seems to me preeminently a novel about a place, and seems to me so successful because it communicates your nostalgic feeling for that place. A country house in the south of Ireland. I always felt that I know that house myself just as I feel with Proust that I've actually lived at Combrey or Balbec, and, of course, Joyce's Dublin. I read *Ulysses* long before I ever went there, but I felt I knew Dublin almost as well as my own home town. I think really this is my favourite kind of novel. That's probably why I particularly like *The Last September*. Of course, in some of your novels and stories there's a kind of extra reality because I happen to know the places you write about.

Bowen: You do. Yes, of course, *The Death of the Heart* would be an outstanding case. It's a little seaside part of the village where it is right in [. . .].

Brooke: Yes, I do know Seale-on-Sea, though that's not its name. That terrible house called Waikiki on the sea front. I walked by it only the other day.

Bowen: You did. *The Death of the Heart* seemed[7] to me to have gathered so many legends. Some of them, where I'm concerned, rather misleading. I've heard it, for instance, called a tragedy of adolescence. I never thought of it in that way when I wrote it, and I must say I still don't see it in that way now. The one adolescent character in it, the young girl, Portia, seems to me to be less tragic than the others. She, at least, still has a hope and she hasn't atrophied. The book is really a study. It might be presumptuous of me to call it a tragedy of atrophy, not of death so much as of a death sleep. And the function of Portia in the story is to be the awake one; in a sense therefore she was a required character. She imparts meaning rather than carries meaning. Yes, I required her, I needed her so I assembled her. I took her face, for instance, from the face of a young girl I saw for a moment in a shop.

Brooke: [. . .]

Bowen: Yes, once the face was there Portia went on acquiring life and inevitability as a character should, indeed as a character has to. But I had already, I should tell you, for some time been in deliberate pursuit of Portia for my purposes when I happened, by chance, to see that young girl's face. I think, too, another thing, that it's been on the strength of *The Death of the Heart* that I've come to be called a novelist of sensibility. Actually, it never has been my wish either to generate sensibility or to play upon it, or indeed to exhaust it. In fact, sensibility in itself for its own sake seems to me neither here nor there as a subject and often in excess rather tedious in real life.

Brooke: The word's been overdone rather by reviewers, hasn't it?

Bowen: Yes. It's a key word now, but to return to its place, it has a place, for me a great place, but as a medium one might say, and a medium which can be put to immense use. It's a kind of an element in which things stand out dramatically and clearly and above all with significance. Just as the landscape, for instance, stands out most sharply in a certain peculiar light. As a matter of fact you, Jocelyn, must know that yourself, because in that novel of yours, *The Scapegoat*, you use the sensibility, or at any rate the raw jaggedness of that unhappy boy.

Brooke: Yes, I think that's more or less what I was doing in *The Scapegoat*. For me character, I think, is very often, if not always a vehicle for presenting landscape and atmosphere through a particular type of sensibility as you say. I find that what interests me most often is the relation between a personality and a landscape. As you say, sensibility casts a kind of light on the surroundings. And, incidentally, that reminds me of something else. How important the quality of light is in your work. It has been noticed before, I think, and I think that critics have commented upon it. What do you think about that?

Bowen: Yes, they have. It has been remarked on and until it was, I myself hadn't been aware that it was so outstanding. There is a case of unconsciousness coming in. Now I can see what has struck you and has struck other people.

Brooke: Yes, certainly . . .

Bowen: The part that light plays in my books. This may be due to two things. One the purely physical fact that I am extremely short-sighted and therefore tend to see everything at a first glance either as a sort of dazzling blur or in a mass of shadows, and the other was already suggested by the critic, who being Irish himself spotted the thing in me. In Ireland, as you may have noticed, light is a factor, immense factor; it's always changing and it conditions everything by its changes. It can range from the almost magical, really almost celestial to starkly, grimly, grittily ugly. And the light determines one's mood, one's day, really one's entire sense of the world.

Brooke: It's very important in Ireland, I know, I can quite understand that.

Bowen: Having come from there myself now, wherever I am, I can't escape from almost a fatalistic susceptibility to light.

Brooke: Yes, I think you once told me, too, that you used to paint and draw a lot when you were a child. That made me wonder, rather, if you hadn't been a writer whether you might not have been a painter instead, perhaps you're a painter [. . .].[8] This might possibly account for your interest in life, and in landscape generally.

Bowen: Yes, I think it would. I did originally see myself as a painter, did desire to be a painter, and had I become one I know what my subject would be. I can see, in fact, my unpainted picture, and perhaps that concentration of vision, which I might have had as a painter, which a painter has, has accounted for this fact that really the short story which was my first choice of form is really, I think always, the natural and the attractive one to me. That intensity which one can have, in the concentration of the short story.

Brooke: Yes, much more pictorial altogether.

Bowen: At the same time there's something against it. The short, short story, I don't now ever find perfectly satisfying. It somehow cheats me of something, it excludes something.

Brooke: Yes, yes, I find exactly the same thing. I think the only ideal length for a story, surely, is what they call the long short. Or what's called in France a *conte*, or *nouvelle*.

Bowen: Yes.

Brooke: Publishers in England, unfortunately, loathe them and they won't accept them at any price, which is a pity.

Bowen: Yes, it is a pity. Because certainly I do share your feeling for that form. I know well pieces of work of mine that have most nearly wholly pleased me, or I might almost say most nearly rejoiced me, have always been[9] long short stories. "The Disinherited," for instance, or I don't know, "Ivy Gripped the Steps," or "Summer Night," or "The Happy Autumn Fields."

Brooke: Yes, I agree. "Ivy Gripped the Steps" fits into its length exactly. It seems to me exactly the right length for it. One so often feels that the professional novelist spins out his material to eighty or a hundred thousand words simply because his publisher and the circulating libraries require it. Whereas really the same material could be quite adequately and better dealt with in fifty or even twenty-five thousand. Incidentally, I do feel something of the kind, if you don't mind my saying so, about your last novel, *The Heat of the Day*. I don't mean that it should have been a short story, even a long short story. But it did strike me rather as containing a lot of material which could have provided you with several long shorts. It didn't seem to me quite to hang together, and I think I felt about it that perhaps it was written rather too consciously. Even the quality of the prose seemed to me over-elaborate. Or rather elaborated for its own sake. The feeling one gets, or I get at least, with the later Henry James. I'm probably wrong about this, because the book was very highly praised and I may just have a blind spot about it. I may have missed something. Parts of it I did like immensely. Horrible house, Holme Dene, somewhere in the Home Counties, I think.

Bowen: Another horrible house.

Brooke: It should have been in Surrey, I feel, but it wasn't. And the scene in the blacked-out café where nobody seems to know quite why they're there or where they're going seemed to me to be a most terrifying vision of a sort of neon-lighted, chromium-plated limbo full of lost souls. It's a thing, by the way, that I've always admired tremendously in your work. This feeling of a latent horror beneath quite banal and ordinary surfaces[10] of life. One gets the same thing a lot in some of Forster's novels, you remember: *Howards End* and *The Longest Journey*. One example occurs to me especially amongst your novels, the chapter in *Friends and Relations* where Lady Elfrida takes the children out on a hot thundery afternoon in the country town, you remember. The whole passage has a most sinister tone, and yet it's only by its,[11] nothing particularly sinister about it, really. It's just this subtle underground kind of suggestion by which it's built up. And then, of course, the storm breaks. The emotional storm that is, and one's plunged suddenly into what Forster once described as "a world of telegrams and anger." Yet one had no hint of what was actually going to happen. One only had this latent sense of evil, piling up below the surface. You know what I . . .

Bowen: Yes, I know what you mean. I want to go back to that, it interests me. I do want to say one thing about *The Heat of the Day*.

Brooke: Yes, I think you should. I think I was rather rude about that.

Bowen: I want to talk to you about that because I want to try and explain something to myself. I think I must say that the apparent disjection between the characters and scenes in *The Heat of the Day* was to a certain extent intended. I wanted, I was aiming to give an effect of fortuity, of a smashed up pattern with its fragments invecting on one another, drifting and tapping rather like the broken ice which I described in the opening passage ten years before in *The Death of the Heart*.

Brooke: Yes, with the two people standing on the bridge in Regent's Park.

Bowen: Yes, I wanted to show people in extremity, working on one another's characters and fates all the more violently because they worked by chance. I wanted the convulsive shaking of a kaleidoscope, a kaleidoscope also in which the inside reflector was cracked. And other thing remember[12] that the centre of *The Heat of the Day* was a love story, the rest of the plot germinates, comes out of the love story, and love, especially when it is coupled with fear, any kind of fear, makes its own scene, makes the landscape again, a Caligari-like, subjective, exaggerated, highly defined, perhaps slightly-out-of-the-true world.[13] About the writing itself, a certain overstrain which you felt, which a great number of other people have been aware of, probably came from a too high tension from my trying to put language to what for me was a totally new use, and what perhaps was, showed itself to be a quite impossible use. And yet, do you know, I shall always be glad that I at any rate tried to write *The Heat of the Day*. To go back to what you said about the horror beneath the surface – it sounds alarming – yes, I suppose I have always been aware of that, or I've been aware of it, that something, something that emerged in my writing. For that reason, that very reason, the maintenance of the surface as a subject fascinates me. In fact, the more the surface seems to heave or threaten to crack the more its actual pattern fascinates me. What do I mean by the surface? Civilisation, any kind of control. I just said that I should not personally consider myself a novelist of sensibility. I should if I were asked about myself rather call myself a novelist of behaviour. This turns back to something that may seem quite off the point. As a child I got a terrible scare from the Halley Comet, 1910 wasn't it?[14]

Brooke: Yes, I'm sure it was 1910, because I remember being furious because I was too young to have seen it . . .

Bowen: Well, you certainly missed there an excoriating nervous experience. A little friend of mine at the day school I was at at Folkestone took me aside and told me that this comet was at any moment going to hit the earth, that it was whistling towards us and that all the grown-ups knew that the collision and the demolition were inevitable. They were keeping it from us, and we children had not been told.

Brooke: Good heavens, I'm rather glad I missed it. Well, that's rather the position we're all in nowadays. We're all sort of waiting for disaster but the grown-ups won't tell.

Bowen: I think the Halley Comet panic was so intense for me that it finally and forever exhausted my fear of impact.

Brooke: Sort of immunised you, really.

Bowen: Yes, immunised. I could say that it had two other effects. I've remained impressed by people's formidable capacity for silence, for keeping a secret, and not less by their power of acting up, of behaving as though nothing were the matter.

Brooke: Yes, one still is surprised by it. It just struck me as a very good example of that in *The House in Paris*: the unspoken dread felt by the children; the sense that grown-ups weren't telling one things.

Bowen: Yes, and when they aren't told, how do children make things out? It seems to me that children, very suspicious, are arbitrary in their observations.

Brooke: Yes.

Bowen: Don't you think? They can be so acute and they can show great blanks, times when they don't seem to have registered at all. Has it ever seemed to you that artists are a bit like that?

Brooke: I think very much so, yes, I think there is a parallel. One could quote Proust again as an example. We seem to keep dragging him in, but Proust used to say, if you remember, that he was a very bad observer of the social scene. He never noticed details in the journalistic sense, like a society novelist. Yet one knows the amount of observation in his books is enormous. One can only imagine that it was largely unconscious at the time. That he only recollected it in tranquillity. As he said the memory is like a photographic plate which has to be developed and may, and often does develop in patches. I think this would apply to the child's memory and the artist's, don't you agree?

Bowen: Yes, Jocelyn, I was very much caught by a phrase in one of your books, "the haunted coastline."

Brooke: Oh, yes.

Bowen: You feel that a tract of land interlocks with an acute phase of personal memory.

Brooke: Oh very much so.

Bowen: You will agree that it comes again as one goes on in life. What could be a sort of extra dimension by being associated with the acute awareness of childhood. My impression is that in our dwelling on childhood we are really more than anything hankering to recapture some particular faculty that childhood had. So many other periods of one's life are comparatively boring to remember, in fact, so boring that one often simply fails to remember them. That's one reason why I never could, I know, write autobiography. You do. How do you get round this?

Brooke: Well, I don't know. I suppose it's something to do again with this business of selective memory, but I agree it would be very boring to have to write a completely factual account of one's own life leaving out nothing. Yes, I think one can only write autobiographies selectively, leaving out the bits which one finds boring. The patches which don't develop properly on the photographic plate. So really, I think we get back to the fact that the act of writing, for you and me anyway, is an interior process, depending on a patchy and obsessional kind of memory, largely associated with place and landscape. Of course, a psychologist probably would explain the process in terms of neurosis and unconscious complex and so on, but I always feel myself that this kind of explanation is only partial. It can explain the how but not the why. All we know, really, I suppose, some people have this strange compulsion to write as others have to compose music or paint pictures, and they continue to have it apparently, however unpropitious the state of the world may be. Goodness knows it's bad enough.

Bowen: Yes. We shall have to stop in a minute. Let's arrive at one thing, as far as anything can be arrived at. Is art really rooted in obsessions? Is in fact obsession the cause of art? As far as I'm concerned I can't leave it at that, no. I can't ignore an enormous element of pleasure in the contemplation, in the very performance. I'm convinced that writers, or painters, like composers, really do intensely enjoy themselves.

Brooke: Oh yes, one does enjoy it.

Bowen: And if they don't do anything else they communicate by what they paint, or write, or compose, at least some degree of what has been their own enjoyment. I think art's sociability. I think it all links up with the enormous human fact that it's for pleasure. However bad the times, hundreds and thousands of people simply do enjoy themselves dancing, going to the races, strolling about on fine days, falling in love. They enjoy themselves more than they know, and more than perhaps they probably dare admit. One could say that the artist's only unlike his fellow man in being able to know to what degree, or at least to some degree how much he enjoys himself. If he dares to say so he's probably accused of fiddling while Rome burns. I still think that having to face that charge is better than taking up the morose, alternative attitude of here am I while Rome fiddles. I do. It may be fair enough. It is fair in these days to expect the artist to show credentials, everybody's expected to show credentials . . .

Brooke: Yes, alas we are.

Bowen: One thing I'm sure that he should not be edged into doing, that is to profess a misery he does not feel.

Do Women Think Like Men?

Young: In general everyone is prepared to recognize that men's and women's minds are apt to work differently. Miss Bowen and Mrs. Vallance must forgive me if I say that when we say of a man that he thinks like a woman we don't mean it as a compliment. I think we mean that, like a woman, such a man usually spoils his argument or a chain of reasoning by bringing in personal and irrelevant details.

Mabbott: But are personal details always irrelevant?

Bowen: Surely not. Everything will depend, won't it, on the line of argument? If we are drawing conclusions from certain mathematical assumptions, or calculating probabilities in statistical terms, then personal details like the colour of the eyes of one of the mathematicians would be totally irrelevant and would spoil the argument. But if we are concerned to discuss a problem of conduct, whether somebody shall or shall not behave in a certain way, then I think as many circumstances as anyone can recall about that somebody and the other people concerned may very well be to the point. If men think of women as likely to introduce irrelevant and personal details we should certainly think of men (shouldn't we, Mrs. Vallance?) as likely to make an argument unreal by being too abstract.

Vallance: I think we should. I suspect that we think of men as taking to reason merely as a game, which they are willing to play for the sake of the game and without much regard to the consequence.

Young: I think I can bear that out. I have talked about this to women sometimes. What they have told me is that they consider that the weakness of the man is that he will insist on giving reasons for what he does or thinks, and that the reasons are usually wrong.

Mabbott: Meaning that a man is apt to put so much faith in reasons that he will draw them from anywhere in order to make out a case. Yes, I think that's true. If we think of men's aptitude as an ability to pursue a line of abstract thought, how would you define woman's gifts?

Bowen: Flexibility, quickness in the uptake, sensitiveness and a sympathetic attitude towards the other person's point of view.

Vallance: I agree with you. Comparing her with a man, I'd be inclined to say the woman was more receptive and kept her feet planted better on the ground. I was at a party the other evening and our hostess made us play one of those games which are supposed to require lots of concentration. Somebody read out fourteen different clues in a situation. It was supposed that by listening to them carefully we should be able to answer any unexpected query which was put to us at the end. It began like this: A train carrying passengers was travelling from Euston to Liverpool. The guard, the engine-driver and the fireman were called Smith, Jones and Robinson, but not respectively. So it went on, the guard collecting tickets and talking to the passengers, who also had names and were travelling to and from different places. Then came the last clue and the question: Smith played billiards with the fireman – what was the name of the engine-driver? And immediately a woman's voice said: "Smith, of course." Everybody looked up in consternation. "What do you mean, Smith?" someone said. And the woman replied: "Smith was the name of the engine-driver." Everybody was rather indignant, and the man who propounded the game said: "She's quite right. Smith is the engine-driver's name." "But how did you know it was?" we all asked. "You certainly haven't had time to work it out." The woman looked a bit embarrassed. "Work it out?" she said. "I didn't work out anything, but I did hear John ask at the end what was the engine-driver's name, and having heard that Smith played billiards with the fireman, well, I knew of course that no one else on the train would know him well enough to play billiards with him."

Mabbott: What a nice story! And perfectly typical of a woman. She got the answer by going down quite another path from the one intended. And a much quicker path, as it turned out.

Bowen: It would be all right if there were always alternative paths.

Mabbott: Are you sure that there aren't?

Vallance: I think he'd be a bold man, or woman, to say so.

Young: Yes, I should like to suggest that the network of associated ideas differs in men and women.

Vallance: You mean that the connections of ideas can be distinguished in men's and women's minds?

Young: Yes, and not only that, but that the principles of selection are quite different and I believe we have already put our finger on the difference when we said that men liked rather to deal with topics in general, and women rather in particular, terms.

Bowen: And which is the more useful?

Young: It will depend on the task in hand. We might fall back on that image of ours of the pyramid of knowledge whose base is made up of particular facts and whose apex is the absolutely general idea. When we are concerned with marshalling detail on or near the base line we might expect women's gifts to be useful, but should look to men to help us as soon as the problem has become generalised.

Vallance: And what does the image mean when translated into actual instances?

Young: That the field of the woman is wherever individual men and women count as such, and have to be handled or dealt with as such. Men come into their own when the individual as such ceases to be important and gives way to the general principle. Roughly speaking, I should give women the field of social relations and men the field of administration.

Mabbott: I think that's right. We shall want the generalising abilities of the man's mind not only in the pursuit of abstract knowledge in history, science, economics and so on, but in the construction of the systems of law, justice, education, transport and that sort of thing – the systems within whose frames we live. But we must not forget that individual men and women have to live in these systems, however elaborate they are, and as you said, Young, it's in the business of relating these individual lives to one another that women's gifts can play so large a part.

Bowen: And what is it that you think endows us to play a specially useful part in social relations?

Mabbott: Partly, I should say, your distrust of generalisation, and that distrust is in personal relations, of course, the saving grace, and there's also the extraordinary range of your particular observations. Generalisation we are agreed in thinking is the man's characteristic, and must always be carried through at the expense of the particular instance. I should say that a woman had an extraordinary knack of not neglecting the particular instance, but of taking close notice of it and of storing it away intact for future use.

Young: And the lengths to which women can carry this gift are sometimes quite extraordinary. I'll tell you a story which illustrates the point. I remember coming up from the City to have lunch one day and somebody coming up to me on the Underground platform and saying, "Excuse me, but aren't you Mr. Jacks?" I told him I wasn't and got into the train, and presently the man came up to me again in the train and said, "Excuse me, but I can't help thinking I've met you before somewhere." I rather impatiently told him that I couldn't remember him and I turned away. At lunch I sat next to an Austrian lady who had entertained me once in her house in Vienna. To fill up a pause in the conversation I told her about the man who had spoken to me in the train, and she said at once, "I wonder if it was the man whom I introduced you to in Vienna who was looking for a job?" and it came back to me in a flash that it was that man, but by what power had she at once thought of this man and suggested him to me?

Bowen: The stock answer would be, of course, by intuition. But what is intuition?

Young: In this case I expect that the tone of my voice when I told her of this man on the platform probably reminded her of the way I had spoken of the man in Vienna. I wonder if it is anything more than a quick summary of half-remembered, remembered, or perhaps even forgotten experiences?

Mabbott: I should say that that was a very serviceable description of it. Certainly it would fit in very beautifully with what we have been saying about the woman's gift for paying attention to the particular. Man, as we have said, being less interested in the particular, squeezes it dry if he uses it at all and incorporates it as a dead instance in the walls of his theory. The woman, because she attends to it so closely at the time, perhaps, manages to keep the life in it and to bring it out instantly and powerfully just at the right moment. I should say that she had a specific talent for keeping her thought alive with experience, and of bringing her past experience to bear in her present consideration of any problem.

Young: I wonder if this is part of what I have always thought, that women have a larger sense of responsibility.

Mabbott: Do you mean that women's sense of responsibility is deeper and graver than men's?

Young: I should have thought so. I wonder if Miss Bowen and Mrs. Vallance would agree to that?

Bowen: I think I should. It's part of what I meant, I think, when I said at the beginning of this discussion that men seemed to *think* so often, to generalise, to think abstractedly, for the fun of it, as if reasoning were in the end a game. Turning live issues too quickly into generalisations does seem to me to show a lack of responsibility. I think it's what your women friends meant when they told you, Mr. Young, that men were always looking for reasons for what they think and do.

Vallance: I agree most strongly too. I think we have more sense of responsibility than men, and I think it probably comes from bearing children. It's very difficult for us to think of life as a game. We haven't, as it were, time to play. There are so many things we actually have to do: cooking the meals, feeding the children, mending the clothes, and so on and so on. I think that most women do think of generalities and general conceptions as a snare and a delusion. Men have such a free way of talking about things like courage and honour and nationality, for instance. When a man talks of Germany a woman at once thinks not of Germany but of the German men and women of whom she knows Germany to consist. I believe that most women think of the war as men's work, and the result of men's way of thinking, as if men had let their differences grow larger and larger, into carrying more and more general significance, until the conflicting aims which we, as women, would have tried to reconcile at the root had grown into immense clashes of systems of thought and honour which couldn't issue except in war. Yes, it's as if we had made the mistake of letting one of our children's bad digestion and temper produce such quarrelling and violence in the house as to end by everything in the house being broken up and smashed to pieces.

Young: No doubt women will always look on men as children. And they are quite right. We both begin as babies, but girls grow up and boys never do. Still it is man's power of generalisation that has created the great systems of thought and knowledge, and into them there is no passport except what men call reason. I remember taking part in a discussion on this subject some years ago. Somebody said: "Do you think when a man says two and two are four that he means the same as when a woman says it?" And somebody answered: "They mean the same thing, but the truth is that a woman would not think it worth saying." His answer seemed to me very suggestive, and I've taken it to mean that we've been stressing here that a woman distrusts what is only formal. Once upon a time I remember walking down a lane in the twilight with a woman when a car suddenly came up behind us. We were walking rather to the middle of the road. "Step right!" I said, and the woman hesitated and moved first to one side and then to the other. Talking about it afterwards she said that like most women she always had to think which was her left hand and which her right. I remember being told as a boy that when the canal bargemen give over their boats to their women folk to steer they put up a loaf of bread on one gunwale and a jug of beer on the other and say, "Steer to the loaf, steer to the jug."

Bowen: I should call that a very practical plan. What use is a general principle, then?

Vallance: But you must remind us, Mabbott, what all this has to do with philosophy.

Mabbott: It has a great deal to do with philosophy. Whether or not we learn to distinguish between the processes of men's and women's minds will decide a good many of our educational problems, for instance. Are we going to understand giving equal opportunities of education to men and women to mean that women should be educated on the same lines as men?

Vallance: Won't that depend partly on whether women are being educated to earn their own living?

Young: Not if in virtue of the distinction between men and women's powers we learn to make use of and pay for women's particular abilities in the profession. For example, I should like to see women much more widely employed in the administrative grades of the Civil Service, on the grounds of their quicker perception of individual and personal qualities. On the higher administrative levels, where the sphere of operations is larger, we require the masculine, generalising mind. Most of the Secretaries will, I suggest, be men, but a great many of the Assistant Secretaries will be women.

Bowen: I wonder where one draws the line?

Mabbott: Everything depends, I suppose, as Young says, on the size and the sphere of operations. The smaller the sphere the more the particular will count.

Vallance: I suppose that does not mean, in the end, that we're going to have to limit women's gifts to the home?

Mabbott: Not at all. Do you remember Homer Lane's account of the little law court set up by the children in the model reformatory? The boys occupied the judgement seat to start with, but they were soon deposed by common consent in favour of the girls on the grounds that the girls, instead of formulating general rules of punishment, knew better how to adapt a special punishment to each offender in turn. Two children might commit the same crime, but they wouldn't be awarded the same punishment by the girls. No, each would be given the punishment which the girl knew each particularly disliked. I expect you'd agree, Mrs. Vallance, that women had given in too much during the last twenty years to rationalising in the treatment of their children.

Vallance: Yes, and even of the newly born. I and my contemporaries all tried to bring up our babies according to the precepts of a well-known baby specialist from America,[1] who had planned a programme for young things all round the clock. Fifteen minutes at half-past six were set aside marked "Artless Baby Prattle."

Bowen: Where does the specifically female sphere of influence begin and end?

Young: It all depends how far women's sympathies and interests can be extended. I was saying, I think, that the higher levels of administration require the generalising mind which we have agreed to think typical of the male. Women judges could do their work in a court which was directed to individual reformatories, but a universal conception of justice must work by principle and not by individual instances. But I should never admit that this means in the end that women's power should be limited to the home. I think we agreed earlier that the woman's gift for appreciating particulars and her ability to use them made her invaluable wherever the matter in hand involved personal relations. That is to say that it seems to me capable of being exercised in far wider spheres of society than the home.

Vallance: One has only to think of someone like George Eliot to realise how wide her sphere of influence can be made.

Young: Now Mabbott, sum up.

Mabbott: You asked me, Miss Bowen, what were the philosophical implications of the distinctions we have been trying to make. I said that they obviously very closely concerned theory and practice in education. Young has pointed out that they bear very directly also on theory and practice in administration. But they have another bearing still, which perhaps philosophically is the most important. And that is what these distinctions seem to suggest about the nature of thinking itself. Many people suppose that generalising is the only method by which a chain of thought can be carried on and developed. We didn't get very far in this discussion without discovering that women distrusted generalisation. Certainly it is dangerous. It has a way of leaving reality out of sight. It all depends, as we have said again and again, on where it's applied. Still, dangerous or not, it would be no use if there were not alternative methods of advance in thought and argument. I believe myself that no greater mistake can be made than to suppose that thinking is a matter of pure generalisation. I think that this is altogether too narrow a conception of reasoning, and that it leads in the end to every sort of error in judgement and to the construction of all sorts of false philosophical theories. For the present, I think we might suppose that the distinctions we have made here have been useful in showing that women's powers, sensitive, receptive, intuitive, are in their own spheres just as fruitful and have just as much right to be called true forms of thought.

Do Conventions Matter?

Mabbott: Every society has found it necessary to conventionalise certain kinds or aspects of behaviour.

Bowen: It's obvious why, I think. What an appalling waste of social energy if every man and woman had to decide for himself or herself what was the appropriate behaviour to adopt in any given situation, and what a danger of being misunderstood.

Noad: Yes indeed, as people often are in foreign countries. Radically misunderstood. I remember a distinguished visitor and his wife coming to a small out-station in Africa, where the people wore no clothes at all. In preparation for their arrival, the local District Commissioner had issued out to all the people a yard of calico, lest the susceptibility of the lady should be shocked. The people all turned up on time, as appointed, wearing the calico, but round their heads. But accidents apart, I still think that convention is not only a safeguard but an immense economy of effort.

Bowen: Yes, and it also makes it possible for me to predict what other people are going to do, and to adjust my own behaviour accordingly.

Pryce-Jones: Unlike a rather ridiculous example of the contrary which I remember seeing once in an opera house, when a horse which had been borrowed from the local circus recognized one of the tunes and behaved according to the conventions of the circus – which, of course, it knew by heart – rather than according to the conventions of the tenor on its back. The result was that instead of carrying the tenor in triumph up to the steps of the cathedral, the horse rose slowly on its hind legs, advanced, pawing the air, and, needless to say, crashed through the cathedral altogether.

Bowen: That is an extraordinarily good example, because humans, when they are over-conventionalised, do begin to look a little like animals at a circus.

Pryce-Jones: I can think of humans embarrassing each other in much the same way. In some parts of the Sudan, it is the custom of one tribe for the men to wear a string of beads round them and the women nothing, where a comparatively few miles away, the exact opposite is the custom – the women wear the beads and the men nothing.

Mabbott: And do you remember Sir Thomas More's account of the visit of the Ambassadors of Britain to the Council Chamber of Utopia? These ambassadors arrived laden with heavy gold chains and the jewelled insignia of their office, and they were dreadfully embarrassed when the councillors of Utopia rose to their feet and burst into laughter, and this was because adults in Utopia had long since given up attaching any importance to childish gauds and trinkets, and they could only conclude that Britain had seen fit to send, instead of councillors, children or lunatics.

Bowen: Yes, we have called conventions an economy and a guide, but it is obvious that unlike, or conflicting, sets of conventions can complicate relations rather than make them easier.

Noad: So that if the world is trying to widen the order of its society, the local conventions must somehow give place to a larger set of conventions to which all peoples can reconcile themselves.

Bowen: And not only when it's a question of relating one country to another. Conventions can enormously slow down the real integration of any given society by prolonging through the outward symbol, sectional interests, class interests, geographical customs and all that sort of thing which keep people apart long after their common sympathies should have brought them together.

Mabbott: Yes, it is a question of flexibility and of paying as much, and no more, respect to conventions than they deserve. But there are certain fundamental conventions which are quite free from emotional colour.

Noad: Would money be an example of a convention of this kind? And would language be another?

Mabbott: Certainly, and perhaps the most fundamental of all. And that also varies from place to place and from time to time, but it's a universal convention.

Pryce-Jones: What you mean, then, is that anything is a convention which has an agreed importance or significance attached to it which isn't, so to speak, intrinsic or proper to the thing itself. A half-crown piece isn't, for example, worth half-a-crown, and it might be exchanged for five or ten shillings if we agreed to accept it as a token of so much value.

Mabbott: Yes, and the same with words. There's nothing in the letters t-a-b-l-e which make it necessary that they should stand for a table, but we agree none the less, that a table is what t-a-b-l-e shall refer to.

Bowen: And you think that with the necessary modifications for particular cases the same thing holds for conventions of any and every kind?

Mabbott: I think so.

Noad: You offered us a tentative definition of convention, Pryce-Jones, as something to which we agreed in attaching a significance which doesn't belong by its own nature to the thing itself. Well, if no particular importance belongs to any conventional act as such, why do we agree to attach importance to it far beyond what it deserves?

Pryce-Jones: I wonder if a distinction between means and ends would help us there?

Bowen: Surely not, or at any rate, we can hardly pretend that people do look upon conventions as a means to an end. That is to say, whatever they ought to do, people do, in fact, insist on attaching quite an absurd importance to the conventional act itself.

Mabbott: Still, I think you are right, Pryce-Jones, that we can make use of this distinction between ends and means. Though as you say, a man feels uncomfortable if he turns up somewhere in the wrong clothes, or feels ashamed of himself if he talks as though there were only men in the room when women are present, without thinking about the value of these conventions, yet I do think the source of their authority, the origin of their status, is the fact that they are means to ends beyond themselves. A convention is something to which people agree as a basis on which they can enter into relations with one another. A convention is one more example, surely, of the common ground which relates the individual to the society he lives in. A convention is something which makes it possible for us individually to meet and to have to do with one another. If it weren't for our agreeing to attach the same meaning to the same words, we couldn't talk to one another or make any exchange of ideas. If we didn't agree to accept tokens of money for such-and-such values, we couldn't buy or sell to each other or enter into commercial relations.

Noad: That seems clear enough. But then, as you said, it does still seem that some conventions are more fundamental than others. Are we to feel ourselves bound to stick to the more superficial as well as the more fundamental conventions on the ground of their being equally entitled to respect as a means of social relations?

Mabbott: No, surely not. The fact that conventions are conventions and not laws suggests at once that we are entitled to some sort of discrimination and choice. It's open to society to codify and impose the whole sanction of law and order on any principles of social behaviour which it thinks fundamental enough to deserve the authority of law.

Pryce-Jones: And one country varies very much from another, doesn't it, in the range of its law. Some countries, like France, incline to carry the business of law-making into all sorts of particular matters of social behaviour which we in this country, for instance, prefer to leave unregulated.

Mabbott: Yes, it would be matter for argument at what point the sanction of law should best give place to the weight of public opinion. Obviously, if the law were to carry its authority into every single social activity, no change could take place in society at all, except by a revolution.

Pryce-Jones: So that in the end, you mean, it might need

a *coup d'état* to change a fashion in hats or the length of a woman's skirt.

Bowen: It seems then, that conventions rule over that part of social life which is still open to change. Can we argue from this that our conventions are keeping us back, so that the more we can dispense with them, the freer we can be to make steps forward?

Mabbott: Again I suppose it's a question of degree. We must not forget that there are large spheres of human behaviour where even the sanction of conventions doesn't run, where you and I and everybody else is free to do exactly as he or she chooses. And since this is so, we can safely assume that there are good reasons for conventions being authoritative where they are and for stopping where they do. We should all agree, I suppose, that it would be disastrous if the influence of conventions were to disappear at one stroke from society.

Pryce-Jones: I suppose that would represent something like a landslide in social behaviour. After all, people sometimes go abroad just in order to be able to live for a short time among other people who don't expect them to behave in any particular way. We all know what happens then. A man feels free to drink champagne and behave in Boulogne in a way that he wouldn't feel free to behave at all in Bournemouth or Bexhill.

Noad: Yes, I've seen the same sort of thing in Africa on a larger scale. One sees white men behaving in an altogether deplorable way, sometimes, among natives, on the assumption that the African will not know what sort of conduct is expected of the white. And I've seen native people making use of the same sort of licence among Europeans.

Bowen: Let's admit that we couldn't expect any good consequences from a wholesale lifting of conventions. But aren't we still, Mr. Mabbott, in the light of what you said about conventions not being law and therefore being in a sense optional instead of arbitrary, under the obligation of subjecting all our conventions to a very close scrutiny?

Noad: In order, you mean, that we can make quite sure that they are not holding us back?

Mabbott: I think you are quite right. But we must recognize that the critical attitude towards conventions must influence our judgements as well as our behaviour. We are most of us ready enough to depart from the conventional ourselves while we are much less ready to be tolerant towards other people.

Bowen: Yes. I suppose that the strength of conventions can be attacked and weakened, so to speak, at both ends. I mean, you can either attack the convention by direct assault, by refusing to obey it, by acting contrary to it and persuading as many other people as you can to do the same, or you can attack it on the flank by suspending judgement, in the negative way, by refusing to add the weight of your own disapproval to the general weight of public opinion.

Noad: And I should think that none of us would be in any doubt as to the relative wisdom of the two strategies.

Bowen: I suppose the flank attack is safer, but is it as effective? It's a strategy which seems to require a much larger striking force. Comparatively few people can cause a disturbance and attract a large amount of attention by flouting convention in the act, but it requires a very large number of people indeed to affect public judgement by merely judging tolerantly, or refusing to judge at all.

Mabbott: Yes, it does require a large number of people, but surely that's just what a convention deserves before it is changed. A convention being, by our own definition, something to which a large number of people agree.

Pryce-Jones: How much have the great flouters of convention achieved – people like Shelley and Byron and Oscar Wilde?

Bowen: Surely Shelley didn't so much flout public opinion as ignore it? And what about Florence Nightingale – wasn't she effective? And weren't Shaftesbury and Wilberforce?[1]

Mabbott: But they were fighting on much better ground. They were attacking more important conventions than Byron or Wilde, and I should have thought that their convictions were much more sincere. Still, in spite of a few noble exceptions, I should be inclined to agree with Noad that the suspension of judgement and the tolerant attitude was a better method of attack than the direct one on the conventions of any generation.

Pryce-Jones: That's an opinion which people generally reach late rather than early in their lives.

Noad: But would there be any harm in the young recognizing more commonly than they do that conventions are much less hindrances or stumbling blocks than tools in the hand?

Bowen: No, that's what he ought to recognize. I don't think we have yet succeeded in showing quite clearly enough how conventions are aids rather than hindrances to social life.

Pryce-Jones: We have admitted that trying to make a clean sweep of conventions is apt to lead to nothing better than a dissolute life whether it happens at Boulogne or in the middle of Africa.

Bowen: But that was an example of people using the absence of public opinion as an opportunity to do exactly the opposite of what conventions previously held them to. The point I want to bring out is that if society, or any section of society, because it was out of patience with the restricting influence of its conventions, were to try and make a new life possible, by sweeping away the conventions it knew, it would have to be content with stepping down from the level of culture it had been accustomed to to a primitive state of life.

Pryce-Jones: As, in fact, some sects have found to their cost. Think of institutions like Emerson's Brook Farm,[2] or even Salt Lake City, which have limited themselves to a primitive form of social life in their attempts to set themselves free to carry out their ideals.

Mabbott: Yes. To take a single example, it would be like men and women who had found the conditions of married life irksome thinking that they could develop happier relationships with one another by scrapping all the conventions of marriage. Discredit the convention of marriage, and it would obviously take society a very long time to develop again all the subtleties of love and affection which the marriage tie has made possible.

Bowen: That would be like a composer thinking that in order to write a new symphony, he must have a new scale, or double the number of notes on his keyboard.

Pryce-Jones: Like, say, Arnold Schoenberg – he might spend the whole of his life developing a system and leave himself no time to put those systems to any real use.

Noad: The fact is, of course, that the art of life, just like the art of music or the art of poetry, depends much less on brand new invention than on the power of making new distinctions on the basis of what has already been established.

Mabbott: Yes, the new ground is won by profiting from other people's discoveries and experience, not from going back to where they started and trying to cover the whole ground from the beginning oneself. Conventions live not on the strength of what they put a stop to, but on the strength of what they make possible. But if we are going to call conventions a tool, there's a wrong way of using them – not for what they make possible but because they are conventions.

Noad: I'm still thinking of the consequences we talked about of anything like a complete lifting of the authority of convention. Doesn't Nazi Germany give us an example? I suppose one naturally looks on the middle or professional classes as the backbone of any society, since it is in them, speaking by and large, that the great majority of general conventions are rooted. Now, as we know, the standing and influence and almost the existence of the professional classes in Germany were undermined and smashed by the currency inflation of 1922. With the disappearance of the professional classes in Germany the great body of social traditions disappeared too. And the pattern of social behaviour was left in the hands either of the few powerful and pushing people, who asked no better than to sacrifice the whole of society to their own ambitions, or the younger generation who had no respect for tradition. I believe the disappearance of the professional classes, and with them the disappearance of the great bulk of organic social convention explains the pace at which Hitler and his Nazi adjutants were able to corrupt the standards of German society.

Mabbott: I think that an extraordinarily good example. It is important, as you said, Miss Bowen, that we should subject our conventions to scrutiny and criticism. For if, as you suggest, Noad, the body of convention represents an organic tradition with which we cannot dispense, yet, on the other hand, particularly when the pace of life changes as radically as it does nowadays, our particular conventions do get out of touch with contemporary ideals and needs. It would be difficult, I suppose, to find another period in history when the conventions of one generation have been as drastically modified as in our own day. But there is such a thing as changing them too fast to be safe, though it doesn't matter how fast one particular set of conventions gives place to another so long as continuity isn't lost in the sense of value that underlies the conventions. Conventions and values react upon one another. Conventions express values, but they also tend in their performance to modify the values themselves. If too large a body of convention is suddenly scrapped, the underlying standard of values may, as it were, be snapped off and broken in two. Then society loses, as we say, its sense of value altogether. It can no longer take people's behaviour as a guide to what matters. It no longer knows what one thing does matter in comparison with another, and then in the confusion and disorder that follows, the interests of society are sacrificed to the ambitions of those who are strong enough and ruthless enough to usurp power.

Conversation on Traitors

Annan: Tonight we're going to talk about traitors, and talk in the sense that we're really going to simply have a conversation about them. It's natural that they've been very much in our minds, not only because of the Nunn May and Fuchs trials, which Moorehead has written a book about recently, but also because of the whole combine of the traitors – the Communist traitors and the Fascist or Nazi traitors during the war – people like William Joyce, for example, and also the American, Ezra Pound, the poet, and also traitors perhaps in the remote past. We want to think about what we mean by the word "treason" and to consider all sorts of questions about loyalty to one's country and the conflicting loyalties which come up and make one sometimes feel that a man, though he was a traitor to his country, had done the right thing. For instance, a controversial case which comes to my mind is one of Sir Roger Casement in the First World War. He was an Irishman. Can you tell us, Miss Bowen, about him?

Bowen: Yes. Roger Casement, who might be said to have

betrayed the country which had honoured him and in which he had worked, which was England, in the interests of Ireland to whose cause he became so deeply attached. He conspired during the war, just before the 1916 rebellion, with Germany, hoping to enlist help from Germany, hoping to bring in the Irishmen who'd served in British regiments on the Irish side. He was captured during a landing in Ireland, trying to stop the 1916 rising, and he was hanged as a traitor. In the view of his own country he was a true patriot; in the view, inevitably, of the British, he had used the honour and prestige in which he was held as a smokescreen.

Annan: Yes, it's exactly that sort of conflict that I was thinking about when I was talking a moment ago. Balchin, do you think one can define treason in any way which is satisfactory?

Balchin: I think it's very easy to define treason, but I think we must distinguish between treason and traitors and treachery. Treason is a legal concept. It is legally definable and to me, at least, a traitor and treachery are not legally definable concepts but essentially emotional ones. It is possible to say, with certainty, that a man did or did not commit treason. But I submit that not every traitor commits treason and that not everybody who commits treason is necessarily a traitor. If I had to attempt some sort of definition I think it would be something like this: that treachery and a traitor always deal in secrecy. Merely to oppose the views popularly held in your country is not treachery, if you do so openly. Treachery involves a double-facedness, a two-way deceptive operation. Though I don't say that this is any more than a cock-shy definition, it seems to me to involve some failure of what one feels ought to be a natural loyalty. I don't think that there can be any doubt that if a man acts against the interests of his own native country, or say, his own family, we have a feeling that some natural law has gone wrong, and it seems as though treason, nearly always, and treachery of all kinds, usually, arises from some deep-rooted conflict, emotions, which I think is a point you made very clearly in your recent book, Moorehead.

Moorehead: Yes, I think that all the people I wrote about were caught up with this – well, perhaps not Pontecorvo because we don't really know about him – but they were caught up with this problem of double loyalty. Their real shortcoming, probably, is that they never really worked things out for themselves.

Perhaps it was because they lacked some settled conviction which they ought to have grown up with, ought to have known about, through their training. Perhaps they were overtaken by the chaotic moment of history in which they were living. But I did feel, all the way through, when I was doing the research for this book, that we were up against something new in the world here, that here was a type of traitor who had immense things to betray, immense secrets, and although perhaps others will disagree with me, I think that did put them into a new category.

Annan: Would you say that it put them in any different category from, say, Roman Catholics in the days of the Reformation? Surely there was the same adherence to some international concept?

Moorehead: Classically, perhaps not, but in their consequences – in the consequences of what they did – I think they were immeasurably more important to the future history of mankind.

Annan: Pragmatically more important but not ethically more so?

Moorehead: No, not ethically, no, I'd agree with you there, not ethically.

Bowen: Do you think that the scale of the betrayal – the size of the issues at stake, such as atomic secrets – determines the scale, the size, the magnitude or the ability of the traitor?

Moorehead: I think it does, to some extent. I think the schoolboy who cheats at school, although ethically he may be doing no more and no less than the traitor who gives away the atomic bomb, nevertheless can be corrected and the consequences of which – of what he does – are so much less.

Balchin: Well, I agree that between cheating at school and betraying the secrets of the atomic bomb there's obviously a great difference, but historically it seems to me that the two – that when you compare treason, shall we say, at the time of the Gunpowder Plot with treason such as Nunn May committed, there isn't really a distinction there.

Annan: You say one is more important than the other, but each generation in history thinks that its own problems are as important as any other generation in history. I don't really think that that's the distinction. I think the distinction is one though which is what was in the mind of the men when they did it; and one of the two points I think you made was this question of whether conscience – whether if you say, "well, I really thought that this was the right thing to do," justifies you; and I believe that you'd held that that was not so, and that you weren't justified merely by standing on your conscience?

Moorehead: Yes, I've been much taken up by this point.

Annan: Well, Moorehead can tell us. What do you feel?

Moorehead: Well, I think the words at issue were these: I wrote that Fuchs was basically a man who would refer to his own conscience first and society afterwards. It's possible I should have expanded that or even re-written it in a different way. What I was really getting at was this: I do think that a lot of people have not competent consciences. I don't altogether believe that we are born with a correct knowledge of right and wrong, for ourselves, and still less for society at large. I think our consciences have to be educated, and I would not like to countenance a world in which we upheld the right of every man to obey his own conscience and do precisely what he liked. I think that way chaos lies.

Balchin: But if you extend your principle there, are you suggesting that a man should never do so?

Moorehead: Certainly not – certainly not. I think that he should consult his own conscience and consult the traditions of the society in which he's living; he should perform the same operation – the one operation at the same time.

Balchin: That's quite reasonable, but it rather is liable to lead us to the feeling that if the man eventually agrees with us, he's consulted his conscience and tradition properly; if he disagrees with us, he's not done so. You see, I don't agree with you that the collective conscience of society is really a very useful weapon; I don't think that society, collectively, has a patent right in all ethical principles.

Annan: But Balchin look, I mean[1] you were saying really that when Count Stauffenberg[2] tried to blow up Hitler on the 20th July that we're very likely to say he was not a traitor. He was quite right to do that because we merely think that it was a good thing to have blown up Hitler. But when Nunn May gives away atomic secrets of this country and of America that he was wrong, simply because it was against our own country's interests. Is that the point you're making?

Balchin: Yes I am, I am saying that. I have no doubt that

society has the right to protect itself against anybody who disagrees with it, as long as it doesn't take a high ethical line which seeks to suggest that what was in fact purely pragmatic had some ethical basis to it, one is – society is allowed to dispose of awkward individuals.

Bowen: What about the man who is genuinely unaware of society, the man who lives in a private world, a cerebral world, the highly concentrated scientist, leading practically no conscious life outside his laboratory, sacrificing quite often personal relationships, pleasure, the normal contacts of life? He may well – and I imagine one [. . .] of it, his particular influence, in Fuchs,[3] until his final discovery of working relationships, personal relationships at Harwell which made him withdraw. There was an instance of a man to whom society was only a theory, or principle, an abstraction surely, whereas his own conscience was a burning force in him which involved his intellect, I should say from his own showing.

[Talking together]

Bowen: . . . his intellect, but it involved it.

Balchin: It's a little dangerous to suggest once again that everybody who doesn't agree with us is in some way intellectually unbalanced. It may be true: it's a failure of adaptation to disagree with society. But what I object to is the implication that the majority verdict in ethical matters is necessarily the correct verdict, as opposed to the necessary practical one.[4]

Moorehead: Balchin, could I put this to you? Are you willing to support the right of everybody to obey their consciences, even though they may be traitors?

Balchin: Yes, I am, because it seems to me that a man's own conscience is in the end the most reliable guide he's got. It may lead him to the wrong conclusions. It may certainly lead him to socially undesirable ones. But I don't feel that he has any other reference on which he can really rely.

Bowen: What about the conscience of the unstable person, which is bound to tilt and veer according to his emotional reactions, or when he's moved or . . .

Balchin: Then he must change his mind[5] when his mind changes. He can do no more.

Annan: That's what Luther said when he said, "God help me, but I can no other."[6]

Moorehead: Certainly.

Bowen: Yes.

Annan: I wonder if we could simplify this a little bit by my putting what is really rather an unfair question. Do you defend the right of Fuchs to do what he did do?

Balchin: Yes, most certainly.

Moorehead: Well . . .

Annan: Now on what grounds, Balchin?

Balchin: On the grounds that using such intellect as he had got as well as he could, he arrived at one time at the conclusion that he should pass this information to what was at that time a friendly power. He later decided that he was[7] wrong and confessed. It seems to me that it's difficult to see how the man could have followed his conscience very much further. Fuchs in a sense was right to do what he did. I also defend society in its treatment of him.

Bowen: Yes, that seems fair enough. Also he was not bound in any way, apart from a serious question of oaths, to this country. He was German by birth; he was Russian by affiliation of ideas. The reproaches that were levelled on him – the lack of gratitude and lack of loyalty – were based, I think, on conventional ideas of gratitude and loyalty, which are spontaneous things. It must be exceedingly difficult for a person displaced by forces outside himself, from his own country, to form a spontaneous, genuine, heartfelt attachment, I should imagine. From what one saw of émigrés, evacuees, and placeless persons – displaced people during the war – they did not have a naturally warm or spontaneous feeling. It was a feeling of bleak necessity to be in the country you were in.

Moorehead: Nevertheless, Fuchs had been for many years in this country and had become a British citizen.

Balchin: Yes.

Moorehead: And he gave out that he would be loyal in all his actions to the laws of this country.

Balchin: Yes, it was a failure of contact. That I would entirely agree is inexcusable.

Annan: You see he signed the Official Secrets Act and broke that. In other words, he disobeyed the ethical principle that promises must be kept.

Moorehead: More than that, he pretended to be a friend and he wasn't a friend.

Balchin: That is my point about a double-dealing attitude being one of the basic things. But of course there have been plenty of instances in history in which people have acted in a two-faced way, or broken their oaths, for what they conceived to be good reasons and we now tend to admire them. It's worth remembering that George Washington was an oath-breaker in that sense.

Bowen: Yes.

Annan: And of course it was one of the terrible problems that faced Frenchmen during the recent war. Should they break their oath – French officers for example – should they break their oath to Marshal Pétain? A great many of them decided, of course, they couldn't because this oath was binding on them. The thing that worries me, you see, about this conscience business is this: it's perfectly right it seems to me to say that a man's conscience must be his guide. And from there you can go on, as you did, Balchin, to say Fuchs in a sense was right to do what he did. But the question I'm worried about is this: the rightness or goodness of an action depends on its probable consequences. Now is there evidence that these people, such as Nunn May and Fuchs, had ever really considered the probable consequences of their action? In all its variety, you see there were a great many things they had to consider. They ought to have considered not only whether in fact their action of betraying these secrets was going to make the world a better place, but, for instance, how this would react in Fuchs's case, how this, his action, would react on fellow refugees. I mean doesn't it make us – for instance, that action of Fuchs's – suspicious of people whom we don't really know much about, because they've come from a foreign country and settled here? Now it seems to be a very bad state of mind to be in when we're suspicious of people, and Fuchs's action helped people to become more suspicious.

Balchin: But you can't provide for every contingency of that kind, I mean during the war, you assume that the people who are in your army will fight on your side, but there are instances where you hand a man a rifle and he immediately shoots the man in the next bed. That is an occupational risk. You can't provide for every contingency of that kind.

Annan: No. I wasn't suggesting that. But what I was really asking was had these people, whom we call traitors, had they really considered the consequences of their action, and I believe that they hadn't. Simply to say, "Oh, they were Communists," and therefore the whole problem of the matter was solved for them, all they had to do was owe allegiance to the Communist Party, that to my mind is not really facing the problem; it's a way of getting out of it.

Balchin: Would you agree, Moorehead, that Fuchs certainly seems to have thought about this enough, even if he thought about it badly?

Moorehead: Yes, he thought about it very deeply and very inadequately. I don't think we ought altogether to dismiss this factor. There is a tremendous attraction in just the villainous act of being a spy. I know this is rather a light point, but I think it ought to be borne in mind, and I think that Fuchs, who found himself in the possession – in the possession of a great secret, was immensely attracted by the whole paraphernalia of giving it away, and by so doing taking a hand in the control of the world. I think there was slight megalomania in it.

Bowen: I was interested when you described him as an addict who said that after those – that period of abstention when he failed to contact those Russian agents . . .

Moorehead: Yes.

Bowen: . . . he returned almost against his will, against his newly developing social conscience – as an addict returns to a drug or a person returns to a vice.

Moorehead: Yes – yes I think he did. I think he did. And I think that was a time of torment to him – the torment probably that the drug addict knows when he's breaking off his habit and discovering a new one. And Fuchs in the end, of course, was undone by the fact that he at last began to understand some of the simple loyalties of living with other people – a factor which he'd never considered before.

Bowen: He did say of himself, didn't he, in the confession though, that – "I found I myself had been made by circumstances . . ."

Moorehead: Yes he did. That's why I said his conscience ought not to have been his guide.

Bowen: No.

Balchin: No, what would you suggest should have been his guide?

Moorehead: I think that probably if he had had a more fortunate training and lived in a more fortunate period of history, of course the problem wouldn't have arisen. Perhaps there was no hope for Fuchs – perhaps he was inevitable. But what I would not defend is the right of these odd people to consult their consciences when their consciences are not competent – certainly not competent to legislate for the world at large.

Balchin: But you see that's very difficult, because as far as I remember, one of the main charges against the people tried at Nuremberg was that they had failed to consult their consciences in these matters. There was a letter, I think, from Lord Wright in the *Times* the other day pointing out that a man cannot plead superior orders as a defence in a war crimes trial.[8] And as far as I can see one of our great objections to the Germans we tried at Nuremberg was that they'd accepted the view of the society in which they lived, and the Government of that society, when their consciences ought to have told them otherwise. Now either people should use their consciences, or they shouldn't, but you can't have it both ways.

Moorehead: Yes, but Balchin, surely at Nuremberg the issue didn't turn on conscience. Surely these men were tried on the basis of whether or not they obeyed international law, international practice, not their own consciences.

Balchin: But surely a man either obeys orders, or the orders of the government or society in which he lives. Or else he consults his conscience and says, "No, I know this is wrong."

Moorehead: Well, as I understand it, at Nuremberg these men were asked, "Did you not feel when you were given this monstrous order to do away with so many children in the gas chamber, or whatever it was, that this was an affront to accepted international practice?" They were never asked was this an affront to your conscience.

Balchin: Really, were they seriously expected to understand international law?

Moorehead: Well I don't mean that . . .

Balchin: Surely what they were asked to understand was human decency . . .

Annan: Yes, exactly . . .

Moorehead: But that's conscience, not law.

Annan: Oh no, human decency isn't conscience.

Moorehead: Oh no, conscience – conscience might be something quite different.

Bowen: Well, surely it's a sort of rule of thumb for conscience, isn't it? I mean it's a reference in those problems of conscience in which we all at times find ourselves, and tend to become purely subjective. The only reference we have is to try the thing out on somebody else, try and see if one saw so-and-so behaving in that way, how would one judge them. I mean the idea of the rule, the elementary rules of the thing not being done, or being morally distasteful to do, exist outside oneself. One may occasionally break them down. One may say, "Yes that thing is distasteful, but I think I am right." But they do exist, and they are in a normal situation expected to prevail – like the case of putting children in a gas chamber.

Annan: But . . . Balchin, yes, go on.

Balchin: I would like to take up Moorehead's point that human decency is not relative to human conscience. What is it relative to?

Moorehead: What, the conscience?

Balchin: No, human decency. I mean what defines it?

Moorehead: Well let me ask a question of you in answering that. What do you suppose the conscience was of a sixteen-year-old Nazi boy in 1945 – a boy who'd only grown up under Nazi laws? Was it the same sort of conscience as, say, an English boy, or an American boy would have had?

Balchin: Certainly not. But you are assuming that conscience is purely a thing injected by training.

Moorehead: Not purely – no. All I want to suggest is that we are born with consciences. But they in themselves are not adequate; we do need the instruction of the traditions of the society in which we are living.

Annan: But what it really is, it seems to me, that you have various ethical principles – I mean, for instance, one norm of human behaviour in an ordinary civilised country is that a soldier is obedient to orders. That is a norm of behaviour – but there are others – and that may conflict with other principles – namely, not to commit murder and it is murder, for instance, to put defenceless children into gas chambers – and these conflicts of loyalty occur – and when they occur it's very unpleasant for us. But we have to decide which duty is more binding upon us.

And it seems to me that with traitors what often occurs is that they have not really thought out which duty is more binding upon them.[9]

Balchin: Or having thought it out, have arrived at what is the socially inconvenient conclusion.

Annan: That is true too.

All: Yes. Yes.

Bowen: But suppose, Mr. Annan, they're not qualified. Suppose they're so unequally developed – to get back to my idea of the driving of an obsession which deforms the reasoning faculty, or which draws the natural emotion out of them – that you can have a person bordering on the insane who has the whole machinery for instance – who has the fine brain, but owing to some displacement of the normal faculties through being obsessed, through a single-minded burning thing, which has – to put the thing practically – driven out this sense of cruelty or the sense of responsibility, or the sense of society – then[10] you have in that person a particular case. These men, Nunn May and Fuchs might be people normally slightly disabled in that way and placed anyhow in what might[11] be called an inhuman situation for even an ordinary human being. I mean they have at their disposal a thing so enormous to play around with.

Annan: Yes – certainly – and one may have compassion for someone in that position, and one may say this man had not the faculties which one may expect an ordinary human being to have. But it doesn't alter the fact that what he did was wrong.

Bowen: No.

Annan: The action can be wrong. The man you may have[12] compassion with. No. The question really also seems to me is to whether there is – there are some standards which we may have lost today, or which are different today which has made people potentially be traitors more than they were, shall we say, fifty years ago. I mean for instance, the question of what is the honourable thing to do. I'm reminded, I mean, particularly because a few – some years ago – E. M. Forster made a splendidly provocative statement in which he said that if I had to choose between betraying my country and betraying my friends I hope I should have the guts to betray my country.[13] It was words something to that effect. I mean that is the thing where it seems to me that Forster was thinking in terms of – that he might be placed in a position where what his country was doing he would think was really a bad thing, and that he would feel a higher loyalty to friends in whose integrity he believed.

Bowen: Yes. The point of integrity is important because, isolated, that sentence could give the impression that one was to be subject to one's affections, to one's affinities, to one's adherences, to one's personal emotions, and reply purely emotionally from the idea of failing a single, or group of dear human beings, and prefer to sacrifice his country. But being him of course the idea of integrity is implicit, isn't it?

Balchin: Yes. One of the things which I find trying about this is the fact that people seem to assume that right and wrong are things which are easy to see. But one sees a game of football with one side wearing one coloured shirt, which is right, and the other side wearing the other coloured shirt, which is wrong. Now it may be for more fortunate people that the colours of the shirts are clearer than[14] to me. I may be morally colour-blind. But my problem has always been, not so much to support the right, but to decide what the right was. And what I find a little distressing about a good many discussions of this subject is that people assume that there is some automatic way in which one knows what is right and what is wrong; and that that automatic way is the way society thinks. Now I disagree; I think it is possible for a man entirely, sincerely, using all brains and all the effort he can, to arrive at what is socially the wrong conclusion. I think society is entitled then to punish him, imprison him, or do what it likes; but not to get on to the high ethical horse of assuming that what it thinks is right with a capital R, as opposed to being necessary socially. Which is to me a different issue.

Moorehead: I'll agree with you entirely there. But all I . . .

Annan: Can you develop it, Moorehead? Go on.

Moorehead: Yes. But all I would bring in – perhaps I'm repeating myself here – is that while society is never an adequate guide in itself, neither is conscience.

Annan: Well I would say conscience is, provided it is instructed by the intellect.

Moorehead: Provided it's instructed.

Balchin: But by whose intellect do you . . .

Annan: By the man's intellect.[15] It isn't merely a question of saying, "I want to do this, and I'm sure it's right." You have to consider the consequences of your actions, and you then have to begin to think, to ratiocinate. I don't say we do this all the time, because of course we act in accordance with the ethical norms of society. But when one is faced with a real conflict of loyalties, then one has to begin to think.

Balchin: Well I fear that people do think and reach the wrong conclusion. I don't believe that the people do these things light-heartedly; I believe they think with everything that they've been given, and that is where your point, Miss Bowen, about malad-justment – society – comes in.

Bowen: Yes – yes.

Balchin: Where there is a failure to adjust to the society in which you find yourself. And certainly I agree with you that that must be profoundly true, the people who in some instances, as we tend to forget, are not even operating in their own language.

Bowen: Yes.

Annan: But Balchin where I thought you put it unfairly was to say this idea – that whatever society thinks is right – should be attacked.

Balchin:[16] Of course it should. What society thinks is right is not necessarily right. And in fact the greatest moralists have been those who have attacked what society thought was right. But they attacked it openly and said what they thought and they argued it out, and in fact by so doing I mean they changed what people thought was society.

Bowen: They declared war on society instead, before carrying on an act of war . . .

Moorehead: Exactly, yes exactly.

Annan: Now, if you're going to be a traitor, and to carry on this thing in total secrecy, you have got to be very, very certain indeed, and have considered the whole thing carefully before you go into it. Or at any rate that's what I feel. You may argue that it was right for Casement to act as he did, but it certainly requires a very careful examination before, in secrecy, you commit these acts.

Bowen: Yes.

Moorehead. I would agree with you.

Balchin: The Cambridge Heretic Society has a rather inter-esting motto, that progress is only achieved by heresy. It is, of course, a fairly lighthearted motto, there is just enough to it to make it rather important, and to make it rather important to realise that all the major changes in society have been brought about by people who in their day were regarded as pretty deplorable. The secrecy aspect of the thing, as I mentioned in the first place, is the one where I think I agree with you Annan. Once one – if one declared war on society openly, and is prepared to take the consequences, well. But the business of smiling and stabbing is a thing, I think, which we all find emotionally and morally revolting.

Moorehead: Yes, but you've got to make the distinction between the revolutionary and the traitor: the revolutionary, of course, being the man who declares himself. I think there's some point here in the story of Speer, isn't there, in Germany.

Balchin: Oh yes, rather.

Bowen: What was that?

Balchin: Well, as I remember it, Speer was – let's see he was Minister of Production, wasn't he actually . . . [17]

Annan: He was Hitler's own personal friend and protégé. Towards the end of the war he decided that Hitler's policy was no longer possible for Germany and he did a very interesting thing. He went away and actually made recordings of the speeches that he wanted to broadcast when the downfall of Hitler came. He considered an attempt on Hitler's life and generally acted in a way which was traitorous to Hitler, to whom he'd sworn an oath. But having done so, he did the awfully attractive thing of going back and telling Hitler that he had done so.

Bowen: Yes, that was it.[18]

Balchin: Which was, I think, being a loyal man backwards so to speak.

Bowen: Yes. It was truth in reverse.

Balchin: Yes.

Bowen: But then you get the argument of the person who is convinced, as Fuchs particularly must have been – morally convinced – that he was in a right cause in a hopelessly weak position. He might have acted like the scientists in your book, *A Sort of Traitors*, as his senior Sewell did, contemplating this act of defiance. He didn't think that Fuchs's temperament was totally different from your men – Sewell's – and he therefore thought here he was unarmed, single with only his conviction of the right. Therefore, when it gets back to the question of the means justifying the end – but his means to do what he considers right – was at the cost of honour. I feel that he probably is a man of sensibility of his own kind, he had a conception –

Balchin: Yes, certainly.

Bowen: He seemed distracted. He smiled and stabbed because he thought it was essential; it wasn't that he wanted to stab, but he thought something was gained by the stab. It was a Brutus act.

Annan: Well I wish I thought that they had thought as much as this. You see I feel they didn't; I feel that they drifted into a treachery. Yes, and that seems to me to be a very poor state of mind to be in,[19] indeed. I mean where you just drift and let[20] things take, and then suddenly you find that a Russian has come up to you and given you so many dollars in a whisky bottle. I mean really if you don't think what is – are going to be the consequences of your actions in all their – in all detail, you must try and foresee all these things.

Bowen: You think that it's cumulative treachery, that it can begin in small ways by a small cheating, a small going back on one's words, small infidelities to friends, small – well, small betrayals in the realm of the personal life.

Annan: Yes – yes – and all in – I mean if they really do think in terms of loyalty to an ideology. Now loyalty to ideologies it seems to me is loyalty which makes less appeal to me than loyalty towards friends. And that if you are not certain where you stand in an honourable position towards your friends, whoever they may be at the time, you may find yourself, it seems to me, in grave moral difficulties. That is to say, liable to do things which are really dishonourable and would be dishonourable if you thought about them.

Bowen: When you say ideology, are you certain that in the case of a lot of these people sold out to Russia it hasn't been an idealisation, not only of an ideology but of the actual spiritual force which they imagine to[21] be there, the extraordinary hold that Russia has had – we knew it through the writings of the Russians –

Annan: Yes, of course.

Bowen: And that it is typical of the raceless person, like the thing in the Bible about here we have no abiding city but we seek one to come.[22]

Annan: Yes – yes indeed.

Bowen: This seems to be the ideal world, this almost – the general impulse of the creation.

Moorehead: I think these atomic spies are in a special case, you see. They well might have been zoologists, or biologists, in which case we would never have heard of them, because the experiments they would then have made would have not been capable – perhaps biology is an exception – but in general would not have been capable of affecting mankind – mankind's detriment – but they were physicists; they had this immense power. They suddenly found themselves, as it were, going up and up into the material world, making more and more discoveries until at last they arrived at the point which I think Windward Roed[23] makes in his book, where they could in fact destroy the world, or pretty nearly so. This was the moment when they turned around and looked over their shoulder and said, where is the ethic for this, where is the law and order? And understandably they said, well, here is Marxism, at least this is a neat and tidy system by which we can govern this monstrous thing. Therefore let us have a look at Marx; let's see if we can't help Marx. Let's help Marx's disciple, Russia. And I think this puts them into – as a very special category of traitors.

Annan: Well is it really so different from other categories in which men have – for belief in a set of ideas – have betrayed their country. I mean is this so different from what a Catholic would have felt in the early days of Protestantism in England – the Reformation?

Moorehead: Perhaps not.

Annan: I mean the Catholics who, for instance, were engaged in aiding and abetting the Spanish Armada, believed no doubt heart and soul that they were doing what was right.

Bowen: Yes.

Annan: Because they admired and upheld the Catholic way of life, as opposed to a different way of life.

Moorehead: I don't think the issue put before was quite as drastic as this one.

Annan: You see I think you think – I mean when you said, "what about destroying the world" – you'll forgive me if I say – I think that's rhetoric, I mean in fact we don't know[24] if the world will be destroyed by this – I mean it wasn't really.

Moorehead: But you don't get my point there . . .

Annan: Well no, I don't . . .

Balchin: Oh, I think I see Moorehead's point there. He is saying that a physicist was placed suddenly by the work on atomic fission in an entirely special category, and I think that's obviously true. Because if you notice, having been a Communist and changed your mind, it's not only a harmless thing to do if you're a poet or a writer, but nowadays a very profitable one as far as I can see. The only thing is,[25] there's no money in it: never having been a Communist at all.

[Laughter]

Balchin: But a large number of people, after all, in the days when Fuchs was considering Russia as a friendly power were also considering Russia a friendly power and writing poems about it. Nowadays they write poems to explain how they came to fall into this error, but unfortunately, as you say, they hadn't got anything very important to give away.

Moorehead: Thank you, Balchin. You've put it much better than I could.

Bowen: About – if it isn't too late to start this – is what might be called a perverted patriotism, as explained by Whittaker Chambers in the trial when he was brought to charge against Alger Hiss in describing his movement of the Communists, that he had joined the Communist Party to undermine the existing state of life in America because he loved America and he believed it was for the good of the country he loved, that it should go through this drastic experience to be remade. I don't know if that is too special a case to quote, but you could have a man forced into a course of action for the traitor or the traitorous person, the destructive person in the name – in the name of a form of rebuilding of [. . .] recreation of the country he loved. Just as people can do drastic things to each other – hurt each other because they believe it will attain some good for the person hurt.

Balchin: I am worried by your point, Annan, and your conviction that these things arise because people hadn't used their brain. It seems to me that that's a very comfortable thought, but I personally don't believe it. I believe they may have arrived at inconvenient answers, but I can't somehow see this business of treachery on a large scale creeping up on one by accident, as it were. I don't think the people you wrote about, Moorehead, really bear out that impression.

Annan: Well, ethical problems are very difficult. Philosophers who have dealt with these problems had to think very, very hard about them. You can arrive at good conclusions about problems of conduct only by analytical thought, that it is not merely a question of saying, "I think this is right, I really feel it deeply, I must do this." That is the mainspring of action, but you must then go a stage further and think of the consequences of the action, and it isn't that I'm saying, "Oh, everything will be all right if people thought harder." It's if people thought more accurately, and that they were trained to think more accurately. Of course we know that all of us probably sitting round this table might very well come to wrong conclusions about an ethical problem, a moral problem, if it's put to us. But we should realise I hope – well, I think, that it needed some thought, that it wasn't automatic reflex action. And that is what I think is the danger so much of both the Fascists', which was an irrational philosophy, and the Communists', which, though it has a rationalistic basis, is nevertheless – provide a set of answers which you need only convince yourself are true, and then you've done with thinking.

Bowen: Yes, quite.

Moorehead: That's the danger of the matter. And that's what I meant when I talked about thinking harder about it.

Annan: Yes.

Moorehead: If I could just take up Balchin's point just for two words here. To my mind, you see, Fuchs was hopelessly out of date. Any average character, any normally well-informed man should have seen by 1945 or '46 that the Russians were going a different direction to the direction we imagined they were going in 1943. But they failed to understand this. This is where they went wrong, they were out of date.

Bowen: How can that be? How can this tendency to wrong thought leading to treachery, this emotional slip – are we to think that it spreads? How is it to be coped with? I don't mean that we are breeding a whole generation of traitors, but it's alarming to find this capacity for treachery; this uncertainty of – for the loyalty this break with honour is spreading.[26] Can that be checked?

Annan: Well I would say it can only be checked if people

consider carefully what is honourable. Why they have a duty to be loyal to their country, or if necessary, not to their country – I mean why they should break that loyalty. But it is a question in which you've got to heighten your moral sensibility, so you've got to be aware that an awful lot of questions arise if I am to do this act.

Bowen: Yes.

Annan: That's what I really feel about it. Honour, to discuss at least what is honourable, is important, and that I think perhaps is not done by people because it's not put in simple terms. The simple terms of – is Brutus an honourable man.

Frankly Speaking: Interview, 1959

First Interviewer: Miss Bowen, my name is Bowen as yours is, but I don't think we're related – my father was Welsh.

Bowen: Well, my family came from Wales, from the Gower Peninsula, but my ancestors went to Ireland with Cromwell, so I have one nationality overlaid on another, but I feel I have Welsh roots.

First Interviewer: It seems to me, Miss Bowen, that it's very important to you to be related, that your books have continuity, that you're much concerned with continuity.

Bowen: Yes, I am. I think the family thing, or an equivalent of a family thing – though I think one can have too much family if one's Irish or Welsh – I think it inbreeds in one some sort of idea of connection and relationship and cause and effect: because somebody did something, somebody did something else. I don't know if that's what you mean about its being important[1] for me to be related, but I do have a sense of relationship, not necessarily to people but between one event and another, one influence and another and so on.

First Interviewer: Well, in your books – your books are some-times hauntedly – the rooms are sometimes haunted by presences –

Bowen: Yes –

First Interviewer: – of ancestors . . . a ghost quality in the work.

Bowen: It is. And I think it's a thing that anybody who has it feels, and wants to break out of really, because my idea of a life isn't at all to live in haunted rooms. It's an inherited idea of life – to be not haunted in the gibbering sense with skulls, I mean, but life in pre-inhabited places.

First Interviewer: But you have written a book about your family stretching back to Cromwellian times, in Ireland?

Bowen: Yes, I did.

First Interviewer: Did that release you from the ghost?

Bowen: Yes, I think it – I really rather think it did, you know. It was a kind of clearing off of a lot of things, and it was also extremely interesting to research into a perfectly obscure but fairly, I suppose, typical Cromwellian family and treat them as if they were historic characters, that is to say, research into them.

Second Interviewer: A feeling of course for the ghost is very Irish. Do you feel yourself Irish, or, if I may use the word, Anglo-Irish, I mean, do you feel yourself at one with . . .

Bowen: Oh, I feel Anglo-Irish. A race inside a race – there's absolutely no doubt about that.

Second Interviewer: How do you feel then about the Irish? I remember in one of your books – *The House in Paris* – you say the Irish are only truly Irish when they have someone to be Irish at.

Bowen: Well, I think that's true – I think I've got a sort of – I think the Anglo-Irish are a sort of race carved out of two races, and it would be too simple to say that I've been Irish in England and more English in Ireland. But I'm extremely conscious of the Irish Irish, and feel they are a pure race. But I'm afraid I'm a hybrid. I don't think I have an inferiority because of it. I think the Irish are an overpowering race if they concentrate there too much, and that's why the half of me – the Irish half – has always overflowed into England, into America and to any place. I mean we do need a big – we need expansion.

Second Interviewer: As an Anglo-Irish woman – I'm an Anglo-

Irish man – do you ever feel concerned for your separation from the Irish? Let's say like Louis MacNeice expressed it when he said "that he's the Rector's son and banned forever from the candles of the Irish poor"? Have you felt that?

Bowen: No, I haven't, I think I'm a naturally separated character in any case. I mean, I'm absorbed with what I'm doing at the time. I'm perfectly happy in any country, any place. I'm in a way rather unstuck – I mean unlocated, and I don't think that ever has troubled me.

Second Interviewer: Were you fond of your father?

Bowen: I was fond of my father. I was fond of him and admired him, and he was tremendously an idea to me of what a person should be. I didn't see him a great deal as a child, because I was at school, and I think I loved and admired him. An attachment which one has to fathers.

Second Interviewer: Is there an association you feel now to people and things?

Bowen: I think there's an association which anyone who's determined to be a writer creates around themselves. I don't believe you can be webbed into any society and be a writer.

Second Interviewer: But there is a source, isn't there? I mean, the adult writer is one thing but the child belongs to a place.

Bowen: Yes, certainly that.

Second Interviewer: Now when you were in Ireland, coming back to this Anglo-Irish separation, did you feel separated from the children of the Irish poor, the whole life?

Bowen: No, I don't think so, because when you're a child, you're a child with any other children. I've played with some – I mean any other children who came in the yard, in the garden, were children with me. I think the fortunate thing about being a child, unless you live in high-class society, is that anyone of your age is, as it were – although I hate the word – a group, a race, a class with you, almost. And you feel a natural alliance with any child that was vaguely against anyone who isn't a child. I remember Stephen Spender in his early poems writing, I think it was a sonnet, beginning "My parents kept me from children who were rough."[2] And nobody stopped me playing with any child at all.

Second Interviewer: And no feeling the other way round – non-Protestants told to keep away from that nasty Protestant child?

Bowen: No. There was no sign of that.

Second Interviewer: Later on, at the time of the Troubles? You must have been, how old – eighteen?

Bowen: I am the same age as the century, so that in 1919 and 1920 I would have been nineteen and twenty, and I was partly in Ireland and partly in England, and though it sounds a very unsympathetic thing to say, I was really more interested in my own problems and involved in being nineteen and twenty and whether I would succeed in being a writer or not. But I did live of course under the feeling that our house might be burnt down, which gave me an early feeling of detachment. But you don't have any sort of material detachment.[3]

Second Interviewer: But these people who might have burnt your house down would have been these very children you've been speaking about?

Bowen: Yes, but then we'd all grown up, and I think that one of the principles I accept in life is a sort of natural separation as one grows older in time, like the fingers when they leave the palm of the hand, they naturally separate.

Second Interviewer: Did you ever feel like hiding your face in Ireland?

Bowen: No, not for a moment. No.

Second Interviewer: They threatened to burn down your house, didn't they?

Bowen: Yes. But my life . . . the Anglo-Irish . . . you have a foot in each country, a foot on each side, which sounds an extremely uncomfortable physical metaphor when you think how wide the Irish Sea is. But also I've been to school here, my friends were here, my ambitious life centred on London. I don't know that it does for people who are young now, like I was. It seems to me you can be in any place, divided between the Irish landowner and the person who wanted to be in Paris or wanted to be in London. So half the time I lay in bed in County Cork thinking, "Is there somebody going to burn the house?" and half the time I thought, "Well, when I'm back in London I'll see So-and-so." It's most unheroic, but it's true.

First Interviewer: Were the Irish at other times very affectionate to the Anglo-Irish?

Bowen: Yes.

First Interviewer: Brendan Behan, you remember, described

an Anglo-Irishman as an Englishman on a horse. That was very affectionate. You played as a child with the little Dohertys and little Flanagans.

Bowen: Yes.

First Interviewer: But when the trouble came and you and they were both older in 1920, did you still keep in touch with them?

Bowen: No, I don't think it was a problem at all. But meanwhile I had been in England – I'd been to school in England – the people that I met and played with, my contemporaries, were the people with whom I had sat in classroom – they were the people with whom I had spent the holidays, they were English children, and I accepted them. They were people to ride out on a bicycle with in the holidays, and so on. And you don't really think in terms of the loyalties, or the past you are allied to, with anyone who is around at the moment. These children whom I played round the house with had been superseded by the chance of circumstance by English children and English young people.

First Interviewer: How far has all that early life in Ireland affected your work?

Bowen: If it doesn't sound too cosy – a sort of terrain of imagination. And it also gave me the thing about seeing England from the outside. Almost all the novels I wrote except two and some short stories are set in England. And I wouldn't dare to compare myself to Henry James, but I think it's quite interesting that some of the novels about the English have been the work of people who can remember seeing England consciously. I remember when I first came to England and drove in a cab across London, and woke up in a London house, and thought, "I'm in England, I'm in England – how exciting, how striking, how extraordinary." It gave me an angle on England.

First Interviewer: Fascinating, your mentioning Henry James. How far has he been your master, your model, how far has he influenced your writing?

Bowen: I admire him in the dramatic way. I can't read the more complicated books. I haven't ever read *The Ivory Tower*, he's quite beyond me there, I really belong to *Portrait of a Lady*. I wouldn't care to read him while I was writing a novel myself because I think his type of style is extremely infectious.

First Interviewer: It is, and I'm not surprised that you found it so.

Bowen: I know one novel I wrote in which his infection showed – though you can't say it's like catching measles, because it's a splendid style, but it's a dangerous style.

First Interviewer: One has noticed it. Who else influenced you?

Bowen: Well, really the influence nobody ever spots is[4] the Dickens novels. I think I've been most influenced by Dickens and nobody would have ever guessed. I mean, that sounds an exaggerated thing to say, but it isn't. Those novels were read to me before I was able to read at all, and that romantic feeling for haunted places and those obsessed characters and that burlesque comedy . . .

Third Interviewer: Am I wrong in suspecting a touch of Meredith?

Bowen: No, I don't think you are at all. I didn't read any Meredith until I was seventeen and then I read Meredith solidly for about three or four years. I've read the same ones over again – I've only read about six of them. I think he was a terrific influence.

First Interviewer: How did you arrive at writing? Was it slow and careful?

Bowen: As a little girl I was precocious in my drawing and painting in an Edwardian way. I thought I would be a painter and then I found that was no good at all, I was following a blind alley. And then I started by writing poetry because that was easier on the clothes. But I've always found it extremely hard to write. I mean, I can't pretend it was easy, but I started when I was about nineteen, I think, and set myself on and on and on writing these short stories.

First Interviewer: And taught yourself, did you, word by word?

Bowen: I think to a great extent taught myself by imitation. I don't think it's a thing to be ashamed of. In reading any of my early stories – in fact it goes on for a jolly long time – it may still for all I know – I can still see streaks or threads and patches of other influences of other people. I think when you get started – for my generation, my kind of writer, it was one way to teach yourself. You became aware of influences anyway – it was one pattern of one's imagination. It was rather like a palisade round a young growing tree, you knew that you felt secure in other people's work.

Second Interviewer: You know, what you haven't said is *why* you started writing as a young girl. You've said *how*, but not why.

Bowen: Why? I think – well, *that's* more a how than a why. I think it was an extension of the thing that has been said before, of the imaginative play thing a child has – that life isn't amusing enough, so you build it up with imagination of your own. An intense desire to do something, or make something. The great aim of anyone who has ever written a book is the desire to add to these things.

Second Interviewer: A desire to add, or a desire to be a writer? It is important.

Bowen: I would say a desire to add more.

First Interviewer: Something that no one has yet done?

Bowen: To *do* something. Writing appealed to me as a way of doing something that hadn't ever been done before, because nobody but me could write the particular thing that I would write. Other people could write . . . but it was one of the few things *one* could do, short of painting or composing music. It was the inventive thing. I don't think it appealed to me as a personal thing. I mean, when people say, "I want to write, I want to express myself," I don't honestly think I thought of it in that way, but it was a desire to do something that hadn't ever been done.

First Interviewer: A desire to do something or a desire to say something?

Bowen: To do something.[5] I mean, when I've been talking in places in central Europe and places abroad about the novel, the European attitude to novels always results in somebody, whose point of view I immensely respect, getting up and saying, "Have you a message in your work, what do you fundamentally say?" And I've always had to say that what I do say I say unconsciously, or I say it out of the general authority of a writer, to which all writers have access. But with me it was much more a desire to do something like picking one's way through a wood or staking a claim on something. It was much more the desire to *do* than to *say* – the desire to *make*, in a way. I mean, as I wrote my first stories I remember seeing the books that I had – good, bad and indifferent in the shelves of the room I was in – and thinking they were concrete objects and feeling I wanted to cause one more of those to be there.

First Interviewer: Do you think that is perhaps fundamental to writing – to make rather than to do?

Bowen: I think it could conceivably be, I had never thought of it before, but it could.

First Interviewer: Well, you're not a feminine – I wouldn't think of you as a woman novelist – but it seems that many women writers have this concern for objects.

Bowen: Yes.

First Interviewer: And also some of it that you have, which is going back into one's own immediate experience – going from one's childhood – the circumstances of one's early life. How much have you done that?

Bowen: I think the circumstances of my own life and my memory and my autobiography were much like a box of bricks, out of which a child might build a building. It's all you have. Or if you're dressing up, someone gives you a trunk of old clothes, and you hunt about in them for the things that will most serve your purpose. But I think I used my experiences for what I wanted to make and do, rather than in order to express my experiences or my family or social or racial background. They were the bag of bricks.

First Interviewer: Well, the gimmick you've just used – a bag of child's bricks – is interesting, because I've always felt about your work the great architectural interest you have. You have lived in a beautiful house – one of the most beautiful houses in Ireland, Bowen's Court, and in your book it was the rooms I admired . . . you put people into rooms and created them about them.[6] Have you got great architectural interests?

Bowen: That's a very acute question, because the profession I did want to have when I was at school was architecture – I wanted to be an architect – but I went no further. I certainly wouldn't have had a great career as an architect, and I realise that I was not mathematical. But my original idea of a career – I was such a lazy girl really that I was not career-minded – but the one thing when I was fifteen and sixteen and seventeen that I did want to be was an architect. I was always drawing elevations and modelling and thinking I'd like to build something.

First Interviewer: Were you conscious in your childhood that you were living in a very beautiful house?

Bowen: It only dawned on me extremely slowly because my

father and mother accepted the house. The governesses or nurses I had as a child spoke of it as "this great, bare house" because at that time Georgian architecture was unfashionable. I mean, all people wanted was an Elizabethan house, covered with ivy and gables, and diamond bay-windows – which are indeed very handsome themselves. But I think it was really only after I'd been to Italy when I was twenty-one, and seen the prototypes from which my house was imitated, that I came back and saw the house objectively, and saw the whole was a beautiful house. Before that, the family attitude was that they were, as I say, fond of it, it's such a dear house, it's our home. But I only came full circle, as it were, around the world, and then saw the house and realised that it was a beautiful house, and I was primarily fond of it for that reason, not for emotional reasons. Not because aunt So-and-so, or great-uncle So-and-so, or great-grandfather had lived there . . . But in spite of the cobwebs and in spite of all the entanglement, it remained the sharp objective thing which was a beautiful house.

Third Interviewer: Have you often lived in beautiful houses?

Bowen: On the whole I have. The only other house which falls into that description was the house my husband and I lived in for eighteen years, which was one of the Regent's Park houses, a Nash house. And the moment I went into that house I wanted to have it . . . Oh, and I lived in a house, one of the Westminster houses, the house of a great-aunt which was in Queen Anne's Gate, and it also was a beautiful house. And my conception of a pleasing, beautiful house is one in which the rooms are repeating shape, the idea of reflection in from trees, through windows . . .

First Interviewer: You lived in Oxford too.

Bowen: I lived in Oxford.[7] We lived surrounded by Oxford, but we lived in the village of Old Headington, in a house which we constructed for ourselves out of an old stable. It was, I think, a beautiful house in a different way. It was more uneven, a house of uneven rooms, low ceilings. It wasn't a quaint house, we made it as un-quaint as we could, but it was in no sense a great house.

Third Interviewer: I want to take up some other aspects. I'm a writer of a different sort: I'm a diplomatic correspondent. Now people accuse us of writing fiction, and we certainly have to deal occasionally with plots. Which leads me up to my question, are you more interested in plots, environment, or characters?

Bowen: Oh plots, first of all.

Third Interviewer: I wouldn't have thought it.

Bowen: Well, environment contributes to the plot. I would say: plot, environment and character. I shouldn't say character last. Perhaps I had better say situation more than plot, and part of a situation to me is where a thing happens.

Third Interviewer: But the sort of thing that strikes me – look at *The Death of the Heart* – is that you are just getting us through to knowing what's happening, and all of a sudden, either you get bored, or something. You just dropped the curtains.

Bowen: Yes.

Third Interviewer: And we never knew what was going to happen further. Now surely that isn't being interested in plots, is it? The plot just banged shut like that. Into the second act, and we . . .

Bowen: Yes, to me that was a plot which had no end – I mean what happened to that child next. It was a really inflated short story, I think, that thing. I could have crystallised the whole of the novel into a long short story, and I think it would have been the better if I had.

Third Interviewer: I just got frustrated, I wanted to know what happened. The plot was just getting exciting, and I felt, "Well, she's not interested in the book."

Bowen: Well, the plot rounded off when she, Portia, the girl, because she was only a child, in a quiet way defeated all those older people when they all sat round the table and said, "What do we do now?" And . . . they were . . . they sent deputations to bring her home, and she came home on her own terms. They had to send the housemaid to bring her back, because they knew very well she would have stayed in that Kensington Hotel with that frantic Major. She had the whip hand over them. I mean it's really a struggle for ascendancy, I think, that story.

First Interviewer: I wonder whether perhaps we ought to make a distinction between plot and narrative.

Bowen: Yes.

First Interviewer: Would you make that distinction? I think I should.

Bowen: Yes, I think plot in the proper sense is narrative. At least – I don't know how you as a novelist see it – I think first of a situation, but around it you must have the story . . . and how you spread the situation into a story and distribute it . . . and what happens, one thing after another, is the plot.

First Interviewer: Is perhaps narrative the mechanism which carries on the plot if the plot is a developing situation? If, you see, you are concerned with a developing situation, and I think you are, then it is the people in the situation which are important, and narrative is a mechanism.

Bowen: Yes, you're perfectly right.

First Interviewer: Isn't narrative the plot in action? In movement?

Bowen: Yes, it's the relating, the narrating of movement, I suppose. It depends on you to tell how that movement moved.

First Interviewer: I'm not trying to pin you down to a definition, you understand, that isn't after all the purpose of our talking to you.

Bowen: No.

First Interviewer: I'm trying to pin you down, if anything, to a way of looking at books.

Bowen: Yes.

First Interviewer: It seems to me that the message that you spoke of, the unconscious, is a kind of point of view which exists, and must exist, in all your books – because you have one, don't you?

Bowen: Yes, I do.

First Interviewer: A way of looking at life. Do you, yourself, find that something has developed in your books, as you, yourself, have grown older? Have you found that way of looking at life a developing thing?

Bowen: I have.

First Interviewer: To what extent have you been conscious of it?

Bowen: I'm only conscious of it when I see the books. I think in the actual course of producing a book, of telling a story, and also of casting the light on events which is part of the telling of the story, however impersonal you try to be, you are evaluating . . . and I think most people can't avoid it . . . The idea of impersonality, total impersonality, objectivity is extremely difficult.[8]

Second Interviewer: Yet you yourself have said earlier on this evening you don't believe you can be webbed into society.

Bowen: No.

Second Interviewer: You don't find that a contradiction?

Bowen: No, I don't think I do, because my way of seeing things is probably a result of happenings, of where I go, of the events . . . It's present experience, plus past experience, probably, one acting on the other. But I think at present it's what is happening in the moment or the day or the month or the year – partly in the world around me and partly how things hit me – how I act on situations in which I find myself.

Third Interviewer: Are you concerned by what happens in the world around you?

Bowen: I'm less so than a number of people. I entirely believe the writers, novelists I've known who have said they've been reduced to absolute silence by the state of the world, and that they've felt before the war, during the Spanish crisis or during the war, or in those years of dismay and uncertainty afterwards, a complete – not through lack of faith in their own powers – but by some feeling that what they are creating is futile, and why go on? It hasn't affected me like that at all, for better or worse. Just as in an air raid, if you were a warden, which I was, you stump up and down the streets making a clatter with the boots you are wearing, knowing you can't prevent a bomb falling, but thinking, "At any rate I'm taking part in this, I may be doing some good." But the actual climate of events, if I may say so, has affected me extremely strongly, I think it would affect any human being. But on the whole I'm much more egocentric – I'm less morally, psychologically sensitive – than quite a number of the novelists I know. I've got a sort of imperviousness. And just as, apart from the work I did during the war for the government, I went on writing and writing away – not, I think, altogether wrongly, but feeling, "Well, this is the one thing I can do and what's the point of stopping it? If it's any good at any time, it's some good now."

Third Interviewer: Have you as a writer ever had to deal with the outside world, as a journalist?

Bowen: I've been a journalist in the sense of asking myself to a peace conference, representing an Irish newspaper. I've been a journalist in doing a good deal of reporting work for the Ministry of Information during the war, of different kinds. I don't know whether that would rank as journalism or not.

Third Interviewer: I meant psychologically dealing with the events going on around you.

Bowen: No. When I was reporting a peace conference there was a good deal of photography of the situation, photography of particular characters as I saw them, the atmosphere of a particular occasion, the circumstances, the surrounds, whatever you call it, of a particular conference room where small debates were taking place. But I had enough sense to know that I ought not to waste space in the columns of the paper by laying down any theory or appearing to act on any information which I would not have, and you would.

Third Interviewer: For whom, then, were you writing?

Bowen: I was writing in this case these three articles for the *Cork Examiner* for the readers in the South of Ireland who take in this far-reaching and important and fair-minded magazine. I wrote for it, since it stood for a certain standard of integrity and accuracy.

Third Interviewer: And did you in fact make any difference in the way that you wrote for that reason?

Bowen: Well, I don't think so, because I was chiefly trying to be comprehensible about the subject. If I had been sent by a weekly – an English paper, either a weekly or a daily – I would have written very much the same kind of articles, for whatever paper I wrote, on the understanding that if that paper employed me they would know that I was not qualified to write from a political or foreign affairs journalistic experience, and if they were prepared to take me on they would merely expect a not altogether unselective photograph, and a picture of events as I saw them, trying to relate what I saw to what I hoped to be the truth.

Third Interviewer: How did you come to be on the Royal Commission on Capital Punishment?[9]

Bowen: It was a surprise and an honour to me to be asked, and I understood that there was a wish to make it representative, and that as the names were drawn up it was found – probably by those who were associated – I don't know whether this is right or wrong – that they wanted to have one more woman on the commission, and they wanted to have a writer because otherwise every profession as far as I know was represented.

Second Interviewer: Interesting?[10]

Bowen: Extremely interesting. Yes, it was an education in the sense of learning not to take an emotional squeamish view of the – I was surprised by how little squeamishness or emotion surrounded the extremely harsh and – what can I say? – agonising material that we handled, and it was – it was frightening, a sense of having a very, very great responsibility. But it was an opportunity to hear any aspect, any question of rights and wrongs, worked over among twelve people who had come into the discussion with open minds, and were bringing whatever we had in the way of judgement and intelligence and some kind of integrity to it.

Third Interviewer: Was it entirely a matter of listening to evidence?

Bowen: No, we went round – we divided into parties of two, and between us saw most of the larger prisons in England and Scotland, because it was a question of a long-term sentence and how much . . . treatment of murderers whose sentence had been remitted would be [?] in the case of suspending capital punishment. Altogether how the problem of the so-called life sentence was resolved, what to do with the people, what their conditions would be, and this included – we spent a great deal of time naturally over the insanity laws and the MacNaughten rules.[11] So we went to [?] and during the three weeks we were in America we saw the larger prisons there in the east, and also went into the question of the criminal insane.

Third Interviewer: You didn't have to see an execution, I take it?

Bowen: No, it was suggested that we should, and we were all prepared to, and it was decided no, and I think possibly rightly, because of the reactions of people who were not conditioned to this.

Third Interviewer: Yes, horrified.

Bowen: Horrified, as it were, as if one were present at an operation, and saw the surgeon make a large incision. It could be argued, though, that the judgement should be by people who could realise the full force of the thing. We inspected the gallows arrangement and in America we saw what to me was the most horrifying thing, the execution place in Sing-Sing; we saw how gallows work, we saw the traps, we saw the cells in which the condemned people are confined, and we saw the whole circumstances and surroundings of an execution.

Second Interviewer: Is it difficult for you to forget this?

Bowen: No – and I don't think I should, but it's in a compartment of my mind. It isn't surrounded by any of the worked-up emotion in which, if I were to read (as I do a great deal) detective novels and crime stories, and you read not only about a murder but about a trial and execution, and your feelings are then churned up in a way which the author intends and which may do no harm. But many of the things I actually saw or learned or knew have an astringent . . . I suppose it is rather like seeing an operation . . . It would probably remain carved out of all ordinary experiences.

Second Interviewer: Have you ever tried to put it out of your mind?

Bowen: No, I haven't at all. Because it isn't one of the few things which I might remember which would fill me with unbearable horror – I can't think of any, but there must have been some in all our lives. But these things do not correspond with that at all.

Third Interviewer: You said that they wanted a woman and they wanted a writer.

Bowen: Yes.

Third Interviewer: In what way do you feel you yourself, as both, contributed most to the report?

Bowen: I had certain . . . every member of the Commission developed some personal line from which they were approaching the problem, and I myself brought in my particular point on one interesting point of law, which is that only physical provocation counts as provocation which can turn murder into manslaughter or make it just another homicide. And it may have been either as a writer and an imaginative person, or as a woman, that to me continuous mental torture is equally provocative . . . In the existing medieval idea, if you pull somebody's nose and the person runs through you with a rapier, the person who uses the rapier is justified. Well, in these days, since on the whole, we don't pull each other's noses, we don't hit each other about, and any kind of physical assault seems fully provocative and the most horrible thing to do to a person.

Third Interviewer: Did you get your way in the report?

Bowen: We recommended the inclusion of verbal provocation. I also objected to the thing by which clemency is more likely to be extended to a man who finds his wife has been unfaithful to him, who finds her in the arms of somebody, whereas a man whose mistress distresses him in the same way is more likely to have the law against him. [Laughter] And I argued that in an irregular relationship, passion and sexual feeling is nearer the surface, and if you were to allow for uncontrollable passion in a husband it is likely,[12] probably, to arise in what is described as a love relationship, whereas in a marriage complicated distress and [?] are involved. It seemed to me confusing to set a value . . .

Third Interviewer: Did you get your way?

Bowen: I think we made – I read the report with great care, and I think we made some reserved remark on this. If any of my colleagues and friends are hearing us tonight, they will probably be in a position to check on that, but they must well remember how the discussions arose.

Second Interviewer: Do you think the Commission was looking for somebody who is concerned with character? Rather than the lawyer or the statistician?

Bowen: Yes, I suppose so, somebody who must be taken to study character, to connect one thing with another. As I have previously said, I don't call my character-drawing character-analysis . . . but still, nobody is practising the trade of a novelist if they do not have some . . . formula, some almost detective interest, in character. And I think on the other side the idea of having two instead of one woman, I mean to bring in the feminine elements – I don't know if people are right in crediting women with commonsense, but there is also the more ordinary . . . say, that if you saw somebody knocked down in the street by carelessness . . . If a husband and wife were walking down the street, you may assume that the man will say "How wrong" and pursue the person who knocked the other person down, and the woman might be said to have the reaction of help and to apply the handkerchief . . .

Third Interviewer: The man gets the number and the woman gives first aid?

Bowen: Exactly, you've summarised it perfectly.

Third Interviewer: Have you done any other public work which –

Bowen: I've worked with some of the County Education Committees, and I worked for three weeks – I beg your pardon, for three successive years – with the Kent Education Committee on a holiday school for teachers in Kent. They asked me to be Principal, which involved no educational thing, but simply taking part in it . . . I have taught in America for short terms, in colleges. I taught for a month in a state university in Madison, Wisconsin. I was teaching English; I was working over stories which people wrote, I was working with composition books. It was strictly known as a senior composition class, and I was really there in the role of a critic, trying as far as I could to make out some general principle out of piecemeal criticism of the stories that came in.

Second Interviewer: Do you like working with young people?

Bowen: I do, yes, because for one thing they keep you up to the mark. In fact, people of anything like my age could only work, I suppose, with young people because with people of anything like my age, there's something wrong with them if they want that from you. I mean, generally the only honest way to work with young people who are beginning to write is if you are somebody with a certain amount of technical and workmanlike experience which, if they care to come and ask you for it, you can hand over. But I can't imagine working with middle-aged people, because they ought to have passed any need for help from me.

First Interviewer: What do you do – this is a flat, personal question – what do you do when you're not writing?

Bowen: I like being out of doors, I like to walk, I like stopping being anywhere near a writing table at all. I don't read a good deal; I tend to re-read. I read in between writing a book or on a holiday, or if I have a cold. It is in my idea a great pleasure to read. I like to go to the cinema, I like to play gramophone records. I like to walk. I haven't had TV in my life for the last year, because I have been in Ireland and we don't have it there, but while I was in America I saw quite a lot. I like it, but I'd much rather go to the cinema. I like a big screen, and I like being packed in among rows of other people, I like to get out of where I am, I still like that. I like . . . the feeling of going in and walking down a place in the dark and sitting down.

First Interviewer: Well, do you like the theatre as much as the cinema, where in a sense you don't walk down?

Bowen: No, really I like the cinema more. It would be idiotic not ever to go to the theatre, but a cinema is more like pure pleasure to me.

Second Interviewer: The isolation of the cinema can be complete, whereas in a theatre you've got the sounds of one's neighbours.

Bowen: Yes, and you have those awful intervals and the lights come on, and you have to stare at everybody – oh well, intervals are useful, because if you smoke as much as I do you can get a minute or two's smoke, but on the whole I like the continuity of the cinema, I like the film and the shorts and . . .

Second Interviewer: And the anonymity? Do you pursue this anonymity at other times in your life?

Bowen: Well, I do, because – that is why I like to be in an immensely big town. I'm extremely happy in New York, I'm extremely happy in London, and the only thing which I find trying in any place in the country – whether it's Ireland, or England, or France, or Italy – is the feeling that you aren't anonymous in a small community. I mean, I'm not anonymous, nobody is anonymous, you walk up a path or a lane, you're going to the village, and it isn't only myself, but it's anybody at all . . . "There goes old So-and-so, what is he up to? What's she buying?" which is in a way intensely human, but also makes you feel like a moth in a lantern or something. Writing is a lonely trade, a very lonely trade.[13] I hate to have to talk while writing. I really would like to be – I would like to go into a comfortable, rather gay country inn for six weeks on end, like various writers who work frightfully hard all day, and then come down into the bar, or the lounge, and talk with anybody who is around. Or I want to go out to a movie, and then play cards or something.

Second Interviewer: When you are writing, how long do you write, how many hours?

Bowen: I write about seven or eight hours.

Second Interviewer: Seven or eight. When do you start?

Bowen: I start about half-past nine or ten. Ideally, I like to start the day so that I start at half-past eight, but I generally start about half-past nine. And on a day that I like to have, I go on to about quarter-past five or six. By which time I think anyone, even if they're thirty years younger than I am, is[14] usually tired. So you want a complete break, you want to go out on the street, or you want to be among a lot of people, but I don't feel like a . . .

First Interviewer: But writing isn't a lonely trade, really I think in some ways a writer is the least lonely person, and when people like [?] talk about "la solitude de l'écrivain," I think it's absolute nonsense. Surely a writer is like one of those curious, tropical plants in the Boys' Adventure stories, which is always reaching out, you remember, and grabbing in the stray traveller, and digesting them, and then eventually a beautiful blossom comes. Surely this is what writers do?

Bowen: Well, I mean the actual workshop conditions of a writer are solitary. I don't know – I'd be interested to know how you work, but the actual conditions of so many hours of work to me are a table and a typewriter, in a room alone, because I find it hard to work. No, when you come out of that you then certainly do want the other extreme – you don't only want it, you have to have it . . . A writer has to have a lot of contacts, lively relationships and then you do pull things in – you're perfectly right – like one of those fly-eating cactuses.

First Interviewer: Quite obviously one has contacts in every part of society, and even the Capital Punishment Commission gave you something which perhaps you didn't even know you were using. Also, perhaps, some of one's contacts are with other writers. You have many famous friends, I think?

Bowen: I have had friends who have become famous – yes, I have.

First Interviewer: And were famous, sometimes, when you knew them?

Bowen: Yes, they were on the way to be – either writers or people at Oxford who have gone on their way.

First Interviewer: But on the other hand you must have often heard it said, as I have, that writing in this country – and probably it's said about every country – is a kind of Old Boy Net; knowing the right people helps things to be published in the right magazines, to have your books published, to have your books reviewed – even, I suppose, to have them sold. How far do you feel there's any truth in this whatever?

Bowen: Well, in my own case it was not true. I had immense hope and encouragement from one writer, forever dear to me as a person, and that was Rose Macaulay. But apart from the fact that she read my stories, and wrote to a publisher, I didn't know a single critic, I didn't know a single person in the literary world. But that was right back, my first book came out in 1923, and I think things were different then . . . But I think now the whole thing, the whole scene, seems more crowded, and I would accept that; and the first thing I would do for any young person, a man or a girl I was interested in who wanted to bring out a book – I would bring them across as far as I could do to critics, or editors, because – well, as I say, there is more of a crowd. I think it's much harder than it was in my day for the perfectly unknown provincial person as I was to break through.

First Interviewer: You don't think it's necessary to know people?

Bowen: I don't – really I think if there's enough force in the work, I can't feel that to fail to know anybody is a handicap, because I've been a reviewer, I know the look of a pile of books and how you review, and you turn them over and you look through and you suddenly find something, and you feel, "Now I want to read this." And it may be a first book that has got no buildup, it isn't by young So-and-so, who somebody asked you to be kind to. It's that you see an unmistakable layout in the page, you hear a voice, you – no, you don't hear a voice, perhaps that's wrong. But you feel an impulse behind it, you feel interested and drawn in.

Second Interviewer: You've just given thanks to Rose Macaulay for help that she gave you. Do you ever feel the best way for you to pay your debts to Rose Macaulay is to help the –

Bowen: I certainly do. I feel I owe that back as a debt.

Second Interviewer: Yes, and that is really the principle of what one calls the Old Boy, isn't it?

First Interviewer: I don't think I do call that the principle of the Old Boys at all. I think that what I was suggesting is that there are people who quite honestly believe that there is a kind of literary establishment centring on the two Sundays and the two weeklies, and if you do not please it you cannot get anywhere. I don't believe this to be true myself, and within your own experience I was wondering what you felt about it.

Bowen: I feel that it is a bit true. I remember we were not called the Angry Generation, but I remember how mad angry I was when I was young, when I wrote stories and sent them to magazines who claimed they wanted new talent, and back it came, and always it seemed to me the same old crowd, Uncle Tom Cobley and all, the same names again. I think I was conscious of an establishment then, and I think there is an establishment now.

First Interviewer: Do you belong to it?

Bowen: I wouldn't say I did. I've never belonged to any group. I was thinking about the great elder group, to me, the people in Bloomsbury. I think they were not wielding particular power, but they were creating influence. I wouldn't say my generation were so much of a group and, so far as we worked our way along, that Graham Greene or Evelyn Waugh or Henry Green or Rosamond Lehmann has[15] a certain prestige and influence; but I wouldn't say that the establishment consisted of the novelists who were at work so much as the critics and the circle which they create.

Second Interviewer: An establishment open to the talents – and you were one of the talents that got through?

Bowen: Yes!

Notes

The Confidant

"The Confidant" bears no resemblance to the short story called "The Confidante," which was published in *Encounters* in 1923. Although Bowen clearly means that Hermione is the confidante, she writes the noun without the terminal "e" that would indicate the appropriate gender. Bowen worked on this radio play under the guidance of Eddy Sackville-West. Writing to Bowen from Devonshire on 9 September 1943, Sackville-West offered advice on the script:

> I think this promises very well indeed. I have, however, two rather important criticisms, the first of which is fundamental: (1) Surely this thing ought not to end "happily"??! Surely the point of a confidant is that she remains one, renouncing a personal life for a vicarious one. Would it not, therefore, be better if Major Jeremy's intentions were made obvious but were never allowed – either by Hermione or her friend – actually to issue in an offer? The final sequence should, I feel, contain either some new exorbitant claim from a new character, or an impassioned complaint from Mr. Antrobus or Mrs. Billing at any suggestion from H. that she might have something of her own to attend to.
>
> (2) The play is, as it now stands, a good deal too short & has not the weight necessary to make its point felt. I think myself that the extra length ought to come in the first sequence, which is too scrappy & trivial at present. We ought to know a little more about Antrobus. Why not let him get further into his silly story before one of the telephonic interruptions? The plane of light comedy – of farce, if you like – can be sustained throughout this first section; but I think this note of seriousness – of conflict – should enter with Jeremy. There must be a moment when H. consciously chooses what future she is to have – i.e. married life with J. in the Federated Malay States or whatever, or a perpetual round of telephone conversations with A. & Mrs. B *e tutti quanti*.

Apart from these considerations, I certainly think an introductory narration giving a short historic sketch of the confidant would be both useful & amusing.

One other point. Please don't underline words, unless absolutely necessary, & don't put in "expression" directions (e.g. *glumly*), except for the same reasons. These annoy actors & confuse them, & should be left to the producer. (HRC 2.3)

Sackville-West lights on the problematic aspects of the play, including its drawing-room trivialities and fussy stage directions. Pre-empted or broken-off engagements appealed to Bowen; a curtailed engagement darkens the atmosphere of *The Last September* and a broken engagement motivates "I Died of Love." The acoustic possibilities of the radio, especially ringing bells and telephones, make this a play about listening. The play, as Sackville-West observes, is notable for its interruptions. It was apparently never produced. The seventeen-page typescript has revisions written in Bowen's hand (HRC 2.3). All the revisions, none of them substantive, are legible. Some lineation has been altered to render changes from one speaker to another easy to follow. Throughout, I have changed "Mr. A." to "Mr. Antrobus," and I have put the names of speakers all in upper case to be consistent with Bowen's other radio plays.

1. Bowen added by hand the word "too" after "rather," creating the incorrect phrase, "rather too a long story."

New Judgement: Elizabeth Bowen on Jane Austen

"New Judgement: Elizabeth Bowen on Jane Austen" aired on 8 March 1942 on the BBC Third Programme. The play, produced by Stephen Potter, was re-broadcast in the evening of 16 August 1948. In the latter broadcast, Celia Johnson played Jane Austen; Phillip Leaver played Darcy and Mr. Knightly; Carleton Hobbs was the Narrator. A typescript for each broadcast exists. The 1942 version shows changes, some probably made during rehearsals (HRC 2.4). Instructions to give "more expression" to the opening Narrator's speech appear in the margin; cuts to passages from *Emma* and *Pride and Prejudice* tighten the pace. Some of these changes are incorporated into the 1948 transcript; some are not. The 1948 version has been used as the base text. "New Judgement" expands on Bowen's interest in Austen. In Bowen's dramatisation, Cassandra comes across as a biased custodian of her sister's legacy. In the 1948 broadcast script, each speaker is numbered, starting at one, on each page; these numbers make sense only in the context of the legal-size physical sheet on which the original is typed. Punctuation and capitalisation have been retained.

1. Throughout the typescript, "Bennet" is mistakenly spelled "Bennett."

2. The typescript reads "as it its." The 1942 version confirms that "as to its" is correct.

London Revisited: As Seen by Fanny Burney

"London Revisited: As Seen by Fanny Burney" was broadcast on the BBC Home Service on 14 November 1942. The typescript of this broadcast, on seven legal-size pages, breaks off suddenly (HRC 2.3). The rest of the script appears not to be extant in any form, either written or recorded. The play mixes eighteenth-century court life with the motif of travel through time and space. Bowen was keen on time travel in the 1930s and 1940s, as her review of the futuristic film *Things to Come* corroborates. In her short story "Gone Away," first published in 1946, a character named Van Winkle awakens from a sleep of unknown duration to a futuristic, twentieth-century "impression of squares and streets, of soap-clean arcades and polished perspectives, of glass, of dizzying architecture soaring rigid into the mauve-blue sky" (*Collected Stories* 759). To set "London Revisited" in heaven, where Dr. Johnson, Mrs. Thrale, Edmund Burke, and other luminaries preside, is a brave stroke. Fanny leaves heaven to visit blacked-out, wartime London. Time travel accounts for her astonishment over pavement, cars, cigarettes, and traffic lights. The typescript has pencil marks in the margins of the first four pages, most of which advise a lengthy "cut" to talky paragraphs; the producer of this broadcast evidently wanted less historical information and more dialogue to exploit the technical resources of radio.

1. In "Dr. Burney's Evening Party," Virginia Woolf writes that Fanny Burney retreated to "a cabin at the end of her stepmother's garden at King's Lynn, where she used to sit and write of an afternoon till the oaths of the seamen sailing up and down the river drove her in" (*Second Common Reader* 108). Woolf may have been in Bowen's mind as she wrote this passage.

2. Because "four years" does not constitute a "life," the phrase might be better understood as "four years' confinement."

3. The typescript gives "letter" in the singular.

4. The typescript gives "No, I admit no" but "not" might be intended.

5. *Ton*: tone.

6. The script breaks off here.

A Year I Remember – 1918

"A Year I Remember – 1918," produced by R. D. Smith, with a cast of thirteen, was broadcast on 10 March 1949 on the BBC Third Programme. It was re-broadcast the next day. The twenty-page typescript has a few asterisks and circles drawn by hand in the margins, but it is otherwise quite clean (HRC 2.3). Bowen remembered and dramatised events of 1918 at the time that the Second World War was on her mind; *The Heat of the Day* was published on 21 February 1949, just prior to the airing of this play. "I had grown up without having the capacity to feel," she claims in this broadcast. The statement recalls the concluding sentence in the essay "London, 1940": "We have no feeling to spare" (*Collected Impressions* 220). The most successful of Bowen's radio plays, "A Year I Remember – 1918" orchestrates sound, voices, poetry, and music. While Bowen may have been thinking about Tennyson's *In Memoriam* and Rupert Brooke's "Peace," the play resonates most fully with T. S. Eliot's "The Waste Land" in its evocation of missing people, popular music, vernacular speech, and collage effects. Italics and capitals are inconsistent in the script; I have regularised them. Block capitals indicate speakers' voices and directions for sounds; italics, for the most part, indicate tones of voice. Bowen, or the producer, knew the BBC collections well enough to include titles and catalogue numbers for recordings.

1. Now, God be thanked: Rupert Brooke's "Peace." Bowen omits the last five lines of the sonnet.

2. V. A. D.: founded in 1909, the Voluntary Aid Detachment provided auxiliary nursing services during both world wars.

3. Zeebrugge: on 23 April 1918, the British Royal Navy attacked and defeated the German naval forces at Zeebrugge on the coast of Belgium.

4. Bowen inscribed "Insert" in the margin next to this speech, but no insert is included with the typescript.

5. Bowen crossed out "didn't it?" and inserted "I know."

6. Bowen crossed out "all by himself" and inserted a phrase that I cannot decipher. I have, therefore, left the phrase as it originally appeared.

7. The word "Waterloo" is inserted after this exchange on the typescript, with the code "9cR" beside it.

8. Rennie mocks Hook by repeating her language. A page break falls after "Show me the famous victory," which may account for the change in tone.

9. The phrase originally read "over a series of dips and hills." Bowen crossed out "a series," without crossing out "of."

10. *Leinster*: a German submarine torpedoed HMS *Leinster* on 10 October 1918. The official death toll was 501. A German submarine torpedoed the *Lusitania* on 7 May 1915 off the coast of Kinsale, Ireland.

11. Calm is the morn: Tennyson, *In Memoriam* 11. Bowen omits stanzas two and three, as well as the last line of the poem.

Book Talk – New and Recent Fiction

"Book Talk – New and Recent Fiction" was a regular BBC feature. This review went to air on 25 June 1945 on the Home Service. The typescript, on microfilm at the BBC Written Archives, is fairly clean. Bowen added a few handwritten changes and crossed out some passages, possibly to meet time restrictions. I have restored the cancelled passages because they represent Bowen's intentions rather than the time constraints of radio. Nonetheless, deleted passages are mentioned in notes. Building on her reputation as a reviewer for the *New Statesman* and the *Spectator*, Bowen developed an expertise as a radio reviewer notwithstanding her pronounced stammer. On 15 July 1945, she recorded another review for "Book Talk." At the invitation of William Empson, she wrote at least three other book reviews for the BBC Overseas China Service in 1943 (Sellery and Harris 274–5). The distinction between "story" and "history" that Bowen makes in the two opening paragraphs of this review bears on the reiteration of the word "story," as against "history," in *The Heat of the Day*. In that novel, Bowen worries over "where the truth of any story might lie in a universal wartime discourse of story-telling" (Corcoran 169). The discussion of Rumer Godden's *A Fugue in Time* in this review resonates with Bowen's own meditations on houses at the end of the war, as demonstrated in the short story "Ivy Gripped the Step" and the essay "Opening up the House."

1. Two lines, from "we watch them" to "power," are crossed out in the typescript. This correction makes the sentence clearer and avoids the ungrammatical linking of two independent clauses.

2. Bowen crossed out "'Prey' seems a hard word, for" and inserted "But" above the line.

3. Bowen inserted the word "Pause" after this paragraph, perhaps to guide her reading on the air.

4. The comma has been added for sense.

5. The two sentences from "She feels family memories" to "great-grandmother" are crossed out in the typescript.

6. The three sentences from "We see old Sir Rollo" to "despot-father" are crossed out in the typescript.

7. The passage from "lit each year" to "shake with age" is crossed out in the typescript.

8. The passage from "shows herself a disciple" to "She" is crossed out in the typescript.

9. This sentence is crossed out in the typescript, but "stet" has been written beside it in the margin. "Pause" has also been written after this sentence, as a guide to reading.

10. This paragraph, in its entirety, has been crossed out in the typescript.

11. The clause, "for he has refused the traditional unseen child-bride," has been crossed out in the typescript.

The Next Book

"The Next Book" was broadcast on the BBC Light Programme on 13 July 1947. It was re-broadcast on the BBC Overseas Pacific Service in a series called "Famous Writers" on 14 September 1950. The BBC Third Programme saw fit to broadcast it again, nearly fourteen years later, on 15 January 1964. Anticipating the release of *The Heat of the Day* in February 1949, "The Next Book" was also published in *Now and Then*, the promotional magazine for Jonathan Cape (Autumn 1948): 11–13. The published version has been used as a base text. A corrected, double-spaced typescript in 1947 was retyped, with changes, in single-spaced copy for the 1950 broadcast (BBC Written Archives). The only differences between the typescripts and the printed version in *Now and Then* concern punctuation and italics. In the broadcasts, Bowen gives emphasis to words such as "purely" and "mean."

Impressions of Czechoslovakia

"Impressions of Czechoslovakia," a three-page essay dated 15 March 1948, was read by Mrs. Krywultova for the BBC European Service to Czechoslovakia. On 26 January 1948, Audrey G. Anderson, Czechoslovak Programme Organiser at the BBC, contacted Bowen to ask if she would speak about her impressions of Czechoslovakia: "I have been informed by the Foreign Office that you are going to Czechoslovakia on February 6th for a lecture tour. I should be most grateful if, on your return, you would let us have a short script on your most outstanding impressions of that country" (BBC "Scriptwriter" file). Bowen delivered the script in March, after her return from Czechoslovakia, with a brief note to Miss Anderson: "Here is my broadcast. It is difficult to estimate the length suitable for the time; if this is too long it can, of course, be cut" (BBC "Scriptwriter" file). Two successive drafts exist (HRC 2.3). The second version, a blue carbon copy, incorporates manuscript insertions and corrections from the earlier draft. The second version is used as the base text.

1. *The Secret*: Bedřich Smetana (1824-84) is the composer most closely identified with Bohemian national opera. His opera *The Secret* was completed in 1878.

2. *A Year in Bohemia*: probably *Spaliček*, Jiri Trnka's 1947 film featuring animated puppets. *Spaliček* is usually known in English as *The Czech Year*, not *A Year in Bohemia*. The film, famous in its time, won prizes for animation at film festivals in Venice and Paris.

The Mechanics of Writing

"The Mechanics of Writing" exists as a three-page, typed, blue carbon copy in the Rare Books Room in Firestone Library at Princeton University (Leonard L. Milberg Autograph Collection, C0962, box 1). It also exists on microfilm at the BBC Written Archives. This four-minute broadcast, produced by Noreen Purdon, went to air on the BBC Pacific Service on 14 November 1949. The essay was printed in a slightly different form, under the title "Elizabeth Bowen at her Typewriter," in the *Listener* 42.1087 (24 November 1949): 890. In the published version, contractions are spelled out, italics are omitted, and some sentences are deleted. The Princeton University typescript, more representative of what Bowen read on the air, has been used as the base text. Paragraphing follows the Princeton manuscript; the printed text in the *Listener* has only four paragraphs. A few spelling errors and minor punctuation errors have been silently corrected.

1. Jotting down: Bowen's friend, Ivy Compton-Burnett, wrote notes for her novels on small pieces of paper and hid them behind cushions (Spurling 48). Bowen's comment is not, of course, specific to Compton-Burnett.

2. Commas have been added around this phrase for clarity.

Books that Grow up with One

"Books that Grow up with One" exists in four forms. First, there is an eight-page typescript dated "26.9.49" (HRC 2.3). Second, there is a script retyped for broadcast with corrections by hand (BBC Written Archives). Third, the tape of Bowen reading this essay is extant (BBC Sound Archives). Fourth, the broadcast was published in *London Calling* 546 (9 March 1950): 10. The essay was recorded on 5 October 1949 for transmission on 2 November; it was re-broadcast on 3 November on the General Overseas Service, and again on 9 November on the Pacific Service. Bowen wrote this broadcast for a series called "In My Library." In a letter to Bowen dated 19 April 1949, the producer Kay Fuller spelled out the mandate of the series:

> Its aim is to reflect for our English speaking audience throughout the world English writers and books of the past. The framework is that of a distinguished writer or critic selecting from the shelves of her own library three or four of her favourite books or authors; or perhaps talking in a general way about her collection of books. (BBC "Talks" 1)

In order to meet the eleven-minute format, the first three paragraphs and the first sentence of the fourth paragraph were cut from the BBC typescript, as were other sentences here and there. Someone has pencilled "start here" next to the sentence, "There is, for the reader, a hateful sadness . . ." I have used the typescript from the Harry Ransom Center as a base text and noted changes added to the BBC version. The BBC Sound Archives tape of "Books that Grow up with One" indicates just how serious Bowen's stutter was; she labours over words that begin with "t" and "n," such as "T-t-t-tolstoy" and "n-n-n-never." Sometimes she alters phrases at the last moment, as if swerving away from imminent danger.

1. Words, words, words: Hamlet's answer to Polonius about what he reads. *Hamlet* 2.2.192.

2. In the BBC typescript, the passage, "not only have . . . appear," is crossed out and shortened to "the character should have the power to seem to grow."

3. In the BBC typescript, "must" is crossed out and replaced with "should."

4. In the BBC typescript, "conflict" is crossed out and replaced with "struggle."

5. In the BBC typescript, "depth" is crossed out and replaced by "deepness."

6. The HRC typescript gives "of reading," but the BBC typescript, which I have followed in this exceptional instance, gives "we read."

7. In the BBC typescript, these sentences are heavily corrected: "The book is absorbed into the reader. And, also the personality of the reader is at work on the book."

8. In the BBC typescript, the word is emphasised: "*you.*"

9. In the BBC typescript, "page" is singular.

10. In the BBC typescript, "your vision" is crossed out and the phrase, "the addition of *your* experience," written above the line.

11. In the BBC typescript, "comedy of manners" is replaced with "sheer comedy of behaviour." The rest of the line, "on one of her two inches of ivory," is also crossed out.

The Cult of Nostalgia

Bowen recorded "The Cult of Nostalgia" for broadcast on the BBC Third Programme on 26 July 1951. It aired on 4 August 1951 and again on 8 August 1951. It subsequently aired on the BBC Overseas Service to Japan. The essay was reprinted in the *Listener* 46.1171 (9 August 1951): 225–6. The essay exists as a seven-page, carbon-copy typescript (HRC 2.3) and as a seven-page typescript with some handwritten changes (BBC Written Archives). The published version in the *Listener*, used as a base text, incorporates the changes on the BBC typescript. Bowen's tendency to italicise words and to adorn sentences with exclamation marks and dashes is downplayed in the published text. I have left out the inter-titles that an editor added to the *Listener* version.

1. In the *Listener*, the text reads, "on in the increase," which is not in the typescript.

2. An abiding city: Hebrews 13:14.

3. The BBC typescript reads, "we must know and we must judge."

Coronation

Bowen wrote "Coronation" at the request of BBC producer Anne Kallin. In a letter dated 14 October 1953, Kallin proposed that Bowen, along with Rose Macaulay, Ivy Compton-Burnett, and Veronica Wedgwood, might speak "not exactly on 'our New Queen' or any other Elizabeth, (accept [sic] yourself) or on the Idea of Queenship, but something that would be a part of all that, and which you all would enjoy doing. You know how anti-feminist I am, but even I am tickled by the idea of [a] nice, new fresh Queen" (BBC "Talks" file). In the end, only Bowen and Wedgwood participated. The programme was called "For a Sovereign Lady – Some Thoughts on the Coronation." Wedgwood's segment bore the title "Elizabeth" and Bowen's segment was called, simply, "Coronation." Bowen recorded her essay on 13 March 1953, nearly three months before the actual coronation took place on 2 June. The programme went to air on 31 May 1953. The coronation was much discussed in the press – the regalia, the route, the participants, the ceremony – which allowed Bowen to anticipate crowd feeling on coronation day itself. In her essay, Wedgwood compares male and female monarchs; she concludes that a "special mystery" surrounds women who rule. Bowen's essay exists as a two-page, single-spaced typescript (BBC Written Archives). The essay ran 10'37" in its recorded version. It covers some of Bowen's favourite topics of the mid-1950s: the future, children, media. The typescript is relatively free of errors, although Bowen made a few changes by hand in the margins and between lines. Ellipses are Bowen's.

1. Instead of "by," the typescript reads "be," which is no doubt an error.

2. The typescript reads "voices takes up after voice." The phrase, which makes little sense, was corrected by hand, although the "s" on the initial "voice" was not cancelled.

On Not Rising to the Occasion

"On Not Rising to the Occasion" was broadcast on the BBC Home Service on 19 July 1956. Thereafter, the essay was printed in the *Listener* 56 (26 July 1956): 121-22. It also appeared in *Vogue* 129 (15 February 1957): 124–5. Hermione Lee included it in *The Mulberry Tree* (65–9). The focus on incidents and feelings from Bowen's childhood is explained by the focus of the series for which the essay was written:

"Some Horrors of Childhood." Bowen's contribution was the second instalment in the series.

Writing about Rome

"Writing about Rome" was recorded on 1 September 1959 and broadcast on the BBC Home Service on 14 October 1959. B. C. Horton, with whom Bowen was quite friendly, produced the segment. The broadcast lasted 12'40". The three-page typescript has a few spelling and punctuation errors (BBC Written Archives). These errors have been silently corrected. Bowen's *A Time in Rome* was published on 15 February 1960 in the United States and on 4 July 1960 in the United Kingdom. This broadcast, therefore, served as publicity for the book. In *A Time in Rome*, Bowen consults Augustus Hare's *Walks in Rome* as a guidebook (4, 129). She also cites William Story's *Roba di Roma* (151).

1. "Of" has been added.

2. Risorgimento: the movement for liberation and national unification in Italy. The movement ended in 1870 with the seizure of papal possessions and the acquisition of Venice. Bowen apparently uses "Risorgimento" to mean the period after unification is accomplished.

3. "In" has been added.

4. Augustus Hare (1834–1903): author of travel guides about English shires and Italian destinations. *Walks in Rome*, which ran to multiple editions in Hare's lifetime, was first published in 1871.

5. William Story (1819–95): American sculptor and writer, who settled and worked in Rome. *Roba di Roma*, an account of Rome in the nineteenth century, was published in 1862.

6. "I" has been added.

7. The sentence is awkward. If "danger" were replaced with "dangerous," it would make more sense. The repetition of "concerned" might be intended, but it might just as easily be ditto by the typist.

Ireland Today

"Ireland Today," on eighteen pages of yellow carbon paper, is heavily corrected by Bowen in blue ink, with inserts and crossings-out (HRC 6.5). These handwritten changes have been incorporated into the text. Obvious spelling errors have been silently changed: "romantic" is accidentally spelled "romatic"; "niched" is written "nitched." Errors in punctuation and agreement have, likewise, been corrected without comment. Space breaks have been omitted. The date of composition of this essay is ambiguous. On one hand, internal evidence suggests that it was written around 1952 or 1953. Bowen intimates that de Valera has won several by-elections, and she mentions the budget of 1952. De Valera's party formed the government until 1954. Despite these internal clues, the essay might well be a television documentary written in 1960. On 19 September 1960, Bowen was approached by Spencer Curtis Brown, her agent, with a proposition to write scripts for two half-hour CBS documentaries about Ireland:

> Apparently a man with the characteristic name of Isaac Kleinerman wrote to you from C.B.S. in America asking if you could do a commentary to go with two half-hour films on 'IRELAND TODAY' which C.B.S. have made. I gather that the commentary would run for about 15 minutes on each film and they offer $1,200 for each. I imagine that they can arrange a showing of the films in London. They say they have never had any reply from you and quite possibly you have never got the letter. Are you remotely interested in earning £800 in this way? They seem, as always, to be in a great hurry so perhaps you could wire or 'phone me about it. (HRC 11.3; original punctuation)

Bowen accepted the proposal from CBS. Technical questions subsequently arose about "the number of words per minute to be fitted into the different pauses and different times during which the narration can be heard," as Curtis Brown explained to Bowen in a letter dated 19 October 1960 (HRC 11.3). Bowen posted the script to New York in late December or very early January; Curtis Brown acknowledges receiving it in a letter dated 6 January 1961 (HRC 11.3). Charles Ritchie reports that Bowen's documentary on Ireland aired on television on 29 January 1961, for he wrote up the occasion in his diary the next day:

> Last night we had a gloomy little gathering to hear E's script on the TV. It was Ireland "The Smile and the Tear," and the Irish Ambassador was here. They didn't use her script at all. She sat on the sofa drinking martinis and saying at frequent intervals in a sepulchral-furious voice, "I didn't write that, I didn't write that," and finally announced that she was going to use the money she had earned for the script to sue the CBS. (*Love's Civil War* 363)

My attempts to track down "Ireland Today" at CBS have come to naught – so far. The British Film Institute (BFI) owns the first part of a documentary called "Ireland: The Tear and the Smile," produced by Burton Benjamin and Isaac Kleinerman for CBS, hosted by Walter Cronkite, with a script by Elizabeth Bowen. The copy at the BFI, however, is not available for viewing. Nor was I able to obtain it from CBS. Unable to see this documentary, I have not been able to confirm that the script, in whatever form, derives from the typescript in the HRC. In any event, Ritchie's diary entry suggests that Bowen's script was substantially altered. I have adopted the title "Ireland Today" to distinguish this script from Bowen's other essays about Ireland. Sellary and Harris report that "Ireland Today" was broadcast on CBS television on 22 May and 6 June 1947 (276), but I can find no confirmation of this assertion.

1. In the typescript, the phrase "it is still possible" is partially stroked out, creating "it is seems possible."

2. The original phrase, crossed out, reads, "the distances, however clouded by weather, give out towards the horizon a sort of otherworldly gleam."

3. April 1948: in fact, the Republic of Ireland officially came to pass in April 1949.

4. In the typescript, Bowen crossed out several lines after "generation": "*then*, for the first time, had the green-white-and-orange tricolour been unfurled over Dublin. For the sake of the hero martyrs of 1916, there must be . . ."

5. The typescript reads "organisation" in the singular.

6. John Redmond's . . . defeat: John Redmond (1856-1918), an MP for Waterford from 1891 to 1918, introduced the third Home Rule Bill in 1912. During the First World War, he offered Irish support of the war effort, to the point of withdrawing all troops from Ireland and leaving the Volunteers in charge of policing in the northern and southern counties. This offer was widely considered a misjudgement.

7. Treaty: signed in 1921, the treaty formalised the partition of Northern Ireland and the Irish Free State, with the Irish Free State having the status of a Dominion within the British Commonwealth. The Dáil Éirann ratified the treaty early in 1922 by a narrow margin.

8. Initially Bowen wrote "descents," but substituted "accesses" in ink.

9. The crossed-out text modifies this sentiment: "And the story, the

inflammatory notion, the galling feeling of deprivation, will never quite die down while Partition lasts."

10. The phrase could be "by fact," not "in fact." Prior to revisions, the phrase read, "remains in sympathy and by constitution affiliated to Britain."

11. Edward Henry Carson (1854-1935): a Unionist MP, supported the amendment to exclude four Ulster counties from the 1912 Home Rule Bill, then moved to exclude all six Ulster counties in 1913.

12. The typescript reads "coast," which does not agree with "were."

13. The original sentence read otherwise: "A German invasion, a British attempt to seize the Irish ports – going up and up in strategic value as submarine warfare went on – would have been, equally, withstood."

14. Revising, Bowen created a syntactical error. The sentence originally read, "Worst of all, the taboo on judgement [. . .] fostered a listless responsibility." Crossing out "of all" and adding "there was" she should have inserted "which" before "fostered" or corrected the sentence in some other way.

15. The word "the" has been added for sense.

16. Bowen crossed out "of utter provinciality" in favour of "to total insularity."

17. The word "of" has been added for sense.

18. John A. Costello (1891–1976): leader of Fine Gael, headed the government between 1948 and 1951; de Valera and the Fianna Fáil party held power from 1951 until 1954. Costello and the Fine Gael resumed power from 1954 until 1957.

19. Spanish-advised: de Valera's father was Spanish; his mother was Irish.

The Daughters of Erin by Elizabeth Coxhead

Bowen's review of Elizabeth Coxhead's *The Daughters of Erin* exists as a typescript (BBC Written Archives) and as a recording (BBC Sound Archives). Minor variations occur between the written and spoken versions, mostly in the form of cuts. In the recorded version, Bowen reads fluently without hesitation or stammers. According to information contained in the contract for this review, she received 15 guineas plus expenses to travel from Hythe to London to record the segment (BBC "Rcont" file; contract dated 8 June 1965). Minor handwritten changes on the typescript have been incorporated into the text.

1. The phrase, "is – I would argue – still," is crossed out in the typescript, which renders the sentence ungrammatical. I have restored it.

2. And also intrinsically . . . genius: these two sentences were cut in the recorded version.

3. In the recorded version, Bowen says "came and met," instead of "met."

4. In the recorded version, Bowen substitutes "hears" for "gathers."

Panorama of the Novel

"Panorama du roman" was published in French in a special number of *Fontaine* 37–40 (1944): 33-43. Pier Ponti translated the essay from English. It was reprinted in *Aspects de la littérature anglaise 1918-1945*, edited by Kathleen Raine and Max-Pol Fouchet (Paris: Fontaine, 1944): 30–9. It was also published in German in *Die Neue Zürcher Zeitung: Literatur und Kunst* 168 (4 October 1947): 1–2. In the absence of any extant English version, I have translated the French essay back into English; I make no claims, however, to duplicating Bowen's inimitable style. In the French version, verb tenses often run to the pluperfect, where English uses the simple past. I have reorganised clauses or added explicit clarifications where the French text remains implicit. The ellipses throughout the essay are Bowen's. This survey of the English novel between the wars comprises one of her most comprehensive statements about modern fiction – its chief practitioners and its social shortcomings. Notably, she says nothing about her own remarkable novels written in the 1920s and 1930s, nor does she mention Henry Green's novels. As in "English Fiction at Mid-Century," a 1953 essay that covers some of the same ground as "Panorama of the Novel," Bowen expresses her distaste for the psychological novel in the 1920s and 1930s: "For the greater part of the inter-war years, subjectivity hazed over the English novel" (*People, Places, Things* 322). During the Second World War and the postwar years, Bowen brooded on civic responsibility and social drama, which she understood in the context of emerging internationalism. In his introduction to the issue of *Fontaine* dedicated to English writers, Fouchet writes, "Nous connaissons trop peu, à moins d'être spécialistes, les littératures de nos voisins pour ne pas tenir à nos préférences avec une force inversement proportionelle à notre information [Except for a few specialists, we know too little about the literature of neighbouring countries to hold onto our prejudices with a strength inversely proportional to the information that we possess]" (149–50). This issue of *Fontaine* included translated contributions, some of them posthumous, from T. E. Lawrence, D. H. Lawrence, T. S. Eliot, Thomas Hardy, W. B. Yeats, Lytton Strachey, George Orwell, Stephen Spender, and others. In his introduction, Fouchet offers these writings "sous le signe de la liberté, comme un fervent témoignage d'amitié spirituelle entre deux grands peuples [under the sign of liberty, as fervent testimony to the spiritual friendship between two great peoples]" (152). From the end of the Second World War, Bowen offers an incisive reckoning of detachment, aesthetics, and accomplishments between the wars. She must have written this essay – as she often did write literary essays – without all of her books, for she assigns the wrong dates to many novels.

1. *The Waves*: the French version assigns *The Waves* a publication date of 1930. It was published in 1931.

2. *Portrait*: the French version assigns *Portrait* a publication date of 1922, with *Ulysses* coming thereafter. But *Portrait* was published in 1916 and *Ulysses* in 1922.

3. *Howards End*: the wrong date, 1912, is given in the French version.

4. A note in the French text states that this sentence was written in French in the original: "Cela correspondait peut-être à un besoin tourmenté de solution."

5. Bowen returns to Flaubert's idea of the novel as "psychological overflow" in "The Poetic Element in Fiction."

Subject and the Time

Delivered as the "Blashfield Address" at the American Academy of Arts and Letters and the National Institute of Arts and Letters, "Subject and the Time" was subsequently published in *Proceedings, Second Series, Number 4: American Academy of Arts and Letters* (New York: National Institute of Arts and Letters with the Evangeline Wilbour Blashfield Foundation, 1954): 22–8.

The Poetic Element in Fiction

"The Poetic Element in Fiction" exists in two carbon copy versions, one revised, the other untouched (HRC 7.3). Emendations on the initial two pages of the first carbon copy version have been incorporated into this text. Other minor changes have been made for clarity and common sense, principally spelling and preposition usage. Faint question marks in pencil appear over the words "creases" and "Piast," but they are not in Bowen's hand. They may have been added by a typist. In a letter dated 22 December 1950, someone at the Curtis Brown Literary Agency sent Bowen a "copy of the lecture" that two "girls from the Ambassador Office Service worked on." The author of the letter, whose signature is illegible, writes that the typists found that "the record was, in places, unintelligible. They did the best they could and this is the result" (HRC 7.3). As the opening sentence indicates, this speech was delivered in a lecture series, quite possibly in 1950, since Curtis Brown forwarded her this typescript in late December 1950. The lecture was apparently delivered from notes, recorded, then sent to be typed. The typists were somewhat careless with spelling and punctuation. The syntax, reflecting oral delivery, is loose and sometimes ungrammatical. "The Poetic Element in Fiction" evokes, in phrase and by name, Percy Bysshe Shelley, but does not otherwise engage the relation of poetry to prose. Bowen bids a formal farewell to certain stylistic manœuvers of high modernism: complication for its own sake; technical virtuosity in the use of language; Eliot's claim that poetry ought to be at least as well written as prose. Bowen recognizes Joyce's and Stein's experimentalism as valid ways to access experience, but she does not admire the "sacrifice of intelligibility" that experimentalism entails. Unambiguously she prefers James and Proust.

1. This sentence originally read, "It became the document." The word "document" is crossed out and the phrase "character of a" is inserted with a caret. Although deleted, "document" belongs in the sentence.

2. The passage, before being revised, emphasised class position:

> the novel in its time came into being as an outstanding human acquirement 200 years ago, in the age of reason, the age of liberalism, the age when the cramping hold of the court circle on imagination had gone. And here and in Europe there came into being this group of people, aware of themselves, aware of their place in society. It was reasonable in its intentions – the novel. It stood for rationality and for exploration.

An awareness of continental differences – Bowen uses the phrase "here and in Europe" – indicates that she addresses an American audience.

3. The word "an" has been added.

4. After this sentence, another, crossed out, raises the topic of

language: "And it was dominated by the wise air of rationality that no zone of human experience need remain outside the power of language and the hold of imaginative art."

5. Extensive handwritten corrections end at this point in the typescript.

6. The two women who typed this script may have misread the original. "Piast" was a dynasty of Polish kings and dukes (962–1675), but that reference makes no sense in this context. Bowen appears to mean a French author. "Proust" might be intended, but the typists had no difficulty with his name later in the essay, and, moreover, the context indicates an eighteenth-century example, not a twentieth-century one.

7. The phrase is incomprehensible. The "and" may be superfluous: "a wholly rational order due of man." It is also possible that Bowen meant "of a whole rationale and order due of man," for a faint "e" appears at the end of "rational."

8. The phrase between dashes originally read, "to 'Madame Bovary,'" but the recurrence of "to" in the sentence is excessive.

9. In the typescript, "the" appears after "of."

10. The word "most" has been added for sense.

11. The typescript reads "heat," but "heath" or some other word might be intended.

12. The typescript reads "stone-hinge."

13. The typescript reads "period" in the singular.

14. The typescript reads "general desire for the story in general"; I have removed the first "general" because of its awkward anticipation of the second.

15. The meaning is obscure. Bowen may mean "expressive" or "filled with expression."

16. The intended phrase might be "on a scene or stage from which the ordinary charming scenery has been removed." The odd phrasing might be the result of self-correction during oral delivery.

17. The word "of" has been added after "fact" for clarity.

18. The typescript reads "its," but the pronoun should be plural: "their."

The Idea of the Home

"The Idea of the Home" was given as an address at Barnard College on 10 February 1953. The speech exists in two versions: an incomplete typescript with handwritten revisions (HRC 6.3); and a complete, retyped copy in the Barnard College Archives. Bowen jotted a note on the last page of the incomplete version: "N.B. – the last sheet's missing: I added another end: those last pages are only with Mr. Rauch at Barnard College, Columbia University. I shall have to wait for the proofs from him before this, as an essay, can be complete." On the left corner of the first page, Bowen notes, "*Corrected* (though the copy of this which went to Mr. Rauch was again re-corrected – and more clearly)." Basil Rauch, a history professor and the chair of the American Civilization Program at Barnard, handed over his clean copy of the speech to the president of the college, Millicent C. McIntosh, who deposited it in the Barnard archives. The context of the address – a series about American civilisation – clarifies why emphasis falls on the US in the essay. The HRC typescript is relatively clean, except for the passages where she is at pains to define "home." The typist of the Barnard version some-times Americanised Bowen's spellings, and sometimes left them in their British forms. It is possible that Bowen made changes to the Barnard version herself, but it is also possible that the typist introduced errors while typing. The Barnard typescript, with the final pages included, has been used as a base text. A few obvious spelling errors have been cor-rected. I have amended ambiguous punctuation, especially awkward use of the comma, without annotating every change.

1. Both the HRC and Barnard versions give "never," but Bowen crossed out the "n" by hand in the Barnard version to create "ever."

2. In the HRC version, Bowen writes "spontaneous" above "natural" without crossing out the latter.

3. Currier & Ives: popular, nineteenth-century print company based in New York.

4. In the HRC version, Bowen crossed out "symptomise a certain break with reality" and replaced it with "tend to diverge too widely from reality."

5. The phrase "recollected civilisation" gave Bowen pause. In the HRC version, she tried "remembered civilisation," then "to-be-reproduced civilisation," before lighting upon the final wording.

6. The HRC version reads, "Dare one say."

7. In the HRC version, Bowen originally wrote, "can but be something of an internal tax," instead of "can but impinge upon fundamentals."

8. The HRC version reads "accepted and set community," instead of "*felt* community."

9. In the HRC version, another sentence followed this last, but

Bowen crossed it out: "The answer should be in the affirmative; but how?"

10. The HRC version reads "promise," not "promote."

11. In the HRC version, the word "graciousness" was inserted as an afterthought, which may account for the quotation marks around it.

12. Never-neverland: the imaginary land in *Peter Pan*. Walt Disney's animated film, *Peter Pan*, was released in 1953.

13. Instead of "furnishings," the HRC version reads "furniture," which seems more precise in light of Bowen's subsequent references to furniture.

14. The HRC version reads "cannot longer be sold," instead of "is not to be sold." The HRC version has no paragraph break here.

15. The HRC version reads, without any qualifying adjective, "non-compromisers," not "high-spirited non-conformers."

16. The Barnard version omits the clause "how to share." The typist may have accidentally omitted it.

17. The HRC version reads, "abide by individual choices without declaring those too abruptly."

18. The HRC version reads, somewhat cryptically, "a clearing house of the nature, a hub for contacts not made before." The term "'free zone'" resonates with Cold War political meaning.

19. In the HRC version, this section underwent heavy revision. It originally read as follows: "The home offers itself as a meeting-place for strangers due to become friends, as a clearing house for talk, as a point for contacts. The value of the home is to be judged by its aliveness, its awareness and its expressiveness – and today the world needs the outgoing force. Let America, with her unlost domestic genius see to it that she multiplies such homes."

20. The HRC version reads "strong," instead of "fearless."

21. The HRC version begins the paragraph differently: "The idea of the home moves sometimes a little ahead of, sometimes a little behind reality: we are divided between," then breaks off altogether. For the rest of the essay, only the Barnard version exists.

22. The original is misspelt as "materiel," one of Bowen's habitual spelling errors.

Language

"Language" exists in two very similar versions (HRC 7.3). The first outline has four pages. The second outline, which I have transcribed, has six manuscript pages. Many passages are underlined, sometimes twice. Within reason, I have followed the free-form lineation of the outline. To signal a new sentence or point, Bowen does not necessarily use a full stop, but she does use an upper-case letter. Sections, numbered with Roman numerals and framed by large brackets in the manuscript, are clearly meant as prompts for a public lecture. Internal evidence suggests that Bowen addressed people who teach, for she refers to herself as a writer and then to those who write and teach. In the shorter version of the outline, she has a section called "My experiences in Writing Groups." She may, therefore, have delivered this talk in the late 1950s or early 1960s, after she spent time teaching at Bryn Mawr, University of Madison at Wisconsin, and Vassar.

1. Pleasures: the word is plural in the four-page version, which I have adopted here, but singular, "pleasure," in the six-page version.

2. There is a ditto on "have" in the original.

3. The phrase may be "at least," but "least" is missing in the manuscript.

4. Bowen labels this section VII, when it should be VIII. No further Roman numerals are used in the outline, so I have added them.

5. The dual verbs, "be become," appear in the manuscript.

6. The four-page version concludes differently: "I am convinced that it *is* the desire of *people* to be *articulate*. To make them so is our aim."

The Fear of Pleasure

"The Fear of Pleasure" appeared in *Adult Education* 24.3 (Winter 1951): 167–9. A quarterly published by the National Institute of Adult Education for England and Wales, *Adult Education*, as an editorial note explains in each issue, "is intended to be both a record of activities and an open forum for the discussion of all matters, however controversial, relating to Adult Education." A note in the introduction to the winter 1951 issue states that Bowen's essay was given as an address at Oxford in September 1951 at the annual conference of the National Institute: "Miss Bowen's assertion of pleasure as a positive good which is 'part of the response to the threat of the rational faculties' seems particularly apposite just now. The search for economy in education may all too easily begin at the margins where development occurs" (165–6). It is unclear what supervision Bowen had over the final text. An editorial note explains that the essay is a "summary . . .

compiled from Miss Bowen's speaking notes and approved by her for publication" (167).

1. Golden apples: in Greek mythology, the virgin huntress Atalanta loses a footrace because her competitor, Milanion, casts golden apples in her path, as Bowen recalls in a 1950 review of Eudora Welty's *The Golden Apples*: "those golden apples which, rolled across Atalanta's course as she ran, sent her chasing sideways, and made her lose the race" (*Afterthought* 153).

2. Expense of spirit: Shakespeare, Sonnet 129, "The expense of spirit in a waste of shame / Is lust in action."

A Novelist and His Characters

"A Novelist and His Characters," given as a speech at the Royal Society, was subsequently published in *Essays by Divers Hands: Being the Transactions of the Royal Society of Literature*. Ed. Mary Stoke. New Series. Vol. 36. (London: Oxford University Press, 1970): 19–23.

1. The published text gives "have been *created*," which is clearly an error.

Things to Come

Bowen's review of the film *Things to Come* was published in *Sight and Sound* 5.17 (1936): 10-12. Three stills of spaceships and a giant telescope illustrate the review. Based on H. G. Wells's novel, the 1936 film was directed by William Cameron Menzies, with performances by Ralph Richardson and Raymond Massey. Alexander Korda produced the film, and H. G. Wells wrote the screenplay. In the film, war breaks out on Christmas Day, 1940, and lasts for decades. In the film, "Everytown" is a version of London.

Why I Go to the Cinema

"Why I Go to the Cinema" appeared in *Footnotes to the Film*, edited by Charles Davy (London: Lovat Dickson, 1938): 205–20. The volume included essays by Alfred Hitchcock on directing, Graham Greene on subject matter, John Grierson on realism, and Alexander Korda on British film, among others.

1. Miss Gracie Fields (1898-1979): actress and singer who was

a darling of the music halls. She made a slough of films in the 1930s.

2. *Toupet*: cheek or nerve.

3. Articulated: the published version reads "articulates," but "articulated" makes more sense.

4. *The Informer*: two movie adaptations of Liam O'Flaherty's 1925 novel were released in 1929 and 1935. Bowen probably refers to the latter, directed by John Ford.

Third Programme

Devoted to culture and the arts, the Third Programme went on the air on 29 September 1946, initially broadcasting six hours per day. It survived until 1970, when it was folded into BBC Radio 3. Bowen's essay, "Third Programme," has two distinct incarnations. It appeared under the title "Third Programme" in British *Vogue* (April 1947): 76, 102, 104. Revised, it appeared as "Britain's Wave Length for Intellectuals" in American *Vogue* (15 July 1947): 40, 73. The British version is used as the base text. The American version gives more explanation for non-British readers:

> The big test for any new venture is, I suppose, the kind of publicity it makes for itself as it goes along. The British Broadcasting Company's Third Programme was, is, by every showing a quite new venture, not only in British radio but in radio at all. September 29, 1946, was the day; that day, I cannot imagine that any listener tuning in at 6 P.M. to the wave-length was without some tremor of the dramatic sense. Clocks were set; a queer critical silence pervaded rooms. New aesthetic history was going into the making. ("Britain's Wave Length" 40)

Bowen quotes extensively from George Barnes's "manifesto," as she calls it, in defence of the minority programming. Barnes's statement had appeared in the *Listener* on 26 September 1946. In line with Barnes's view that the Third Programme was intended for the "alert and receptive listener," by which he means the "generally cultivated person," Bowen sees the broadcasts as aesthetic and highbrow, not journalistic or middlebrow. Nevertheless, as Asa Briggs points out, thirty-five per cent of Third Programme listeners in 1949 were working class (83). On its fifth anniversary, E. M. Forster defended the Third Programme on the grounds of quality, not quantity: "Quality is everywhere imperilled in contemporary life. Those who value it, as I do, are in a vulnerable position. We form as it were an aristocracy in the midst of a democracy" (414). Forster is anxious to think of the Third Programme in relation to other available radio services and "the problem of maintaining and extending aristocracy in the midst of democracy" (416). Whether snobbish or edifying, the Third Programme was an opportunity for Bowen. She became a regular contributor of essays, opinion pieces, and conversations. The American version of "Third Programme" is substantially different in its first four paragraphs, then resembles the British text, except in the matter of paragraphing.

Lawrence of Arabia

This promotional piece about David Lean's film *Lawrence of Arabia* appeared in *Show* (December 1962): 66–9, 132. Whereas Bowen claims in "Why I Go to the Cinema" that films relax her, this essay anticipates unrelenting dramatic tension in *Lawrence of Arabia*. The film was a spectacular success and won multiple Academy Awards, including Best Picture of the Year.

1. Desert Rats: the seventh armoured division of the British Army were colloquially known as Desert Rats. They fought in the desert campaign in North Africa in 1941-42.

2. Photographs of T. E. Lawrence and Peter O'Toole in the original publication illustrate Bowen's verbal descriptions.

Downe House Scrap-Book 1907-1957

Bowen's reminiscences about Downe House appeared in this "scrapbook," privately printed to commemorate the first fifty years of the school (Oxford: University Press, 1957): 35–7. Downe House, a girls' school, was founded near Orpington in Kent by Miss Willis and Alice Carver. The school moved to a different location in 1922. As Bowen mentions, this essay complements "The Mulberry Tree," printed in a collection called *The Old School*, edited by Graham Greene. According to Sellery and Harris (122, 225), the essay called "Miss Willis" is an earlier version of the "Downe House Scrap-Book" essay. The two essays have very little in common, except the topic and the first few sentences (*People, Places, Things* 112-13). "Miss Willis" is about the school-mistress, whereas this essay is about Downe House School. The two essays complement each other, without forming a clear stemma. Capitalisation is preserved from the original.

1. British Association: Down House, not Downe House, opened in 1927 as a museum dedicated to Charles Darwin. The site was acquired in 1966 by English Heritage, which manages the house and grounds.

2. Bitha: Bowen's childhood nickname.

3. *Bouches inutiles*: literally, "useless mouths" or "more mouths to feed"; figuratively, unproductive people. *Bouches inutiles* was also the title of a 1945 play by Simone de Beauvoir.

Alfred Knopf

The eight-page typescript of "Alfred Knopf" is faint, making some words and punctuation nearly illegible (HRC 1.2). A few words lack capitalisation, such as "knopf"; others have been misspelled. These errors have been silently corrected. A very few changes to punctuation have been made for the sake of clarity. Because Bowen mentions having known Knopf (1892–1984) for "thirty years," and because the publishing house of Knopf celebrated its fiftieth birthday in 1965, it is likely that this essay dates from that year. As she mentions in this profile, Bowen's first book to be published by Knopf was *To the North*. The professional tie, not without the fringe benefit of friendship, continued until the end of her life.

1. Bowen leaves the date open in the typescript: "(193-)." *To the North* was published in 1932 in Britain; Knopf published it in the US in 1933.

2. A comma after "Blanche" has been removed.

3. The sentence originally read, "he might become bored by the puzzle and give up?" Changing "give up" to "gone home" by hand, Bowen forgot to change the previous verb tense. I have added "have."

4. The typescript reads "to be begin."

5. A comma has been added.

Blanche Knopf

"Blanche Knopf," a tribute to Bowen's friend and publisher, was written for the fiftieth anniversary of Knopf, the publishing house, in 1965. Probably a speech, it parallels Bowen's reminiscences of Alfred Knopf. The typescript of this speech is six pages long (HRC Knopf

Collection 686.1). Blanche Knopf (1894–1966) was a protective, not to say implicated, person in Bowen's life. She wrote many long, impassioned letters to Bowen, not all of which the author deigned to answer. Blanche Knopf also instigated a plan to nominate Bowen for a Nobel Prize, going so far as to solicit letters of support from various writers and academics to further the nomination.

1. A question mark may have been intended here, but conversely the typist may have inverted the phrase "it is" earlier in the sentence.

Confessions

Whereas Bowen answered many questions about her writing habits and personal preferences in literature, "Confessions" sticks to public impingements on the private writer. *Saturday Book* posed this set of nine questions to nine distinguished men and women. Other respondents included John Gielgud and Hermione Gingold. Answers were published in *The Saturday Book: Being the Ninth Annual Issue of this Celebrated Repository of Curiosities and Looking-Glass of Past and Present*, edited by Leonard Russell (London: Hutchinson, 1949): 108–9.

The Cost of Letters

In "The Cost of Letters," Cyril Connolly asked a group of writers six questions about reasonable income and state support in *Horizon* (September 1946): 141–2. John Betjeman, Alex Comfort, George Orwell, Rose Macaulay, Dylan Thomas, Robert Graves, and others responded. Connolly's leading question about the role of the state should be read in the context of the cultural politics of the welfare state. Authors' answers to this questionnaire were reprinted in the anthology, *Ideas and Places*, edited by Cyril Connolly (London: Weidenfeld & Nicolson, 1953): 79–126.

Portrait of a Woman Reading

"Portrait of a Woman Reading" appeared in the *Chicago Tribune Book World* (10 November 1968): 10. The interview, conducted by Charles Monagham, was part of a series called "Portrait of a Man Reading," but the word "Man" was struck out and replaced by "Woman" – for obvious reasons – before going to press.

The Living Image – 1

"The Living Image – 1," broadcast on 4 December 1941 on the BBC Home Service, was part of a series called "The Living Image." Hugh Sykes-Davies mentions painting because the previous broadcast – a discussion among Clive Bell, Herbert Read, and V. S. Pritchett – concerned visual art. The conversation had no subtitle or specific subject. The seventeen-page, double-spaced typescript exists on microfilm (BBC Written Archives). In this conversation, Bowen, citing Vernon Lee and D. H. Lawrence, comes closest to commenting on the rudiments of language: adjectives, infinitives, cadence. The typist's transcription is logical and almost free of amendments. In a very few instances, I have made minor changes to punctuation or capitalisation to clarify meaning.

1. *Arabia Deserta*: Charles M. Doughty's *Travels in Arabia Deserta*, published in 1888, is a masterpiece of travel writing in part because of its idiosyncratic, often inverted syntax. It influenced T. E. Lawrence, who wrote an introduction to an abridged version in 1908.

2. In vain the Tyrian maids: from Milton's "On the Morning of Christ's Nativity," stanza 22. Thammuz was another name for Adonis.

3. *The Use of Words*: Bowen is probably thinking of Vernon Lee's *The Handling of Words, and Other Studies in Literary Psychology*, published in 1923. In that book, Lee discusses the visual force of adjectives.

4. This sentence gave the typist pause. The typist used commas and a parenthesis, but I have opted for dashes to make Bowen's meaning clear.

The Living Image – 2

"The Living Image – 2" was broadcast on 23 January 1942 on the BBC Home Service. The seven-page, single-spaced typescript exists on microfilm (BBC Written Archives). It contains only a very few corrections and erasures. This broadcast develops in different directions to the first discussion. Beales and Davies consume air time with their conversation about readers and money. Nevertheless, Bowen's comments make more precise her position on women's issues, and what she perceived, in 1942, to be out of date in terms of feminism.

1. In the typescript, Bowen makes no prior mention of the Brontës.

It is possible that a portion of the tape was cut before the typist began to transcribe it.

How I Write: A Discussion with Glyn Jones

"How I Write" was pre-recorded on 3 May 1950 for a programme called "Arts Magazine." According to information on the mimeographed transcript, this interview was broadcast on 10 May 1950, from 10.00 to 10.35 p.m. The eight-page transcript is free of corrections (HRC 2.3). Bowen received Glyn Jones's questions beforehand. In a letter dated 7 February 1950, she asked him to send along questions to Bowen's Court after her return from travels in Switzerland and the US: "Would you mind, though, holding the questions over till early April? I shall not have time to deal with anything, intelligently, between now and the time I go abroad at the end of this month. I would, anyhow, rather answer them a little nearer the time" (HRC 10.4). In a subsequent letter, dated 23 April 1950, Bowen writes: "I'd much rather *not* read a passage from my work, but shall be very glad that you should. If so, will you read either the opening of 'Mysterious Kôr' (one of the short stories in *The Demon Lover* collection) or, any passage you like from 'The Happy Autumn Fields' – in the same collection" (HRC 10.4). In this transcription, some punctuation has been altered to enhance the clarity of syntax. A few contractions have been expanded. The transcriber divided some of Bowen's responses into small paragraphs, which I have regrouped into single paragraphs.

1. In the typescript, the first dash appears after "like," but it makes more sense after "novel."

2. The typescript reads "as Flaubert pointed, the contemplation"; adding "out" clarifies the sentence.

3. The words "the" and "is" have been added.

4. Bowen may be thinking of a passage from *Le Temps retrouvé* that she translated, for her own benefit, in the early 1930s. Proust compares the creative writer to a translator: "I perceived, that in order to express these impressions, to write the essential book, the only true book, a great writer has not in the ordinary sense to *invent* (since that book exists already in each of us) but to *translate*. The obligations and task of a writer are those of a translator" (HRC 9.9; Bowen's translation).

A Conversation between Elizabeth Bowen and Jocelyn Brooke

The conversation between Bowen and Brooke was transcribed from a telediphone recording made on 3 October 1950. Two copies of this interview exist, one at the Harry Ransom Center, the other at the BBC Written Archives. Both are fifteen pages long and identical in content. A short extract of this interview was published under the title "The Writer's Predicament" in *Now & Then* (Spring 1951): 17. The BBC version is used as the base text. In a note to Bowen dated 11 October 1950, Howard Newby praised the interview: "Here is the script of your talk. It is so good I think we shall put it out without any cuts in a 35" space" (HRC 2.3). The transcription contains some spelling errors. I have added upper-case letters to titles and made minor adjustments to punctuation where syntax requires it. Where the transcriber separated one speaker's comments into paragraphs, I have made single paragraphs for each question or answer. The transcriber had trouble spelling French words, mostly Proustian terms, which I have silently corrected. At some moments, the transcriber could not understand a word or phrase in the conversation and therefore left ellipses in the text. I have indicated these ellipses with square brackets. Where one speaker trails off and the other picks up, the ellipses, without square brackets, indicate an overlap in voices.

1. Because the transcriber had trouble with French words, it is possible that Bowen said "*donnée.*"

2. "Notes on Writing a Novel" was published in *Orion* in 1945. The transcriber understands the notes as generic: "I believe I've said that already haven't I when I wrote the notes on, for writing a novel."

3. The word "of" has been inserted for sense.

4. The transcriber omitted "Guermantes."

5. The word "to" has been inserted for sense.

6. The transcriber understood the syntax differently: "'most nearly' is writing [. . .] not extremely difficult." I have separated this clause into two sentences, which may be wrong. The word "fiction" may be the omitted word.

7. "Seemed" may be a mistranscription of "seems."

8. The word that the transcriber could not catch might be "manqué." Brooke might also have said, "perhaps you're a painter in words."

9. The transcript reads, "been have always been," which is not correct.

10. The transcript reads "surface," in the singular.

11. A noun is missing. Either the transcriber did not catch it, or Brooke never uttered it.

12. Perhaps the phrase should read, "And another thing, remember, that . . . "

13. Hyphens have been added to "slightly out of the true."

14. Halley's Comet did, in fact, appear in 1910.

Do Women Think Like Men?

"Do Women Think Like Men?" was broadcast on the BBC Home Service on 17 October 1941. A section of the conversation was printed in *The Listener* (30 October 1941): 593-94. In the absence of a taped version, I have used the printed version as the base text. The conversation was part of a series called "Strength of Mind." Perhaps because she was sceptical about the gist of the conversation, Bowen formulates many of her comments as questions directed at her interlocutors. As in other radio conversations, Bowen insists on the particularity of experience as the grounds for moral evaluation.

1. Baby specialist: possibly Dr. Benjamin Spock (1903–98), whose *Baby and Child Care* was first published 1946.

Do Conventions Matter?

"Do Conventions Matter?" was part of a series called "Strength of Mind." It aired on the BBC Home Service on 5 December 1941. Participants were John Mabbott, Lieutenant-Commander J. Noad, Captain Alan Pryce-Jones, and Bowen. Edited, the exchange was printed in the *Listener* (18 December 1941): 823-24. The printed version has been used as the base text. I have made minor alterations to punctuation, mostly the addition and subtraction of commas.

1. Shaftesbury and Wilberforce: Anthony Ashley Cooper, Lord Shaftesbury (1801-85), introduced parliamentary reforms to help factory workers, the insane, and the homeless. William Wilberforce (1759–1833), philanthropist and politician, led the campaign to abolish slavery.

2. Brook Farm: founded in 1841 by George and Sophia Ripley in Massachusetts, Brook Farm was inspired by principles of the socialist concepts of Charles Fourier. Work was to be shared by all farmers in order to allow them time for leisure and intellectual

pursuits. The farm failed in 1847. Although invited, Emerson never joined.

Conversation on Traitors

"Conversation on Traitors," produced by Helen Arbuthnot for the BBC, was recorded on 13 August 1952 and broadcast on 21 August. Bowen was invited on the strength of *The Heat of the Day*, whose central figures are bound in a tragic dilemma of treachery and complicity. Nigel Balchin, a novelist and later a screenwriter, published *A Sort of Traitors* in 1949; Bowen clearly knows this novel, for she mentions it in passing. Alan Moorehead, a journalist for many years on the *Daily Express*, published *The Traitors: The Double Life of Fuchs, Pontecorvo, and Nunn May* in 1952 to considerable acclaim. Moorehead concentrates on "atomic spies" (5) who deal in the secrets of nuclear fission during the Cold War. Noel Annan, having had a brilliant war in military intelligence, lectured on politics at Cambridge University and contributed regularly to the BBC. In the 1950s, Bowen was paying close attention to the Cold War. In July 1953, a year after this broadcast went to air, she published a book review of Whittaker Chambers' *Witness* in the *Observer*. The twenty-five-page transcript of "Conversation on Traitors" at the BBC Written Archives was typed by two different people whose initials appear at the foot of each page. Transcribing from tape presents difficulties, for the typists must decide on syntax, meaning, and punctuation. In order to make the text clearer, I have taken the liberty of altering punctuation and deleting passages in which speakers hem and haw. The tags "I mean" and "I think" cloud meaning; consequently, I have omitted these and similar phrases in some instances. I have not indicated every one of these changes; they are too minor, and such omissions were, moreover, the prerogative of BBC transcribers. Sometimes commas are changed to dashes, semi-colons to full stops. Where speakers adopt a persona and make a statement, I have added quotation marks, as when Annan quotes Martin Luther; these quotation marks do not appear in the typescript. The speakers change their minds about what they were going to say in mid-sentence, which causes incomplete thoughts and sentences. Noel Annan's syntax has a tendency to wind itself up into knots. Sometimes the typists had trouble understanding Bowen's speech and left ellipses; these instances are indicated with square brackets. The "Conversation on Traitors" has the flow of a conversation, with moments of inadvertence, confusion, clarity, and insight.

1. The word is illegible in the microfilm. It has four letters, but might be something other than "mean."

2. Count Stauffenberg (1907–44): initiated a failed plot to kill Adolf Hitler on 20 July 1944. He knew full well that he was committing treason under Nazi law. He was executed by firing squad.

3. The typist could not decipher what Bowen said and left an ellipsis. The phrases "of it" and "in Fuchs" are written in by hand. Despite my attempt to reconstruct the sentence, Bowen's meaning remains elusive.

4. In the microfilm typescript, a note in the margin states, "Insert from last page." I have therefore inserted the last page at this point, for it follows naturally from the conversation about conscience. Nevertheless, everything has been crossed out in the typescript from Bowen's statement, "what about the conscience of the unstable person," down to her amiable "yes." These and other proposed erasures in the typescript may have been used to edit the tape for broadcast.

5. The word is nearly illegible in the microfilm, but it has four letters and might be something other than "mind."

6. "Do" might be missing: "I can do no other."

7. The word "was" has been added.

8. Lord Wright: this letter to the editor appeared in the *Times* (5 August 1952): 5. Lord Wright, previously the chairman of the United Nations War Crimes Commission, argues that, "In all the war trials in the two world wars it was recognized that a plea of superior orders is not in itself a defence if the order was manifestly contrary to the laws or customs of war and humanity."

9. The word "them" has been added.

10. The typescript reads "they," but "then" makes more sense.

11. The word "might" has been added.

12. The typescript has a ditto, "have have," but "may have" makes more sense.

13. In "What I Believe," Forster wrote, "I hate the idea of causes, and if I had to choose between betraying my country and betraying my friend, I hope I should have the guts to betray my country" (*Two Cheers* 78).

14. The word "than" has been added.

15. In the typescript, Bowen was initially identified as the speaker of "It isn't merely," to the end of the paragraph. But her name is crossed out. There is some confusion about who makes this comment.

16. Balchin's name is not given, but Annan's comment was clearly directed to him, and a new speaker is indicated on the typescript by a paragraph break.

17. Albert Speer (1904–81): in addition to being Hitler's preferred architect, Albert Speer was Minister of Armaments and War Production. He was tried at Nuremberg in 1946, and sentenced to twenty years imprisonment for war crimes and crimes against humanity.

18. The word "it" has been added.

19. The word "in" has been added.

20. The typescript reads "left," but "let" is more likely.

21. The word "to" has been added.

22. We have no abiding city: Hebrews 13:14.

23. Windward Roed: unidentified. The name was probably incorrectly transcribed. In a 1945 pamphlet called "Some Political Consequences of the Atomic Bomb," E. L. Woodward, an Oxford professor of international relations, describes the use of atomic bombs to destroy cities as a choice "between good and evil" (5). He accepts, however, "the physicists' assurance that there is, at least as far as can be foreseen, no risk of a general explosion in which all organic life above the deep sea level would be destroyed. This misuse of the atomic bomb is likely to bring local, not universal destruction" (7). The transcriber might have heard "Windward" instead of "Woodward," but "Roed" remains a mystery.

24. The word "know" has been added.

25. The word "is" has been added.

26. The typist left an ellipsis, then filled in the words "break with honour by hand." The words "on us" have been crossed out. The meaning of the sentence, despite these amendments, remains garbled.

Frankly Speaking: Interview, 1959

"Frankly Speaking," a radio interview with Bowen conducted by John Bowen, William Craig, and W. N. Ewer, was taped on 11 September 1959. It was broadcast on 16 March 1960 and 29 March 1963 on the Home Service, and a third time on 16 January 1964 on the Third Programme. Two copies of the transcribed interview exist (HRC and BBC Written Archives). According to a memo dated 22 December 1959, Lorna Moore, Talks Organiser at the BBC, asked that the tape be cut by 2'15" to fit into a suitable block of time (BBC Written Archives, "Talks" file). In the "original uncut transcription," pencil marks slash across passages (HRC 2.3). Bowen or someone else appears to have begun to edit the typescript. Excisions begin at the line, "Do you feel yourself Irish." Segments about the Paris Peace Conference and the Royal Commission on Capital Punishment were also crossed out. Bowen remains poised while facing interviewers' point-blank questions. Whereas she often begins answers with "yes" in her conversations with Jocelyn Brooke and Glyn Jones, she answers "no" to many of the questions that the three interviewers pose in this broadcast. Using the typescript at the Harry Ransom Center as a base text, I have retained the original version of the interview, as against the tentatively edited transcript. Sometimes Bowen begins a thought, then changes her mind, which accounts for moments of drift throughout the interview. Often the transcriber used ellipsis points or dashes to indicate a change in direction. Whereas the original transcriber interspersed Bowen's "yes" and "no" responses within the interviewers' comments, I have set them on separate lines for the sake of clarity. On a few occasions I have altered commas to periods, and only then on occasions when the syntax warrants such a change. Question marks inside square brackets indicate words that the transcriber could not decode.

1. The typescript reads "it's important for me."

2. My parents kept me: Stephen Spender (1909-95) was one of Bowen's friends. "My parents kept me from children who were rough" is not a sonnet, but a twelve-line poem in three quatrains.

3. The sentence is crossed out in pencil in the typescript.

4. The typescript reads "are," which creates an agreement error between subject and verb.

5. The phrase "I never had" is crossed out. The intention might have been to write, "To do something I never had."

6. The interviewer means "created the rooms around the characters." "Them" has two different referents.

7. This sentence is crossed out in the typescript.

8. In a preliminary index that Bowen made for Gustave Flaubert's letters, Bowen created a heading for "impersonality in art" (HRC 6.3).

9. Royal Commission on Capital Punishment: the commission was struck in 1949 and tabled its report in 1954. As Bowen explains, twelve people, herself included, served on the commission, which was charged with investigating the feasibility of modifying capital punishment. E. A. Gowers headed the committee; the other woman who served was Florence M. Hancock.

10. The punctuation could be either a period or a question mark.

11. MacNaughten rules: rules covering a legal defence on the

grounds of insanity. In order to mount such a defence, the accused had to prove a defect of reason or disease of the mind that caused him or her not to know that the act committed was wrong.

12. The word "more" is crossed out before "likely."

13. In the transcript, a square-bracketed phrase follows this sentence: "[Inaudible allusion by an interviewer to the need for talking.]"

14. The typescript reads "are," which does not agree with the singular subject "anyone."

15. The typescript reads "have," but the subject is singular. I have chosen to put it in the present tense, because all of the people Bowen mentions were alive at the time that she gave this interview.

Works Cited

Archives

The Elizabeth Bowen Collection and the Alfred A. Knopf Collection are held at the Harry Ransom Humanities Research Center, University of Texas at Austin; in citations, these collections are identified as "HRC," followed by a box and file number. The Bowen files held at the BBC Written Archives in Reading are identified as "BBC," followed by the name of the file. Most files are identified with a title, such as "Talks," "Scriptwriter," and "Rcont" for "Regular Contributor." Correspondence between Bowen and Morton Dauwen Zabel is located at the University of Chicago Archives. Five letters and a typescript are located in the Leonard L. Milberg Autograph Collection, Firestone Library, Princeton University. Other documents are in the Bodleian Modern Manuscripts collection at Oxford University. The Princeton and Bodleian materials are identified by shelf-marks.

Books and Articles

Adorno, Theodor. "Fetish Character in Music and Regression of Listening." *The Essential Frankfurt School Reader*. Eds. Andrew Arato and Eike Gebhardt. New York: Continuum, 1988. 270–99.

Avery, Todd. *Radio Modernism: Literature, Ethics, and the BBC, 1922–1938*. Aldershot: Ashgate, 2006.

Barnouw, Erik. *Handbook of Radio Writing*. Boston: Little, Brown, 1947.

Bowen, Elizabeth. *Afterthought: Pieces on Writing*. London: Longmans, 1962.

—. "Autobiographical Note." Two versions, dated 1948 and 1952. HRC 1.5.

—. *Collected Impressions*. London: Longmans, 1950.

—. *The Collected Stories*. Intro. Angus Wilson. 1981. New York: Ecco, 1989.

—. "The Cult of Nostalgia." *Listener* 46.1171 (9 August 1951): 225–26.

—. "Desert Island Discs." Interview with Ray Plomley, 11 March 1957. 15 pages, including retakes and deletions. BBC Written Archives, transcription.

—. *English Novelists*. London: William Collins, 1942.

—. *Eva Trout, or Changing Scenes*. 1968. London: Vintage, 1999.

—. "The Idea of the Home." Barnard College Archives. Typescript, 21 pages. 1953.

—. "Ireland Today." Typescript, 18 pages. HRC 6.5.

—. *The Mulberry Tree: Writings of Elizabeth Bowen*. Ed. Hermione Lee. New York: Harcourt, 1986.

—. *People, Places, Things: Essays by Elizabeth Bowen*. Ed. and intro. by Allan Hepburn. Edinburgh: Edinburgh University Press, 2008.

—. *Pictures and Conversations*. Foreword by Spencer Curtis Brown. New York: Knopf, 1975.

—. "Third Programme." *Vogue* (April 1947): 76, 102, 104.

—. *A Time in Rome*. New York: Knopf, 1960.

—. "Vassar Notebooks on the Short Story." HRC 7.3.

—. "We Write Novels." Interview with Walter Allen, 4 May 1955. 8 pages. BBC Written Archives, microfilm.

—. "The World of Books." Interview with Robert Waller about *The Little Girls*, 24 March 1964. 3 pages. BBC Written Archives, transcription.

—. *A World of Love*. 1955. London: Penguin, 1983.

Bowen, Elizabeth, Graham Greene, and V. S. Pritchett. *Why Do I Write? An Exchange of Views*. London: Percival Marshall, 1948.

Bowen, Elizabeth, and Charles Ritchie. *Love's Civil War: Letters and Diaries*. Eds. Victoria Glendinning with Judith Robertson. Toronto: McClelland & Stewart, 2008.

Briggs, Asa. *The BBC: The First Fifty Years*. Oxford: Oxford University Press, 1985.

—. *The History of Broadcasting in the United Kingdom: Sound and Vision*. Vol. 4. Oxford: Oxford University Press, 1979.

Carpenter, Humphrey. *The Envy of the World: Fifty Years of the Third Programme and Radio 3*. London: Weidenfeld & Nicolson, 1996.

Corcoran, Neil. *Elizabeth Bowen: The Enforced Return*. Oxford: Oxford University Press, 2004.

—. *Sunday Feature: Elizabeth Bowen*. BBC radio documentary. With

John Banville, John Bayley, Roy Foster, Victoria Glendinning, et al. 1999.

Crews, Albert R. *Professional Radio Writing*. Boston: Houghton Mifflin, 1946.

Forster, E. M. *The BBC Talks of E. M. Forster, 1929–1960*. Eds. Mary Lago, Linda K. Hughes, and Elizabeth MacLeod Walls. Foreword by P. N. Furbank. Columbia: University of Missouri Press, 2008.

—. *Two Cheers for Democracy*. London: Edward Arnold, 1931.

Foster, Roy. *Life with the Lid Off*. BBC radio documentary. With Victoria Glendinning, Molly Keane, Hermione Lee, Charles Ritchie, et al. 1999.

Gielgud, Val. *How to Write Broadcast Plays*. London: Hurst & Blackett, 1932.

Glendinning, Victoria. *Elizabeth Bowen: A Biography*. 1977. New York: Anchor, 2005.

Ignatieff, Michael. *Isaiah Berlin: A Life*. London: Chatto & Windus, 1998.

Moorehead, Alan. *The Traitors: The Double Life of Fuchs, Pontecorvo, and Nunn May*. London: Hamish Hamilton, 1952.

Ritchie, Charles. *The Siren Years: A Canadian Diplomat Abroad 1937–1949*. Toronto: Macmillan, 1974.

Sellery, J'nan M., and William O. Harris. *Elizabeth Bowen: A Bibliography*. Austin, TX: Humanities Research Center, 1984.

Spurling, Hilary. *Secrets of a Woman's Heart: The Later Life of I. Compton-Burnett 1920–1969*. London: Hodder & Stoughton, 1984.

Thomas, Howard. *How to Write for Broadcasting*. London: George Allen & Unwin, 1940.

Woodward, E. L. "Some Political Consequences of the Atomic Bomb." Toronto: Oxford University Press, 1945.

Woolf, Virginia. *The Second Common Reader*. Ed. and intro. by Andrew McNeillie. 1932. New York: Harcourt Brace Jovanovich, 1986.

Wright, Lord. "Trials for War Crimes." Letter to the Editor. *The Times* (5 August 1952): 5.